SAYONARA, ZETSUBOU-SENSEI

The Power of Negative Thinking

5

Koji Kumeta

Translated and adapted by David Ury
Lettered by Foltz Design

BALLANTINE BOOKS · NEW YORK

A Del Rey Manga/Kodansha Trade Paperback Original

Sayonara, Zetsubou-sensei: The Power of Negative Thinking
volume 5 copyright © 2006 Koji Kumeta
English translation copyright © 2010 Koji Kumeta

Published in the United States by Del Rey, an imprint of The Random House Publishing Group, a division of Random House, Inc., New York.

DEL REY is a registered trademark and the Del Rey colophon is a trademark of Random House, Inc.

Publication rights arranged through Kodansha Ltd.

First published in Japan in 2006 by Kodansha Ltd., Tokyo

ISBN 978-0-345-51636-7

Printed in the United States of America

www.delreymanga.com

1 2 3 4 5 6 7 8 9

Translator/Adapter: David Ury
Lettering: Foltz Design

SAYONARA, ZETSUBOU-SENSEI

The Power of Negative Thinking

CONTENTS

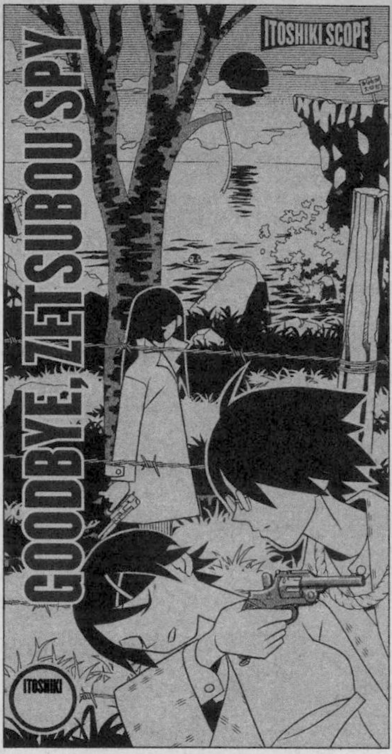
GOODBYE, ZETSUBOU SPY
ITOSHIKI SCOPE
ITOSHIKI

THE STORY SO FAR

Suspected of being the spy who stole Raageru's sacred book, Nozomi is captured and locked inside Doragonia's (of Shibusawa) basement. An interrogator holds a baton to Nozomi's throat. "Tell us where it is, Nyaho-nyaho-tama-kuro!" Nozomi is puzzled, never having heard this peculiar code name. Meanwhile, the count shows up and tells Nozomi, "You're a true Homo Ludens." The count takes a liking to Nozomi, and orders him to put on a weird gadget the likes of which Nozomi has never seen before. Nozomi runs away as the count screams with laughter, "You are wearing the best gadget ever made!" Nozomi runs into a house asking for help and meets an old man who looks like Jiro Shirasu. The old man tells Nozomi, "You have no principles," and teaches him how to make Scandinavian furniture. Meanwhile, a girl is hit by a stray bullet shot by Global Headquarters...

Honorifics Explained

Throughout the Del Rey Manga books, you will find Japanese honorifics left intact in the translations. For those not familiar with how the Japanese use honorifics and, more important, how they differ from American honorifics, we present this brief overview.

Politeness has always been a critical facet of Japanese culture. Ever since the feudal era, when Japan was a highly stratified society, use of honorifics—which can be defined as polite speech that indicates relationship or status—has played an essential role in the Japanese language. When addressing someone in Japanese, an honorific usually takes the form of a suffix attached to one's name (example: "Asuna-san"), is used as a title at the end of one's name, or appears in place of the name itself (example: "Negi-sensei," or simply "Sensei").

Honorifics can be expressions of respect or endearment. In the context of manga and anime, honorifics give insight into the nature of the relationship between characters. Many English translations leave out these important honorifics and therefore distort the feel of the original Japanese. Because Japanese honorifics contain nuances that English honorifics lack, it is our policy at Del Rey not to translate them. Here, instead, is a guide to some of the honorifics you may encounter in Del Rey Manga.

-san: This is the most common honorific and is equivalent to Mr., Miss, Ms., or Mrs. It is the all-purpose honorific and can be used in any situation where politeness is required.

-sama: This is one level higher than "-san" and is used to confer great respect.

-dono: This comes from the word "tono," which means "lord." It is an even higher level than "-sama" and confers utmost respect.

-kun: This suffix is used at the end of boys' names to express familiarity or endearment. It is also sometimes used by men among friends, or when addressing someone younger or of a lower station.

-chan: This is used to express endearment, mostly toward girls. It is also used for little boys, pets, and even among lovers. It gives a sense of childish cuteness.

Bozu: This is an informal way to refer to a boy, similar to the English terms "kid" and "squirt."

Sempai/
Senpai: This title suggests that the addressee is one's senior in a group or organization. It is most often used in a school setting, where underclassmen refer to their upperclassmen as "sempai." It can also be used in the workplace, such as when a newer employee addresses an employee who has seniority in the company.

Kohai: This is the opposite of "sempai" and is used toward underclassmen in school or newcomers in the workplace. It connotes that the addressee is of a lower station.

Sensei: Literally meaning "one who has come before," this title is used for teachers, doctors, or masters of any profession or art.

-[blank]: This is usually forgotten in these lists, but it is perhaps the most significant difference between Japanese and English. The lack of honorific means that the speaker has permission to address the person in a very intimate way. Usually, only family, spouses, or very close friends have this kind of permission. Known as *yobisute,* it can be gratifying when someone who has earned the intimacy starts to call one by one's name without an honorific. But when that intimacy hasn't been earned, it can be very insulting.

Koji Kumeta

SAYONARA, ZETSUBOU-SENSEI

5

The Power of Negative Thinking

Contents

The stories, characters, and incidents mentioned in this publication are entirely fictional.
Originally published in 2006 in Weekly *Shônen Magazine* #1 to #13 (no story was printed in #12).

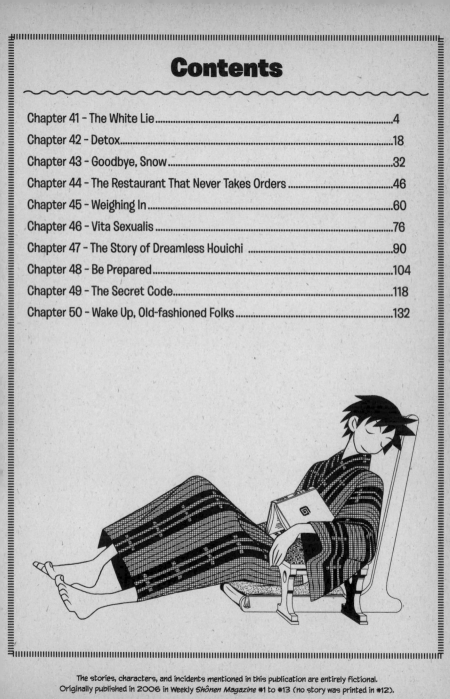

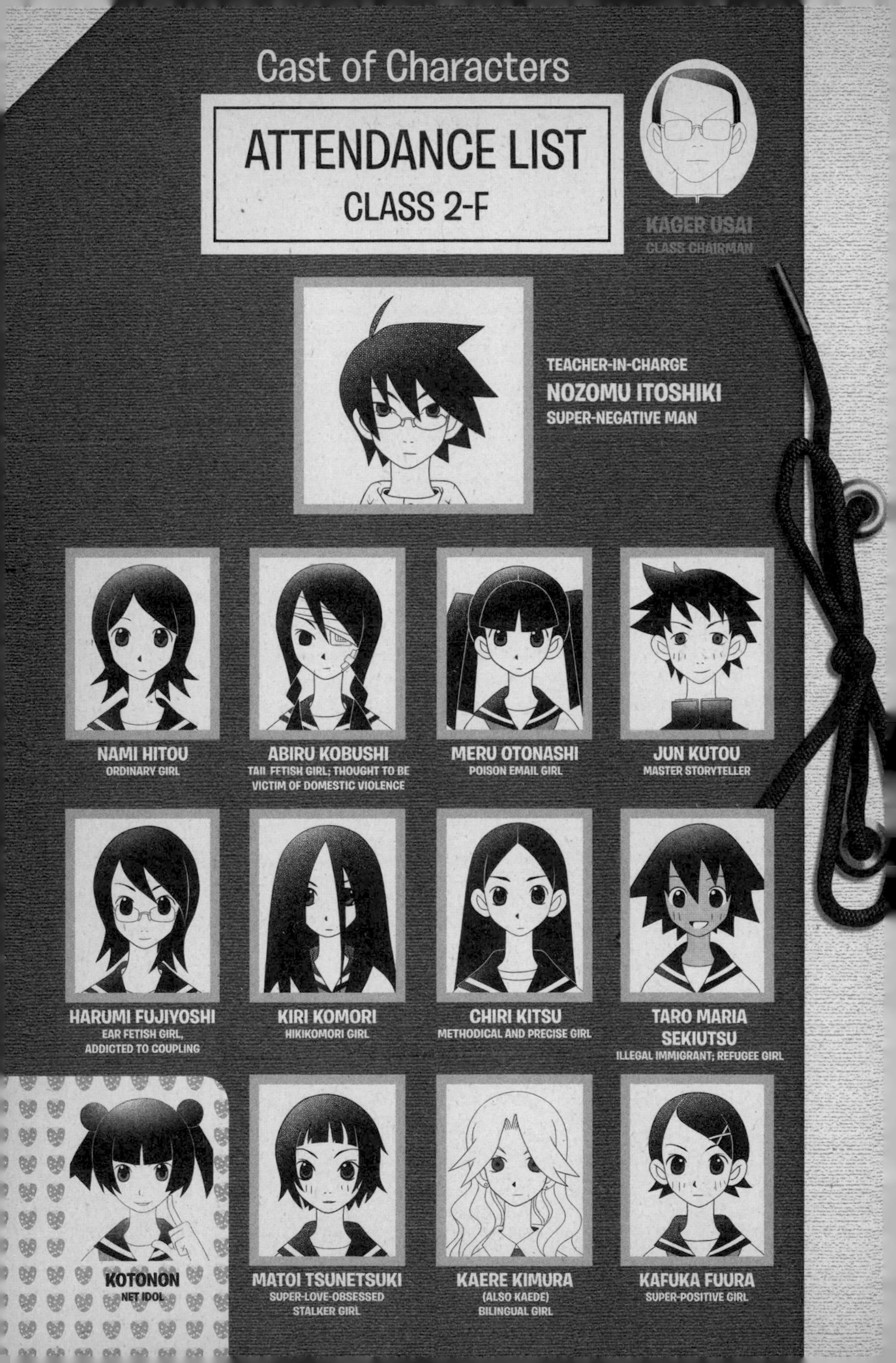
Cast of Characters
ATTENDANCE LIST
CLASS 2-F
KAGER USAI
CLASS CHAIRMAN
TEACHER-IN-CHARGE
NOZOMU ITOSHIKI
SUPER-NEGATIVE MAN
NAMI HITOU
ORDINARY GIRL
ABIRU KOBUSHI
TAIL FETISH GIRL; THOUGHT TO BE VICTIM OF DOMESTIC VIOLENCE
MERU OTONASHI
POISON EMAIL GIRL
JUN KUTOU
MASTER STORYTELLER
HARUMI FUJIYOSHI
EAR FETISH GIRL, ADDICTED TO COUPLING
KIRI KOMORI
HIKIKOMORI GIRL
CHIRI KITSU
METHODICAL AND PRECISE GIRL
TARO MARIA SEKIUTSU
ILLEGAL IMMIGRANT; REFUGEE GIRL
KOTONON
NET IDOL
MATOI TSUNETSUKI
SUPER-LOVE-OBSESSED STALKER GIRL
KAERE KIMURA
(ALSO KAEDE)
BILINGUAL GIRL
KAFUKA FUURA
SUPER-POSITIVE GIRL

CHAPTER 41

THE WHITE LIE

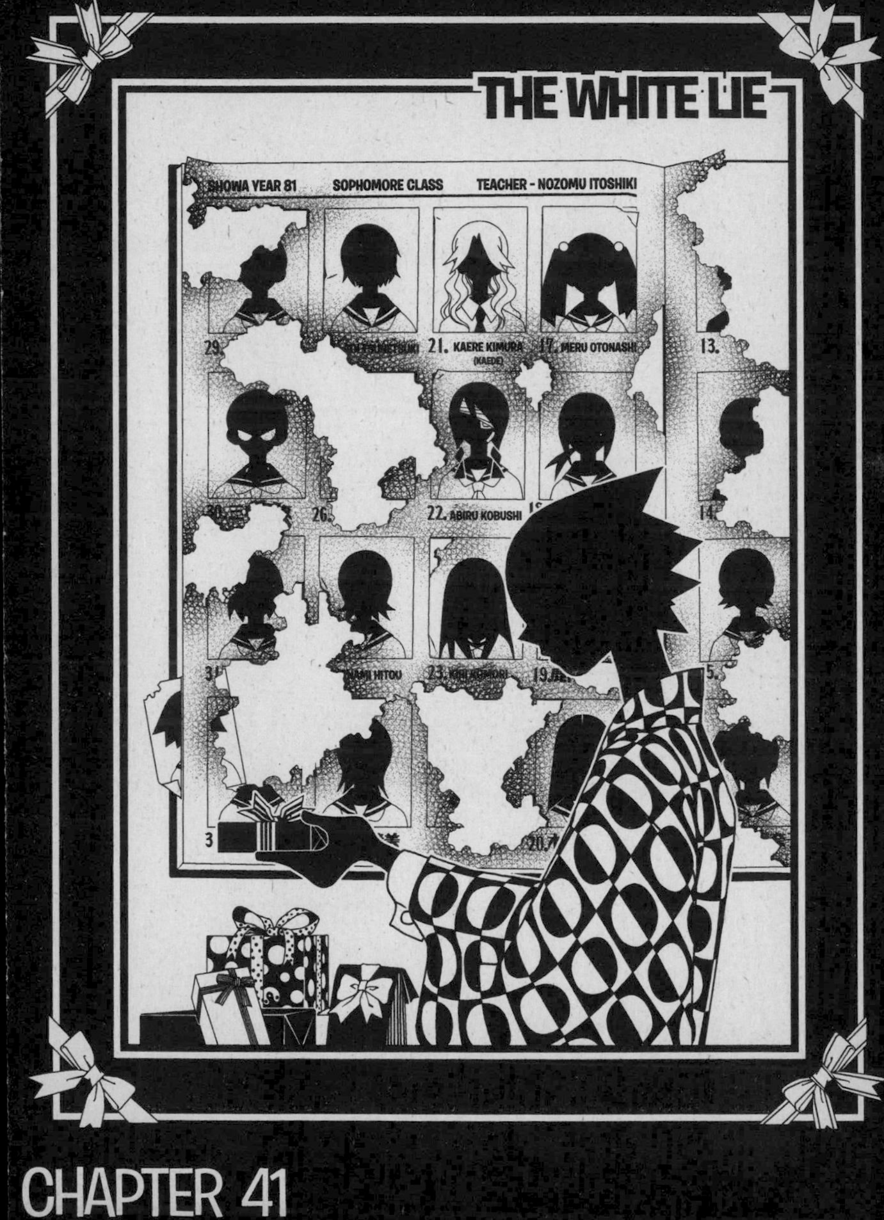
SHOWA YEAR 81
SOPHOMORE CLASS
TEACHER - NOZOMU ITOSHIKI
29.
21. KAERE KIMURA
(KAEDE)
17. MERU OTONASHI
13.
30.
26.
22. ABIRU KOBUSHI
14.
23. KIRI KOMORI
19.
20.

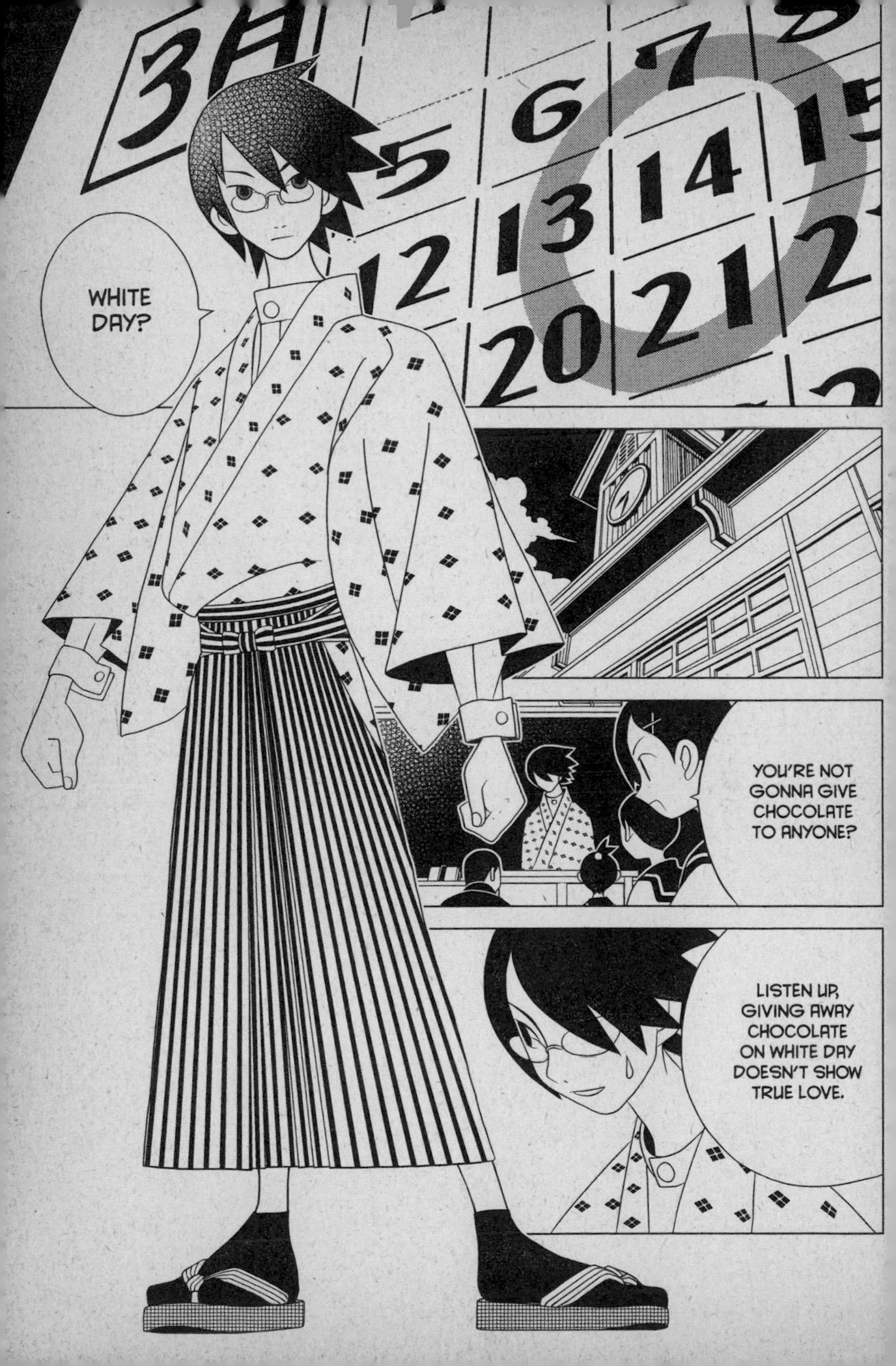
WHITE DAY?
YOU'RE NOT GONNA GIVE CHOCOLATE TO ANYONE?
LISTEN UP, GIVING AWAY CHOCOLATE ON WHITE DAY DOESN'T SHOW TRUE LOVE.

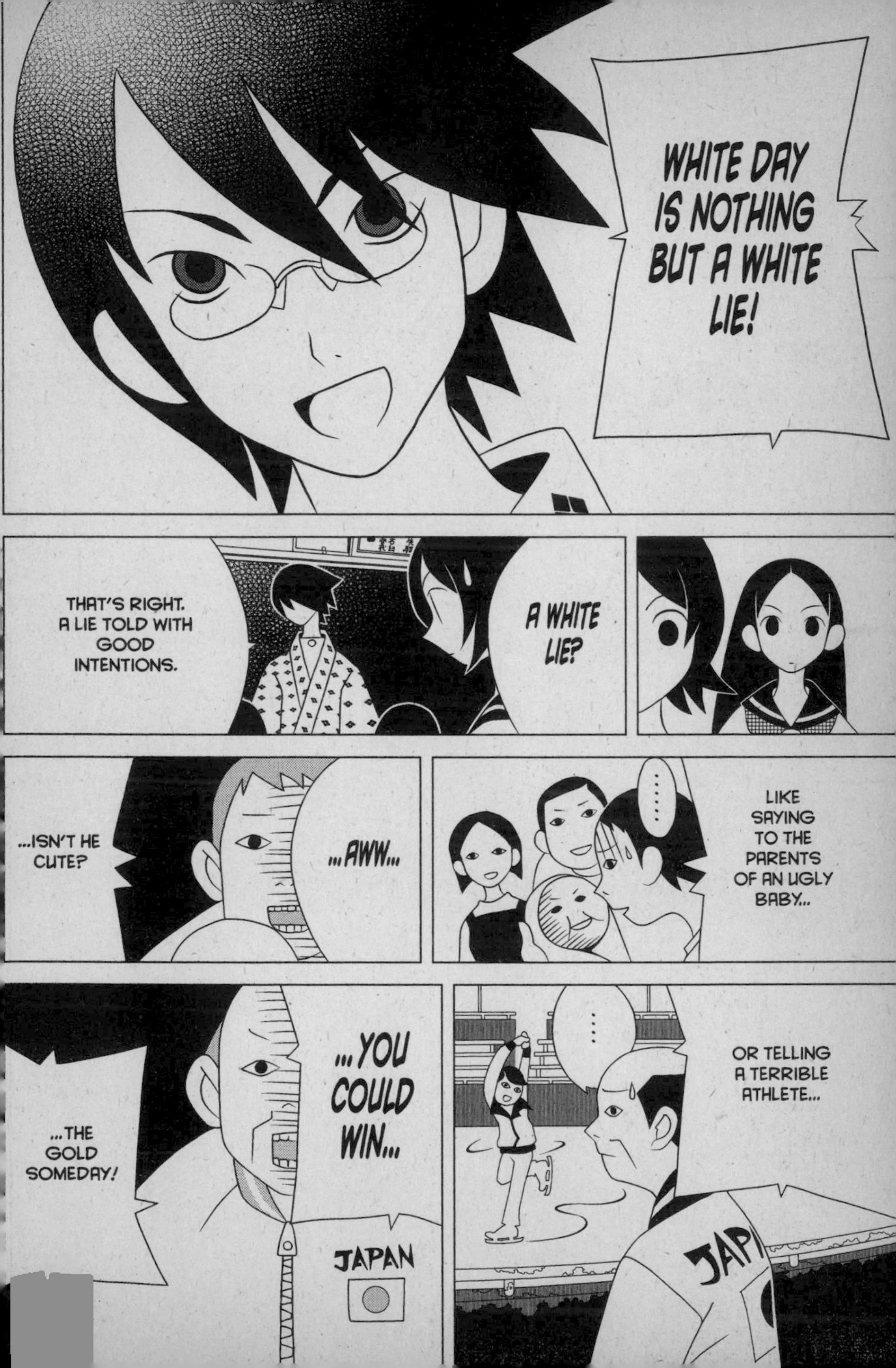
WHITE DAY IS NOTHING BUT A WHITE LIE!
A WHITE LIE?
THAT'S RIGHT. A LIE TOLD WITH GOOD INTENTIONS.
LIKE SAYING TO THE PARENTS OF AN UGLY BABY...
......
...AWW...
...ISN'T HE CUTE?
OR TELLING A TERRIBLE ATHLETE...
....
JAP
...YOU COULD WIN...
...THE GOLD SOMEDAY!
JAPAN

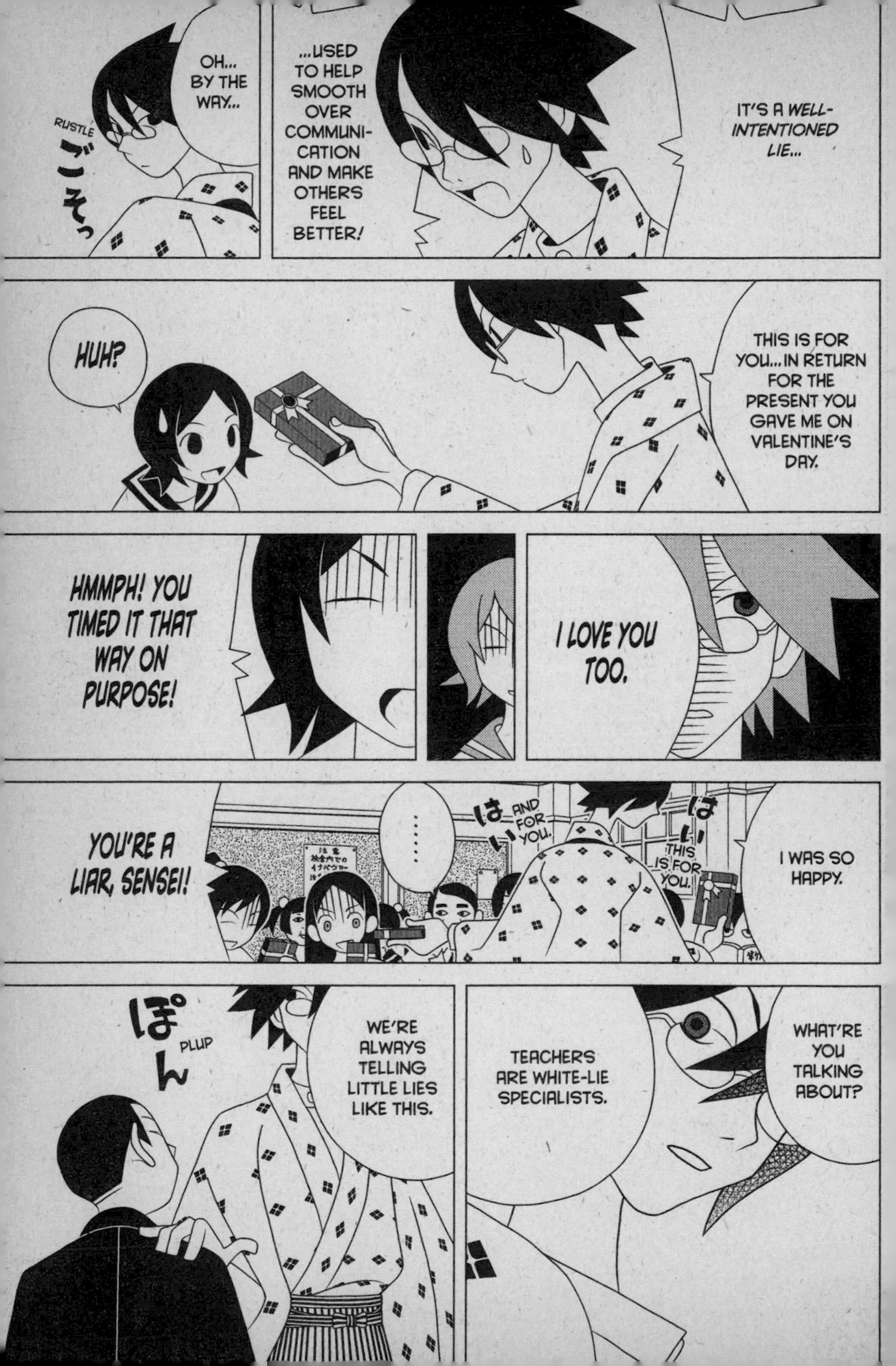
IT'S A WELL-INTENTIONED LIE...
...USED TO HELP SMOOTH OVER COMMUNICATION AND MAKE OTHERS FEEL BETTER!
OH... BY THE WAY...
ごそっ
RUSTLE
THIS IS FOR YOU...IN RETURN FOR THE PRESENT YOU GAVE ME ON VALENTINE'S DAY.
HUH?
I LOVE YOU TOO.
HMMPH! YOU TIMED IT THAT WAY ON PURPOSE!
I WAS SO HAPPY.
はい
THIS IS FOR YOU.
はい
AND FOR YOU.
......
YOU'RE A LIAR, SENSEI!
WHAT'RE YOU TALKING ABOUT?
TEACHERS ARE WHITE-LIE SPECIALISTS.
WE'RE ALWAYS TELLING LITTLE LIES LIKE THIS.
ぽん
PLUP

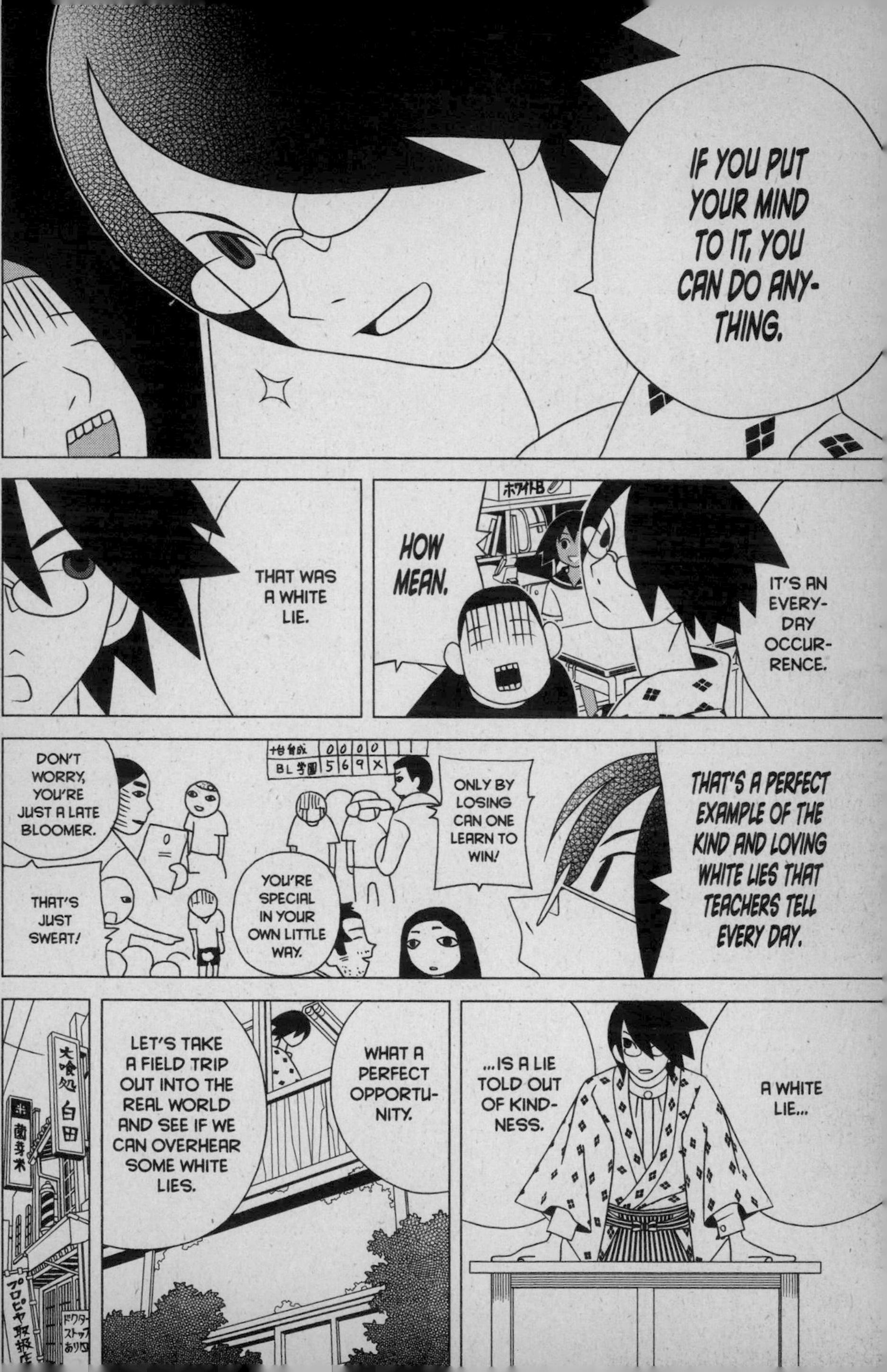
IF YOU PUT YOUR MIND TO IT, YOU CAN DO ANY-THING.
IT'S AN EVERY-DAY OCCUR-RENCE.
HOW MEAN.
THAT WAS A WHITE LIE.
THAT'S A PERFECT EXAMPLE OF THE KIND AND LOVING WHITE LIES THAT TEACHERS TELL EVERY DAY.
ONLY BY LOSING CAN ONE LEARN TO WIN!
YOU'RE SPECIAL IN YOUR OWN LITTLE WAY.
DON'T WORRY, YOU'RE JUST A LATE BLOOMER.
THAT'S JUST SWEAT!
A WHITE LIE...
...IS A LIE TOLD OUT OF KIND-NESS.
WHAT A PERFECT OPPORTU-NITY.
LET'S TAKE A FIELD TRIP OUT INTO THE REAL WORLD AND SEE IF WE CAN OVERHEAR SOME WHITE LIES.
大喰処 白田

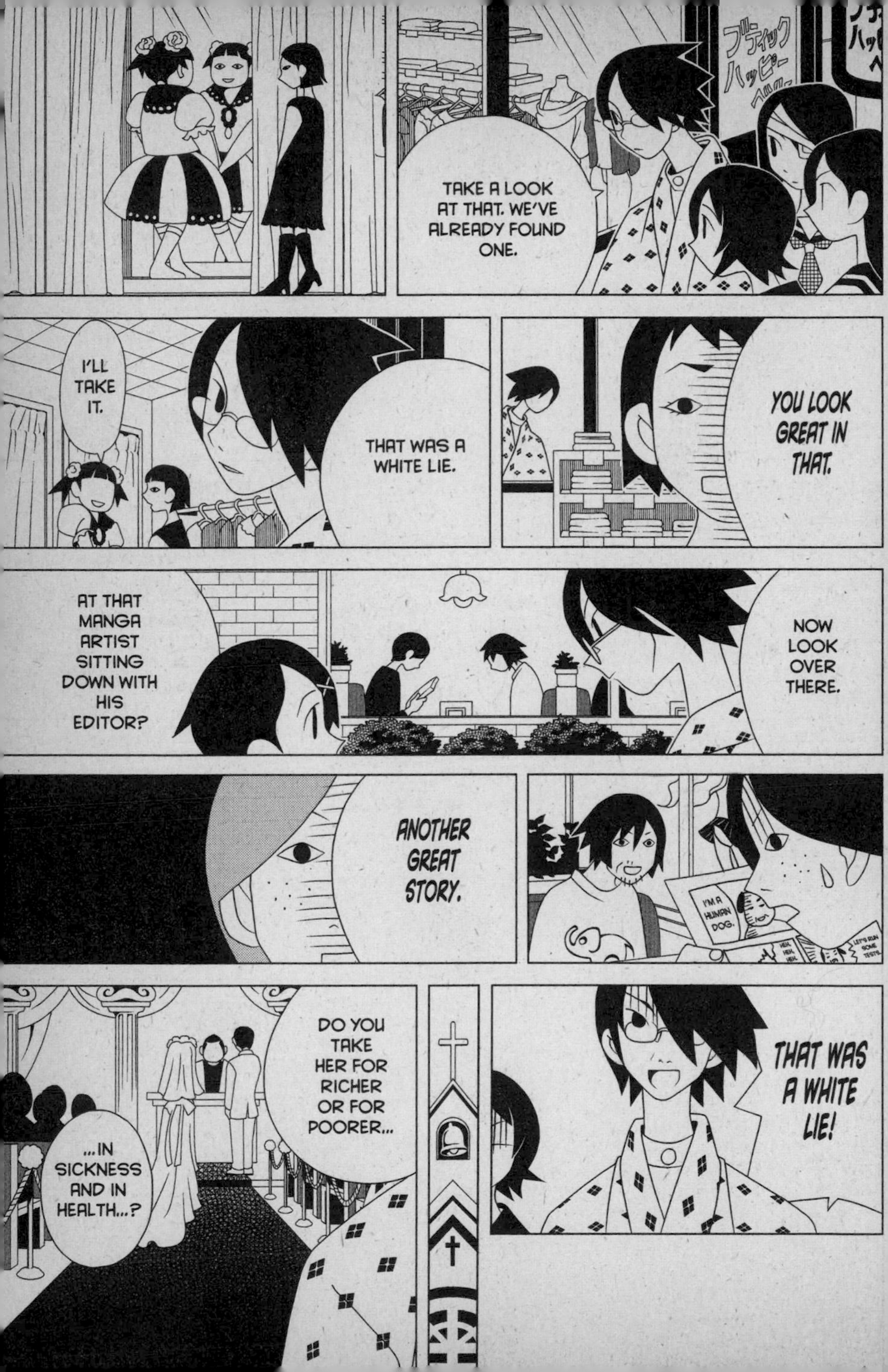
ブティック ハッピー
TAKE A LOOK AT THAT. WE'VE ALREADY FOUND ONE.
YOU LOOK GREAT IN THAT.
THAT WAS A WHITE LIE.
I'LL TAKE IT.
NOW LOOK OVER THERE.
AT THAT MANGA ARTIST SITTING DOWN WITH HIS EDITOR?
I'M A HUMAN DOG.
HEH, HEH, HEH.
LET'S RUN SOME TESTS.
ANOTHER GREAT STORY.
THAT WAS A WHITE LIE!
DO YOU TAKE HER FOR RICHER OR FOR POORER...
...IN SICKNESS AND IN HEALTH...?

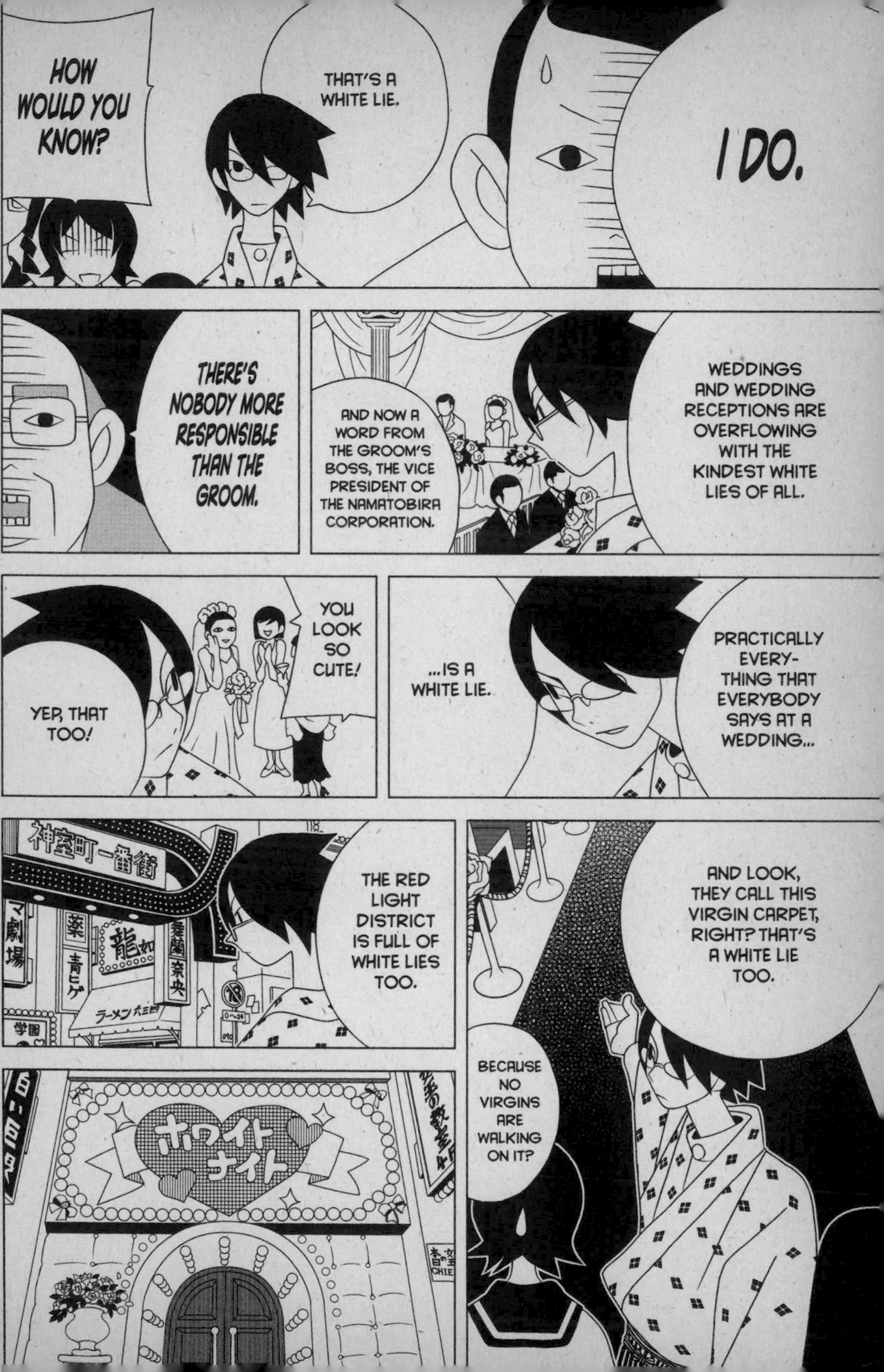
I DO.
THAT'S A WHITE LIE.
HOW WOULD YOU KNOW?
WEDDINGS AND WEDDING RECEPTIONS ARE OVERFLOWING WITH THE KINDEST WHITE LIES OF ALL.
AND NOW A WORD FROM THE GROOM'S BOSS, THE VICE PRESIDENT OF THE NAMATOBIRA CORPORATION.
THERE'S NOBODY MORE RESPONSIBLE THAN THE GROOM.
PRACTICALLY EVERY-THING THAT EVERYBODY SAYS AT A WEDDING...
...IS A WHITE LIE.
YOU LOOK SO CUTE!
YEP, THAT TOO!
AND LOOK, THEY CALL THIS VIRGIN CARPET, RIGHT? THAT'S A WHITE LIE TOO.
BECAUSE NO VIRGINS ARE WALKING ON IT?
神室町一番街
THE RED LIGHT DISTRICT IS FULL OF WHITE LIES TOO.
ホワイト ナイト

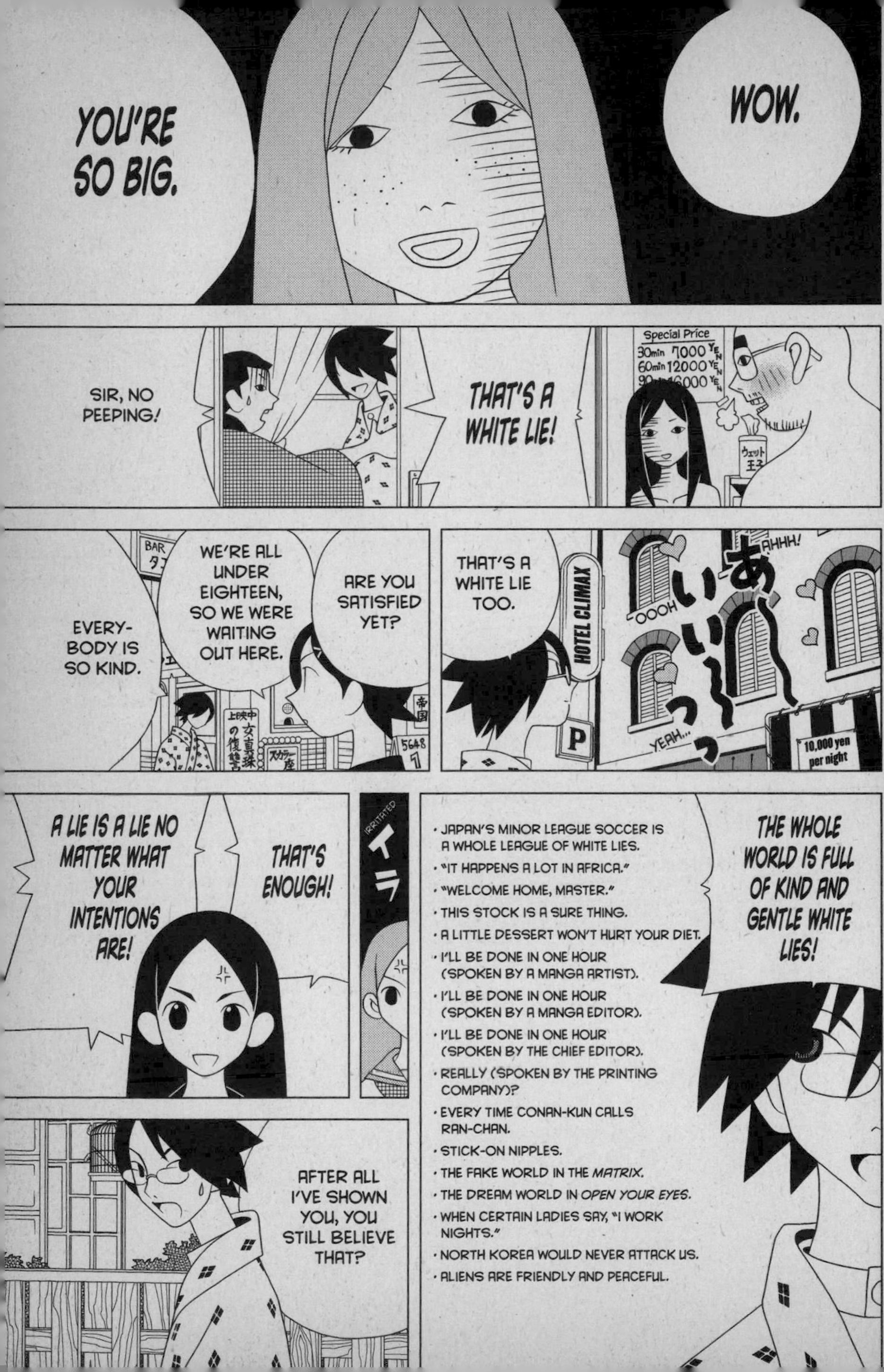

WOW.
YOU'RE SO BIG.
Special Price
30min 7000 YEN
60min 12000 YEN
16000 YEN
THAT'S A WHITE LIE!
SIR, NO PEEPING!
AHHH!
あいい〜っっ
OOOH
YEAH...
HOTEL CLIMAX
P
10,000 yen per night
THAT'S A WHITE LIE TOO.
ARE YOU SATISFIED YET?
WE'RE ALL UNDER EIGHTEEN, SO WE WERE WAITING OUT HERE.
EVERY-BODY IS SO KIND.
BAR
5648
THE WHOLE WORLD IS FULL OF KIND AND GENTLE WHITE LIES!
• JAPAN'S MINOR LEAGUE SOCCER IS A WHOLE LEAGUE OF WHITE LIES.
• "IT HAPPENS A LOT IN AFRICA."
• "WELCOME HOME, MASTER."
• THIS STOCK IS A SURE THING.
• A LITTLE DESSERT WON'T HURT YOUR DIET.
• I'LL BE DONE IN ONE HOUR (SPOKEN BY A MANGA ARTIST).
• I'LL BE DONE IN ONE HOUR (SPOKEN BY A MANGA EDITOR).
• I'LL BE DONE IN ONE HOUR (SPOKEN BY THE CHIEF EDITOR).
• REALLY (SPOKEN BY THE PRINTING COMPANY)?
• EVERY TIME CONAN-KUN CALLS RAN-CHAN.
• STICK-ON NIPPLES.
• THE FAKE WORLD IN THE *MATRIX*.
• THE DREAM WORLD IN *OPEN YOUR EYES*.
• WHEN CERTAIN LADIES SAY, "I WORK NIGHTS."
• NORTH KOREA WOULD NEVER ATTACK US.
• ALIENS ARE FRIENDLY AND PEACEFUL.
IRRITATED
イラ
THAT'S ENOUGH!
A LIE IS A LIE NO MATTER WHAT YOUR INTENTIONS ARE!
AFTER ALL I'VE SHOWN YOU, YOU STILL BELIEVE THAT?

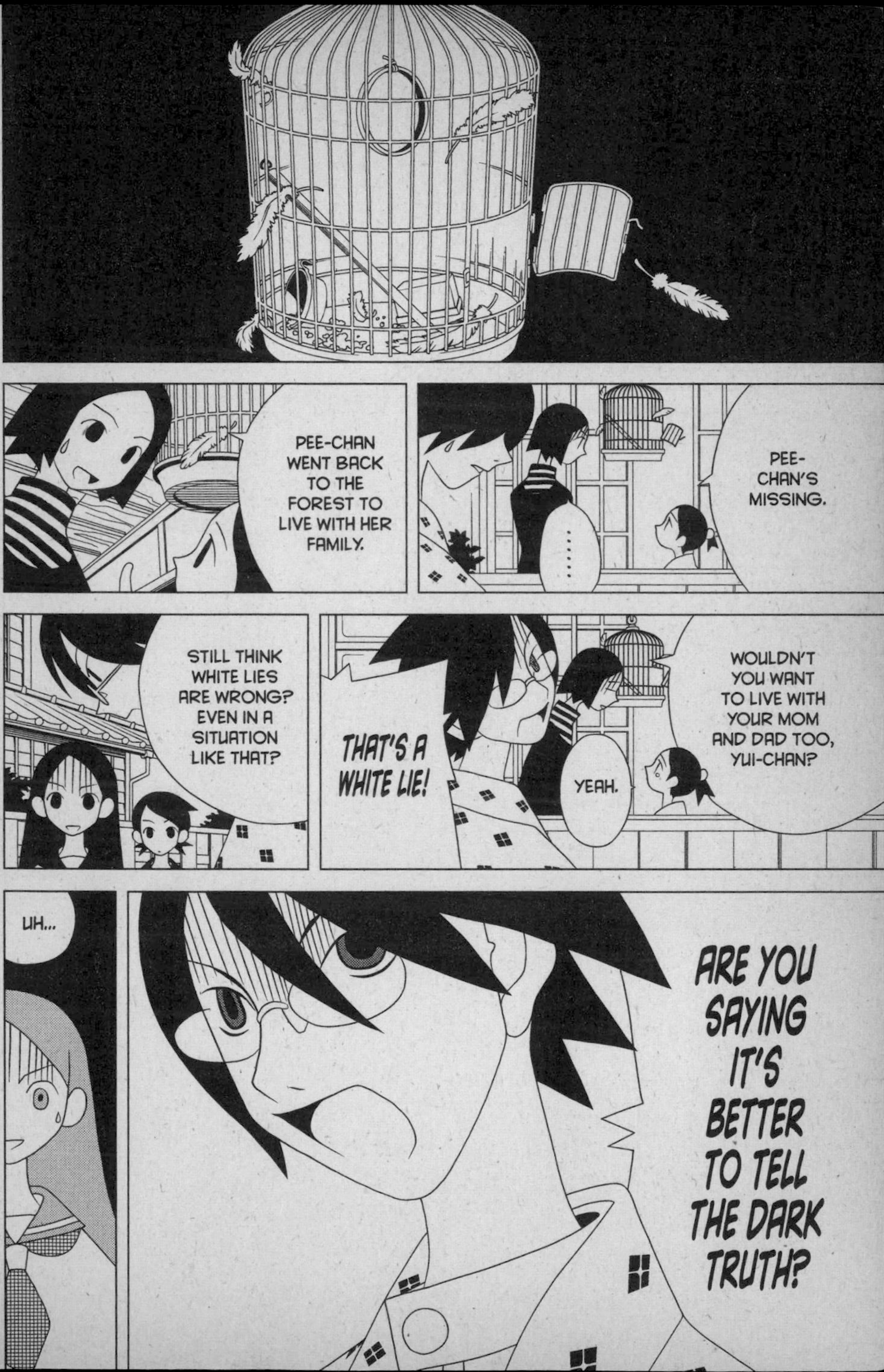
PEE-CHAN'S MISSING.
......
PEE-CHAN WENT BACK TO THE FOREST TO LIVE WITH HER FAMILY.
WOULDN'T YOU WANT TO LIVE WITH YOUR MOM AND DAD TOO, YUI-CHAN?
YEAH.
THAT'S A WHITE LIE!
STILL THINK WHITE LIES ARE WRONG? EVEN IN A SITUATION LIKE THAT?
ARE YOU SAYING IT'S BETTER TO TELL THE DARK TRUTH?
UH...

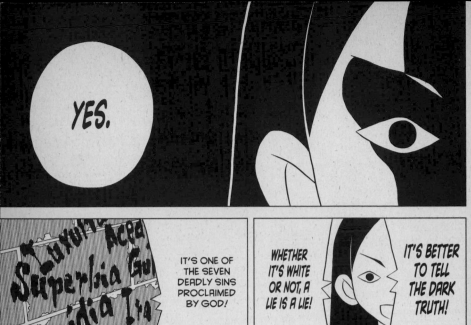

YES.
IT'S BETTER TO TELL THE DARK TRUTH!
WHETHER IT'S WHITE OR NOT, A LIE IS A LIE!
IT'S ONE OF THE SEVEN DEADLY SINS PROCLAIMED BY GOD!
IT'S MY RESPONSIBILITY AS A JOURNALIST TO TELL THE TRUTH!
SINCE WHEN ARE YOU A JOURNALIST!?
しゅたっ
FWUP
AHH... DON'T...
A CAT GOT HER...
わあああ
WAAHH
I WON'T STAND TO HEAR ANYONE TELL A WHITE LIE! NOT ON MY WATCH!
OH NO, WE'RE IN TROUBLE!
WE'VE GOTTA STOP CHIRI!

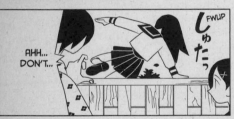

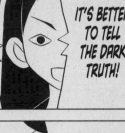

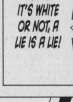

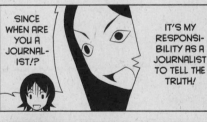

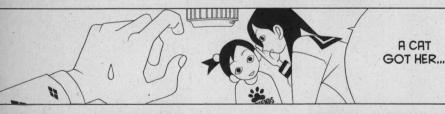

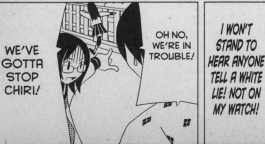

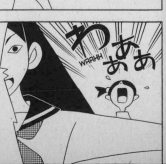

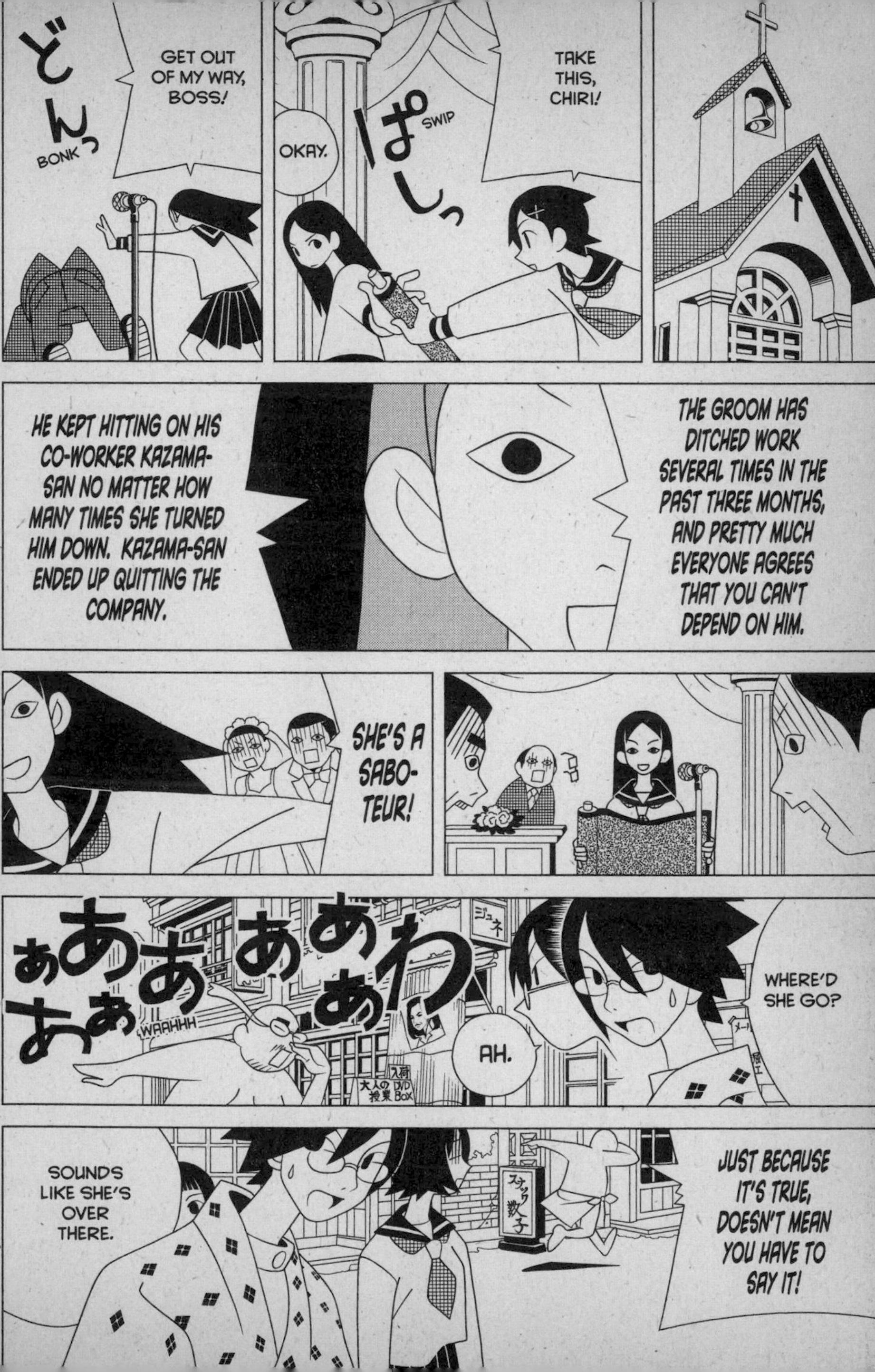
TAKE THIS, CHIRI!
ぱしっ
SWIP
OKAY.
GET OUT OF MY WAY, BOSS!
どんっ
BONK
THE GROOM HAS DITCHED WORK SEVERAL TIMES IN THE PAST THREE MONTHS, AND PRETTY MUCH EVERYONE AGREES THAT YOU CAN'T DEPEND ON HIM.
HE KEPT HITTING ON HIS CO-WORKER KAZAMA-SAN NO MATTER HOW MANY TIMES SHE TURNED HIM DOWN. KAZAMA-SAN ENDED UP QUITTING THE COMPANY.
SHE'S A SABO-TEUR!
WHERE'D SHE GO?
AH.
ジュネ
ぁあああああわ
あぁあああ
WAAHHH
入荷
大人の授業 DVD Box
JUST BECAUSE IT'S TRUE, DOESN'T MEAN YOU HAVE TO SAY IT!
スナック 数子
SOUNDS LIKE SHE'S OVER THERE.

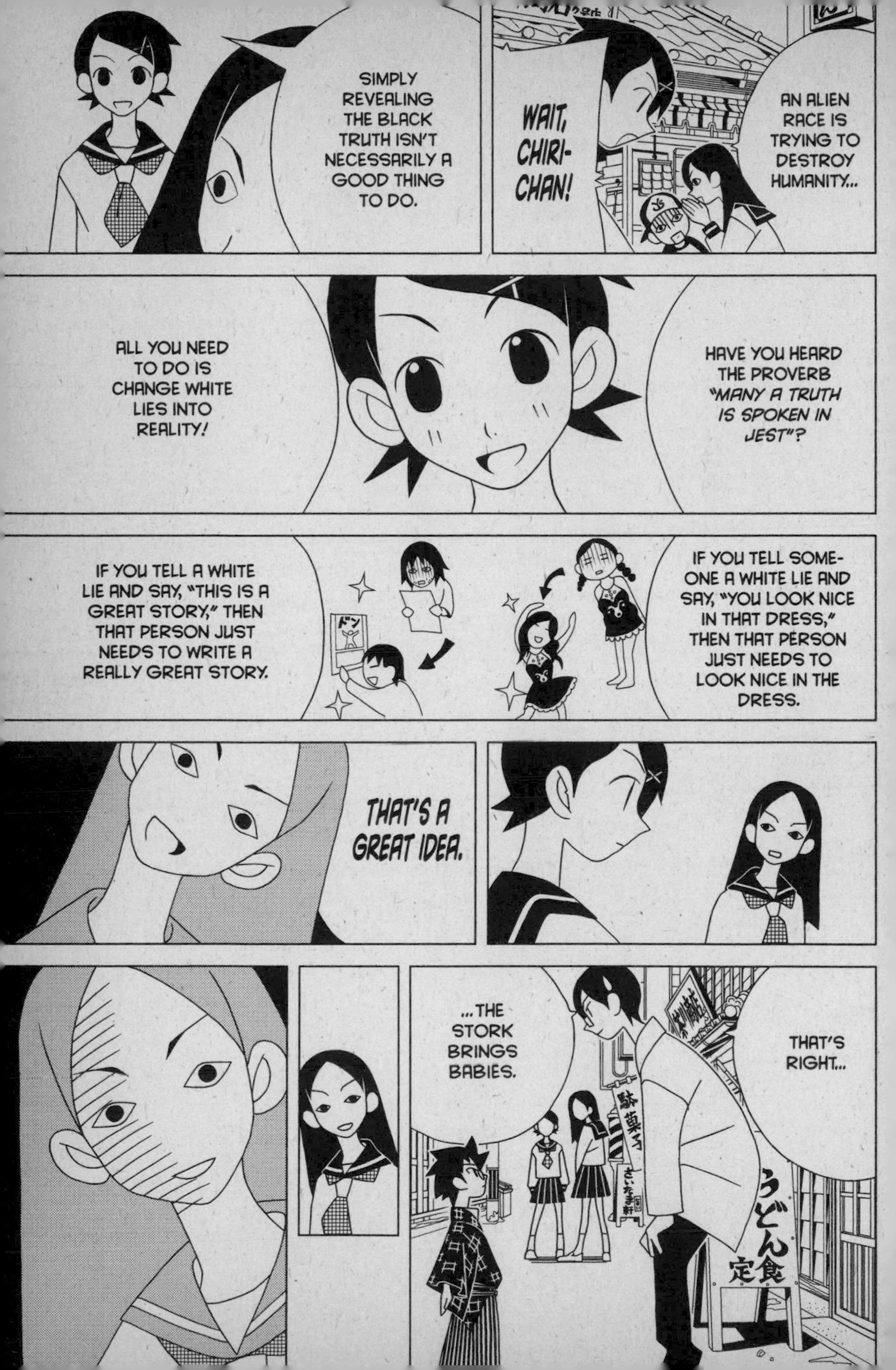
AN ALIEN RACE IS TRYING TO DESTROY HUMANITY...
WAIT, CHIRI-CHAN!
SIMPLY REVEALING THE BLACK TRUTH ISN'T NECESSARILY A GOOD THING TO DO.
HAVE YOU HEARD THE PROVERB *"MANY A TRUTH IS SPOKEN IN JEST"*?
ALL YOU NEED TO DO IS CHANGE WHITE LIES INTO REALITY!
IF YOU TELL SOME-ONE A WHITE LIE AND SAY, "YOU LOOK NICE IN THAT DRESS," THEN THAT PERSON JUST NEEDS TO LOOK NICE IN THE DRESS.
ドン
IF YOU TELL A WHITE LIE AND SAY, "THIS IS A GREAT STORY," THEN THAT PERSON JUST NEEDS TO WRITE A REALLY GREAT STORY.
THAT'S A GREAT IDEA.
THAT'S RIGHT...
...THE STORK BRINGS BABIES.
駄菓子
うどん
定食

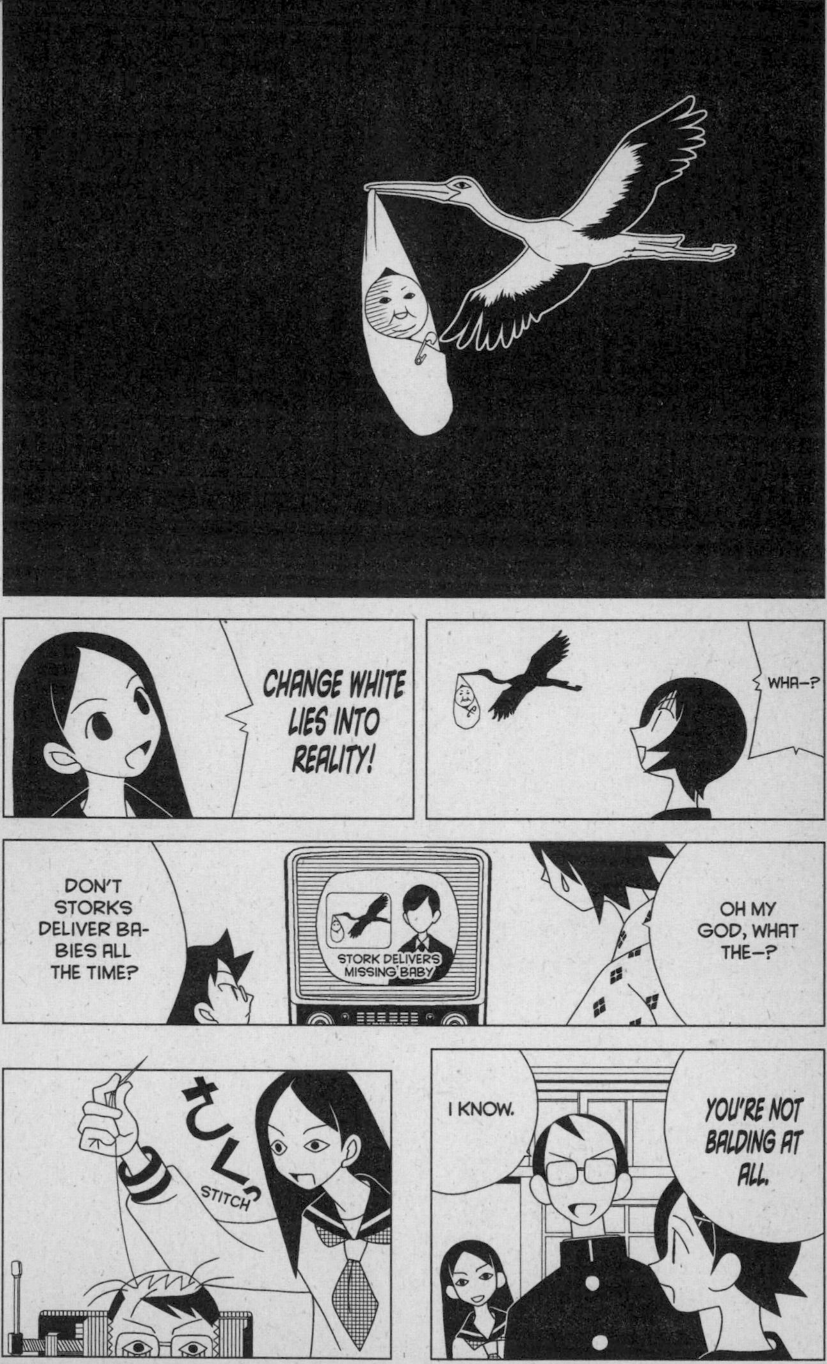
WHA–?
CHANGE WHITE LIES INTO REALITY!
OH MY GOD, WHAT THE–?
STORK DELIVERS MISSING BABY
DON'T STORKS DELIVER BA-BIES ALL THE TIME?
YOU'RE NOT BALDING AT ALL.
I KNOW.
STITCH

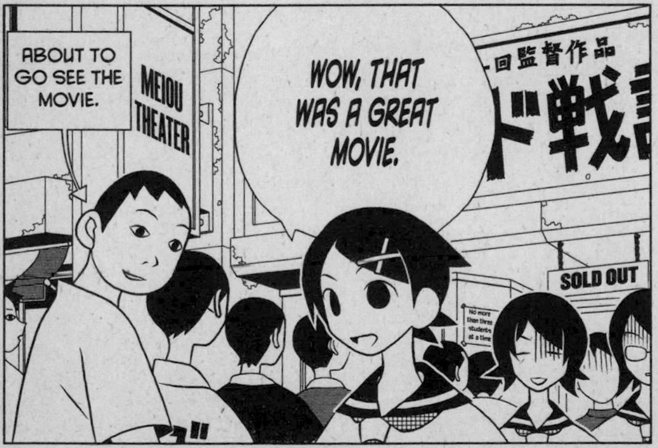
回監督作品
戦
WOW, THAT WAS A GREAT MOVIE.
SOLD OUT
No more than three students at a time
ABOUT TO GO SEE THE MOVIE.
MEIOU THEATER

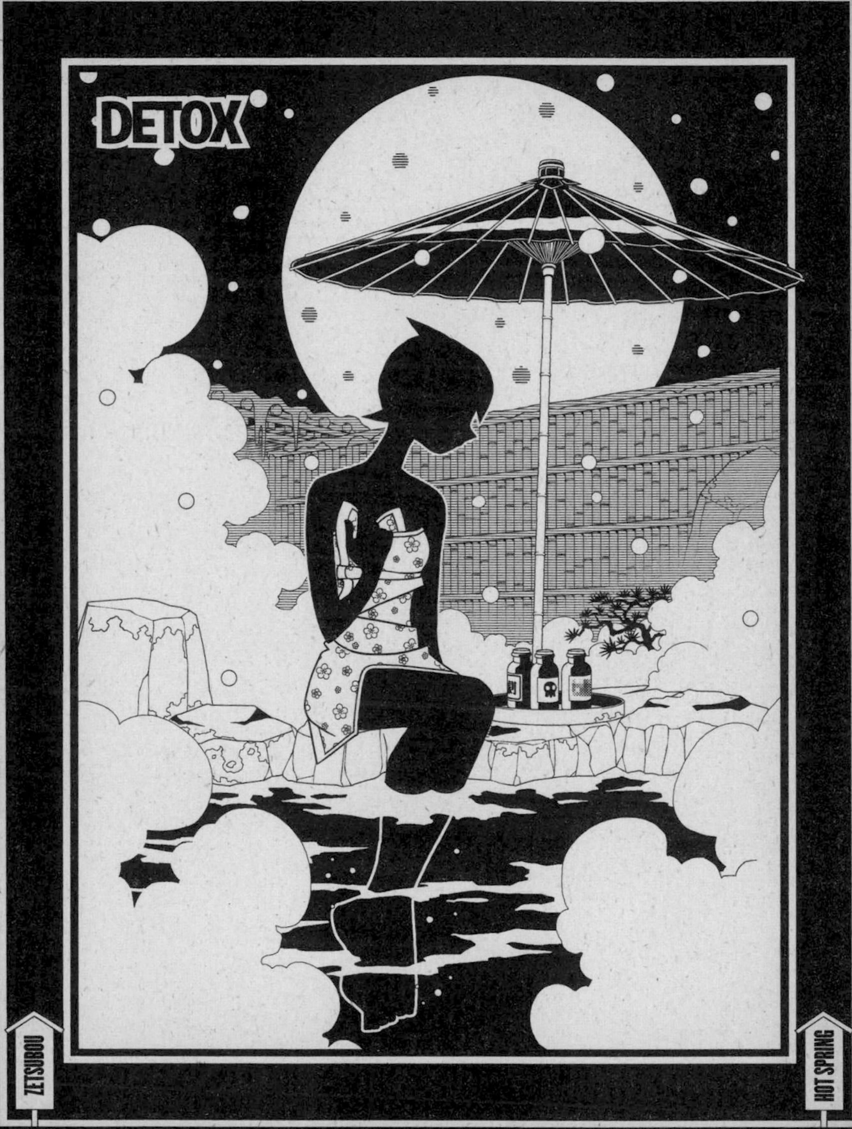
DETOX
ZETSUBOU
HOT SPRING

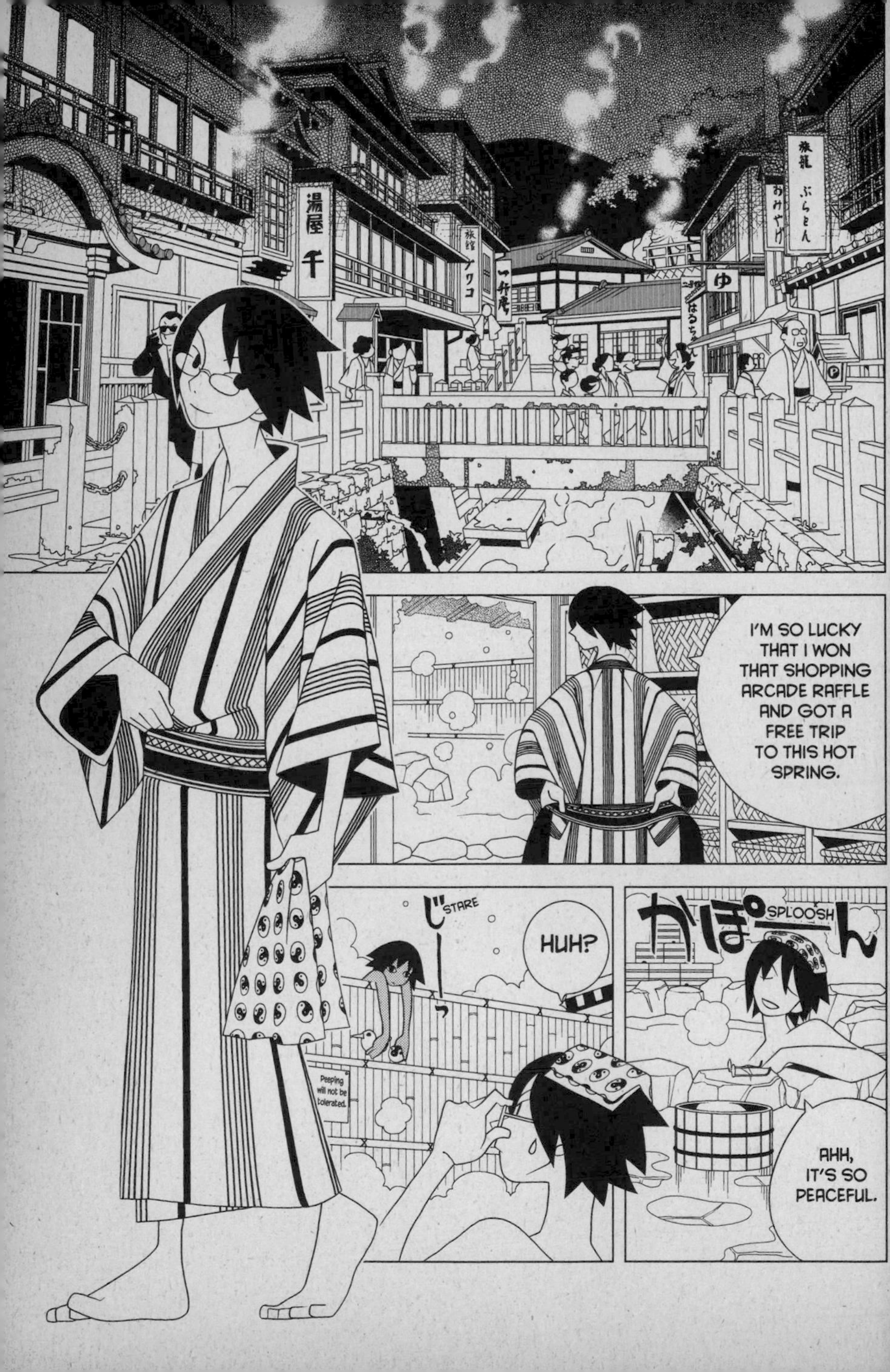

I'M SO LUCKY THAT I WON THAT SHOPPING ARCADE RAFFLE AND GOT A FREE TRIP TO THIS HOT SPRING.
かぽーん SPLOOSH
AHH, IT'S SO PEACEFUL.
じーっ STARE
HUH?
Peeping will not be tolerated.

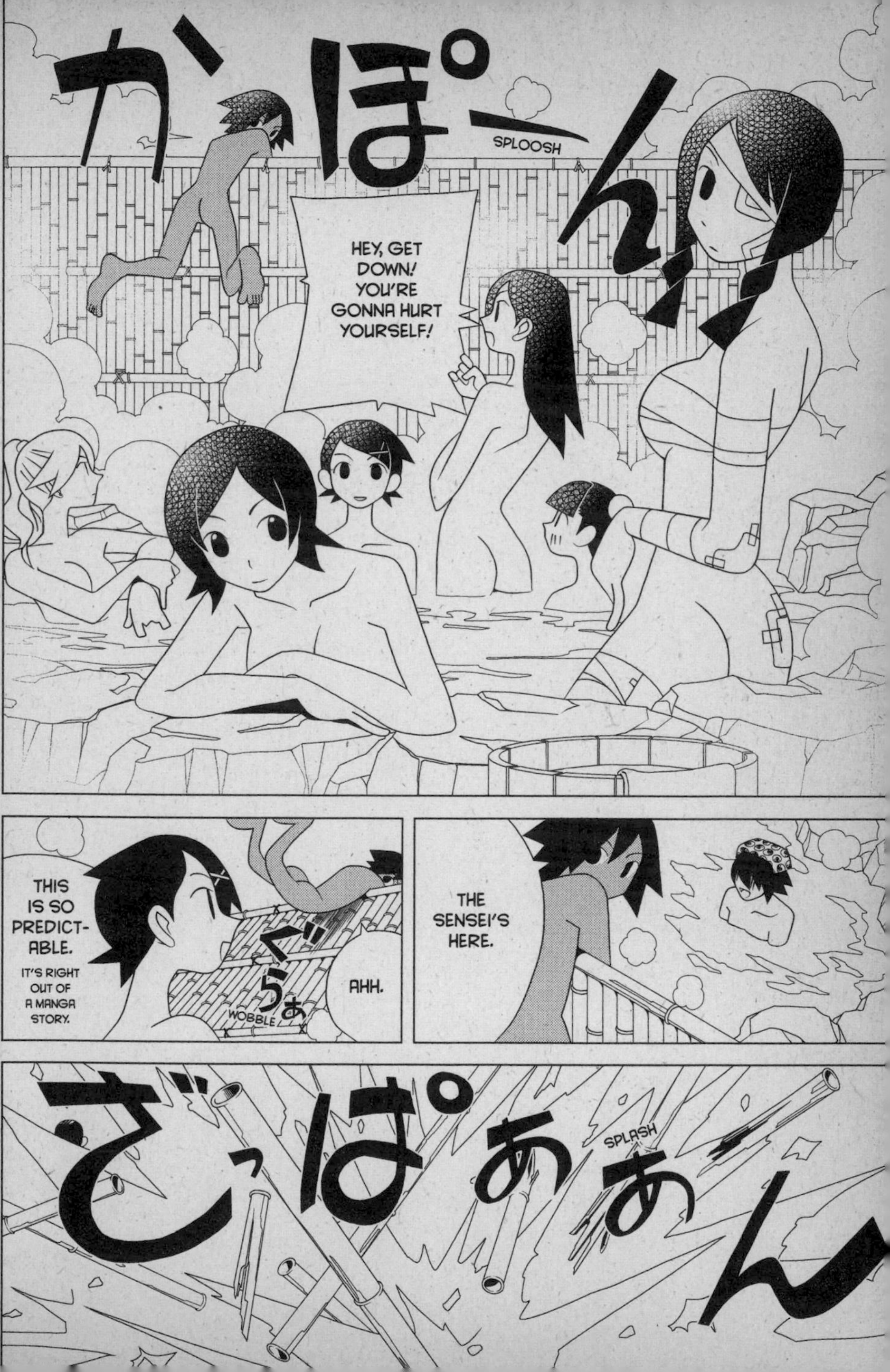
かっぽーん
SPLOOSH
HEY, GET DOWN! YOU'RE GONNA HURT YOURSELF!
THE SENSEI'S HERE.
AHH.
ぐらぁ
WOBBLE
THIS IS SO PREDICT-ABLE.
IT'S RIGHT OUT OF A MANGA STORY.
ざっぱああん
SPLASH

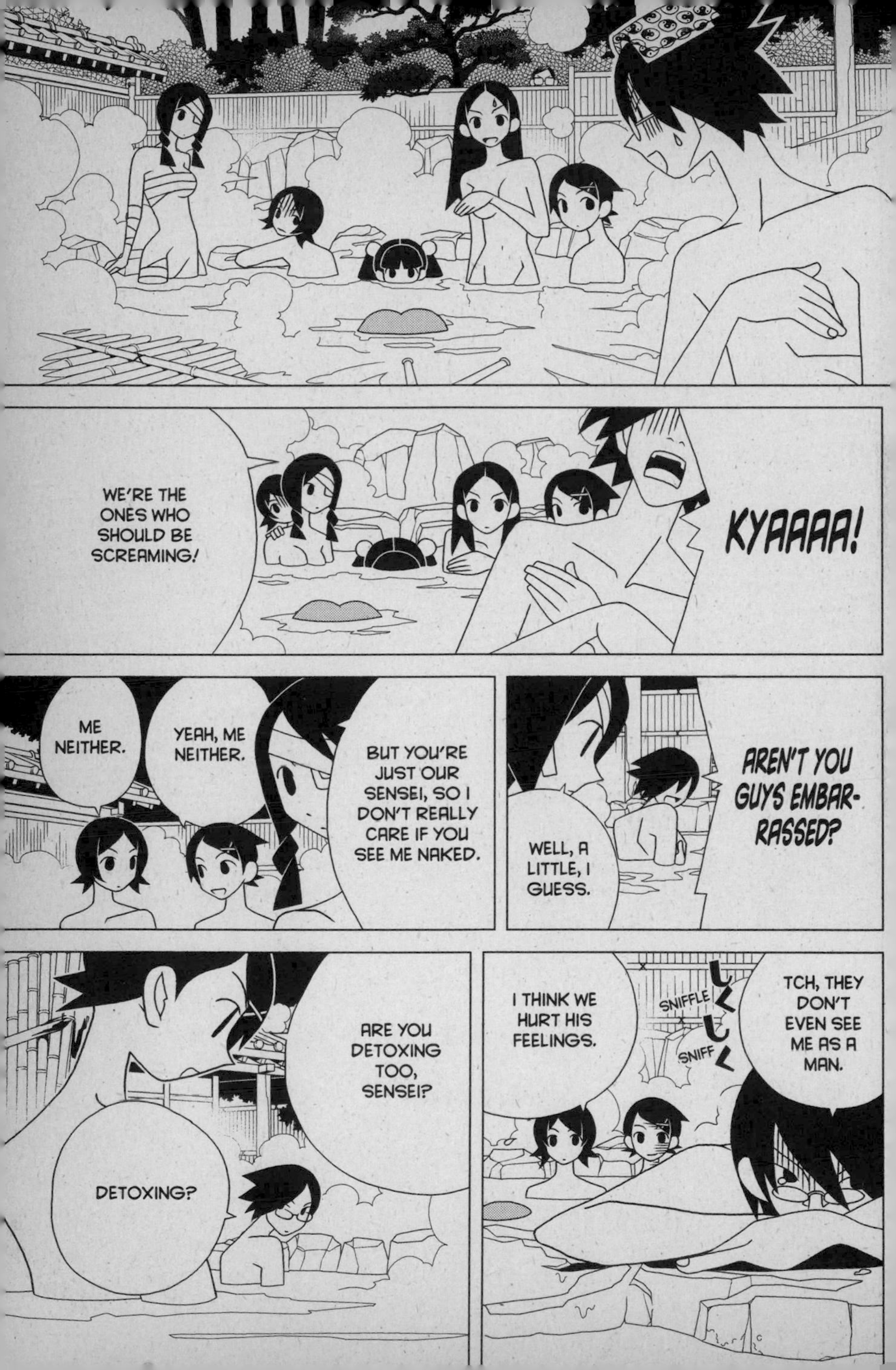
KYAAAA!
WE'RE THE ONES WHO SHOULD BE SCREAMING!
AREN'T YOU GUYS EMBAR-RASSED?
WELL, A LITTLE, I GUESS.
BUT YOU'RE JUST OUR SENSEI, SO I DON'T REALLY CARE IF YOU SEE ME NAKED.
YEAH, ME NEITHER.
ME NEITHER.
TCH, THEY DON'T EVEN SEE ME AS A MAN.
SNIFFLE
SNIFF
I THINK WE HURT HIS FEELINGS.
ARE YOU DETOXING TOO, SENSEI?
DETOXING?

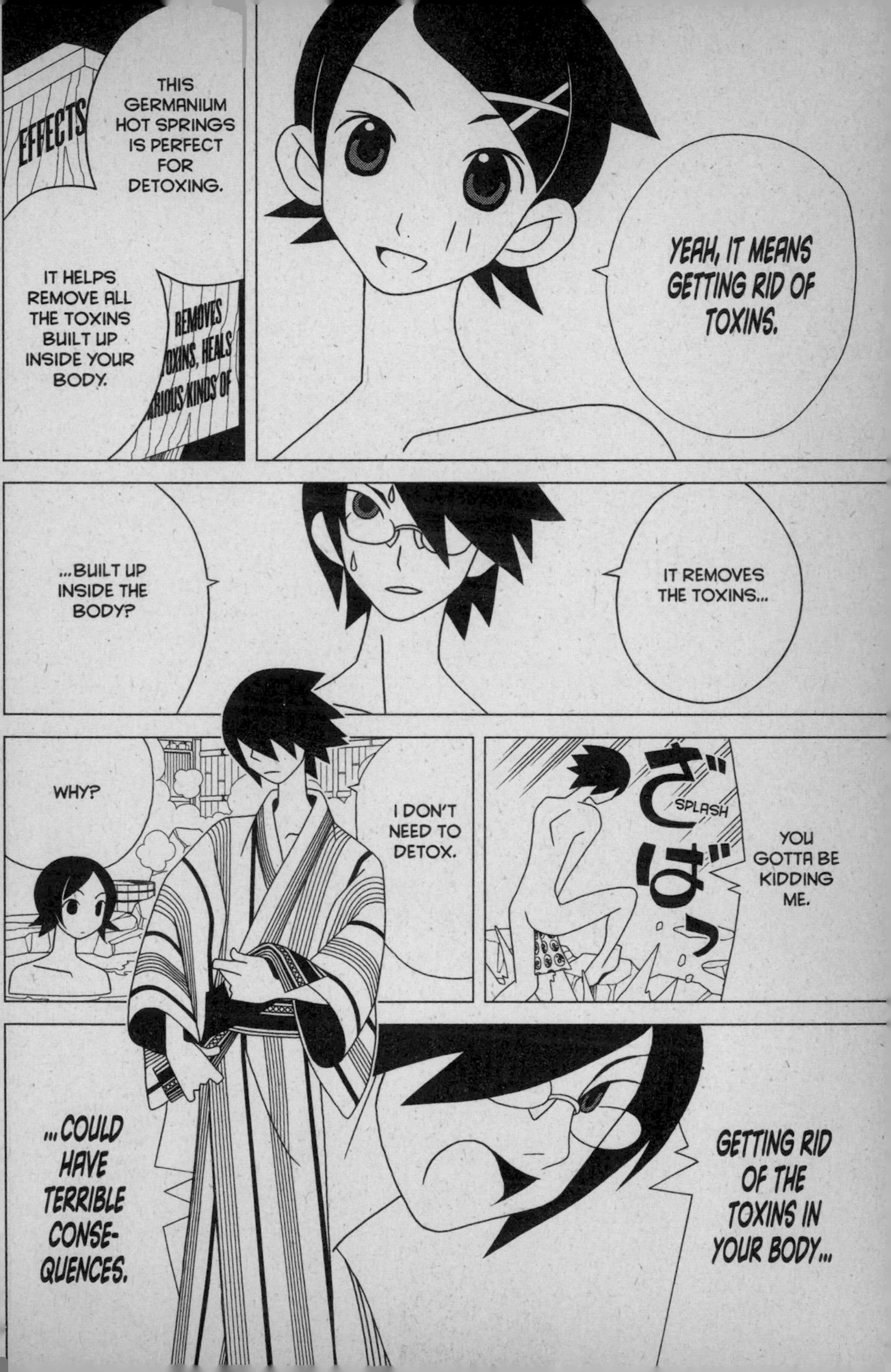
YEAH, IT MEANS GETTING RID OF TOXINS.
THIS GERMANIUM HOT SPRINGS IS PERFECT FOR DETOXING.
EFFECTS
REMOVES TOXINS, HEALS ARIOUS KINDS OF
IT HELPS REMOVE ALL THE TOXINS BUILT UP INSIDE YOUR BODY.
IT REMOVES THE TOXINS...
...BUILT UP INSIDE THE BODY?
ざばっ
SPLASH
YOU GOTTA BE KIDDING ME.
I DON'T NEED TO DETOX.
WHY?
GETTING RID OF THE TOXINS IN YOUR BODY...
...COULD HAVE TERRIBLE CONSE-QUENCES.

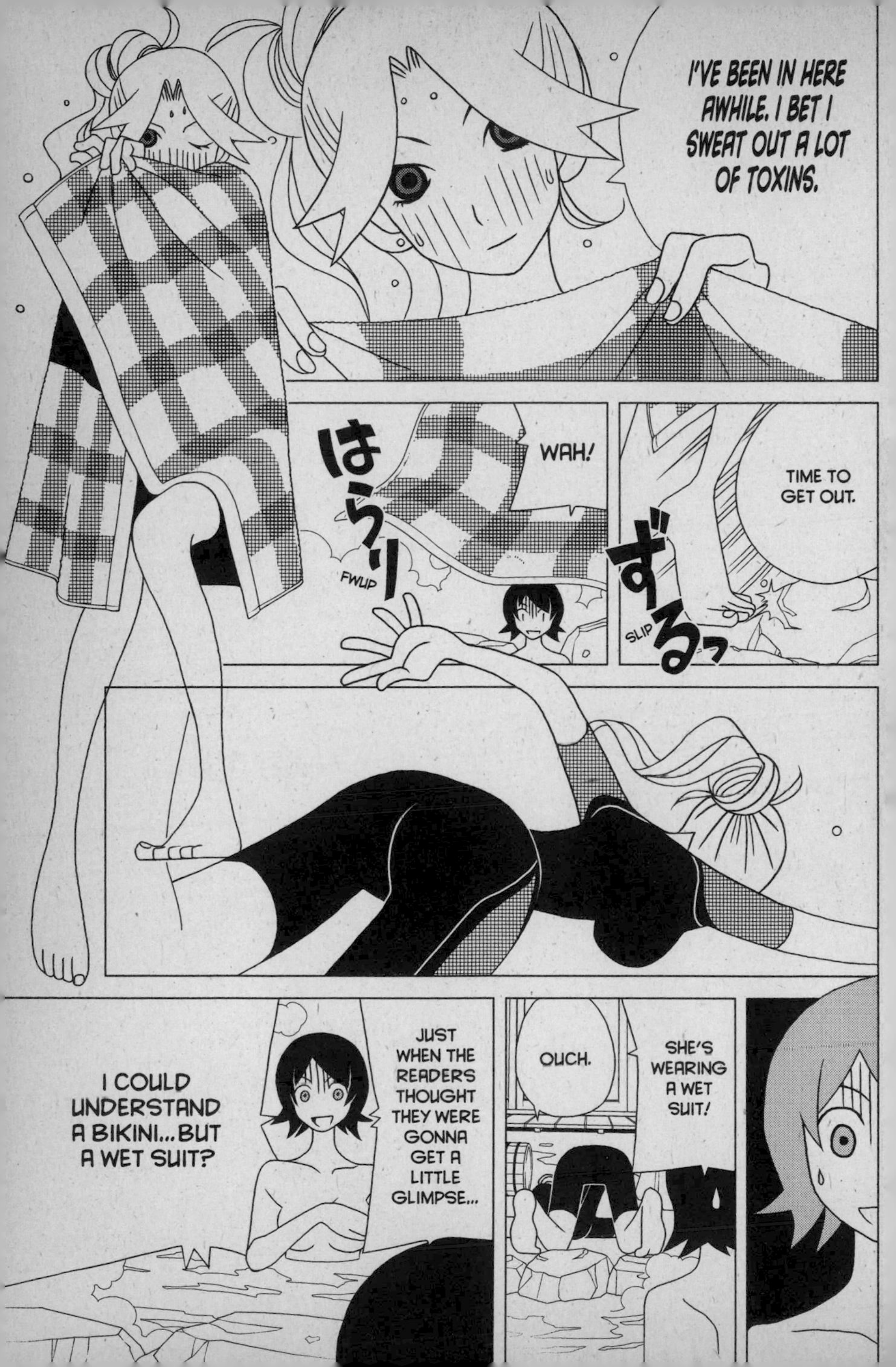
I'VE BEEN IN HERE AWHILE. I BET I SWEAT OUT A LOT OF TOXINS.
TIME TO GET OUT.
ずるっ
SLIP
WAH!
はらり
FWUP
SHE'S WEARING A WET SUIT!
OUCH.
JUST WHEN THE READERS THOUGHT THEY WERE GONNA GET A LITTLE GLIMPSE...
I COULD UNDERSTAND A BIKINI...BUT A WET SUIT?

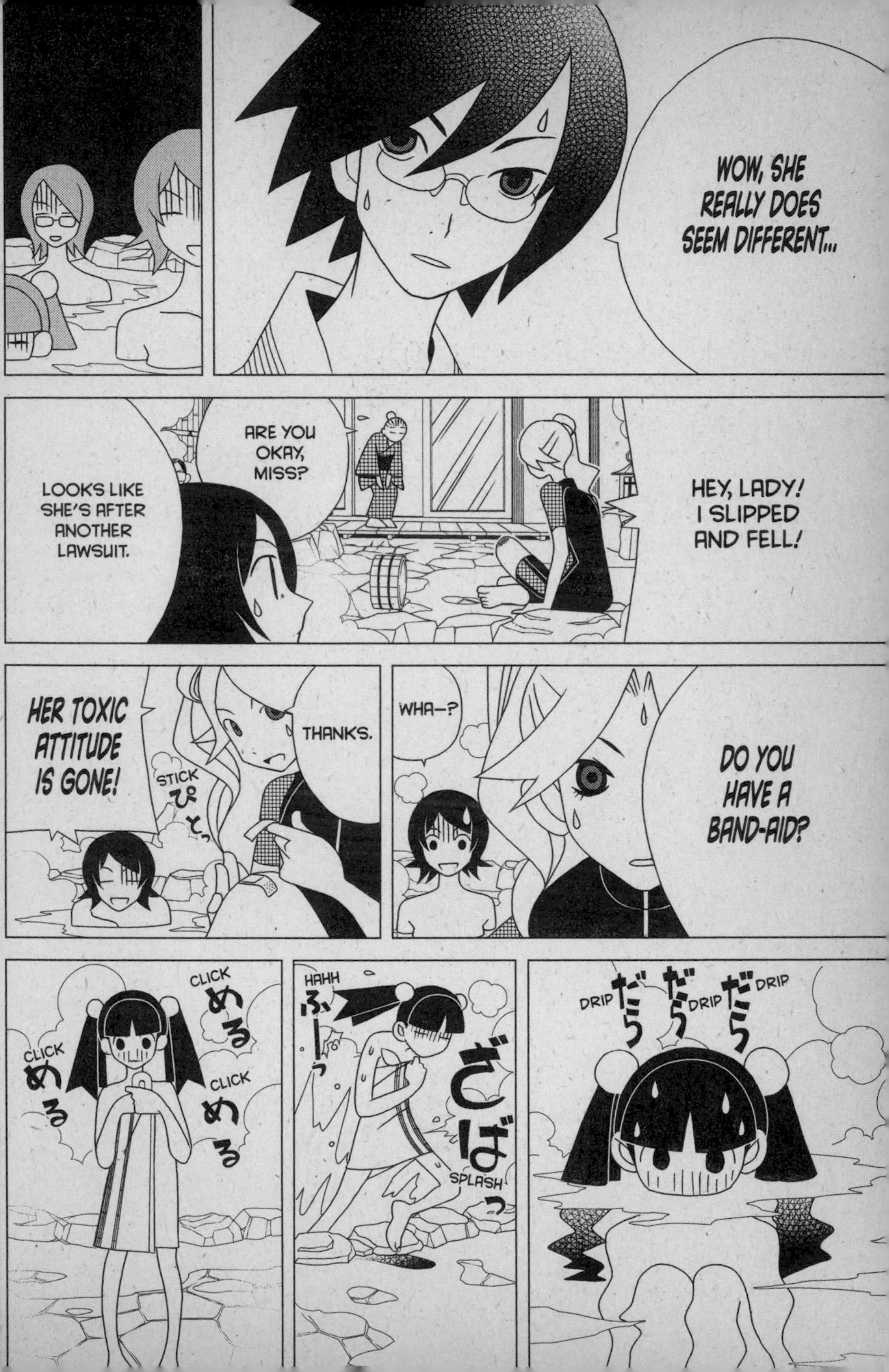
WOW, SHE REALLY DOES SEEM DIFFERENT...
HEY, LADY! I SLIPPED AND FELL!
ARE YOU OKAY, MISS?
LOOKS LIKE SHE'S AFTER ANOTHER LAWSUIT.
DO YOU HAVE A BAND-AID?
WHA-?
THANKS.
STICK
ぴと
HER TOXIC ATTITUDE IS GONE!
DRIP
だら
DRIP
だら
DRIP
だら
SPLASH
ざばっ
HAHH
ふーっ
CLICK
める
CLICK
める
CLICK
める

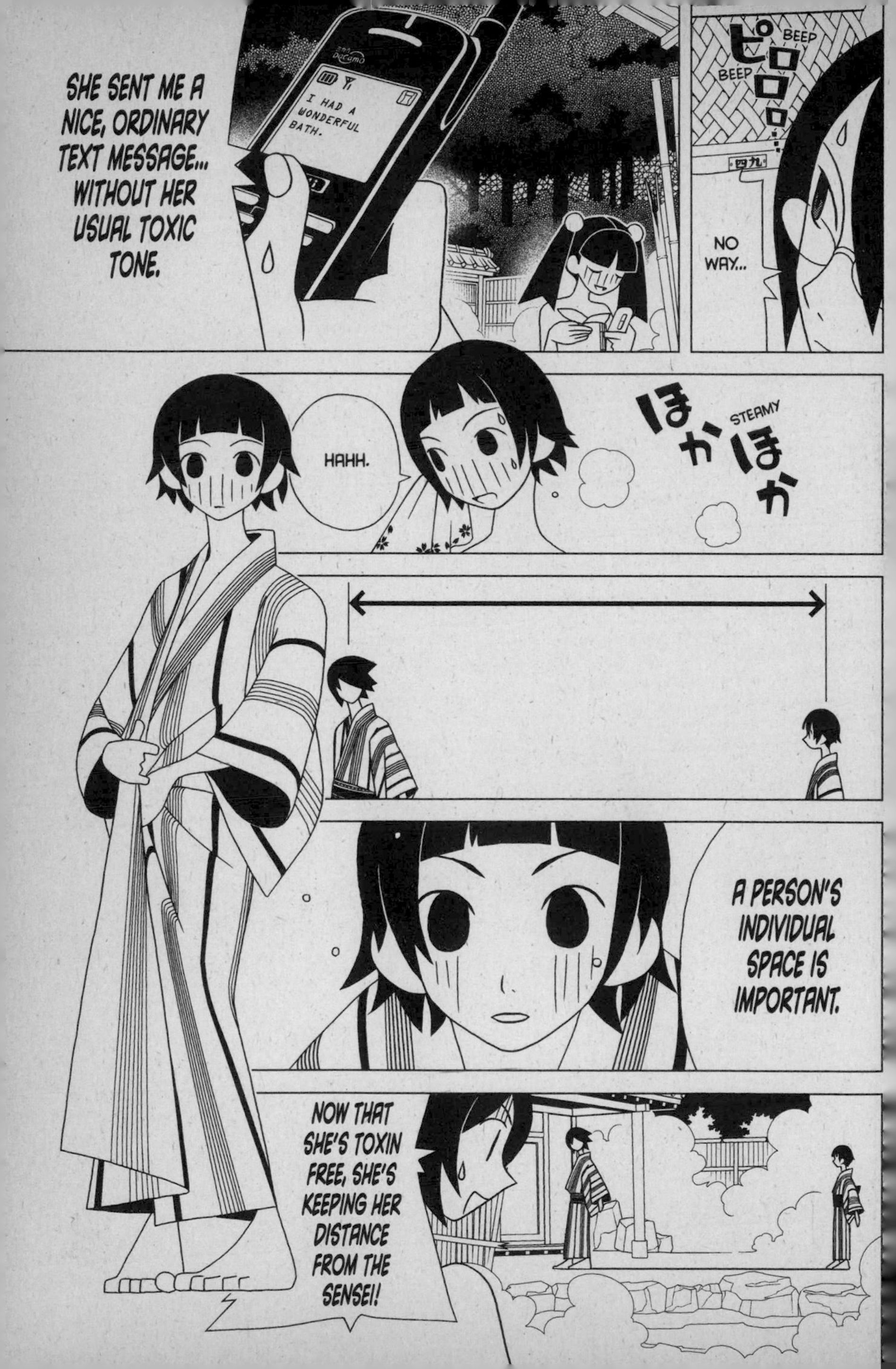
ピロロロ
BEEP
BEEP
NO WAY...
I HAD A WONDERFUL BATH.
SHE SENT ME A NICE, ORDINARY TEXT MESSAGE... WITHOUT HER USUAL TOXIC TONE.
ほかほか
STEAMY
HAHH.
A PERSON'S INDIVIDUAL SPACE IS IMPORTANT.
NOW THAT SHE'S TOXIN FREE, SHE'S KEEPING HER DISTANCE FROM THE SENSEI!

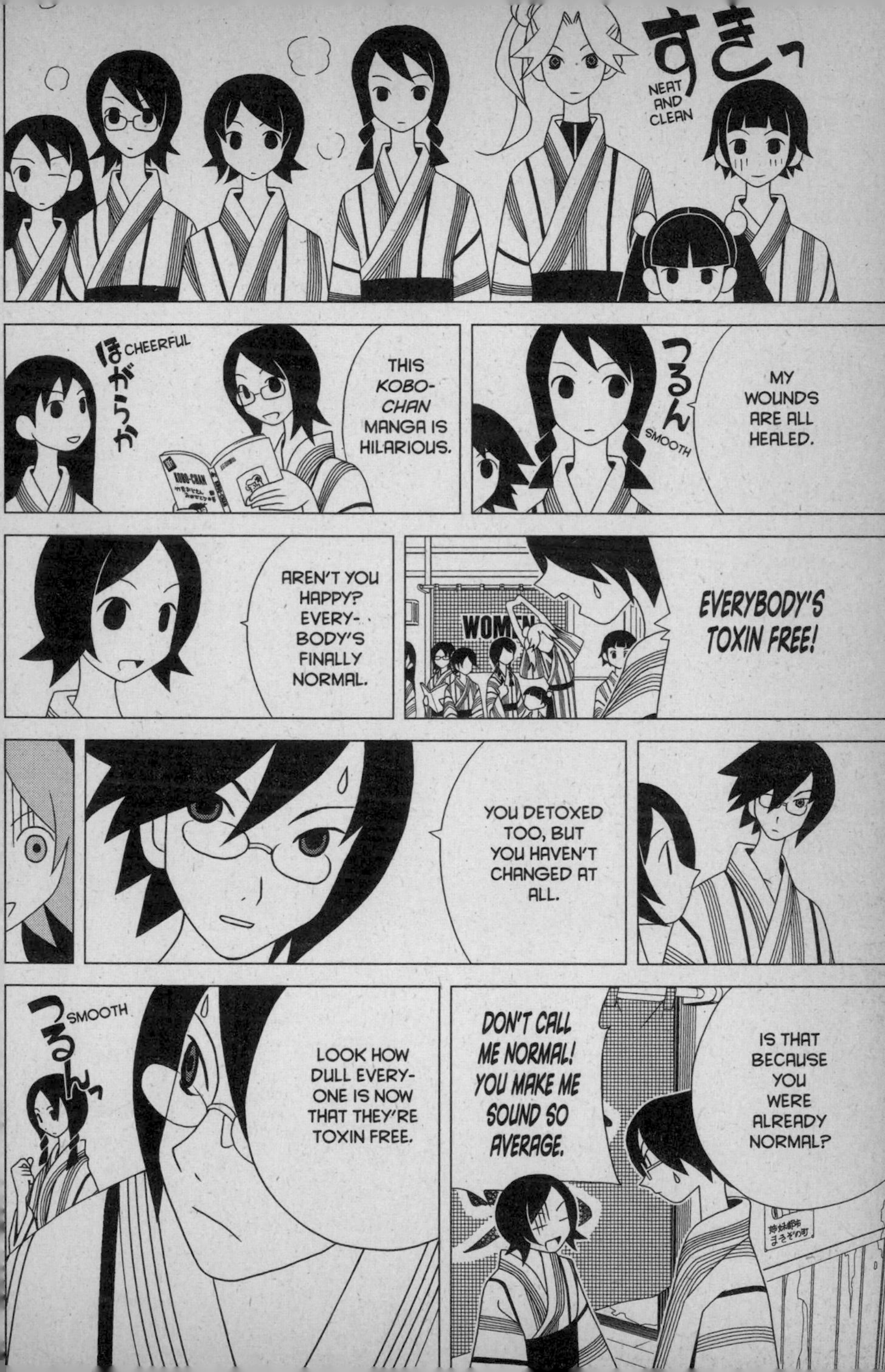
すきっ
NEAT AND CLEAN
つるん
SMOOTH
MY WOUNDS ARE ALL HEALED.
ほがらか
CHEERFUL
THIS KOBO-CHAN MANGA IS HILARIOUS.
KOBO-CHAN
WOMEN
EVERYBODY'S TOXIN FREE!
AREN'T YOU HAPPY? EVERY-BODY'S FINALLY NORMAL.
YOU DETOXED TOO, BUT YOU HAVEN'T CHANGED AT ALL.
IS THAT BECAUSE YOU WERE ALREADY NORMAL?
DON'T CALL ME NORMAL! YOU MAKE ME SOUND SO AVERAGE.
つるんっ
SMOOTH
LOOK HOW DULL EVERY-ONE IS NOW THAT THEY'RE TOXIN FREE.

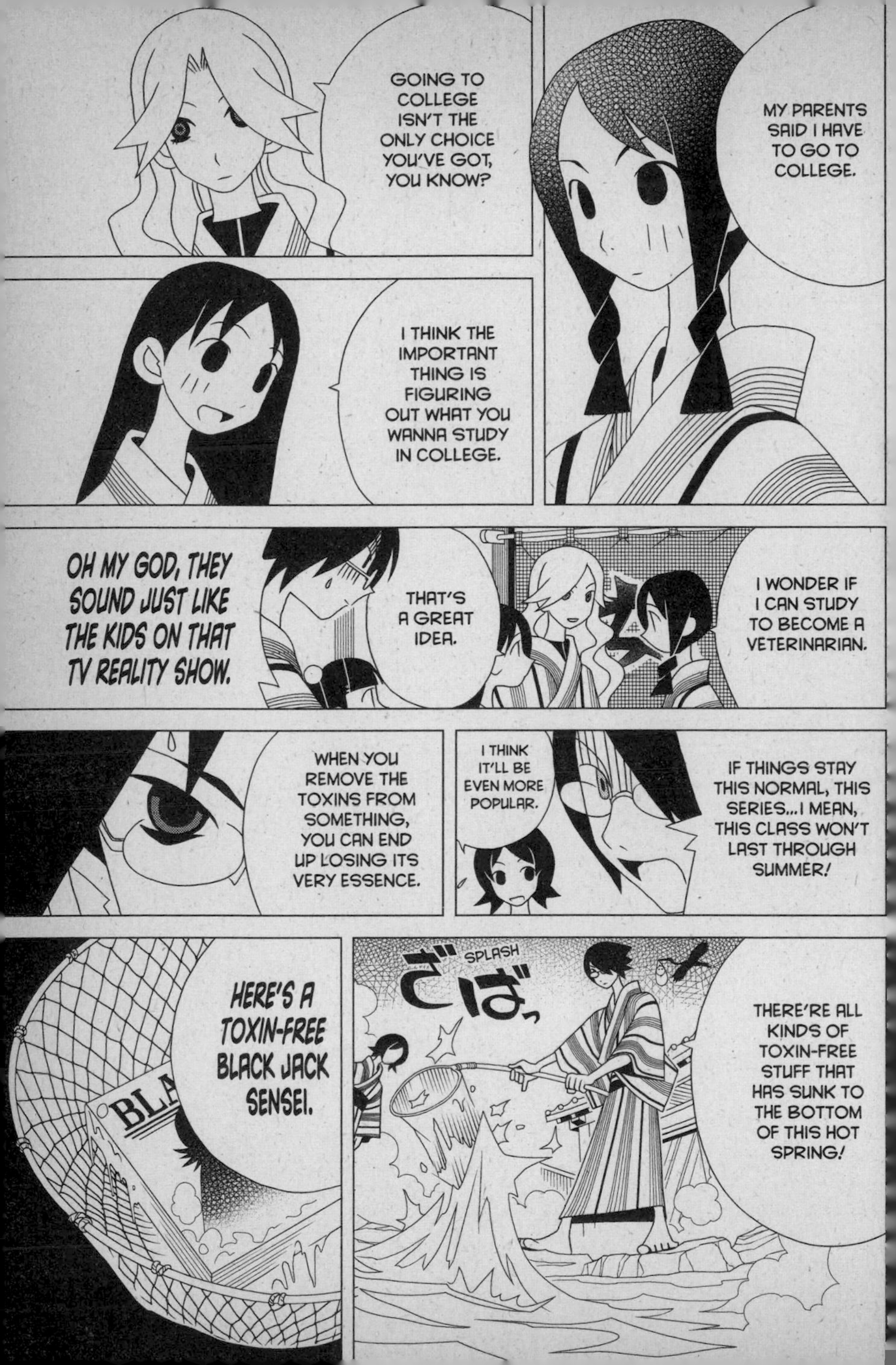
MY PARENTS SAID I HAVE TO GO TO COLLEGE.
GOING TO COLLEGE ISN'T THE ONLY CHOICE YOU'VE GOT, YOU KNOW?
I THINK THE IMPORTANT THING IS FIGURING OUT WHAT YOU WANNA STUDY IN COLLEGE.
I WONDER IF I CAN STUDY TO BECOME A VETERINARIAN.
THAT'S A GREAT IDEA.
OH MY GOD, THEY SOUND JUST LIKE THE KIDS ON THAT TV REALITY SHOW.
IF THINGS STAY THIS NORMAL, THIS SERIES...I MEAN, THIS CLASS WON'T LAST THROUGH SUMMER!
I THINK IT'LL BE EVEN MORE POPULAR.
WHEN YOU REMOVE THE TOXINS FROM SOMETHING, YOU CAN END UP LOSING ITS VERY ESSENCE.
THERE'RE ALL KINDS OF TOXIN-FREE STUFF THAT HAS SUNK TO THE BOTTOM OF THIS HOT SPRING!
ざばっ
SPLASH
HERE'S A TOXIN-FREE BLACK JACK SENSEI.

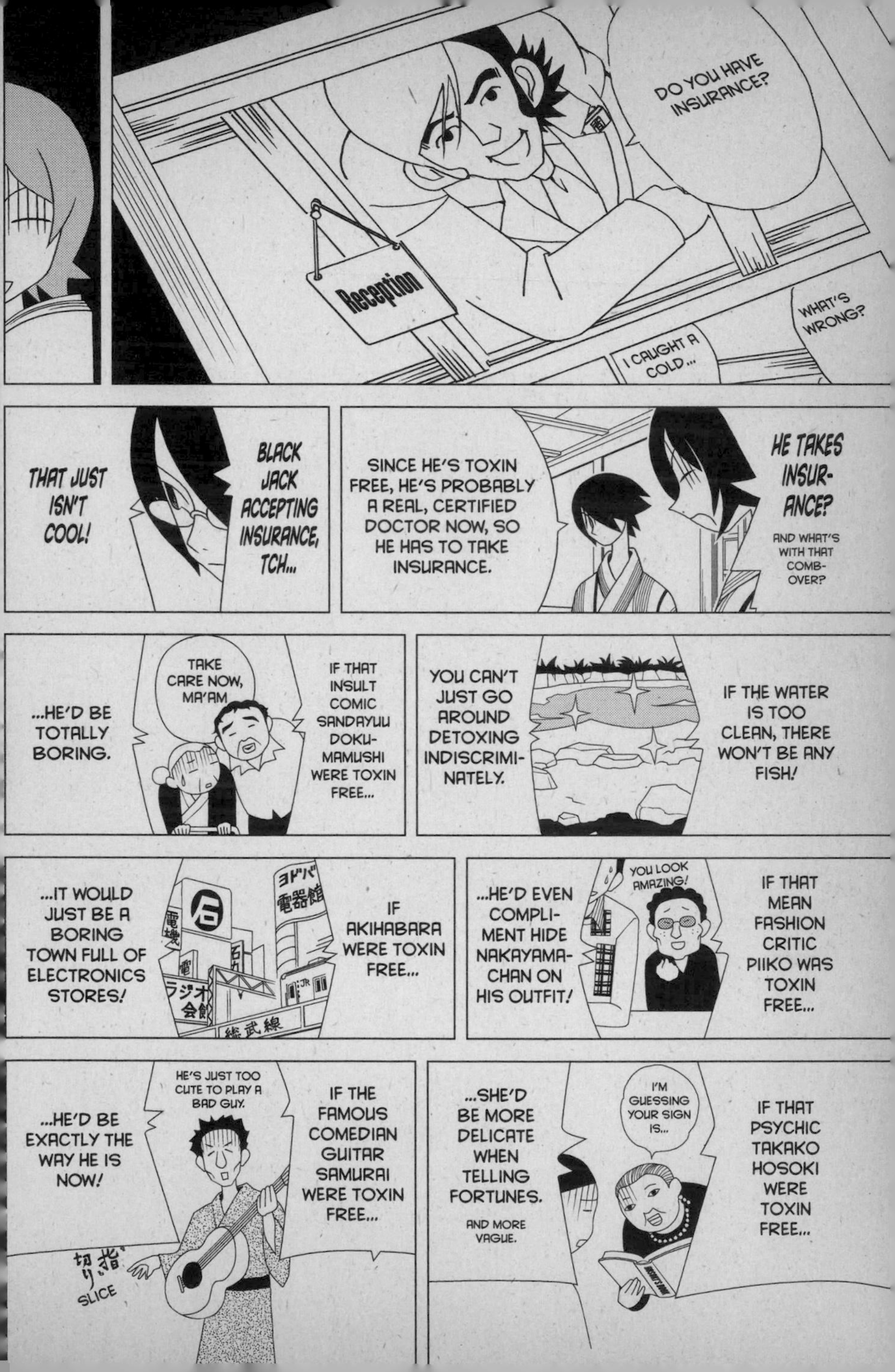
DO YOU HAVE INSURANCE?
WHAT'S WRONG?
I CAUGHT A COLD...
Reception
HE TAKES INSURANCE?
AND WHAT'S WITH THAT COMB-OVER?
SINCE HE'S TOXIN FREE, HE'S PROBABLY A REAL, CERTIFIED DOCTOR NOW, SO HE HAS TO TAKE INSURANCE.
BLACK JACK ACCEPTING INSURANCE, TCH...
THAT JUST ISN'T COOL!
IF THE WATER IS TOO CLEAN, THERE WON'T BE ANY FISH!
YOU CAN'T JUST GO AROUND DETOXING INDISCRIMINATELY.
IF THAT INSULT COMIC SANDAYUU DOKU-MAMUSHI WERE TOXIN FREE...
TAKE CARE NOW, MA'AM
...HE'D BE TOTALLY BORING.
IF THAT MEAN FASHION CRITIC PIIKO WAS TOXIN FREE...
YOU LOOK AMAZING!
...HE'D EVEN COMPLIMENT HIDE NAKAYAMA-CHAN ON HIS OUTFIT!
IF AKIHABARA WERE TOXIN FREE...
ヨドバ
電器館
ラジオ会館
JR
総武線
...IT WOULD JUST BE A BORING TOWN FULL OF ELECTRONICS STORES!
IF THAT PSYCHIC TAKAKO HOSOKI WERE TOXIN FREE...
I'M GUESSING YOUR SIGN IS...
...SHE'D BE MORE DELICATE WHEN TELLING FORTUNES.
AND MORE VAGUE.
IF THE FAMOUS COMEDIAN GUITAR SAMURAI WERE TOXIN FREE...
HE'S JUST TOO CUTE TO PLAY A BAD GUY.
...HE'D BE EXACTLY THE WAY HE IS NOW!
SLICE

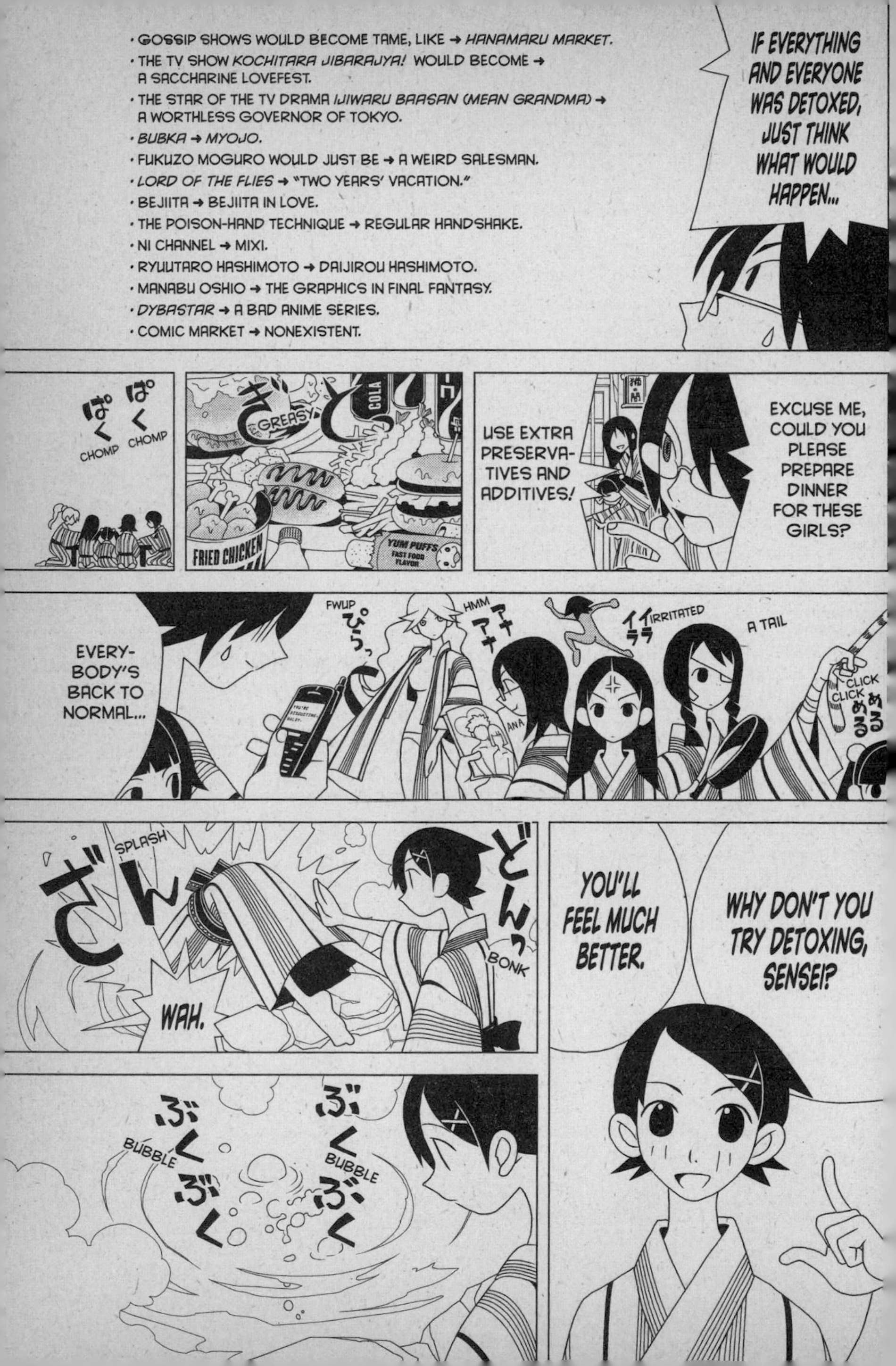
IF EVERYTHING AND EVERYONE WAS DETOXED, JUST THINK WHAT WOULD HAPPEN...
• GOSSIP SHOWS WOULD BECOME TAME, LIKE → *HANAMARU MARKET*.
• THE TV SHOW *KOCHITARA JIBARAJYA!* WOULD BECOME → A SACCHARINE LOVEFEST.
• THE STAR OF THE TV DRAMA *IJIWARU BAASAN (MEAN GRANDMA)* → A WORTHLESS GOVERNOR OF TOKYO.
• *BUBKA* → *MYOJO*.
• FUKUZO MOGURO WOULD JUST BE → A WEIRD SALESMAN.
• *LORD OF THE FLIES* → "TWO YEARS' VACATION."
• BEJIITA → BEJIITA IN LOVE.
• THE POISON-HAND TECHNIQUE → REGULAR HANDSHAKE.
• NI CHANNEL → MIXI.
• RYUUTARO HASHIMOTO → DAIJIROU HASHIMOTO.
• MANABU OSHIO → THE GRAPHICS IN FINAL FANTASY.
• *DYBASTAR* → A BAD ANIME SERIES.
• COMIC MARKET → NONEXISTENT.
EXCUSE ME, COULD YOU PLEASE PREPARE DINNER FOR THESE GIRLS?
USE EXTRA PRESERVATIVES AND ADDITIVES!
ぎど GREASY
COLA
FRIED CHICKEN
YUM PUFFS FAST FOOD FLAVOR
ぱくぱく CHOMP CHOMP
めるめる CLICK CLICK
A TAIL
イライラ IRRITATED
アナアナ HMM
ANA
ぴらっ FWUP
EVERYBODY'S BACK TO NORMAL...
WHY DON'T YOU TRY DETOXING, SENSEI?
YOU'LL FEEL MUCH BETTER.
どんっ BONK
ざんっ SPLASH
WAH.
ぶくぶく BUBBLE
ぶくぶく BUBBLE

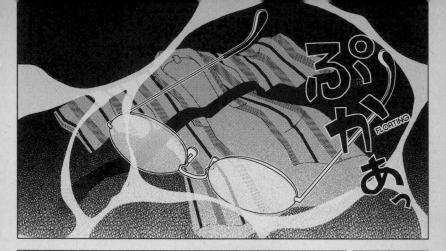

THIS IS ALL THAT'S LEFT OF HIM AFTER DETOXING.

SENSEI...

先生ー

SENSEI...

HIS WHOLE BODY WAS MADE UP OF TOXINS.

WANNA DETOX?

I JUST REALIZED THAT, TO MOTHER EARTH, THE HUMAN RACE IS NOTHING BUT A TOXIN.

BUBBLE

BUBBLE

BUBBLE

BUBBLE

TOXIN-FREE CHIRI-CHAN

ペチャ
CHATTER
ペチャ
CHATTER
THAT'LL BE 1,260 YEN.*
1260円
UH...MY SHARE IS 630...
1260円
JUST GIVE ME 600 YEN.*

*$12.60

*$6

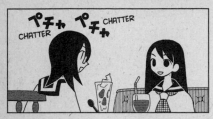

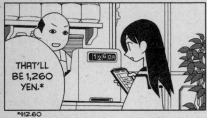

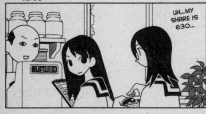

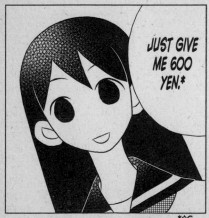

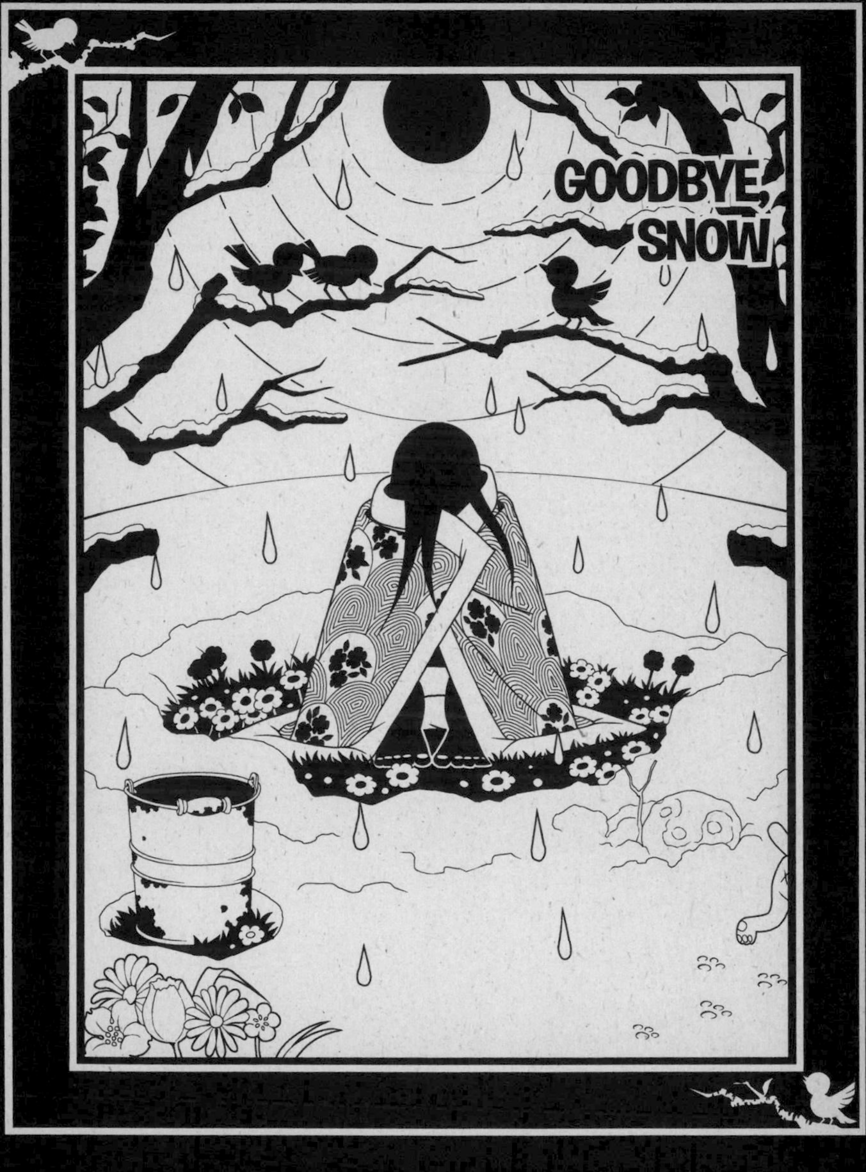
GOODBYE,
SNOW

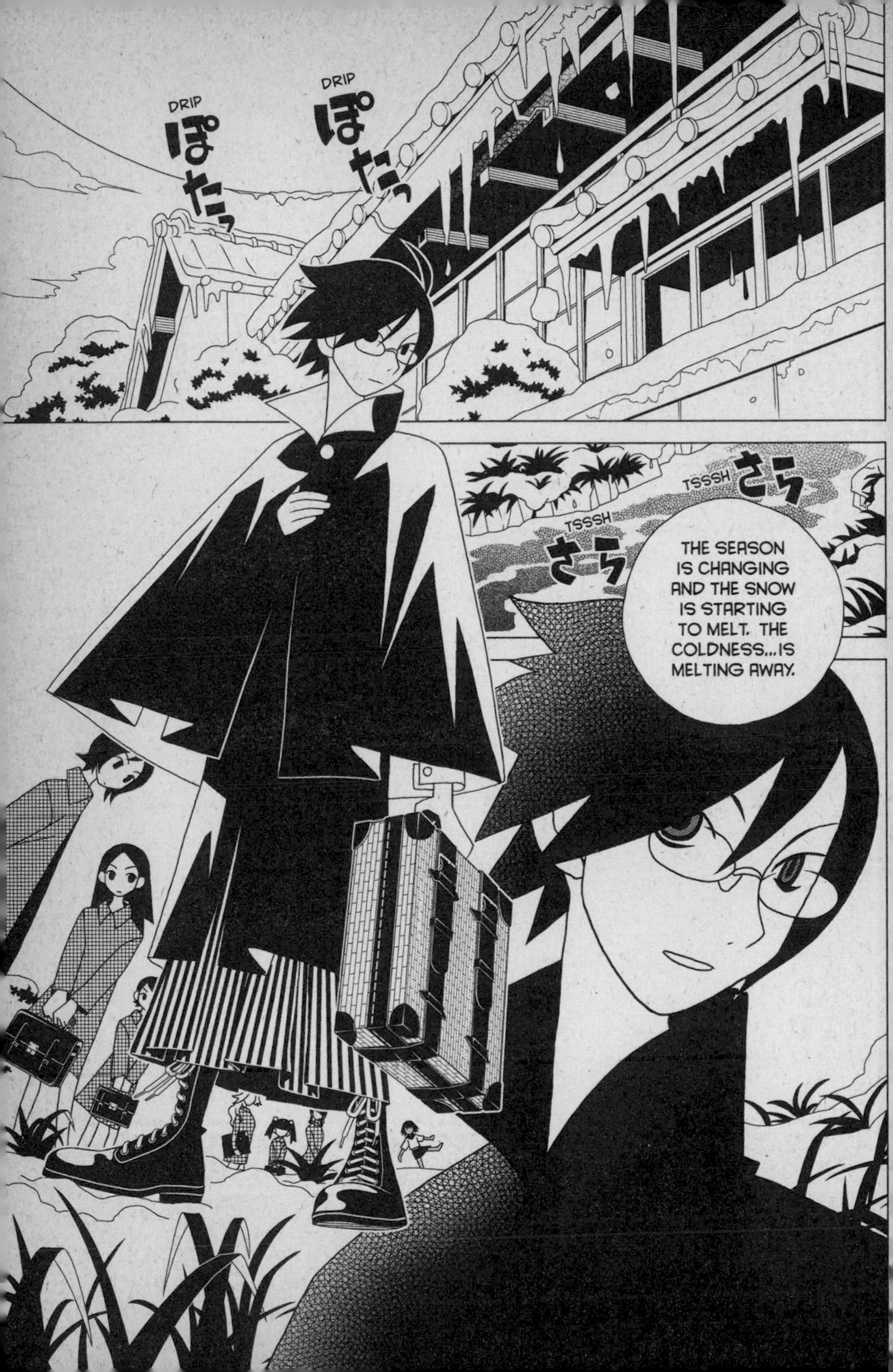
DRIP
ぽたっ
DRIP
ぽたっ
TSSSH
さら
TSSSH
さら
THE SEASON IS CHANGING AND THE SNOW IS STARTING TO MELT. THE COLDNESS...IS MELTING AWAY.

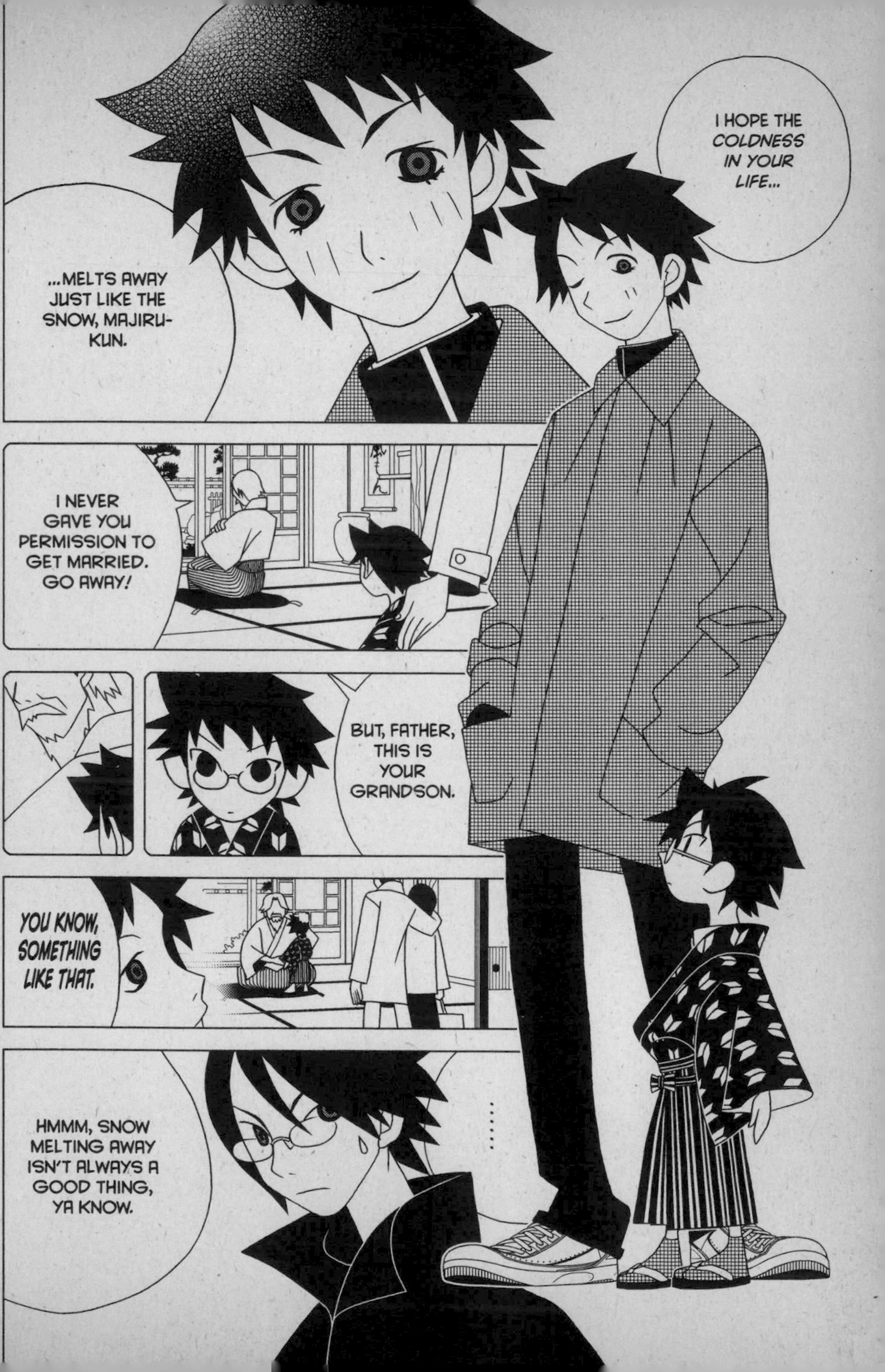
I HOPE THE COLDNESS IN YOUR LIFE...
...MELTS AWAY JUST LIKE THE SNOW, MAJIRU-KUN.
I NEVER GAVE YOU PERMISSION TO GET MARRIED. GO AWAY!
BUT, FATHER, THIS IS YOUR GRANDSON.
YOU KNOW, SOMETHING LIKE THAT.
......
HMMM, SNOW MELTING AWAY ISN'T ALWAYS A GOOD THING, YA KNOW.

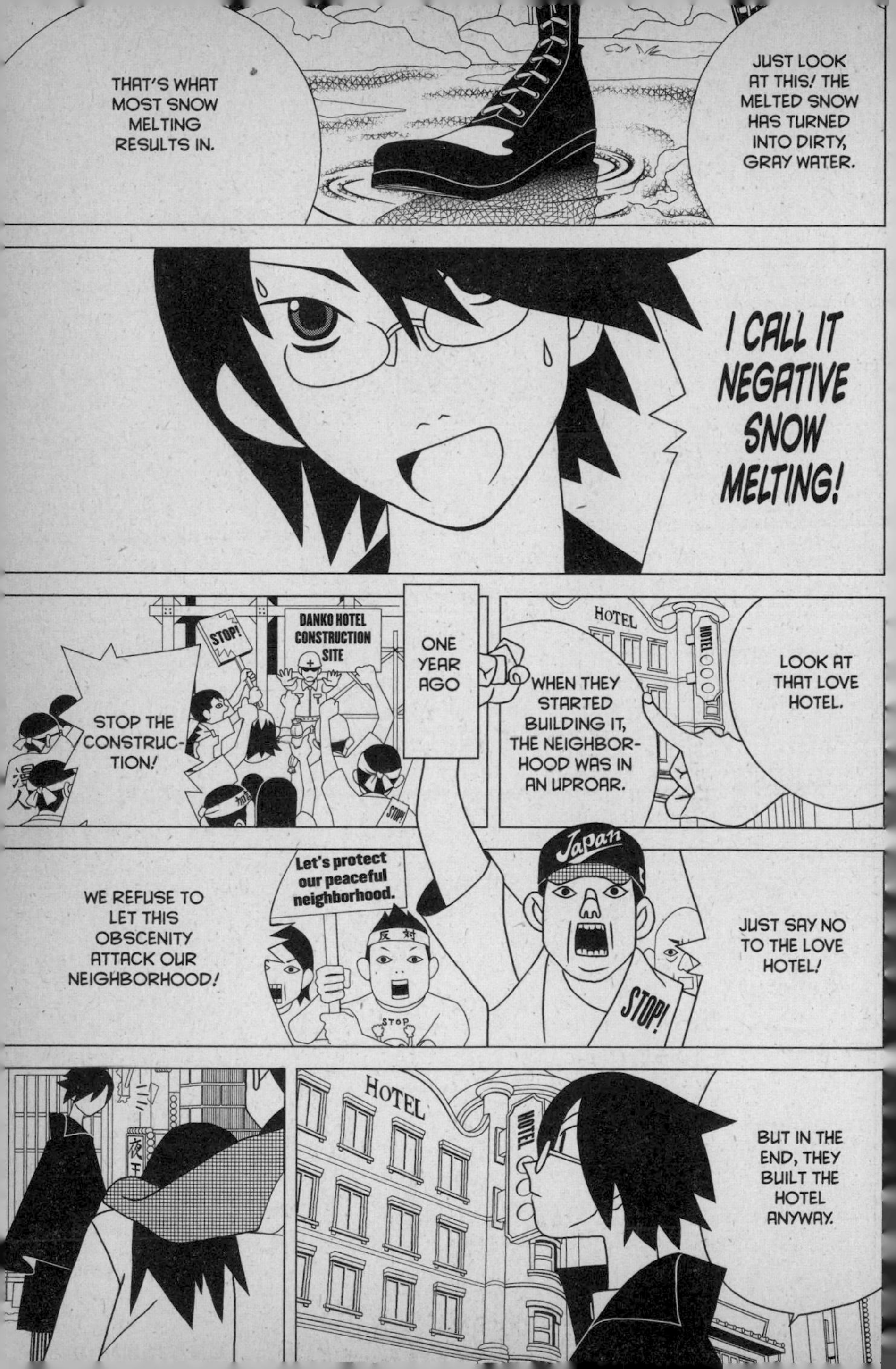
JUST LOOK AT THIS! THE MELTED SNOW HAS TURNED INTO DIRTY, GRAY WATER.
THAT'S WHAT MOST SNOW MELTING RESULTS IN.
I CALL IT NEGATIVE SNOW MELTING!
LOOK AT THAT LOVE HOTEL.
HOTEL
HOTEL
WHEN THEY STARTED BUILDING IT, THE NEIGHBORHOOD WAS IN AN UPROAR.
ONE YEAR AGO
DANKO HOTEL CONSTRUCTION SITE
STOP!
STOP THE CONSTRUCTION!
STOP!
JUST SAY NO TO THE LOVE HOTEL!
Japan
STOP!
Let's protect our peaceful neighborhood.
反対
STOP
WE REFUSE TO LET THIS OBSCENITY ATTACK OUR NEIGHBORHOOD!
BUT IN THE END, THEY BUILT THE HOTEL ANYWAY.
HOTEL
HOTEL

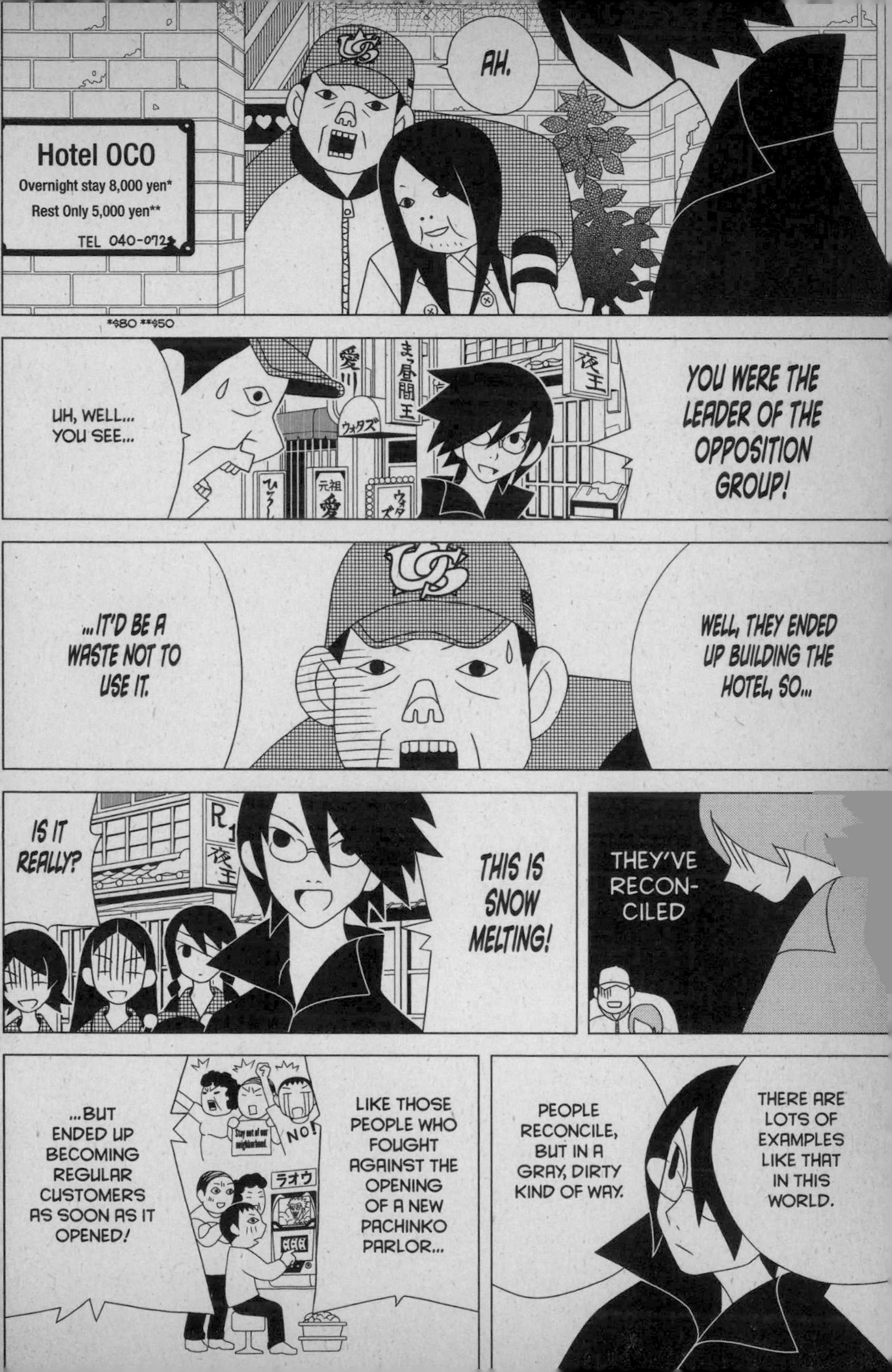
AH.
Hotel OCO
Overnight stay 8,000 yen*
Rest Only 5,000 yen**
TEL 040-072
*$80 **$50
YOU WERE THE LEADER OF THE OPPOSITION GROUP!
UH, WELL... YOU SEE...
WELL, THEY ENDED UP BUILDING THE HOTEL, SO...
...IT'D BE A WASTE NOT TO USE IT.
THEY'VE RECONCILED
THIS IS SNOW MELTING!
IS IT REALLY?
THERE ARE LOTS OF EXAMPLES LIKE THAT IN THIS WORLD.
PEOPLE RECONCILE, BUT IN A GRAY, DIRTY KIND OF WAY.
LIKE THOSE PEOPLE WHO FOUGHT AGAINST THE OPENING OF A NEW PACHINKO PARLOR...
Stay out of our neighborhood.
NO!
ラオウ
...BUT ENDED UP BECOMING REGULAR CUSTOMERS AS SOON AS IT OPENED!

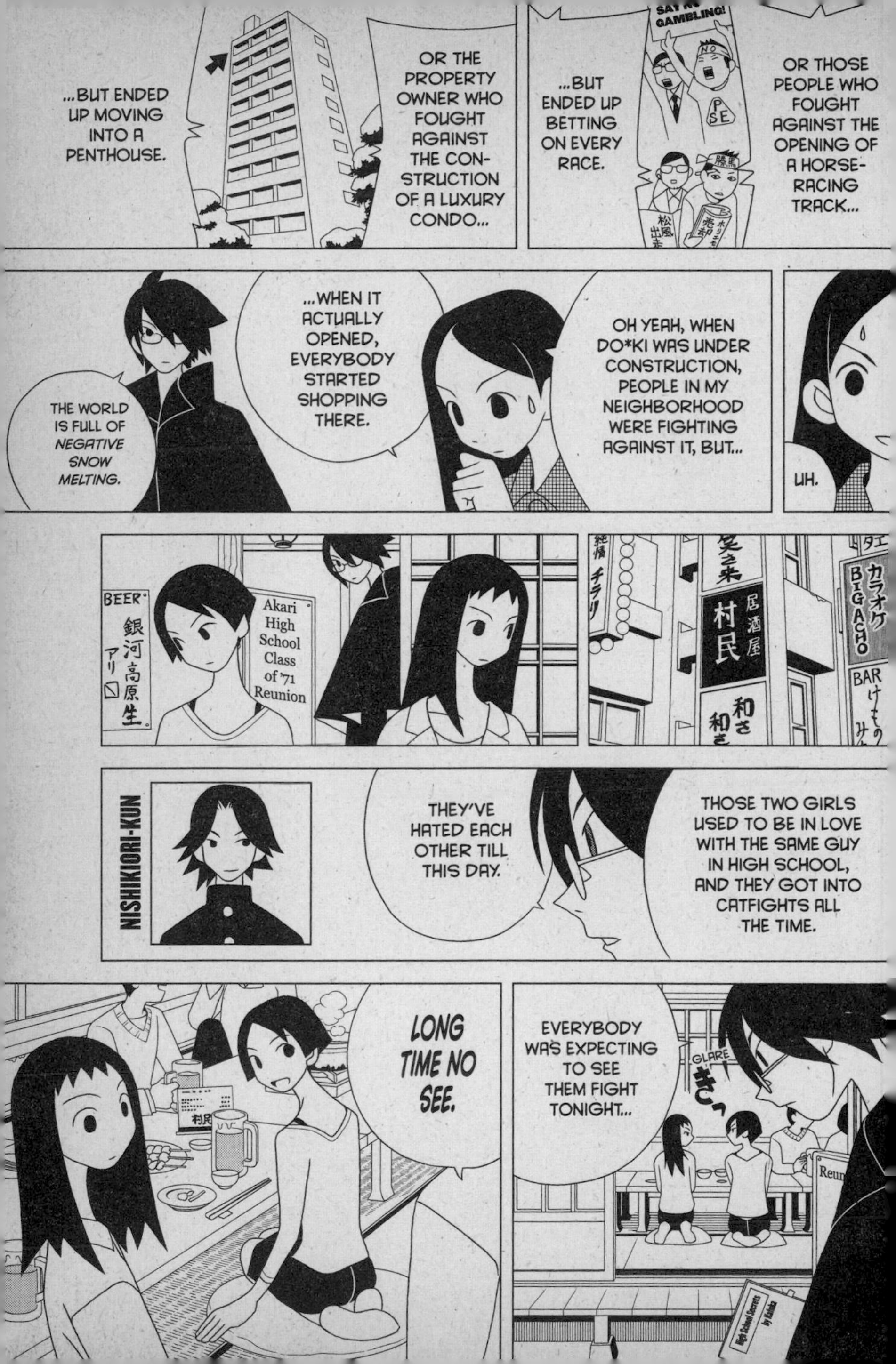
GAMBLING!
NO
PSE
OR THOSE PEOPLE WHO FOUGHT AGAINST THE OPENING OF A HORSE-RACING TRACK...
...BUT ENDED UP BETTING ON EVERY RACE.
OR THE PROPERTY OWNER WHO FOUGHT AGAINST THE CON-STRUCTION OF A LUXURY CONDO...
...BUT ENDED UP MOVING INTO A PENTHOUSE.
UH.
OH YEAH, WHEN DO*KI WAS UNDER CONSTRUCTION, PEOPLE IN MY NEIGHBORHOOD WERE FIGHTING AGAINST IT, BUT...
...WHEN IT ACTUALLY OPENED, EVERYBODY STARTED SHOPPING THERE.
THE WORLD IS FULL OF *NEGATIVE SNOW MELTING.*
カラオケ
BIG ACHO
BAR
居酒屋
村民
BEER
銀河高原生
アリ
Akari High School Class of '71 Reunion
THOSE TWO GIRLS USED TO BE IN LOVE WITH THE SAME GUY IN HIGH SCHOOL, AND THEY GOT INTO CATFIGHTS ALL THE TIME.
THEY'VE HATED EACH OTHER TILL THIS DAY.
NISHIKIORI-KUN
EVERYBODY WAS EXPECTING TO SEE THEM FIGHT TONIGHT...
GLARE
きっ
LONG TIME NO SEE.

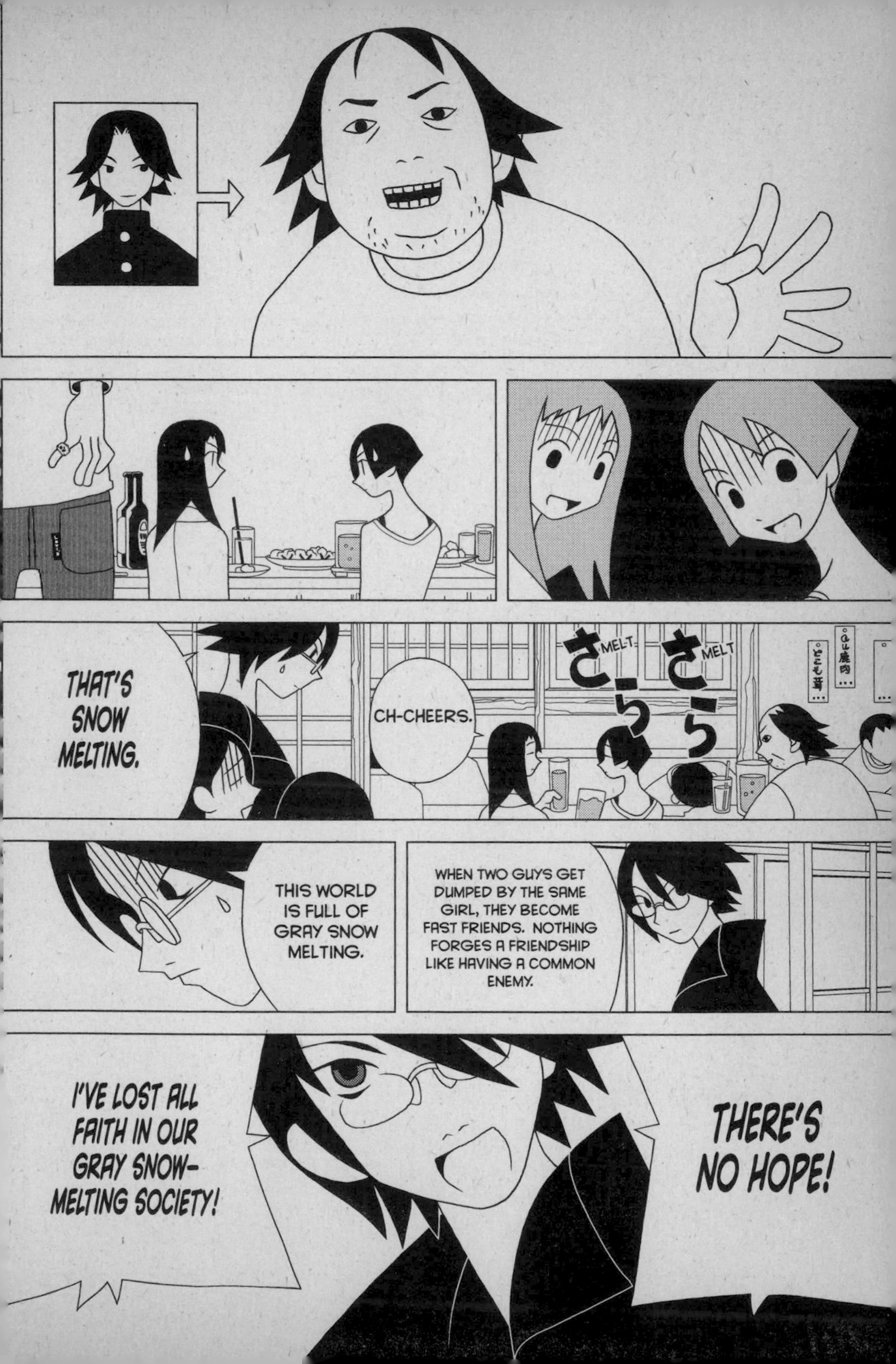

さら MELT
さら MELT-
CH-CHEERS.
THAT'S SNOW MELTING.
WHEN TWO GUYS GET DUMPED BY THE SAME GIRL, THEY BECOME FAST FRIENDS. NOTHING FORGES A FRIENDSHIP LIKE HAVING A COMMON ENEMY.
THIS WORLD IS FULL OF GRAY SNOW MELTING.
THERE'S NO HOPE!
I'VE LOST ALL FAITH IN OUR GRAY SNOW-MELTING SOCIETY!

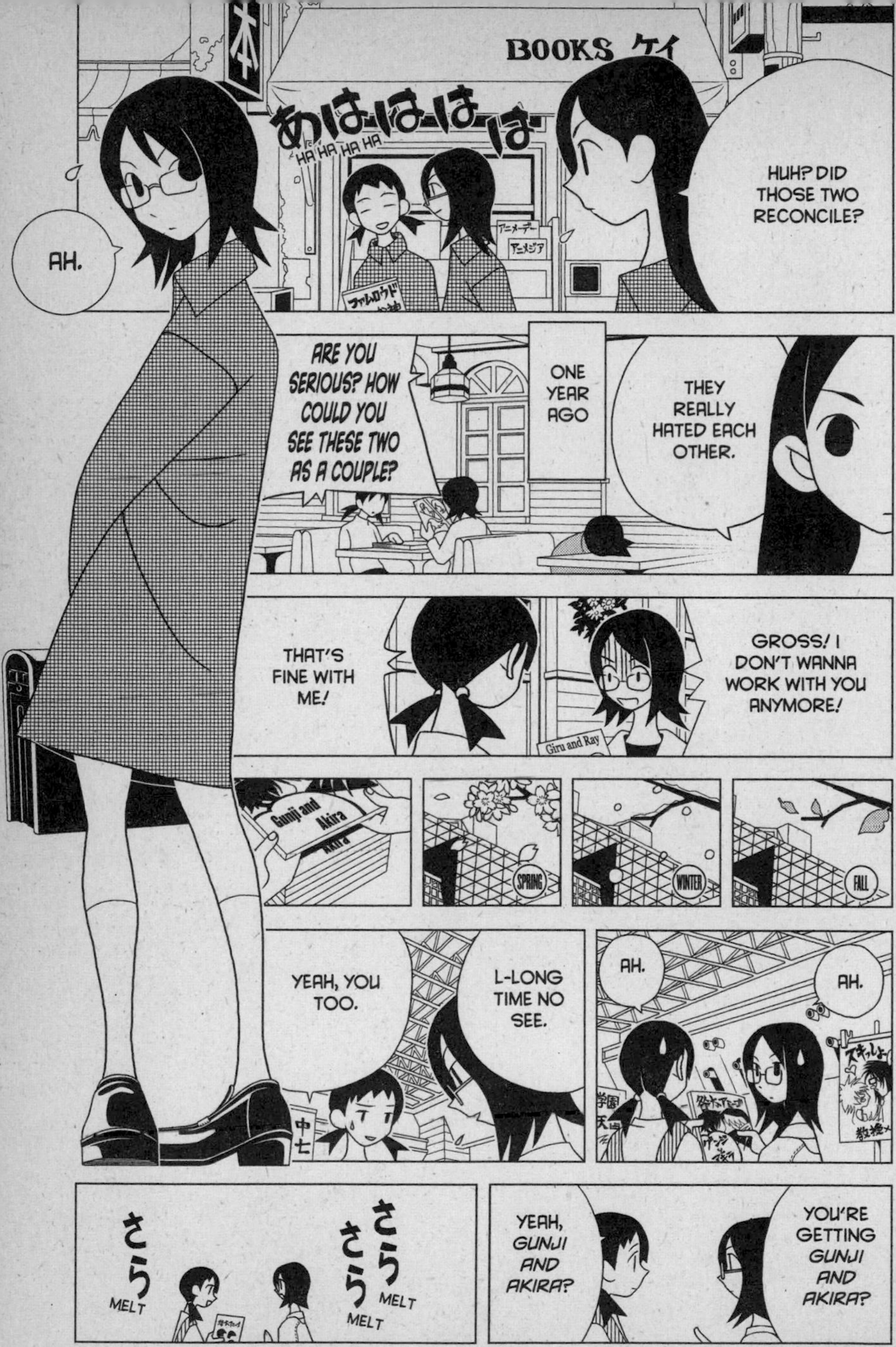
BOOKS ケイ
HUH? DID THOSE TWO RECONCILE?
あははは は
HA HA HA HA
アニメジア
THEY REALLY HATED EACH OTHER.
ONE YEAR AGO
ARE YOU SERIOUS? HOW COULD YOU SEE THESE TWO AS A COUPLE?
GROSS! I DON'T WANNA WORK WITH YOU ANYMORE!
Giru and Ray
THAT'S FINE WITH ME!
FALL
WINTER
SPRING
Gunji and Akira
AH.
AH.
L-LONG TIME NO SEE.
YEAH, YOU TOO.
AH.
YOU'RE GETTING GUNJI AND AKIRA?
YEAH, GUNJI AND AKIRA?
さら さら
MELT
MELT
さら
MELT

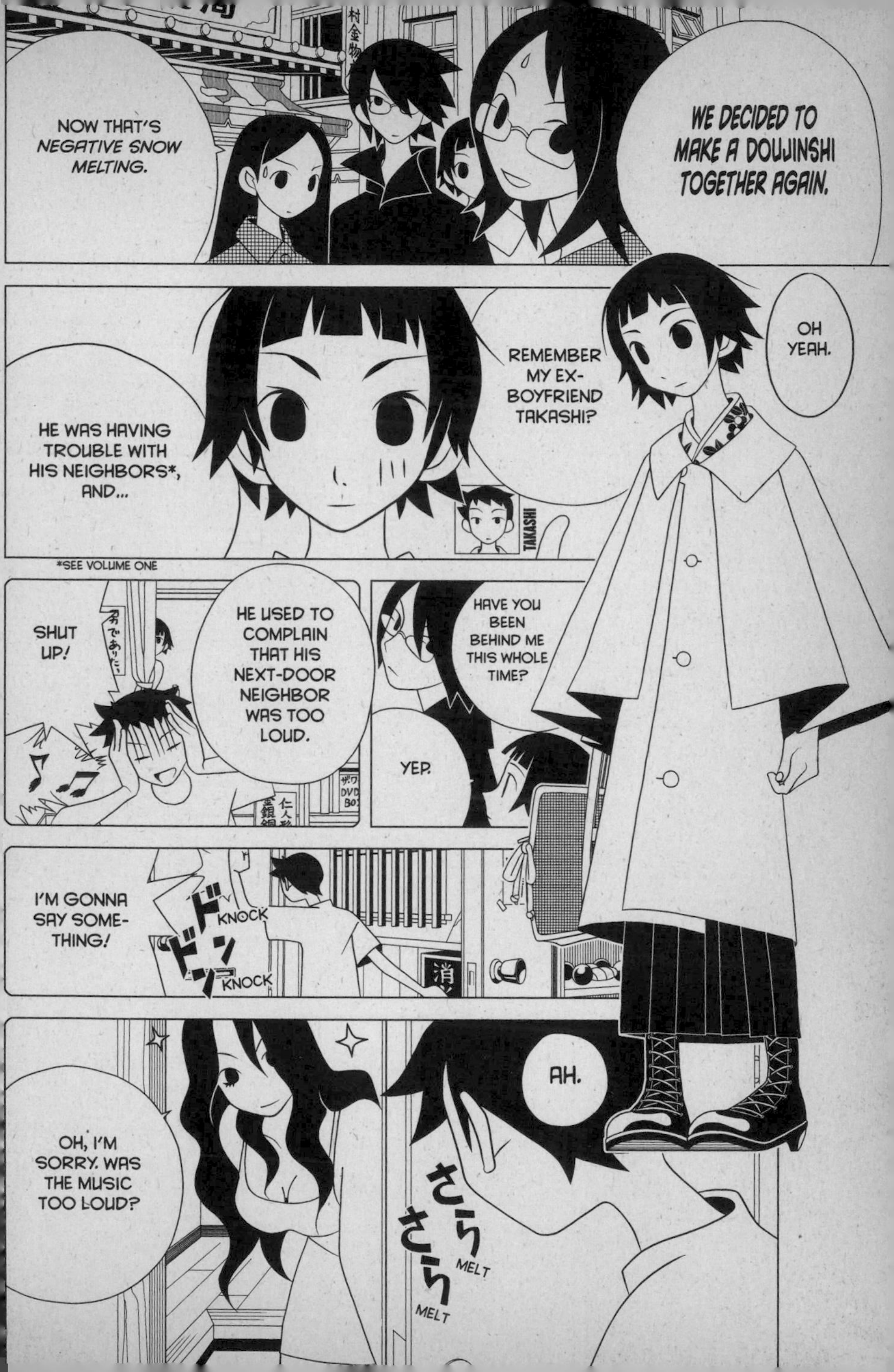
WE DECIDED TO MAKE A DOUJINSHI TOGETHER AGAIN.
NOW THAT'S *NEGATIVE SNOW MELTING.*
OH YEAH.
REMEMBER MY EX-BOYFRIEND TAKASHI?
TAKASHI
HE WAS HAVING TROUBLE WITH HIS NEIGHBORS*, AND...
*SEE VOLUME ONE
HAVE YOU BEEN BEHIND ME THIS WHOLE TIME?
YEP.
HE USED TO COMPLAIN THAT HIS NEXT-DOOR NEIGHBOR WAS TOO LOUD.
SHUT UP!
ドン KNOCK
ドン KNOCK
I'M GONNA SAY SOME-THING!
AH.
さら MELT
さら MELT
OH, I'M SORRY. WAS THE MUSIC TOO LOUD?

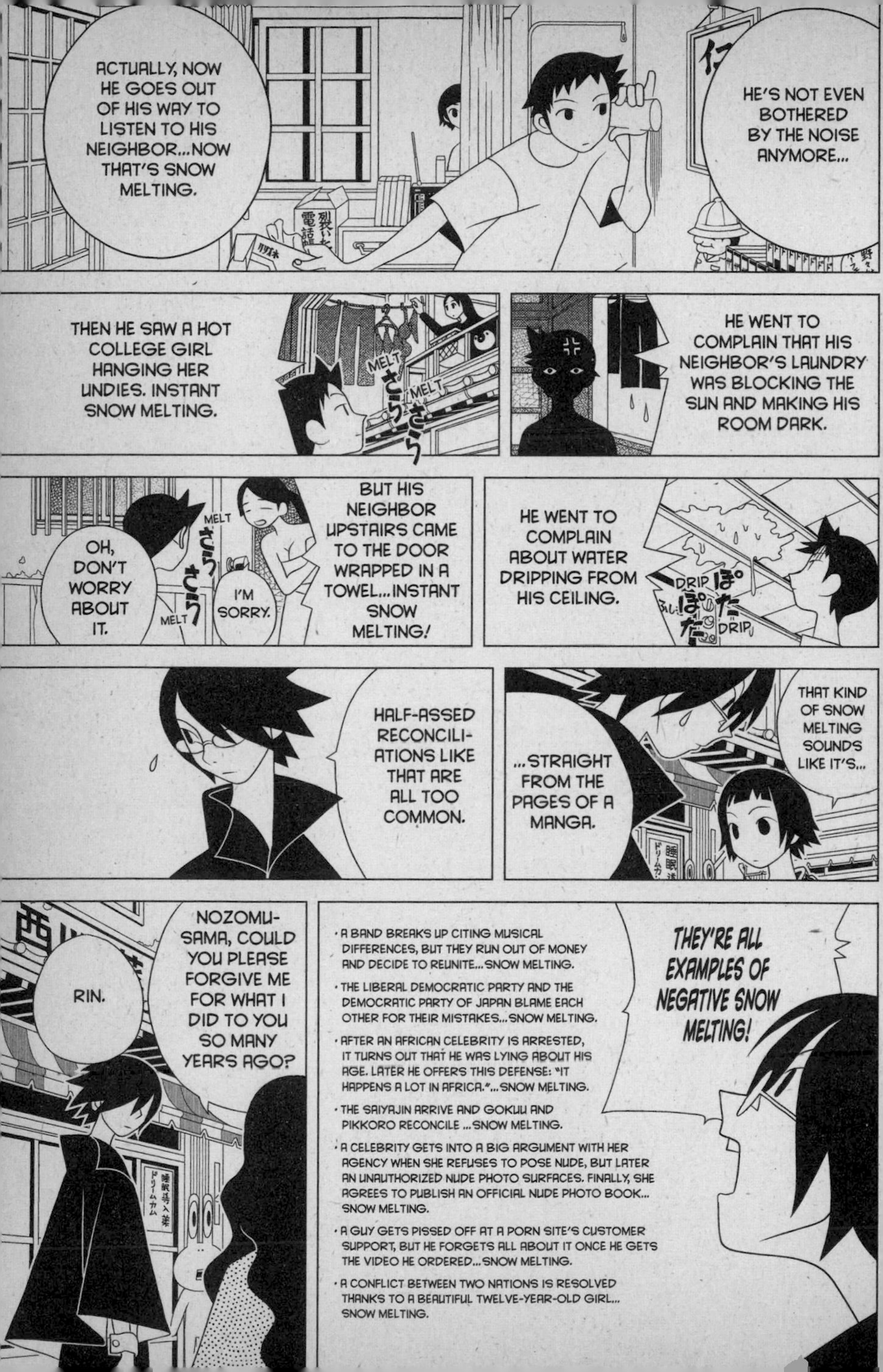

HE'S NOT EVEN BOTHERED BY THE NOISE ANYMORE...
ACTUALLY, NOW HE GOES OUT OF HIS WAY TO LISTEN TO HIS NEIGHBOR...NOW THAT'S SNOW MELTING.
HE WENT TO COMPLAIN THAT HIS NEIGHBOR'S LAUNDRY WAS BLOCKING THE SUN AND MAKING HIS ROOM DARK.
THEN HE SAW A HOT COLLEGE GIRL HANGING HER UNDIES. INSTANT SNOW MELTING.
MELT
MELT
HE WENT TO COMPLAIN ABOUT WATER DRIPPING FROM HIS CEILING.
DRIP
DRIP
BUT HIS NEIGHBOR UPSTAIRS CAME TO THE DOOR WRAPPED IN A TOWEL...INSTANT SNOW MELTING!
MELT
I'M SORRY.
OH, DON'T WORRY ABOUT IT.
MELT
THAT KIND OF SNOW MELTING SOUNDS LIKE IT'S...
...STRAIGHT FROM THE PAGES OF A MANGA.
HALF-ASSED RECONCILI-ATIONS LIKE THAT ARE ALL TOO COMMON.
· A BAND BREAKS UP CITING MUSICAL DIFFERENCES, BUT THEY RUN OUT OF MONEY AND DECIDE TO REUNITE...SNOW MELTING.
· THE LIBERAL DEMOCRATIC PARTY AND THE DEMOCRATIC PARTY OF JAPAN BLAME EACH OTHER FOR THEIR MISTAKES...SNOW MELTING.
· AFTER AN AFRICAN CELEBRITY IS ARRESTED, IT TURNS OUT THAT HE WAS LYING ABOUT HIS AGE. LATER HE OFFERS THIS DEFENSE: "IT HAPPENS A LOT IN AFRICA."...SNOW MELTING.
· THE SAIYAJIN ARRIVE AND GOKUU AND PIKKORO RECONCILE ...SNOW MELTING.
· A CELEBRITY GETS INTO A BIG ARGUMENT WITH HER AGENCY WHEN SHE REFUSES TO POSE NUDE, BUT LATER AN UNAUTHORIZED NUDE PHOTO SURFACES. FINALLY, SHE AGREES TO PUBLISH AN OFFICIAL NUDE PHOTO BOOK... SNOW MELTING.
· A GUY GETS PISSED OFF AT A PORN SITE'S CUSTOMER SUPPORT, BUT HE FORGETS ALL ABOUT IT ONCE HE GETS THE VIDEO HE ORDERED...SNOW MELTING.
· A CONFLICT BETWEEN TWO NATIONS IS RESOLVED THANKS TO A BEAUTIFUL TWELVE-YEAR-OLD GIRL... SNOW MELTING.
THEY'RE ALL EXAMPLES OF NEGATIVE SNOW MELTING!
NOZOMU-SAMA, COULD YOU PLEASE FORGIVE ME FOR WHAT I DID TO YOU SO MANY YEARS AGO?
RIN.

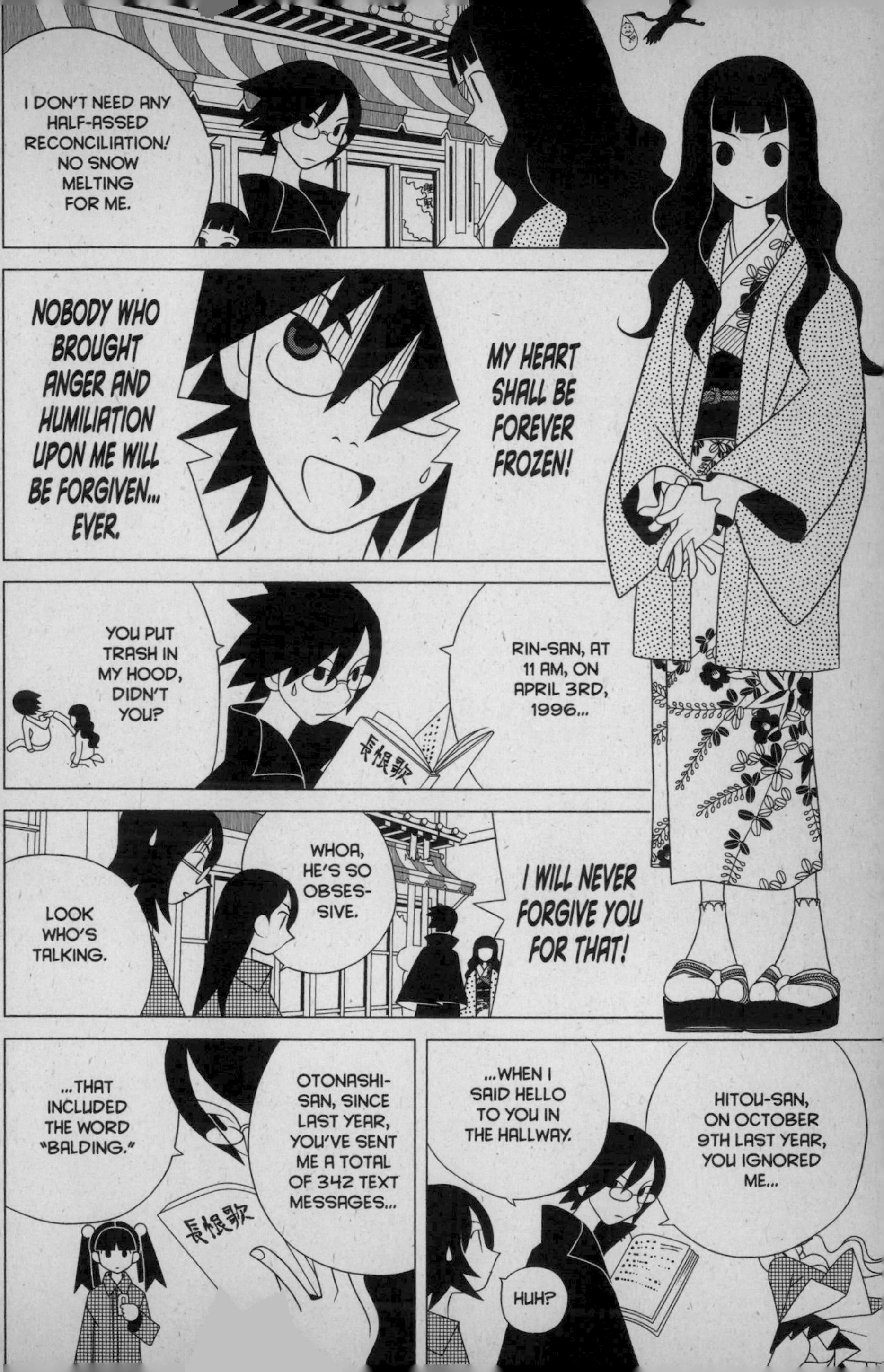
I DON'T NEED ANY HALF-ASSED RECONCILIATION! NO SNOW MELTING FOR ME.
NOBODY WHO BROUGHT ANGER AND HUMILIATION UPON ME WILL BE FORGIVEN... EVER.
MY HEART SHALL BE FOREVER FROZEN!
RIN-SAN, AT 11 AM, ON APRIL 3RD, 1996...
YOU PUT TRASH IN MY HOOD, DIDN'T YOU?
長恨歌
I WILL NEVER FORGIVE YOU FOR THAT!
WHOA, HE'S SO OBSES-SIVE.
LOOK WHO'S TALKING.
HITOU-SAN, ON OCTOBER 9TH LAST YEAR, YOU IGNORED ME...
...WHEN I SAID HELLO TO YOU IN THE HALLWAY.
HUH?
OTONASHI-SAN, SINCE LAST YEAR, YOU'VE SENT ME A TOTAL OF 342 TEXT MESSAGES...
...THAT INCLUDED THE WORD "BALDING."
長恨歌

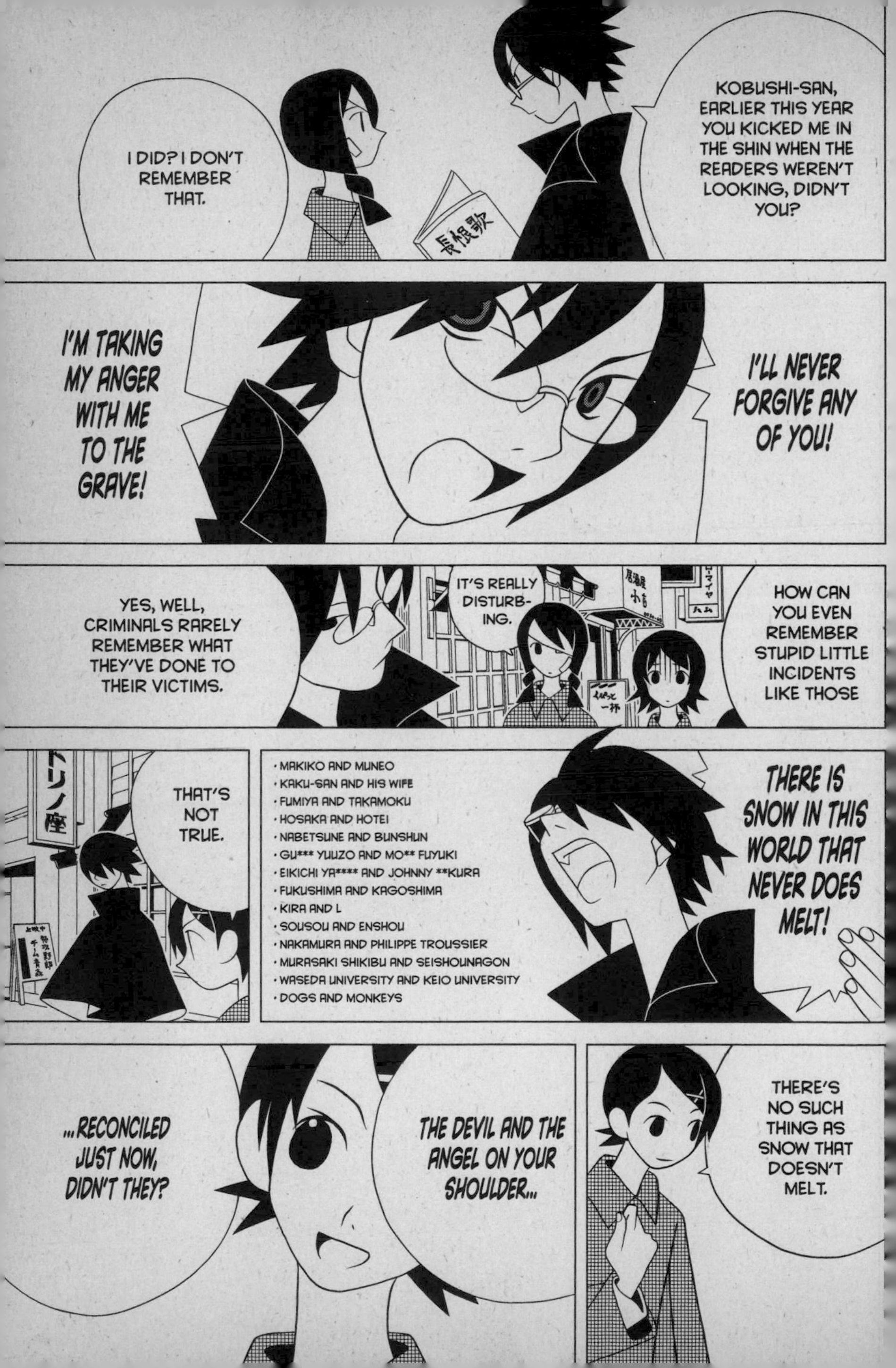
KOBUSHI-SAN, EARLIER THIS YEAR YOU KICKED ME IN THE SHIN WHEN THE READERS WEREN'T LOOKING, DIDN'T YOU?
長恨歌
I DID? I DON'T REMEMBER THAT.
I'LL NEVER FORGIVE ANY OF YOU!
I'M TAKING MY ANGER WITH ME TO THE GRAVE!
HOW CAN YOU EVEN REMEMBER STUPID LITTLE INCIDENTS LIKE THOSE
IT'S REALLY DISTURB-ING.
YES, WELL, CRIMINALS RARELY REMEMBER WHAT THEY'VE DONE TO THEIR VICTIMS.
THERE IS SNOW IN THIS WORLD THAT NEVER DOES MELT!
• MAKIKO AND MUNEO
• KAKU-SAN AND HIS WIFE
• FUMIYA AND TAKAMOKU
• HOSAKA AND HOTEI
• NABETSUNE AND BUNSHUN
• GU*** YUUZO AND MO** FUYUKI
• EIKICHI YA**** AND JOHNNY **KURA
• FUKUSHIMA AND KAGOSHIMA
• KIRA AND L
• SOUSOU AND ENSHOU
• NAKAMURA AND PHILIPPE TROUSSIER
• MURASAKI SHIKIBU AND SEISHOUNAGON
• WASEDA UNIVERSITY AND KEIO UNIVERSITY
• DOGS AND MONKEYS
トリノ座
THAT'S NOT TRUE.
THERE'S NO SUCH THING AS SNOW THAT DOESN'T MELT.
THE DEVIL AND THE ANGEL ON YOUR SHOULDER...
...RECONCILED JUST NOW, DIDN'T THEY?

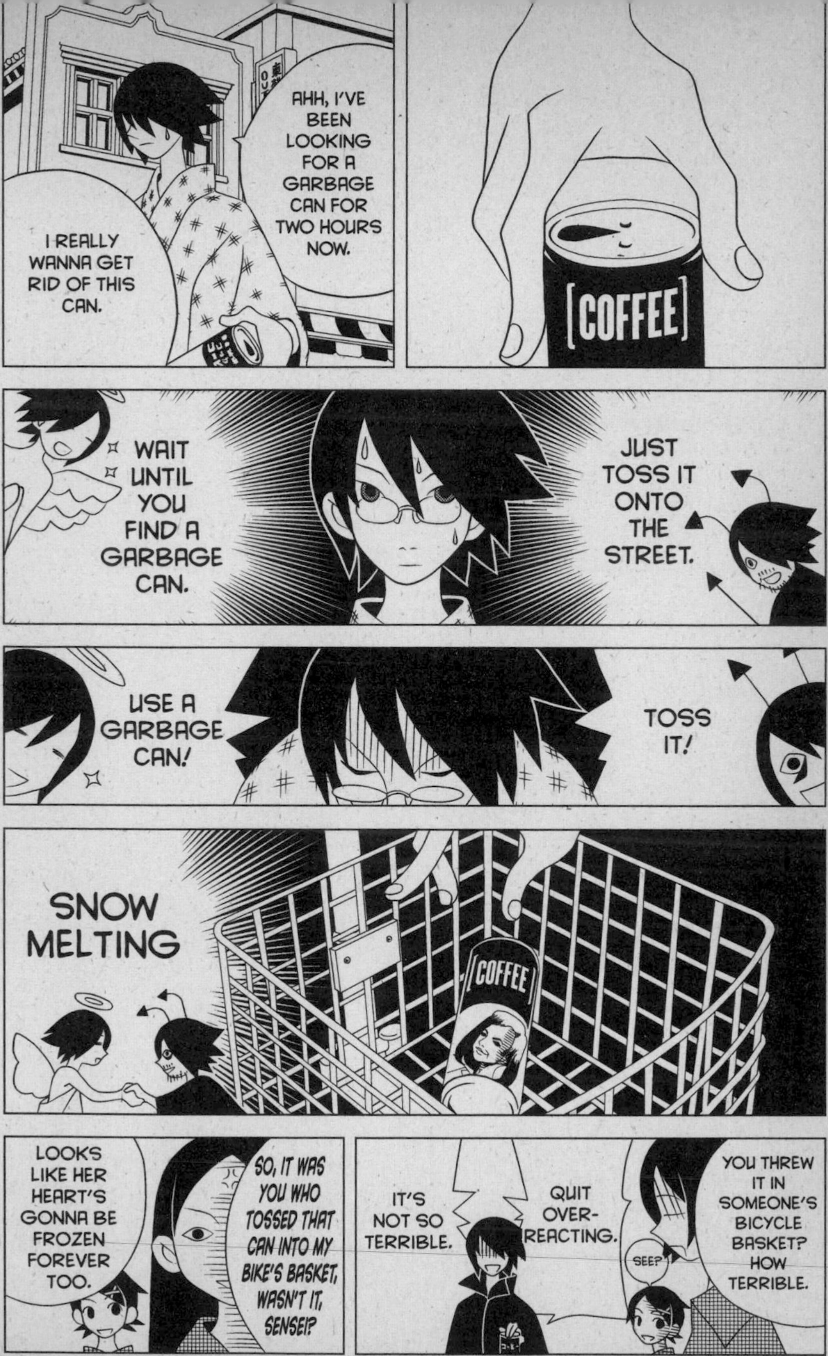
[COFFEE]
AHH, I'VE BEEN LOOKING FOR A GARBAGE CAN FOR TWO HOURS NOW.
I REALLY WANNA GET RID OF THIS CAN.
JUST TOSS IT ONTO THE STREET.
WAIT UNTIL YOU FIND A GARBAGE CAN.
TOSS IT!
USE A GARBAGE CAN!
SNOW MELTING
[COFFEE]
YOU THREW IT IN SOMEONE'S BICYCLE BASKET? HOW TERRIBLE.
SEE?
QUIT OVER-REACTING.
IT'S NOT SO TERRIBLE.
SO, IT WAS YOU WHO TOSSED THAT CAN INTO MY BIKE'S BASKET, WASN'T IT, SENSEI?
LOOKS LIKE HER HEART'S GONNA BE FROZEN FOREVER TOO.

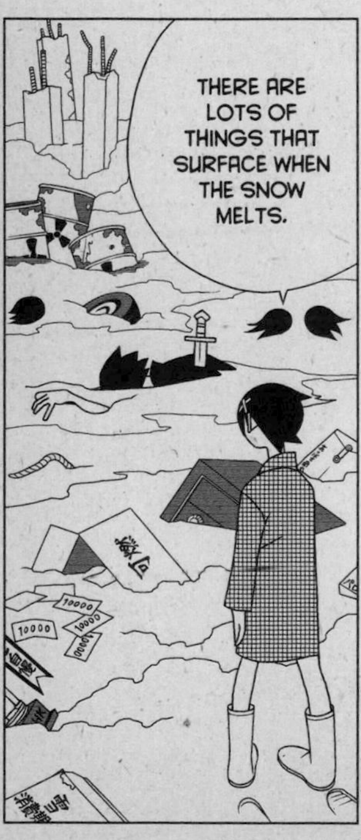
THERE ARE LOTS OF THINGS THAT SURFACE WHEN THE SNOW MELTS.

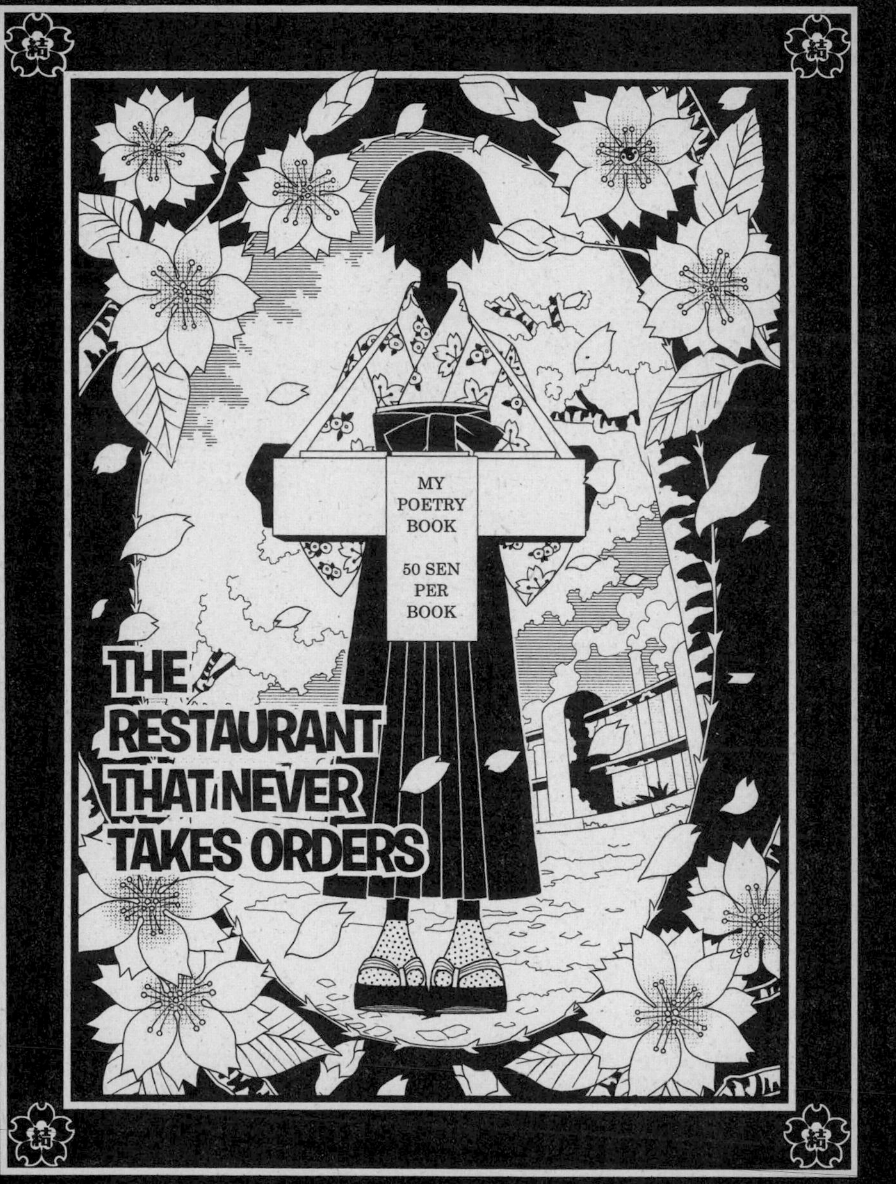
MY POETRY BOOK
50 SEN PER BOOK
THE RESTAURANT THAT NEVER TAKES ORDERS

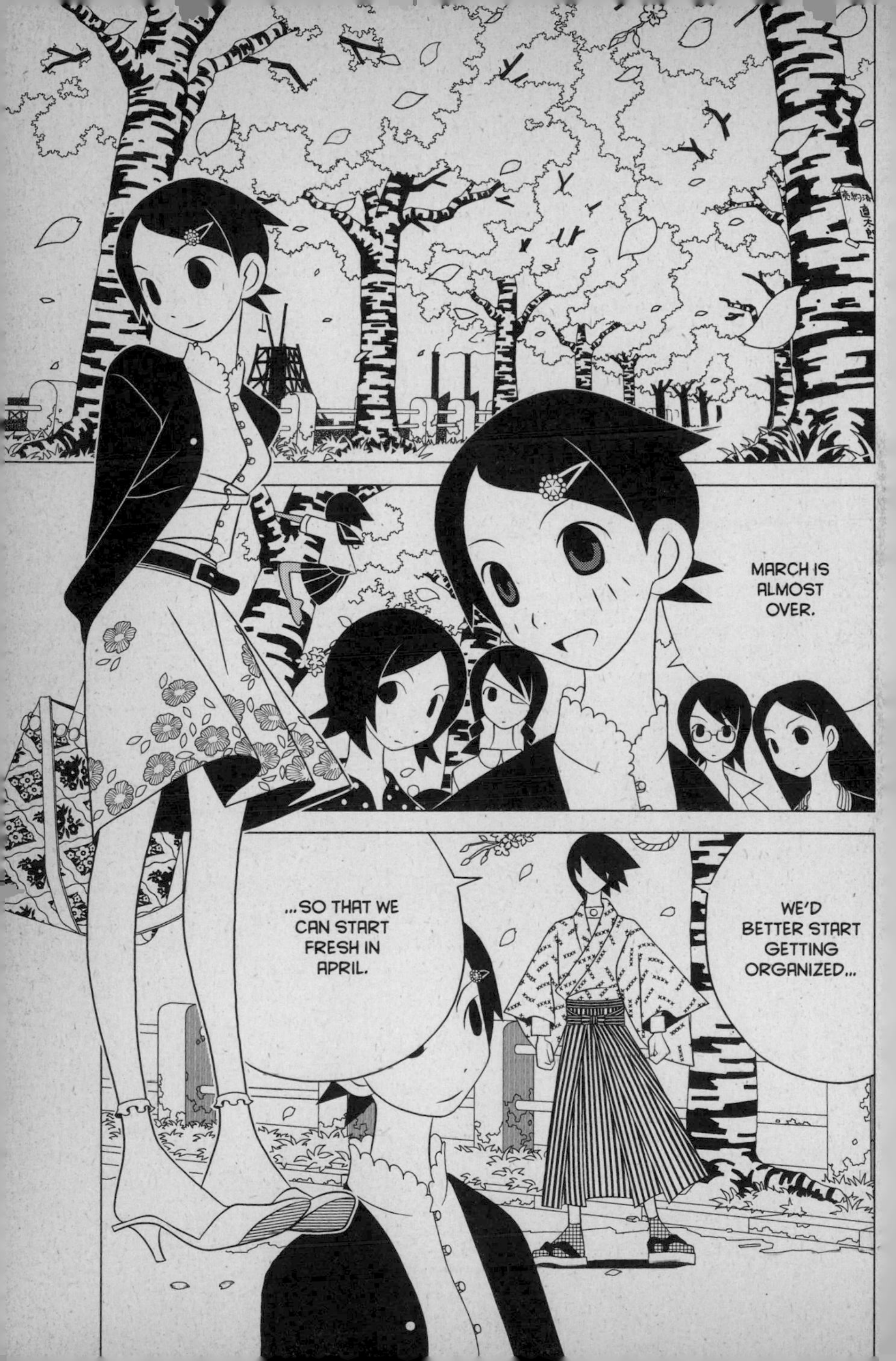
MARCH IS ALMOST OVER.
WE'D BETTER START GETTING ORGANIZED...
...SO THAT WE CAN START FRESH IN APRIL.

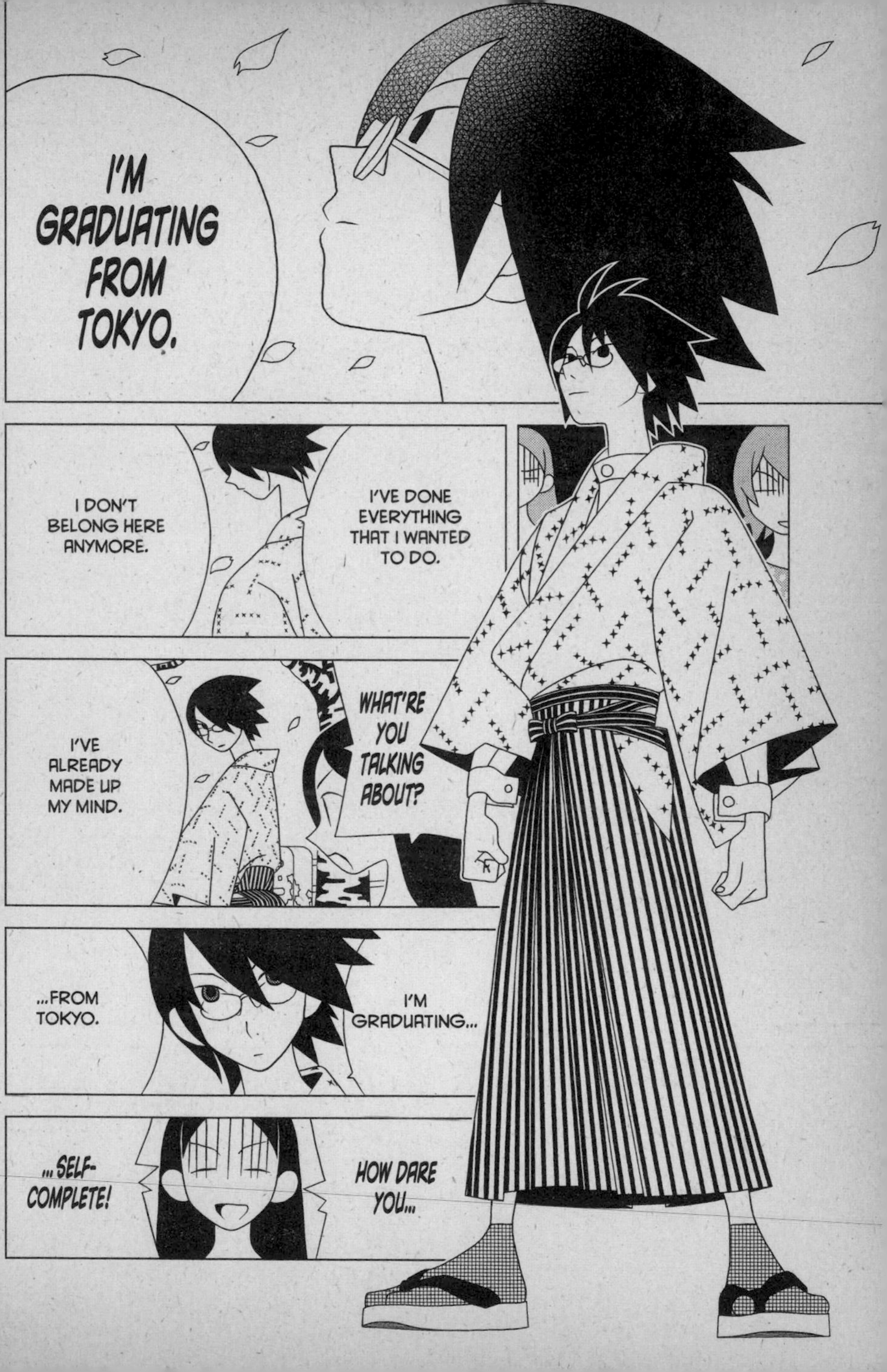
I'M GRADUATING FROM TOKYO.
I'VE DONE EVERYTHING THAT I WANTED TO DO.
I DON'T BELONG HERE ANYMORE.
WHAT'RE YOU TALKING ABOUT?
I'VE ALREADY MADE UP MY MIND.
I'M GRADUATING...
...FROM TOKYO.
HOW DARE YOU...
...SELF-COMPLETE!

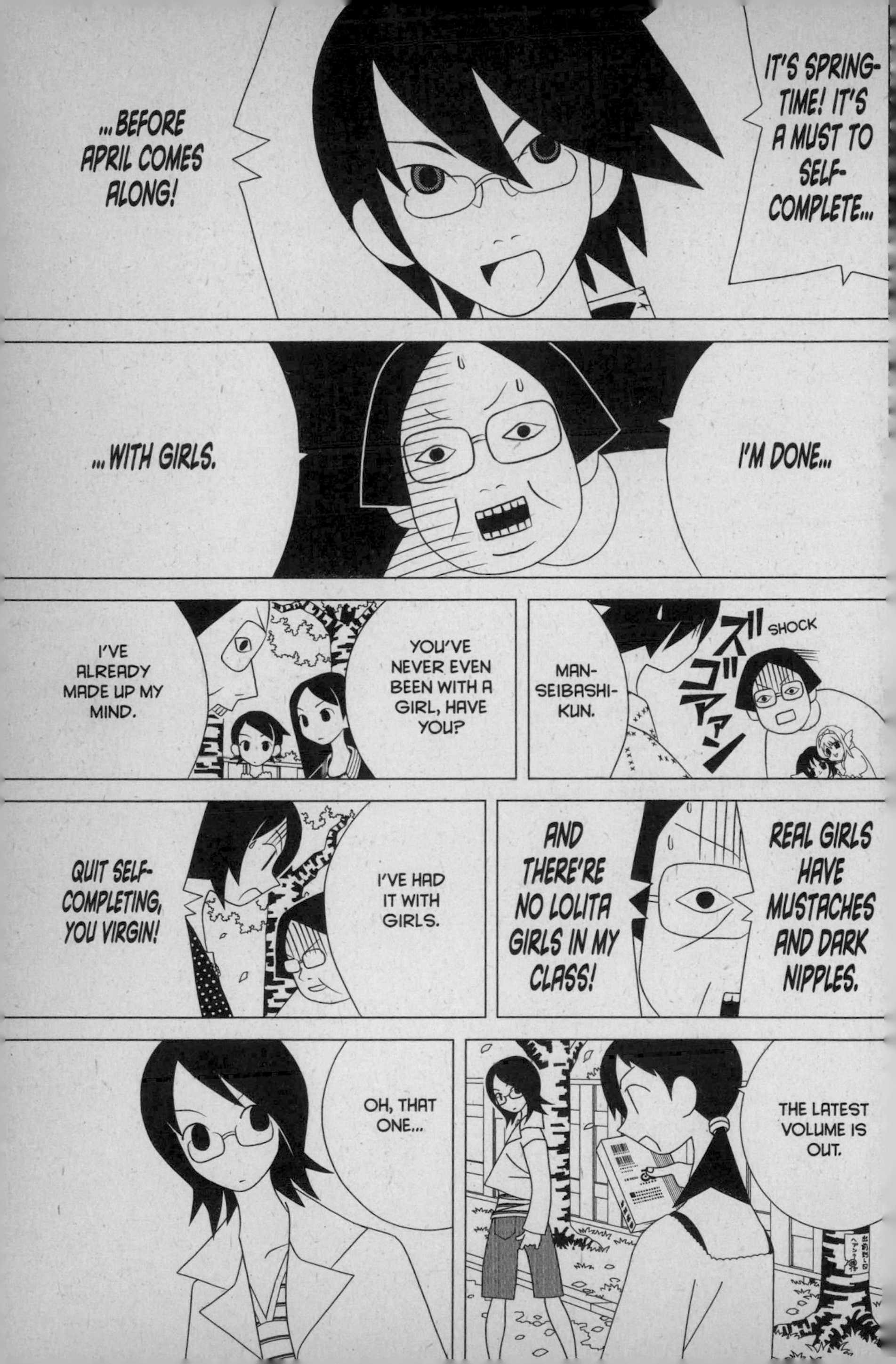
IT'S SPRING-TIME! IT'S A MUST TO SELF-COMPLETE...
...BEFORE APRIL COMES ALONG!
I'M DONE...
...WITH GIRLS.
SHOCK
MAN-SEIBASHI-KUN.
YOU'VE NEVER EVEN BEEN WITH A GIRL, HAVE YOU?
I'VE ALREADY MADE UP MY MIND.
REAL GIRLS HAVE MUSTACHES AND DARK NIPPLES.
AND THERE'RE NO LOLITA GIRLS IN MY CLASS!
I'VE HAD IT WITH GIRLS.
QUIT SELF-COMPLETING, YOU VIRGIN!
THE LATEST VOLUME IS OUT.
OH, THAT ONE...

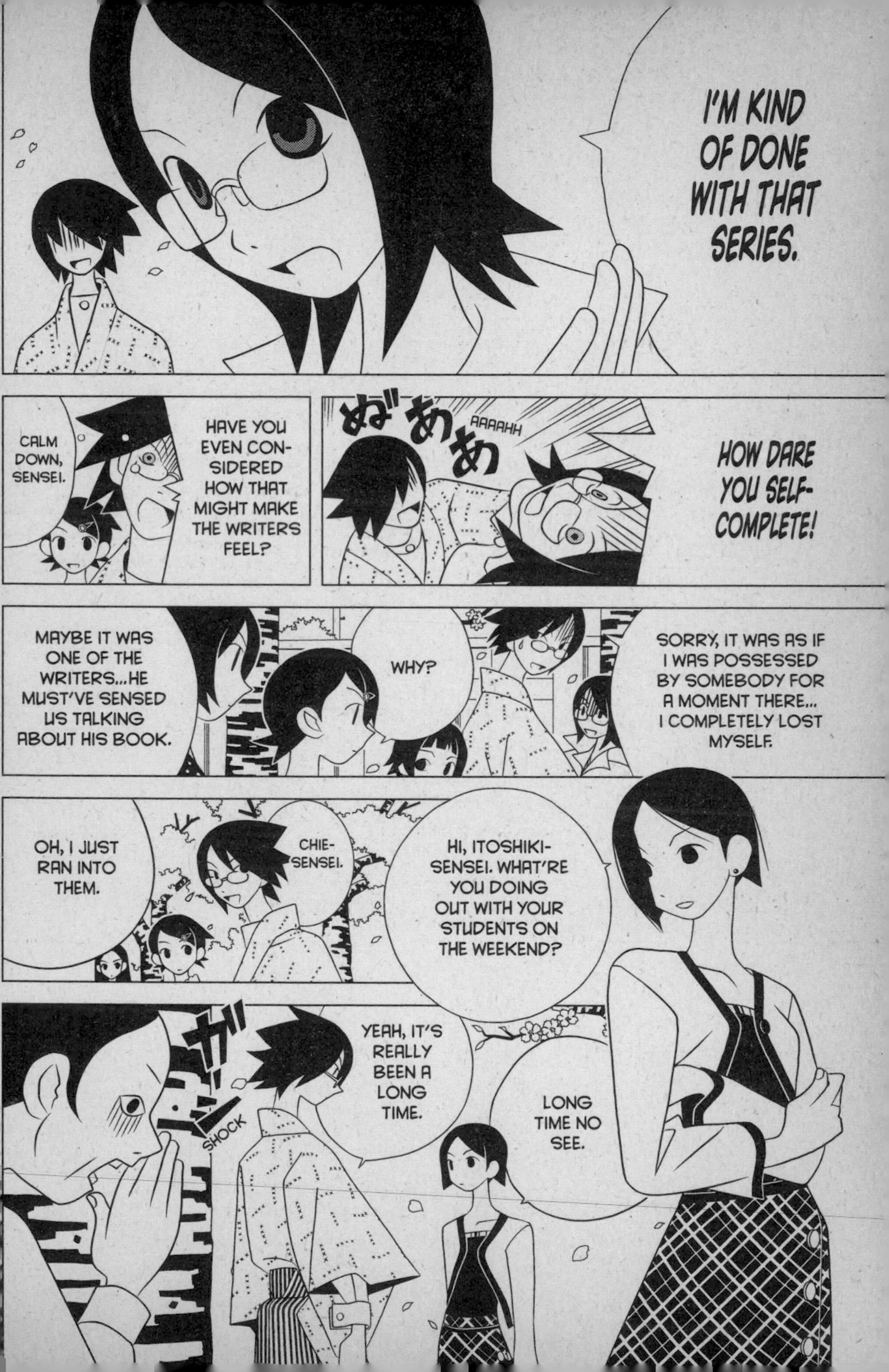
I'M KIND OF DONE WITH THAT SERIES.
HOW DARE YOU SELF-COMPLETE!
ぬ゛あああ
AAAAHH
HAVE YOU EVEN CON-SIDERED HOW THAT MIGHT MAKE THE WRITERS FEEL?
CALM DOWN, SENSEI.
SORRY, IT WAS AS IF I WAS POSSESSED BY SOMEBODY FOR A MOMENT THERE... I COMPLETELY LOST MYSELF.
WHY?
MAYBE IT WAS ONE OF THE WRITERS...HE MUST'VE SENSED US TALKING ABOUT HIS BOOK.
HI, ITOSHIKI-SENSEI. WHAT'RE YOU DOING OUT WITH YOUR STUDENTS ON THE WEEKEND?
CHIE-SENSEI.
OH, I JUST RAN INTO THEM.
LONG TIME NO SEE.
YEAH, IT'S REALLY BEEN A LONG TIME.
SHOCK

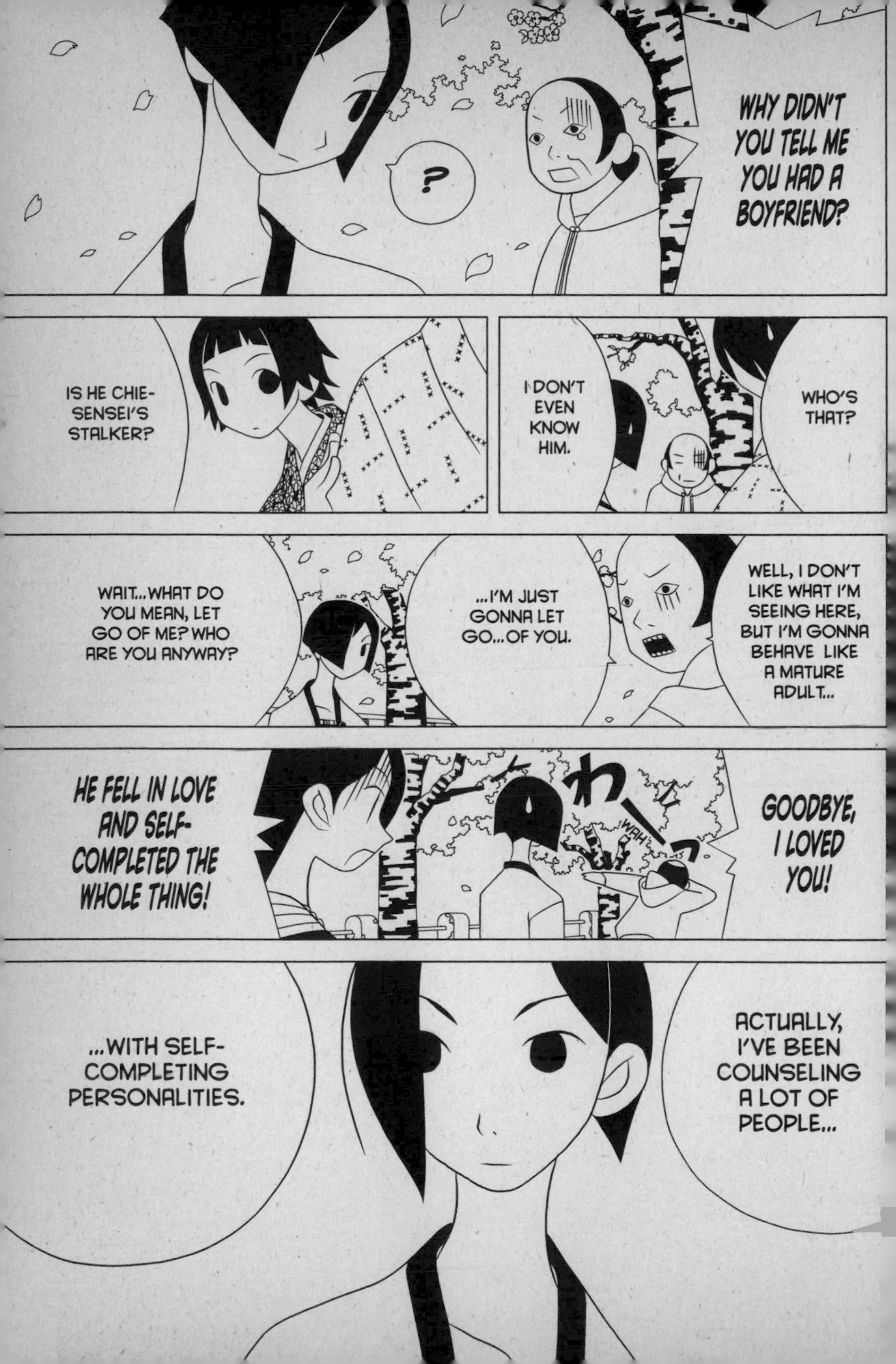
WHY DIDN'T YOU TELL ME YOU HAD A BOYFRIEND?
?
WHO'S THAT?
I DON'T EVEN KNOW HIM.
IS HE CHIE-SENSEI'S STALKER?
WELL, I DON'T LIKE WHAT I'M SEEING HERE, BUT I'M GONNA BEHAVE LIKE A MATURE ADULT...
...I'M JUST GONNA LET GO...OF YOU.
WAIT...WHAT DO YOU MEAN, LET GO OF ME? WHO ARE YOU ANYWAY?
GOODBYE, I LOVED YOU!
わ～
WAH
HE FELL IN LOVE AND SELF-COMPLETED THE WHOLE THING!
ACTUALLY, I'VE BEEN COUNSELING A LOT OF PEOPLE...
...WITH SELF-COMPLETING PERSONALITIES.

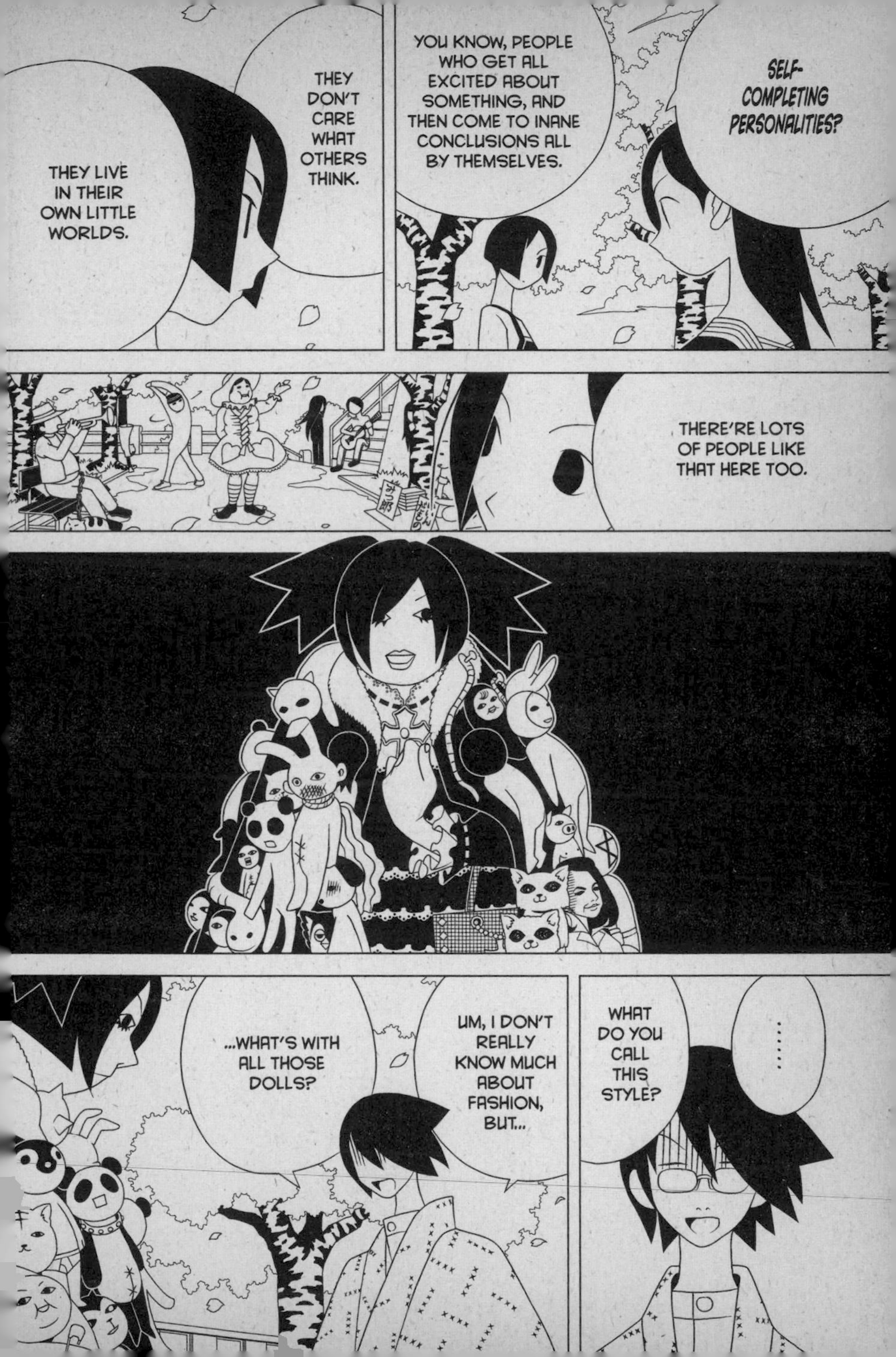
SELF-COMPLETING PERSONALITIES?
YOU KNOW, PEOPLE WHO GET ALL EXCITED ABOUT SOMETHING, AND THEN COME TO INANE CONCLUSIONS ALL BY THEMSELVES.
THEY DON'T CARE WHAT OTHERS THINK.
THEY LIVE IN THEIR OWN LITTLE WORLDS.
THERE'RE LOTS OF PEOPLE LIKE THAT HERE TOO.
......
WHAT DO YOU CALL THIS STYLE?
UM, I DON'T REALLY KNOW MUCH ABOUT FASHION, BUT...
...WHAT'S WITH ALL THOSE DOLLS?

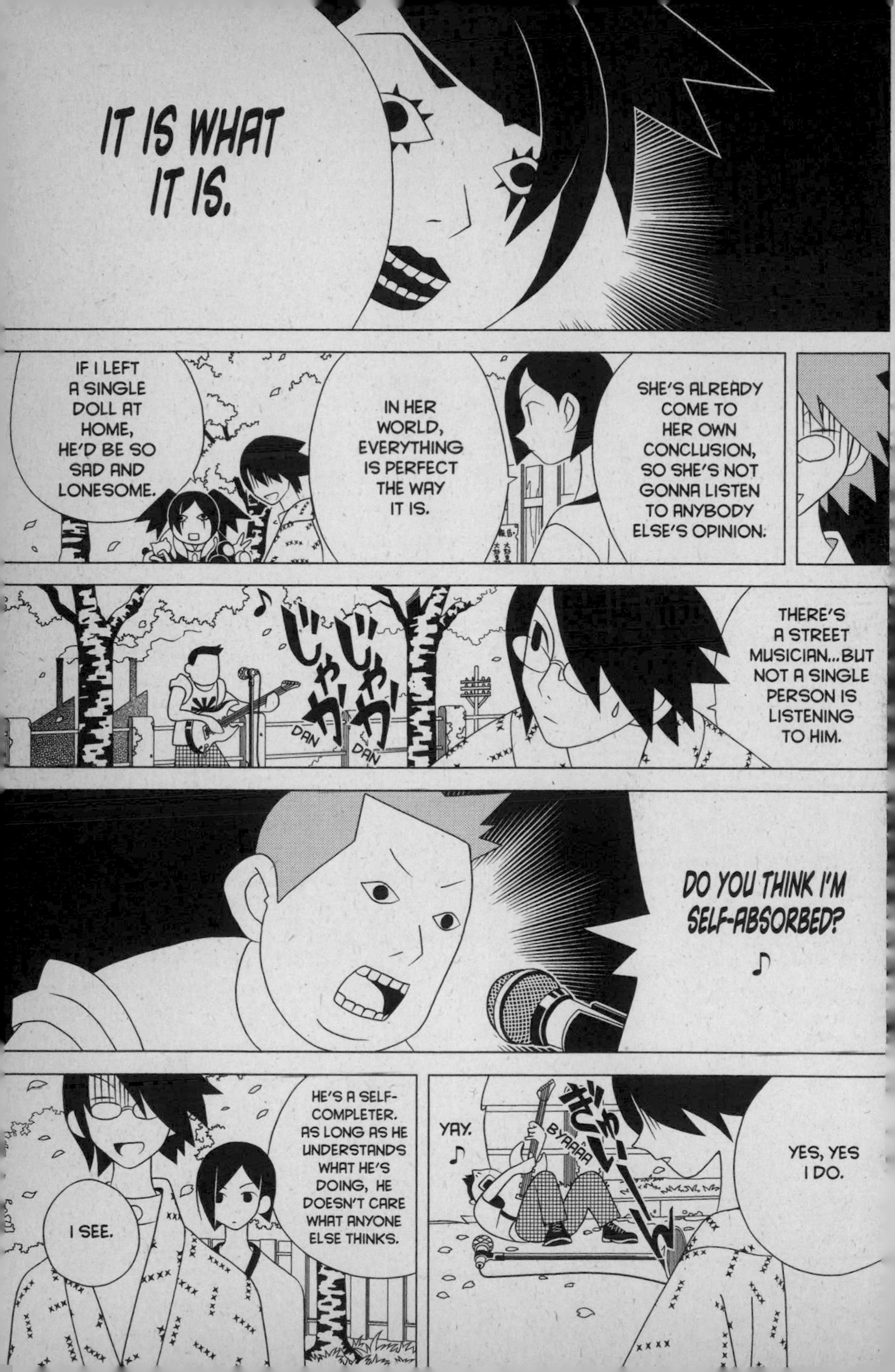
IT IS WHAT IT IS.
SHE'S ALREADY COME TO HER OWN CONCLUSION, SO SHE'S NOT GONNA LISTEN TO ANYBODY ELSE'S OPINION.
IN HER WORLD, EVERYTHING IS PERFECT THE WAY IT IS.
IF I LEFT A SINGLE DOLL AT HOME, HE'D BE SO SAD AND LONESOME.
THERE'S A STREET MUSICIAN...BUT NOT A SINGLE PERSON IS LISTENING TO HIM.
DAN
DAN
DO YOU THINK I'M SELF-ABSORBED?
YES, YES I DO.
BYAAAA
YAY.
HE'S A SELF-COMPLETER. AS LONG AS HE UNDERSTANDS WHAT HE'S DOING, HE DOESN'T CARE WHAT ANYONE ELSE THINKS.
I SEE.

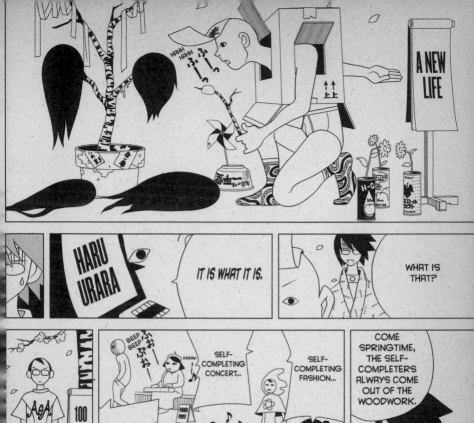

A NEW LIFE

HAAA HAAA

ふーっ ふーっ

HARU URARA

IT IS WHAT IT IS.

WHAT IS THAT?

100 Jokes

SELF-COMPLETING PERFORMANCE!

BEEP BEEP

ふぉーっぷぉ

DREAM

SELF-COMPLETING CONCERT...

SELF-COMPLETING FASHION...

COME SPRINGTIME, THE SELF-COMPLETERS ALWAYS COME OUT OF THE WOODWORK.

FWUP ぽっ

FWUP ぽっ

ぶぉぉぉぉぉっ FWAAHHH

JUST LOOK AT THEM...

SELF-COMPLETING JOKE

THUD ぽんっ

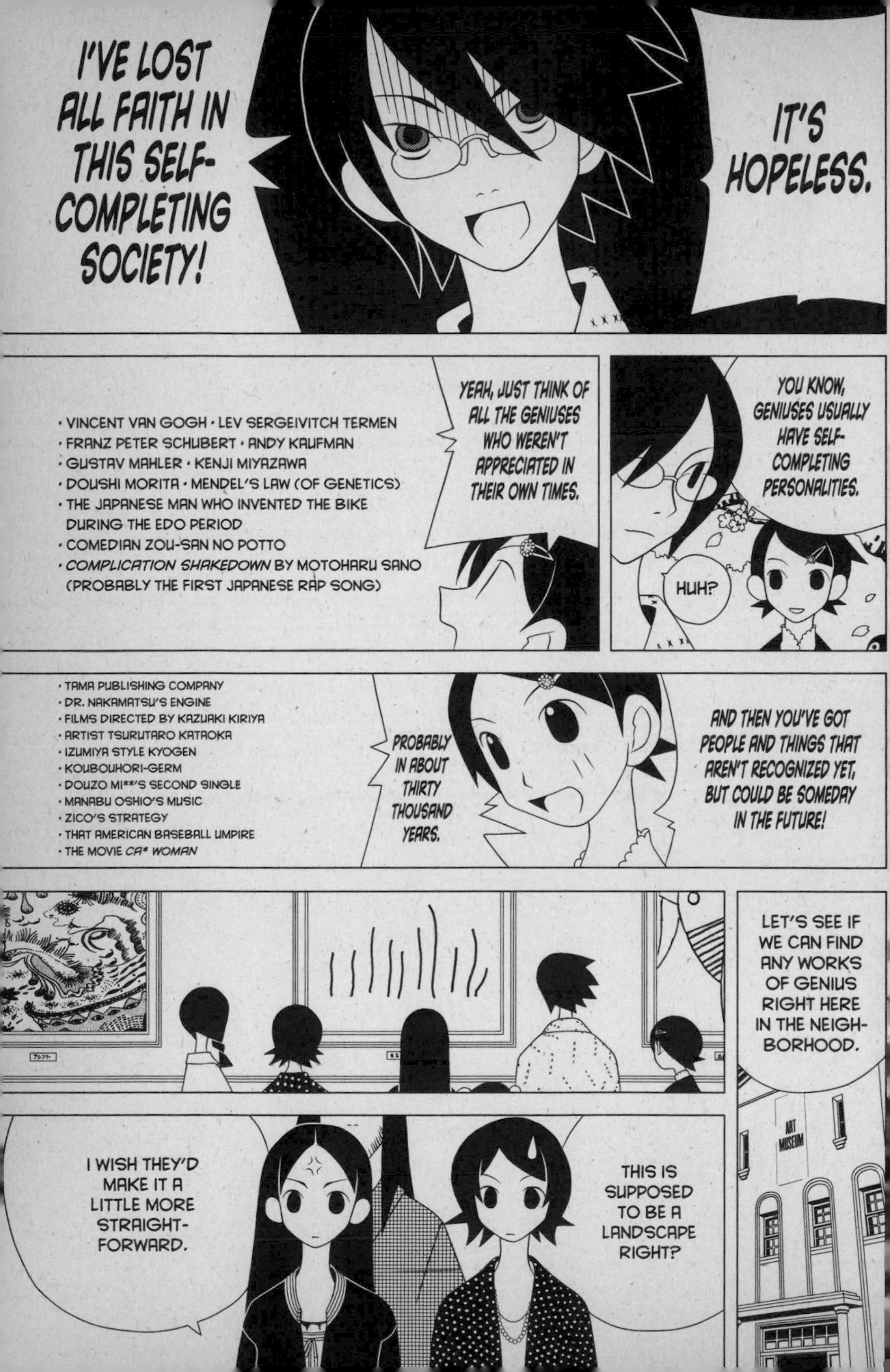
IT'S HOPELESS.
I'VE LOST ALL FAITH IN THIS SELF-COMPLETING SOCIETY!
YOU KNOW, GENIUSES USUALLY HAVE SELF-COMPLETING PERSONALITIES.
HUH?
YEAH, JUST THINK OF ALL THE GENIUSES WHO WEREN'T APPRECIATED IN THEIR OWN TIMES.
• VINCENT VAN GOGH • LEV SERGEIVITCH TERMEN
• FRANZ PETER SCHUBERT • ANDY KAUFMAN
• GUSTAV MAHLER • KENJI MIYAZAWA
• DOUSHI MORITA • MENDEL'S LAW (OF GENETICS)
• THE JAPANESE MAN WHO INVENTED THE BIKE DURING THE EDO PERIOD
• COMEDIAN ZOU-SAN NO POTTO
• *COMPLICATION SHAKEDOWN* BY MOTOHARU SANO (PROBABLY THE FIRST JAPANESE RAP SONG)
AND THEN YOU'VE GOT PEOPLE AND THINGS THAT AREN'T RECOGNIZED YET, BUT COULD BE SOMEDAY IN THE FUTURE!
PROBABLY IN ABOUT THIRTY THOUSAND YEARS.
• TAMA PUBLISHING COMPANY
• DR. NAKAMATSU'S ENGINE
• FILMS DIRECTED BY KAZUAKI KIRIYA
• ARTIST TSURUTARO KATAOKA
• IZUMIYA STYLE KYOGEN
• KOUBOUHORI-GERM
• DOUZO MI**'S SECOND SINGLE
• MANABU OSHIO'S MUSIC
• ZICO'S STRATEGY
• THAT AMERICAN BASEBALL UMPIRE
• THE MOVIE *CA* WOMAN*
LET'S SEE IF WE CAN FIND ANY WORKS OF GENIUS RIGHT HERE IN THE NEIGHBORHOOD.
ART MUSEUM
THIS IS SUPPOSED TO BE A LANDSCAPE RIGHT?
I WISH THEY'D MAKE IT A LITTLE MORE STRAIGHTFORWARD.

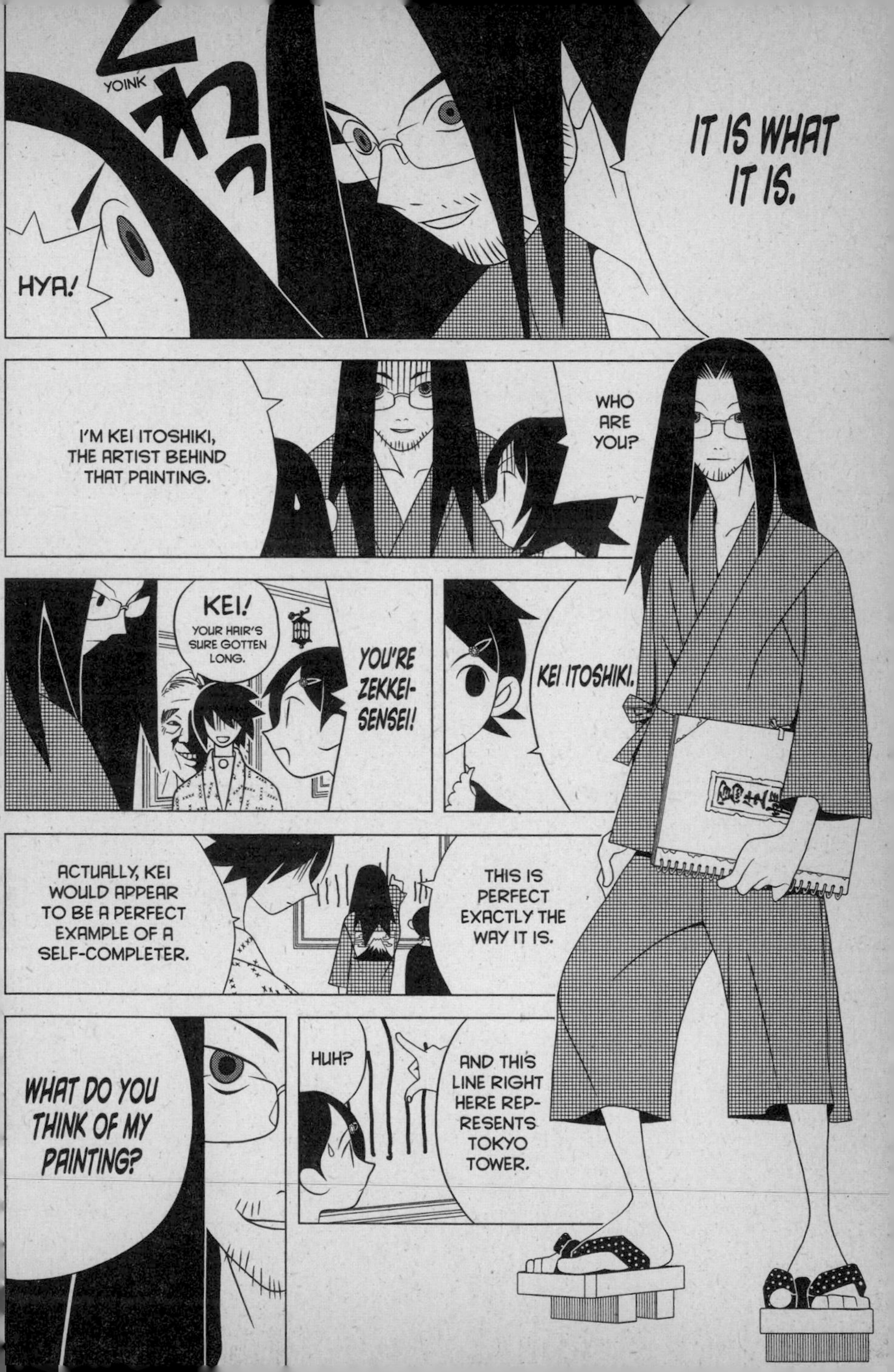

IT IS WHAT IT IS.
YOINK
HYA!
WHO ARE YOU?
I'M KEI ITOSHIKI, THE ARTIST BEHIND THAT PAINTING.
KEI ITOSHIKI.
YOU'RE ZEKKEI-SENSEI!
KEI! YOUR HAIR'S SURE GOTTEN LONG.
THIS IS PERFECT EXACTLY THE WAY IT IS.
ACTUALLY, KEI WOULD APPEAR TO BE A PERFECT EXAMPLE OF A SELF-COMPLETER.
AND THIS LINE RIGHT HERE REP-RESENTS TOKYO TOWER.
HUH?
WHAT DO YOU THINK OF MY PAINTING?

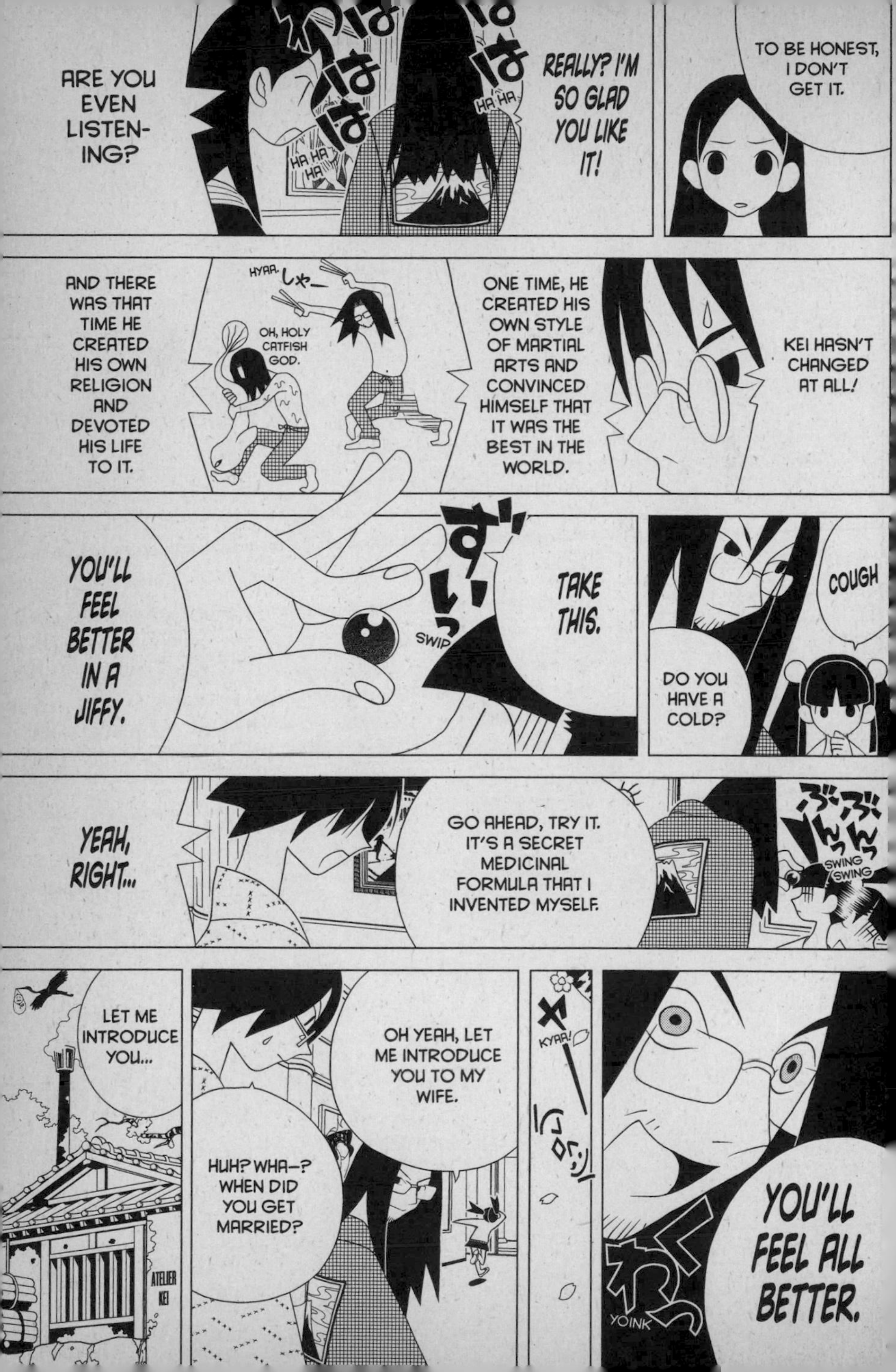
TO BE HONEST, I DON'T GET IT.
REALLY? I'M SO GLAD YOU LIKE IT!
HA HA
HA HA HA
ARE YOU EVEN LISTENING?
KEI HASN'T CHANGED AT ALL!
ONE TIME, HE CREATED HIS OWN STYLE OF MARTIAL ARTS AND CONVINCED HIMSELF THAT IT WAS THE BEST IN THE WORLD.
HYAA.
しゃー
OH, HOLY CATFISH GOD.
AND THERE WAS THAT TIME HE CREATED HIS OWN RELIGION AND DEVOTED HIS LIFE TO IT.
COUGH
DO YOU HAVE A COLD?
TAKE THIS.
SWIP
YOU'LL FEEL BETTER IN A JIFFY.
SWING SWING
GO AHEAD, TRY IT. IT'S A SECRET MEDICINAL FORMULA THAT I INVENTED MYSELF.
YEAH, RIGHT...
YOU'LL FEEL ALL BETTER.
YOINK
KYAA!
OH YEAH, LET ME INTRODUCE YOU TO MY WIFE.
HUH? WHA-? WHEN DID YOU GET MARRIED?
LET ME INTRODUCE YOU...
ATELIER KEI

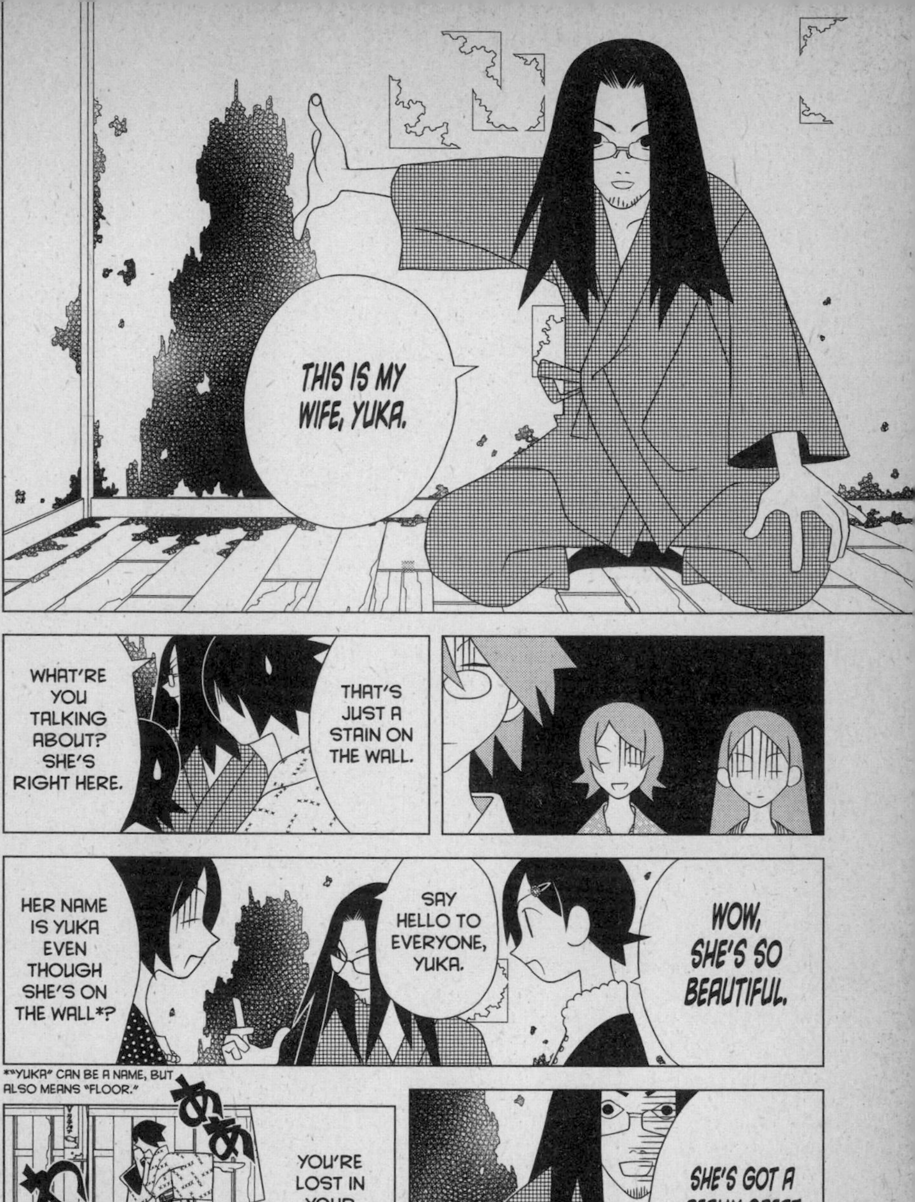
THIS IS MY WIFE, YUKA.
THAT'S JUST A STAIN ON THE WALL.
WHAT'RE YOU TALKING ABOUT? SHE'S RIGHT HERE.
WOW, SHE'S SO BEAUTIFUL.
SAY HELLO TO EVERYONE, YUKA.
HER NAME IS YUKA EVEN THOUGH SHE'S ON THE WALL*?
SHE'S GOT A REALLY GREAT PERSONALITY.
YOU'RE LOST IN YOUR OWN WORLD, KEI.
ああ
わああ
WAAHH

*"YUKA" CAN BE A NAME, BUT ALSO MEANS "FLOOR."

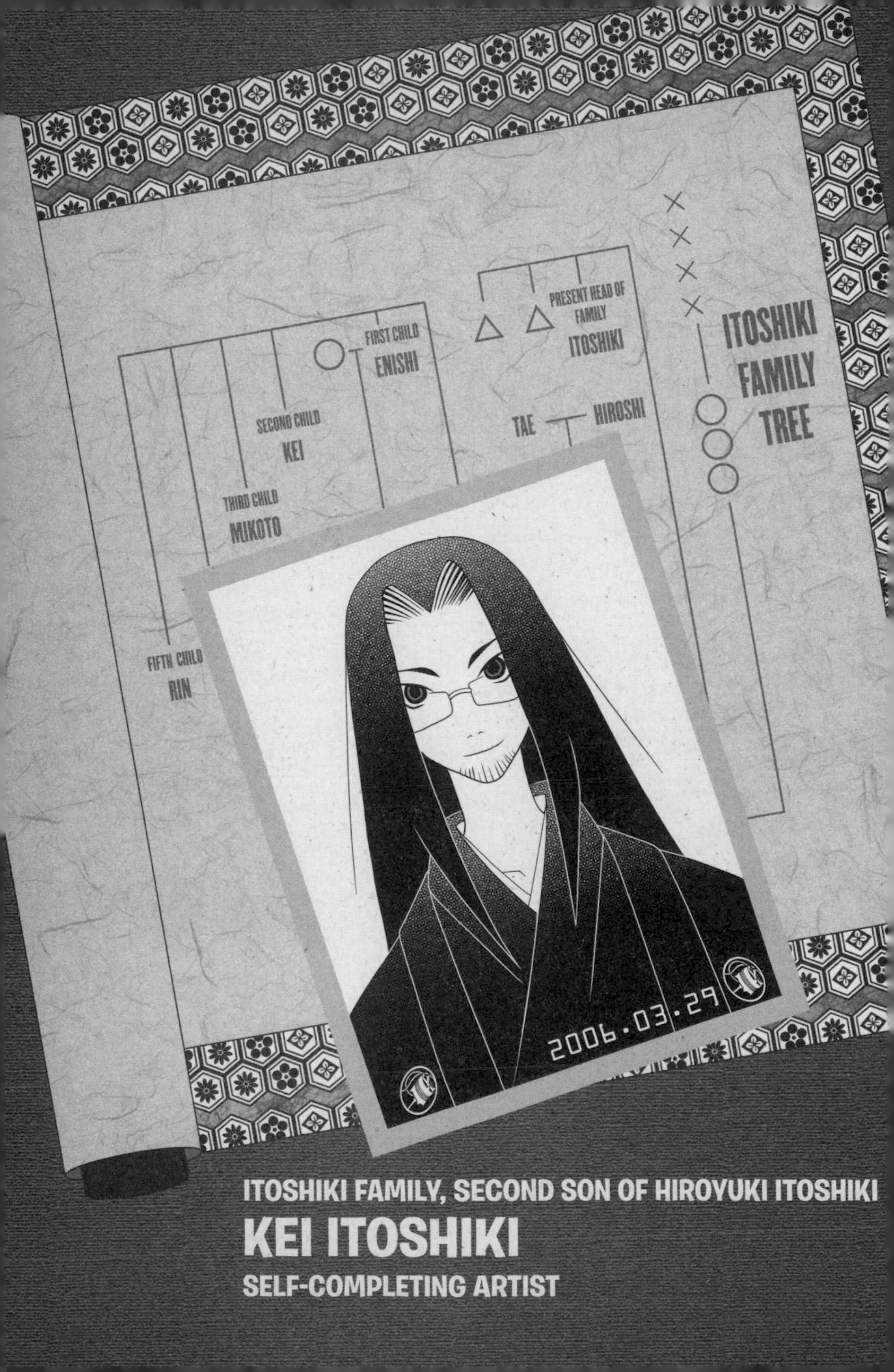
ITOSHIKI FAMILY TREE
PRESENT HEAD OF FAMILY
ITOSHIKI
TAE
HIROSHI
FIRST CHILD
ENISHI
SECOND CHILD
KEI
THIRD CHILD
MIKOTO
FIFTH CHILD
RIN
2006・03・29

ITOSHIKI FAMILY, SECOND SON OF HIROYUKI ITOSHIKI

KEI ITOSHIKI

SELF-COMPLETING ARTIST

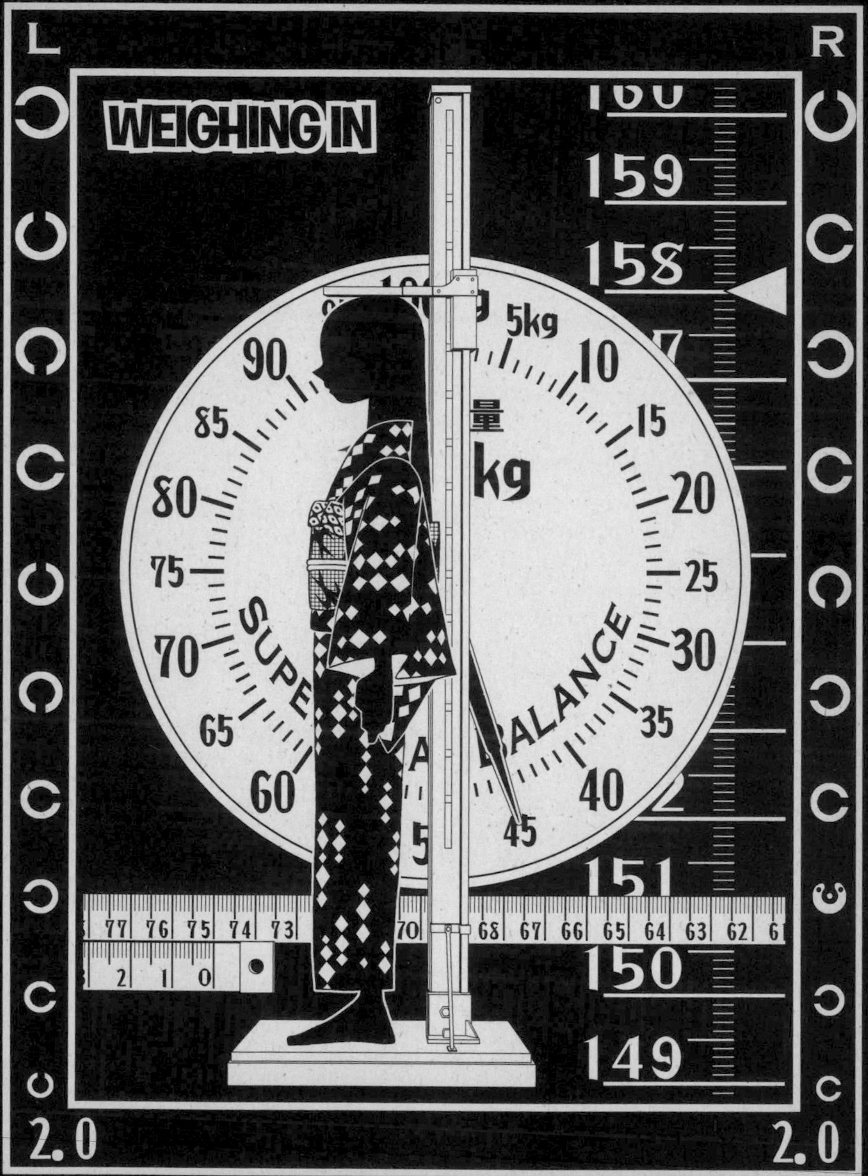

WEIGHING IN
L
R
160
159
158
5kg
10
15
20
25
30
35
40
45
60
65
70
75
80
85
90
量
kg
SUPE
BALANCE
151
150
149
77 76 75 74 73
70
68 67 66 65 64 63 62
2 1 0
2.0
2.0

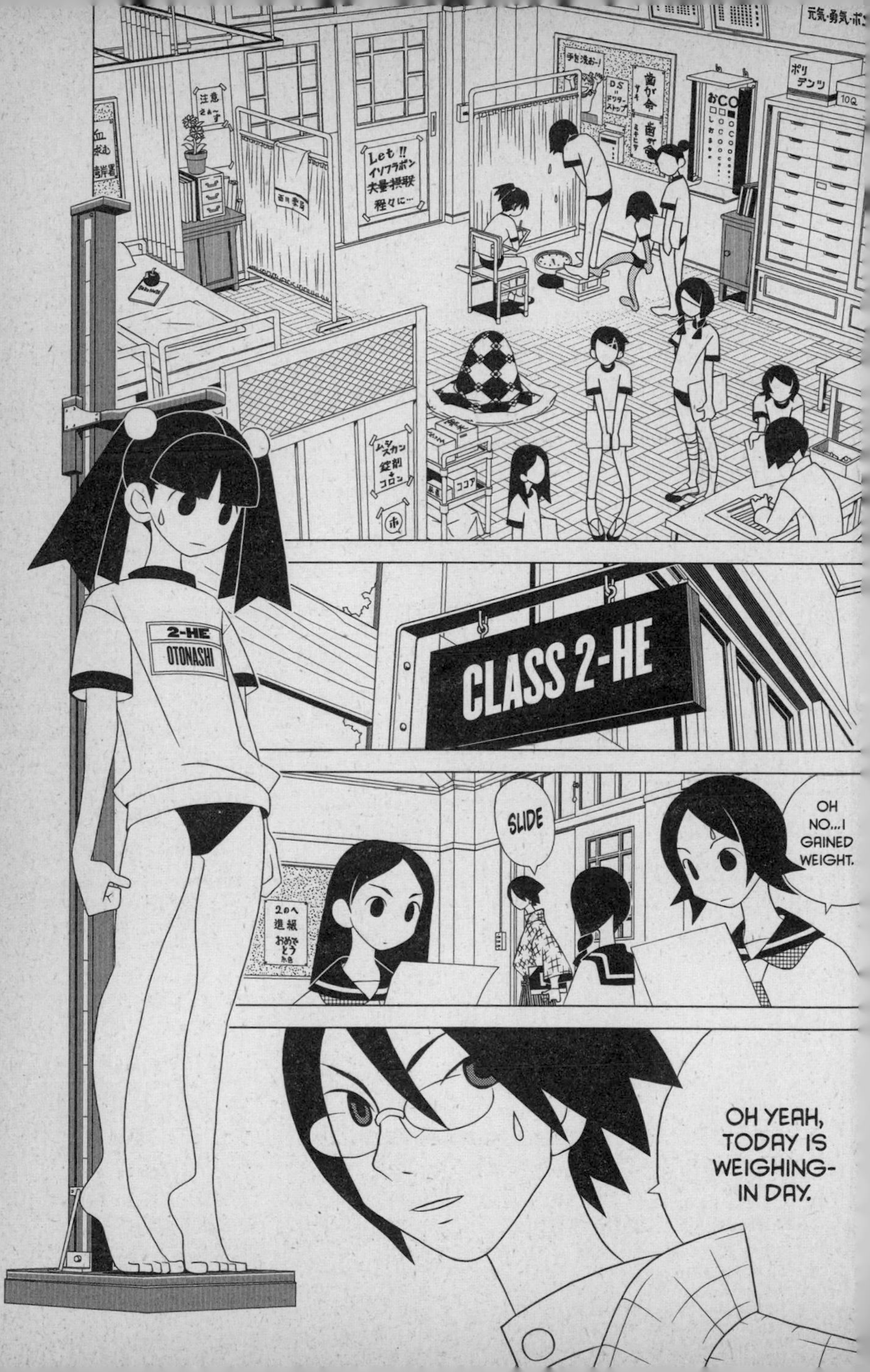
CLASS 2-HE
OH NO...I GAINED WEIGHT.
SLIDE
OH YEAH, TODAY IS WEIGHING-IN DAY.
2-HE
OTONASHI

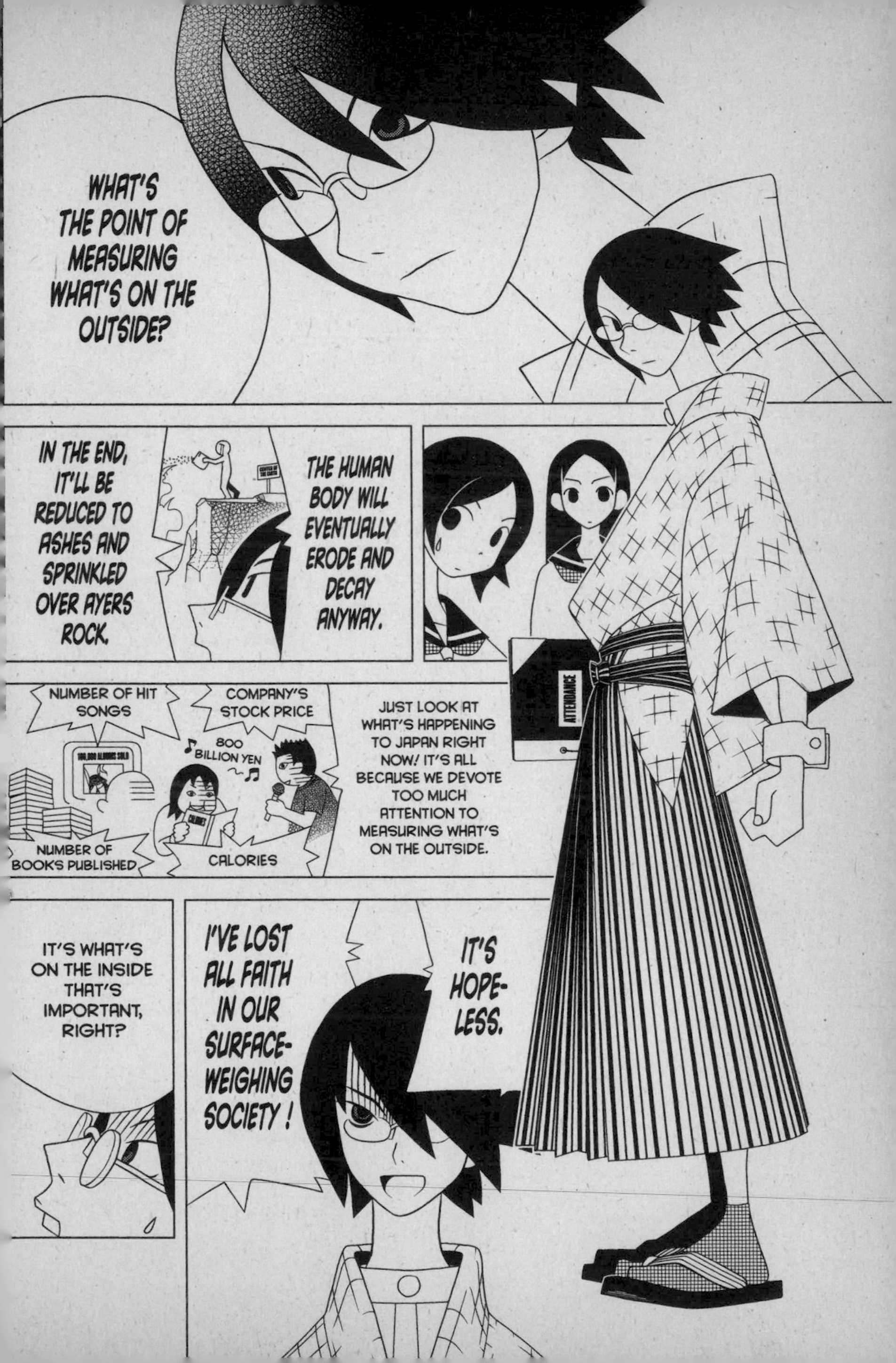
WHAT'S THE POINT OF MEASURING WHAT'S ON THE OUTSIDE?
ATTENDANCE
THE HUMAN BODY WILL EVENTUALLY ERODE AND DECAY ANYWAY.
IN THE END, IT'LL BE REDUCED TO ASHES AND SPRINKLED OVER AYERS ROCK.
JUST LOOK AT WHAT'S HAPPENING TO JAPAN RIGHT NOW! IT'S ALL BECAUSE WE DEVOTE TOO MUCH ATTENTION TO MEASURING WHAT'S ON THE OUTSIDE.
COMPANY'S STOCK PRICE
800 BILLION YEN
NUMBER OF HIT SONGS
CALORIES
NUMBER OF BOOKS PUBLISHED
IT'S HOPE-LESS.
I'VE LOST ALL FAITH IN OUR SURFACE-WEIGHING SOCIETY!
IT'S WHAT'S ON THE INSIDE THAT'S IMPORTANT, RIGHT?

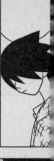

THERE-FORE...
WE'RE GONNA HAVE A MINOTAKE MEASUREMENT DAY!
"MINOTAKE MEASUREMENT"? WHAT'S THAT?
IT MEANS WE'RE GONNA MEASURE YOUR VALUE AS A HUMAN BEING.
I WANT YOU ALL TO KNOW YOUR PERSONAL MINOTAKE MEASUREMENT...
...AND LIVE YOUR LIFE ACCORDINGLY!
THERE'RE LOTS OF PEOPLE IN THIS WORLD WHO DO THINGS THAT GO COMPLETELY AGAINST THEIR MINOTAKE MEASUREMENT.
LIKE PEOPLE WHO PUT A 60-INCH PLASMA TV IN THEIR TINY TATAMI ROOM.
OR BROAD-CASTERS WHO AIR NAUGHTY LATE-NIGHT TV SHOWS DURING PRIME TIME!
OR ELEMENTARY SCHOOL KIDS WHO BRING A BAG OF SUPER EXPENSIVE, GOURMET COOKIES ON A FIELD TRIP.
カンツリーマーム
OR THE GUY WHO TALKS SHIT ABOUT SLACKERS EVEN THOUGH HE HIMSELF IS A TOTAL SLACKER.
WHAT'S WRONG WITH THIS GUY?
WHAT A LOSER.
AGE 28

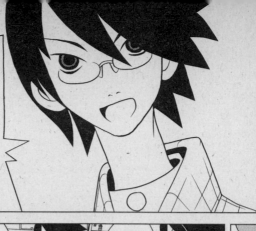

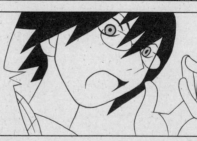

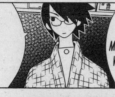

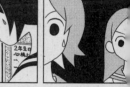

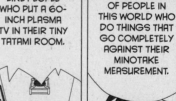

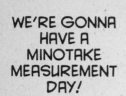

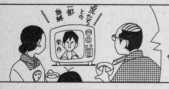

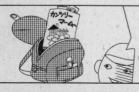

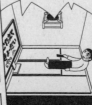

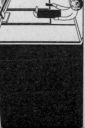

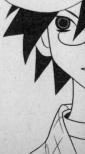

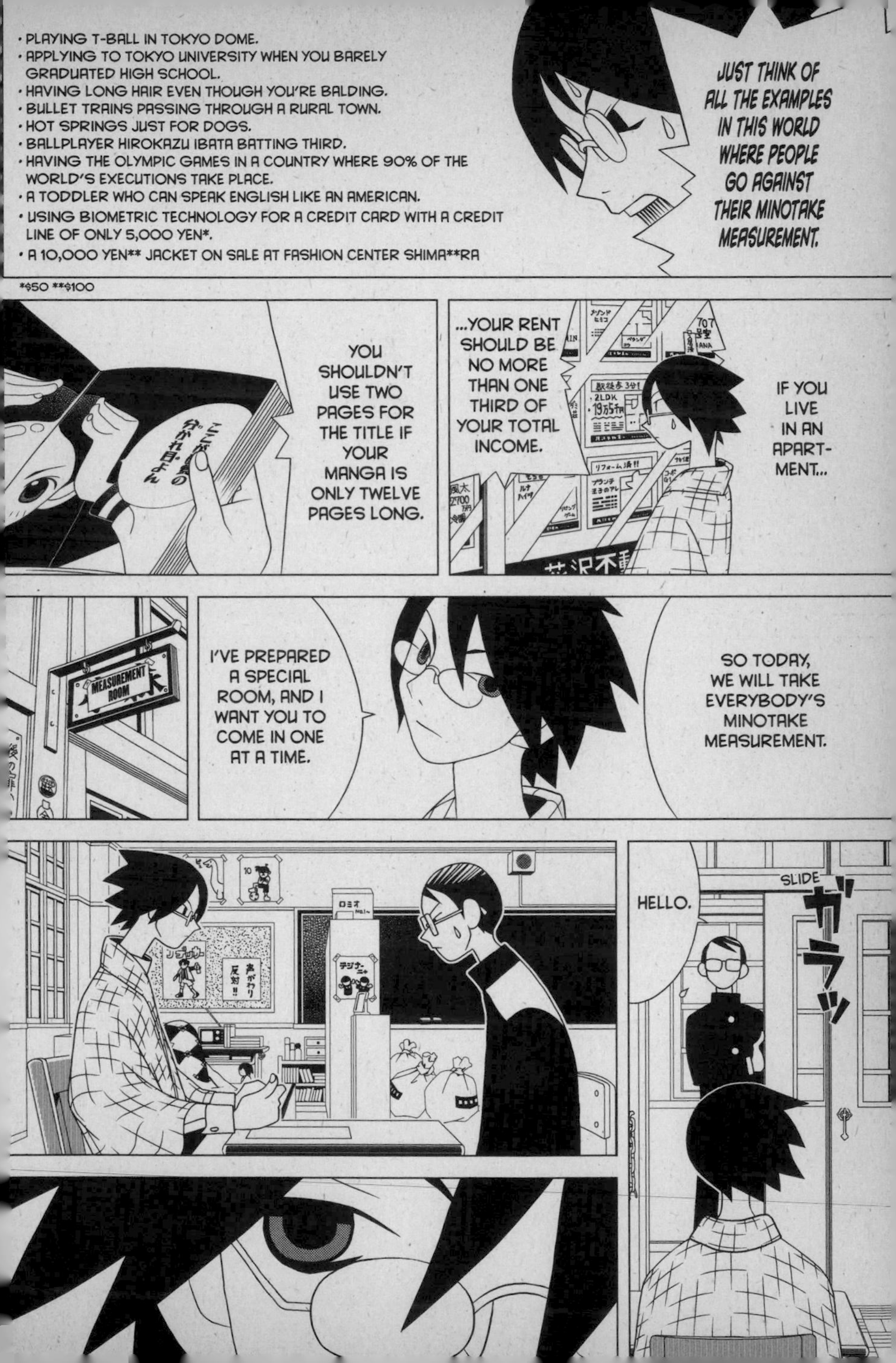
JUST THINK OF ALL THE EXAMPLES IN THIS WORLD WHERE PEOPLE GO AGAINST THEIR MINOTAKE MEASUREMENT.
• PLAYING T-BALL IN TOKYO DOME.
• APPLYING TO TOKYO UNIVERSITY WHEN YOU BARELY GRADUATED HIGH SCHOOL.
• HAVING LONG HAIR EVEN THOUGH YOU'RE BALDING.
• BULLET TRAINS PASSING THROUGH A RURAL TOWN.
• HOT SPRINGS JUST FOR DOGS.
• BALLPLAYER HIROKAZU IBATA BATTING THIRD.
• HAVING THE OLYMPIC GAMES IN A COUNTRY WHERE 90% OF THE WORLD'S EXECUTIONS TAKE PLACE.
• A TODDLER WHO CAN SPEAK ENGLISH LIKE AN AMERICAN.
• USING BIOMETRIC TECHNOLOGY FOR A CREDIT CARD WITH A CREDIT LINE OF ONLY 5,000 YEN*.
• A 10,000 YEN** JACKET ON SALE AT FASHION CENTER SHIMA**RA
*$50 **$100
IF YOU LIVE IN AN APART-MENT...
...YOUR RENT SHOULD BE NO MORE THAN ONE THIRD OF YOUR TOTAL INCOME.
YOU SHOULDN'T USE TWO PAGES FOR THE TITLE IF YOUR MANGA IS ONLY TWELVE PAGES LONG.
SO TODAY, WE WILL TAKE EVERYBODY'S MINOTAKE MEASUREMENT.
I'VE PREPARED A SPECIAL ROOM, AND I WANT YOU TO COME IN ONE AT A TIME.
MEASUREMENT ROOM
SLIDE
ガラッ
HELLO.

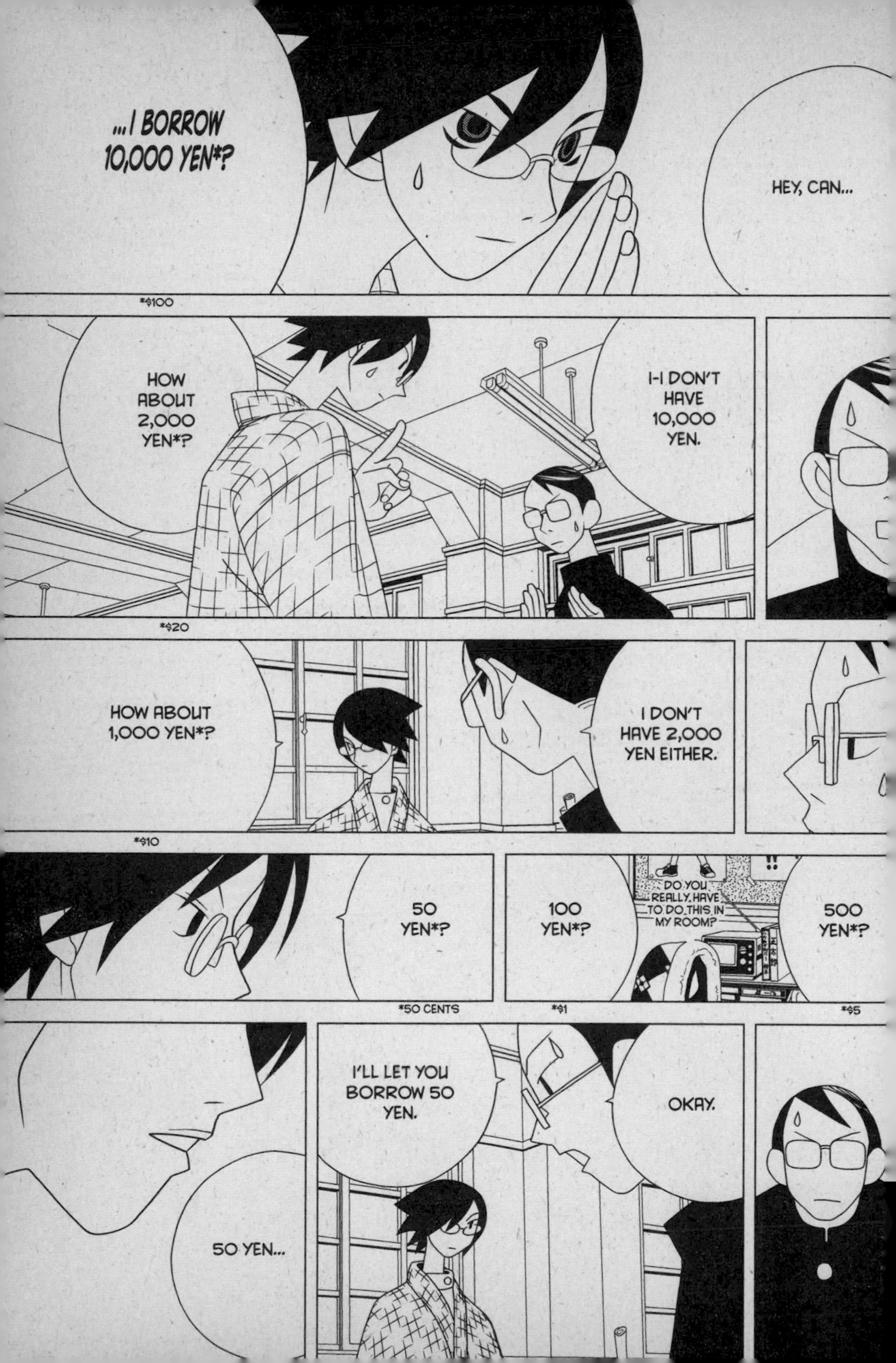
HEY, CAN...
...I BORROW 10,000 YEN*?
*$100
I-I DON'T HAVE 10,000 YEN.
HOW ABOUT 2,000 YEN*?
*$20
I DON'T HAVE 2,000 YEN EITHER.
HOW ABOUT 1,000 YEN*?
*$10
500 YEN*?
*$5
!!
DO YOU REALLY HAVE TO DO THIS IN MY ROOM?
100 YEN*?
*$1
50 YEN*?
*50 CENTS
OKAY.
I'LL LET YOU BORROW 50 YEN.
50 YEN...

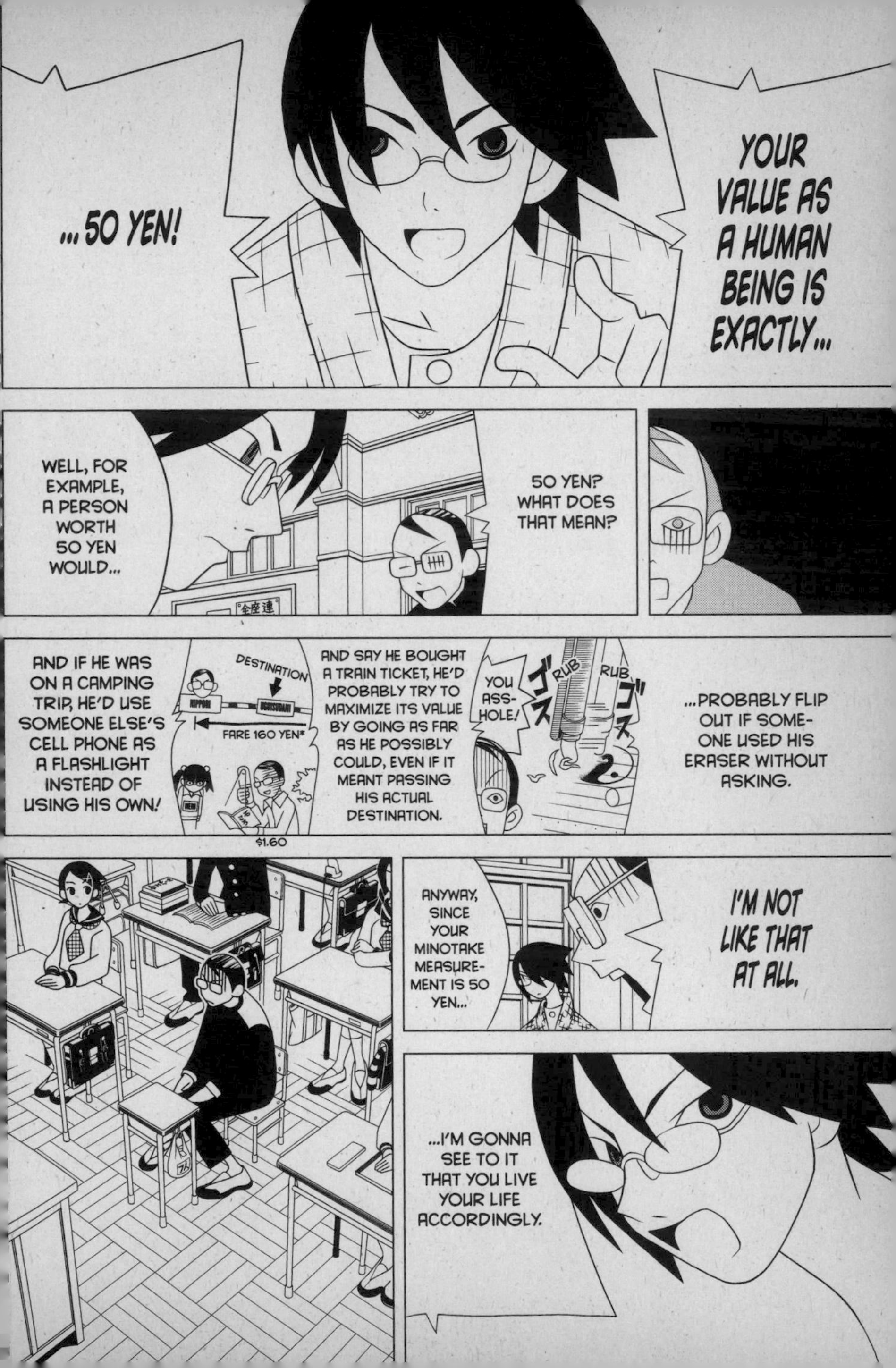
YOUR VALUE AS A HUMAN BEING IS EXACTLY...
...50 YEN!
50 YEN? WHAT DOES THAT MEAN?
WELL, FOR EXAMPLE, A PERSON WORTH 50 YEN WOULD...
全座連
...PROBABLY FLIP OUT IF SOMEONE USED HIS ERASER WITHOUT ASKING.
RUB
RUB
ゴス
ゴス
YOU ASS-HOLE!
AND SAY HE BOUGHT A TRAIN TICKET, HE'D PROBABLY TRY TO MAXIMIZE ITS VALUE BY GOING AS FAR AS HE POSSIBLY COULD, EVEN IF IT MEANT PASSING HIS ACTUAL DESTINATION.
DESTINATION
NIPPORI
UGUISUDANI
FARE 160 YEN*
AND IF HE WAS ON A CAMPING TRIP, HE'D USE SOMEONE ELSE'S CELL PHONE AS A FLASHLIGHT INSTEAD OF USING HIS OWN!
I'M NOT LIKE THAT AT ALL.
ANYWAY, SINCE YOUR MINOTAKE MEASUREMENT IS 50 YEN...
...I'M GONNA SEE TO IT THAT YOU LIVE YOUR LIFE ACCORDINGLY.

*$1.60

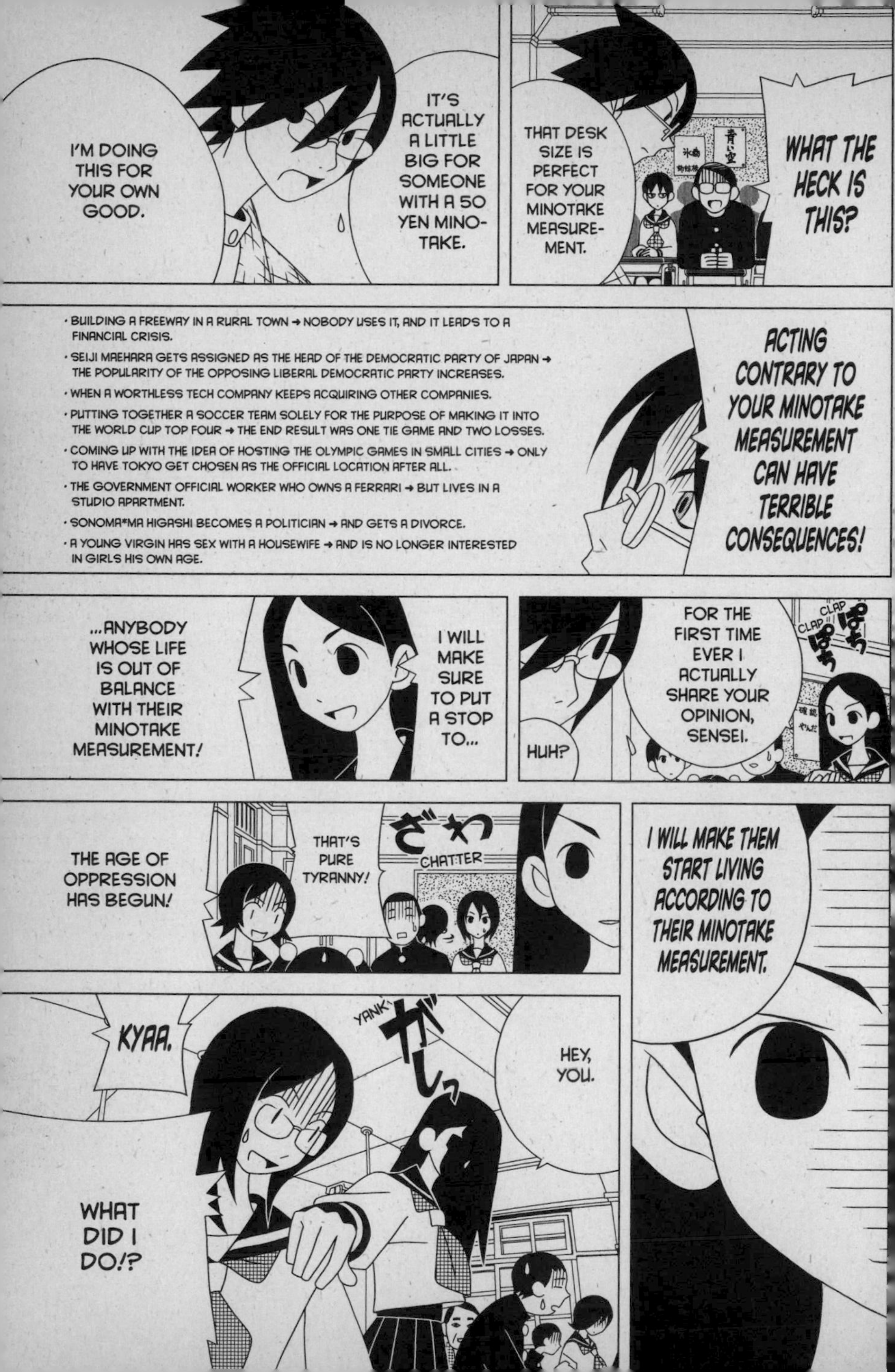
WHAT THE HECK IS THIS?
THAT DESK SIZE IS PERFECT FOR YOUR MINOTAKE MEASUREMENT.
IT'S ACTUALLY A LITTLE BIG FOR SOMEONE WITH A 50 YEN MINOTAKE.
I'M DOING THIS FOR YOUR OWN GOOD.
ACTING CONTRARY TO YOUR MINOTAKE MEASUREMENT CAN HAVE TERRIBLE CONSEQUENCES!
· BUILDING A FREEWAY IN A RURAL TOWN → NOBODY USES IT, AND IT LEADS TO A FINANCIAL CRISIS.
· SEIJI MAEHARA GETS ASSIGNED AS THE HEAD OF THE DEMOCRATIC PARTY OF JAPAN → THE POPULARITY OF THE OPPOSING LIBERAL DEMOCRATIC PARTY INCREASES.
· WHEN A WORTHLESS TECH COMPANY KEEPS ACQUIRING OTHER COMPANIES.
· PUTTING TOGETHER A SOCCER TEAM SOLELY FOR THE PURPOSE OF MAKING IT INTO THE WORLD CUP TOP FOUR → THE END RESULT WAS ONE TIE GAME AND TWO LOSSES.
· COMING UP WITH THE IDEA OF HOSTING THE OLYMPIC GAMES IN SMALL CITIES → ONLY TO HAVE TOKYO GET CHOSEN AS THE OFFICIAL LOCATION AFTER ALL.
· THE GOVERNMENT OFFICIAL WORKER WHO OWNS A FERRARI → BUT LIVES IN A STUDIO APARTMENT.
· SONOMA*MA HIGASHI BECOMES A POLITICIAN → AND GETS A DIVORCE.
· A YOUNG VIRGIN HAS SEX WITH A HOUSEWIFE → AND IS NO LONGER INTERESTED IN GIRLS HIS OWN AGE.
CLAP CLAP
FOR THE FIRST TIME EVER I ACTUALLY SHARE YOUR OPINION, SENSEI.
HUH?
I WILL MAKE SURE TO PUT A STOP TO...
...ANYBODY WHOSE LIFE IS OUT OF BALANCE WITH THEIR MINOTAKE MEASUREMENT!
I WILL MAKE THEM START LIVING ACCORDING TO THEIR MINOTAKE MEASUREMENT.
CHATTER
THAT'S PURE TYRANNY!
THE AGE OF OPPRESSION HAS BEGUN!
HEY, YOU.
YANK
KYAA.
WHAT DID I DO!?

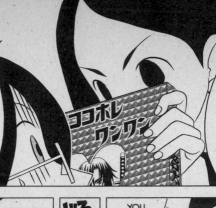

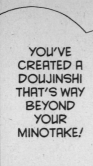

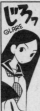

THIS BOOK DOESN'T DESERVE TO BE PRINTED IN HARDCOVER, WITH FULL-COLOR PRINT, A HOLOGRAM, AND A FOLD-OUT POSTER.
ココホレワンワン
YOU'VE CREATED A DOUJINSHI THAT'S WAY BEYOND YOUR MINOTAKE!
SHAME ON YOU!
YOU SHOULD HAVE JUST MADE A BLACK-AND-WHITE ZINE.
シキティーコピー本
じろっ
GLARE
YOU HAVE A CELL PHONE THAT LETS YOU SEND TEXTS UP TO TEN THOUSAND WORDS? THAT'S WAY BEYOND YOUR MINOTAKE.
がしっ
GRAB
ONE THAT SENDS SEVENTY-WORD TEXTS IS MORE THAN ENOUGH FOR YOU!
YOU'RE ONLY IN HIGH SCHOOL, BUT YOU WALK AROUND WITH A DESIGNER HANDBAG?
FORGET THAT, ALL YOU REALLY NEED IS A SHOPPING BAG FROM THE DESIGNER OUTLET.
MATAROU, YOU'RE LIVING A PRETTY MODEST LIFE, SO I'D SAY YOU'RE IN LINE WITH YOUR MINOTAKE.
I DON'T THINK SO.
I'M LIVING BEYOND MY MINOTAKE.

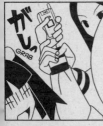

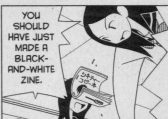

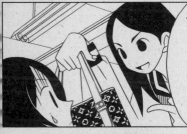

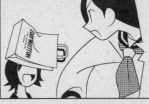

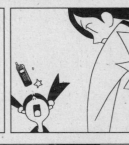

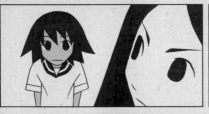

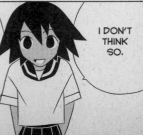

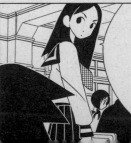

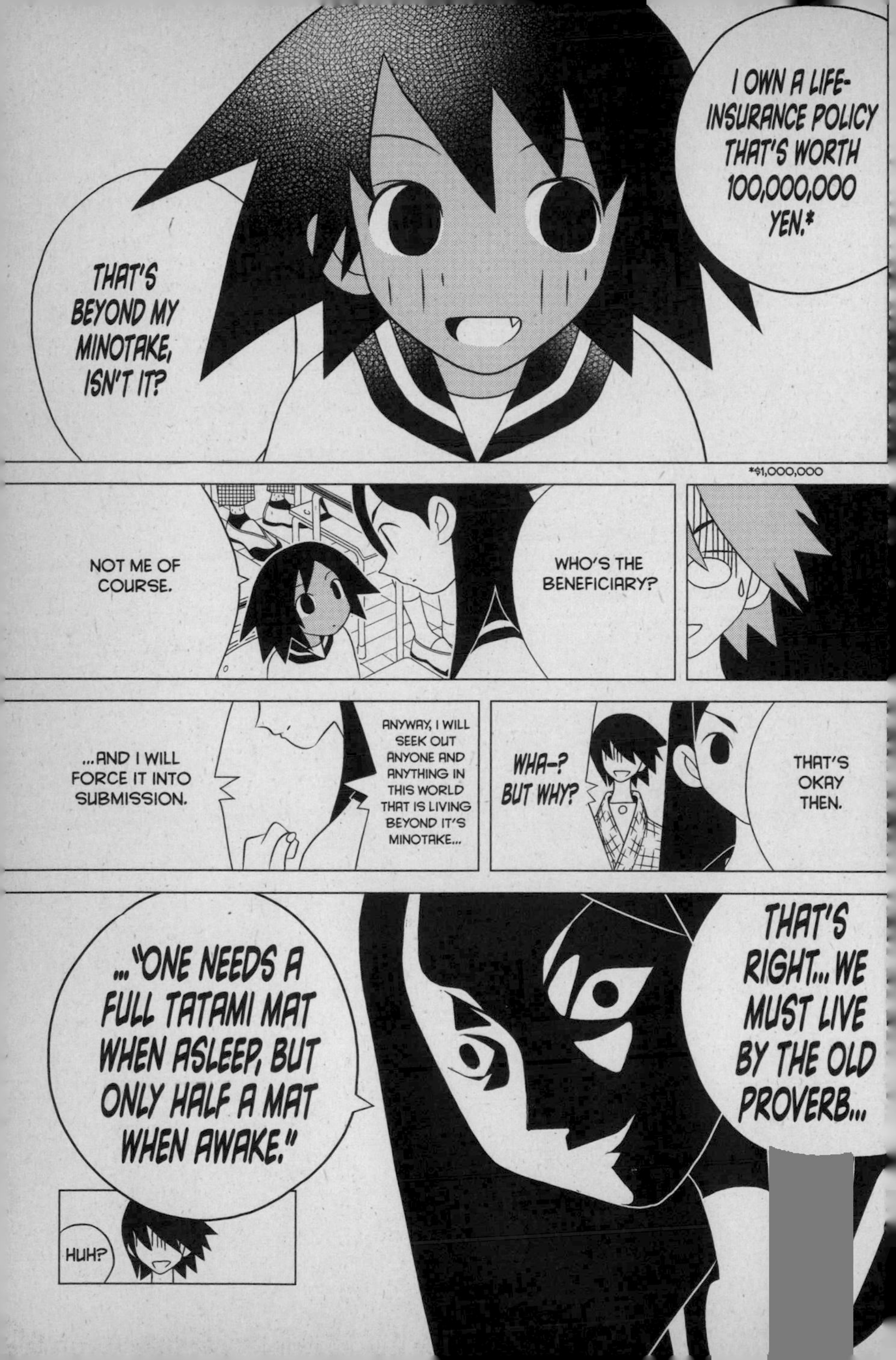
I OWN A LIFE-INSURANCE POLICY THAT'S WORTH 100,000,000 YEN.*
THAT'S BEYOND MY MINOTAKE, ISN'T IT?
*$1,000,000
WHO'S THE BENEFICIARY?
NOT ME OF COURSE.
THAT'S OKAY THEN.
WHA-? BUT WHY?
ANYWAY, I WILL SEEK OUT ANYONE AND ANYTHING IN THIS WORLD THAT IS LIVING BEYOND IT'S MINOTAKE...
...AND I WILL FORCE IT INTO SUBMISSION.
THAT'S RIGHT... WE MUST LIVE BY THE OLD PROVERB...
..."ONE NEEDS A FULL TATAMI MAT WHEN ASLEEP, BUT ONLY HALF A MAT WHEN AWAKE."
HUH?

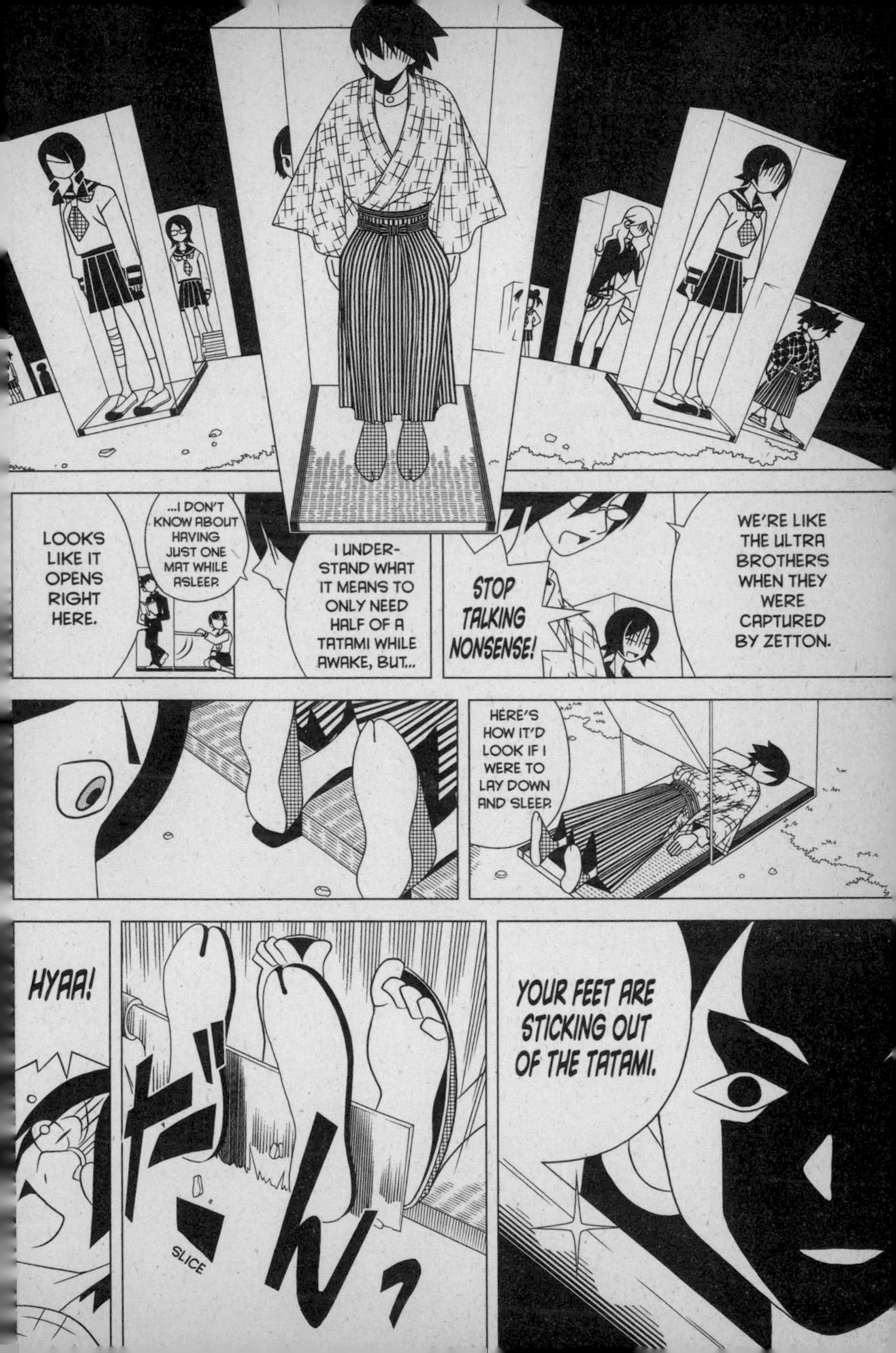
WE'RE LIKE THE ULTRA BROTHERS WHEN THEY WERE CAPTURED BY ZETTON.
STOP TALKING NONSENSE!
I UNDER-STAND WHAT IT MEANS TO ONLY NEED HALF OF A TATAMI WHILE AWAKE, BUT...
...I DON'T KNOW ABOUT HAVING JUST ONE MAT WHILE ASLEEP.
LOOKS LIKE IT OPENS RIGHT HERE.
HERE'S HOW IT'D LOOK IF I WERE TO LAY DOWN AND SLEEP.
YOUR FEET ARE STICKING OUT OF THE TATAMI.
SLICE
HYAA!

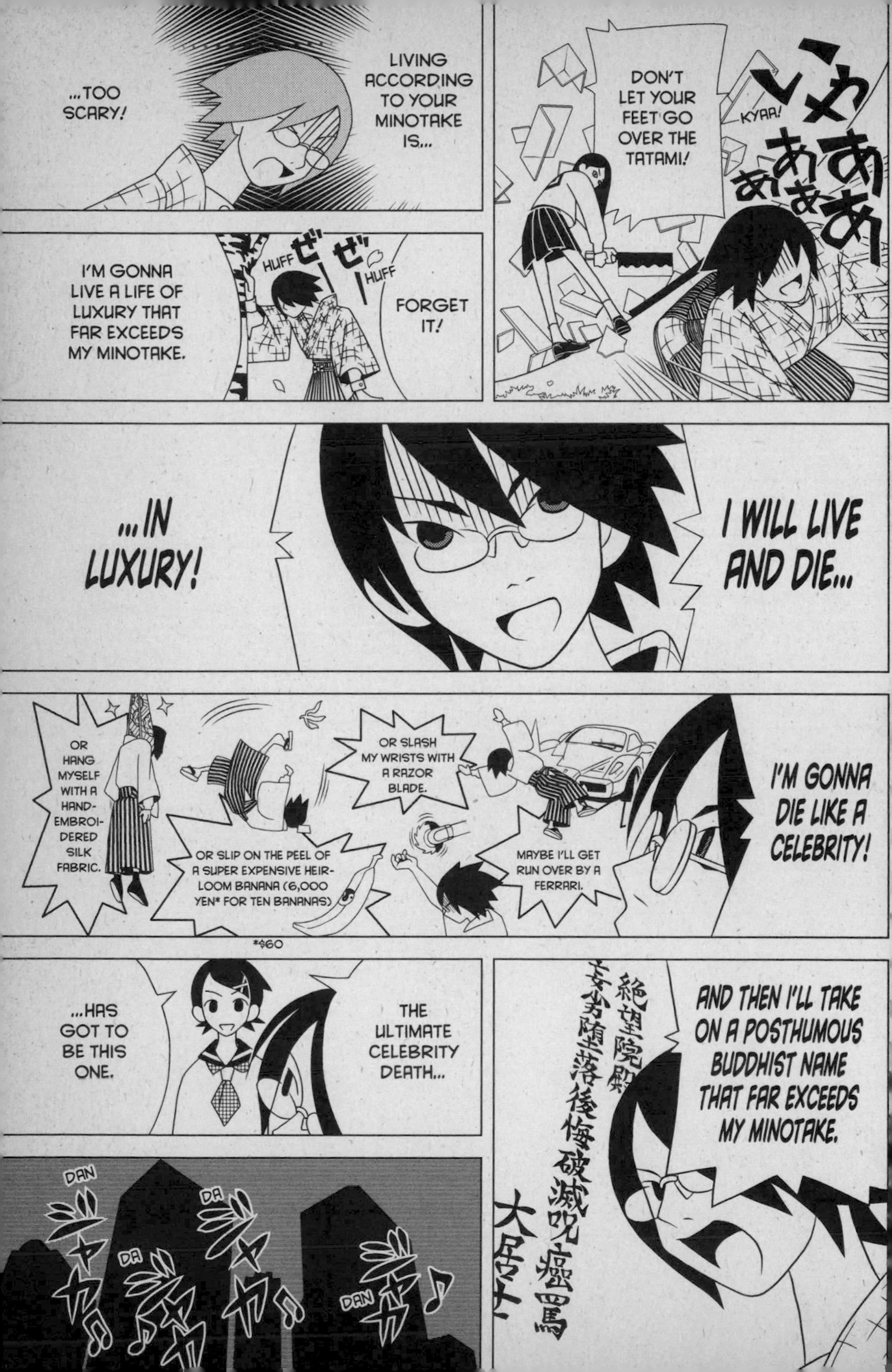
DON'T LET YOUR FEET GO OVER THE TATAMI!
KYAA!
LIVING ACCORDING TO YOUR MINOTAKE IS...
...TOO SCARY!
FORGET IT!
HUFF
HUFF
I'M GONNA LIVE A LIFE OF LUXURY THAT FAR EXCEEDS MY MINOTAKE.
I WILL LIVE AND DIE...
...IN LUXURY!
I'M GONNA DIE LIKE A CELEBRITY!
MAYBE I'LL GET RUN OVER BY A FERRARI.
OR SLASH MY WRISTS WITH A RAZOR BLADE.
OR SLIP ON THE PEEL OF A SUPER EXPENSIVE HEIRLOOM BANANA (6,000 YEN* FOR TEN BANANAS)
OR HANG MYSELF WITH A HAND-EMBROIDERED SILK FABRIC.
*$60
AND THEN I'LL TAKE ON A POSTHUMOUS BUDDHIST NAME THAT FAR EXCEEDS MY MINOTAKE.
絶望院殿
妄労随堕落後悔破滅呪癌罵
大居士
THE ULTIMATE CELEBRITY DEATH...
...HAS GOT TO BE THIS ONE.
DAN
DA
DA
DAN

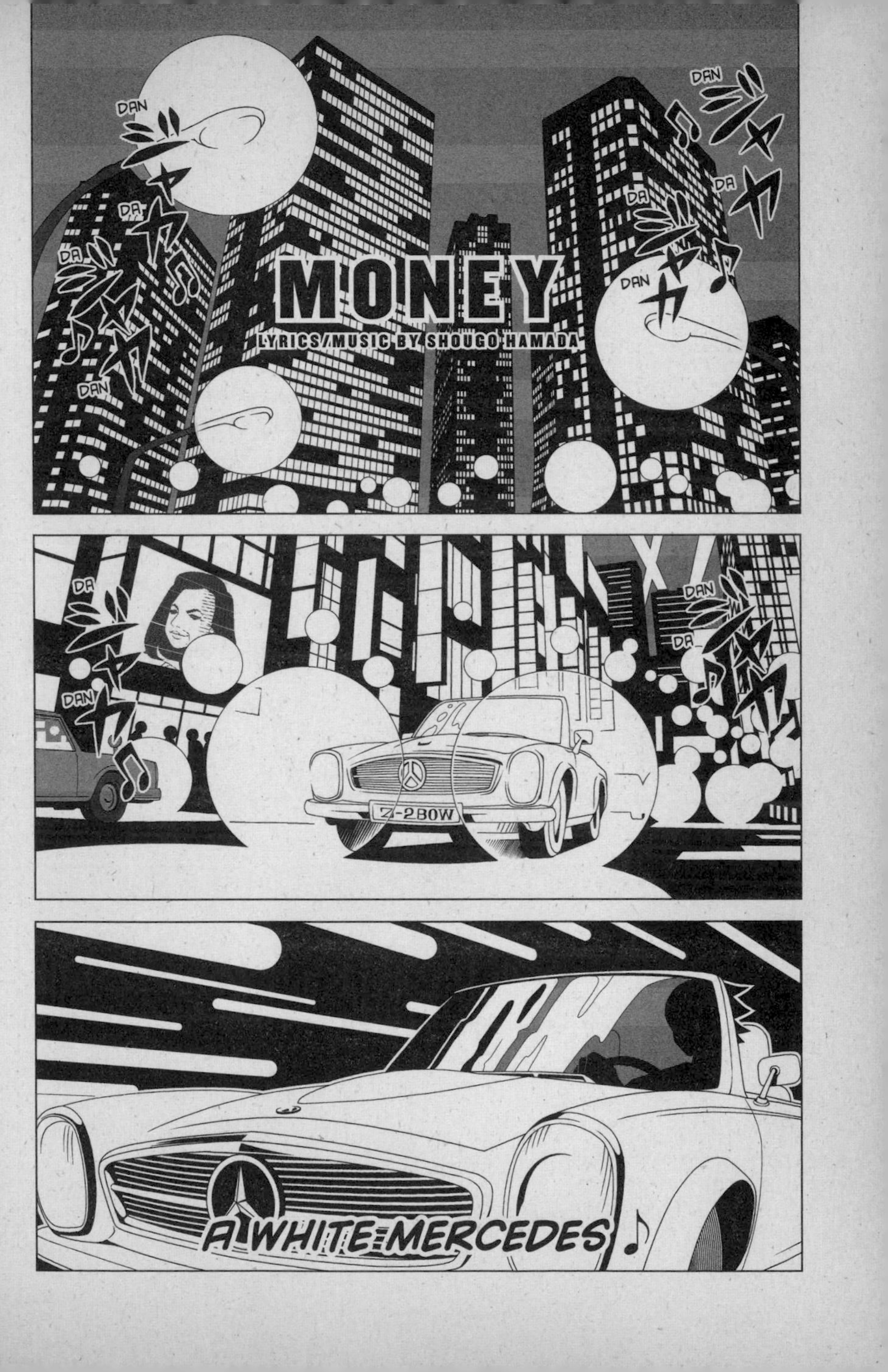

DAN
DA
DA
DAN
MONEY
LYRICS/MUSIC BY SHOUGO HAMADA
DAN
DA
DA
DAN
DAN
DA
DA
DAN
A WHITE MERCEDES ♪

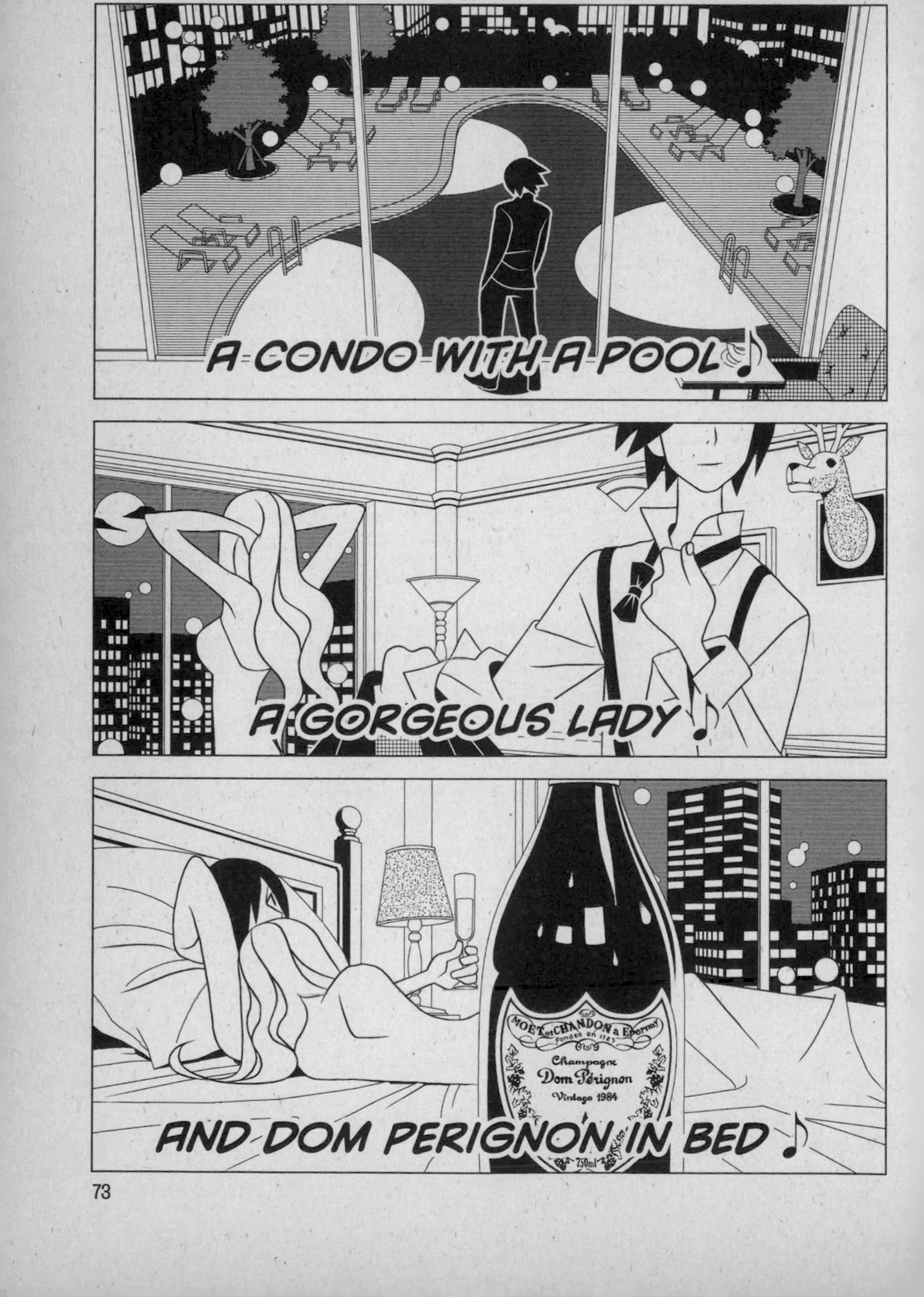
A CONDO WITH A POOL ♪
A GORGEOUS LADY ♪
MOET et CHANDON a Epernay
Champagne
Dom Pérignon
Vintage 1984
750ml
AND DOM PERIGNON IN BED ♪

BUBBLE

BUBBLE

BUBBLE

AND THEN YOU DROWN YOURSELF

...SO I COULDN'T QUITE DROWN MYSELF.

I DIDN'T WANNA WASTE THE DOM PERIGNON...

YOU'RE STILL ALIVE?

HOW CAN DEATH BE SO EXPENSIVE?

AHH...

INVOICE

ITEMS	PRICE
Conde with a pool	
A gorgeous woman (Sofia's Ladies Club)	352,000
Gold Member, 6 hour VIP course	
Extra time charge	
Rental car (white Mercedes)	250,000
Dom Perignon (white)	70,000
Tuxedo (rental)	227,000
*cleaning charge additional	12,390
Bath rental	81,560
Yubari melon	
Render (tip)	68,250
TOTAL	2,000

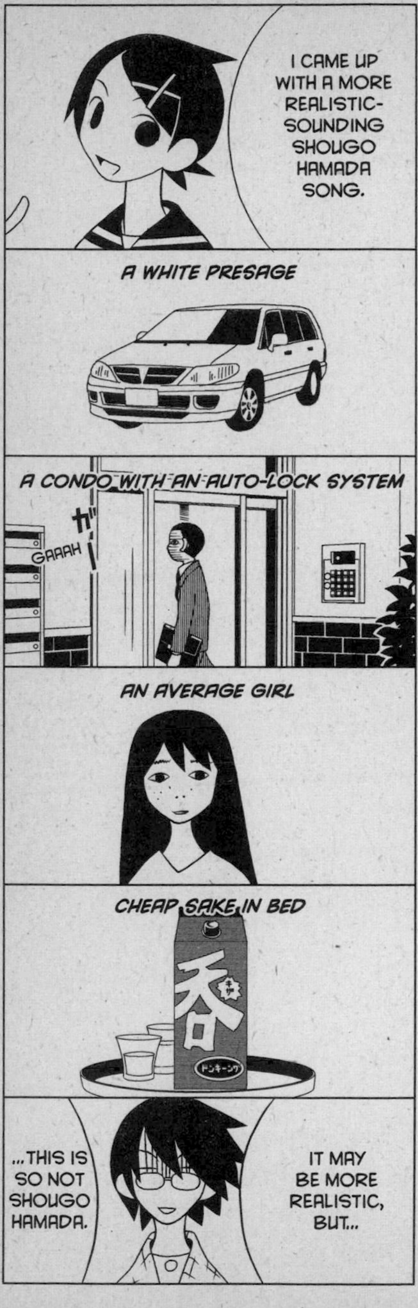
I CAME UP WITH A MORE REALISTIC-SOUNDING SHOUGO HAMADA SONG.
A WHITE PRESAGE
A CONDO WITH AN AUTO-LOCK SYSTEM
ガ
GAAAH
AN AVERAGE GIRL
CHEAP SAKE IN BED
IT MAY BE MORE REALISTIC, BUT...
...THIS IS SO NOT SHOUGO HAMADA.

VITA SEXUALIS

CHAPTER 46

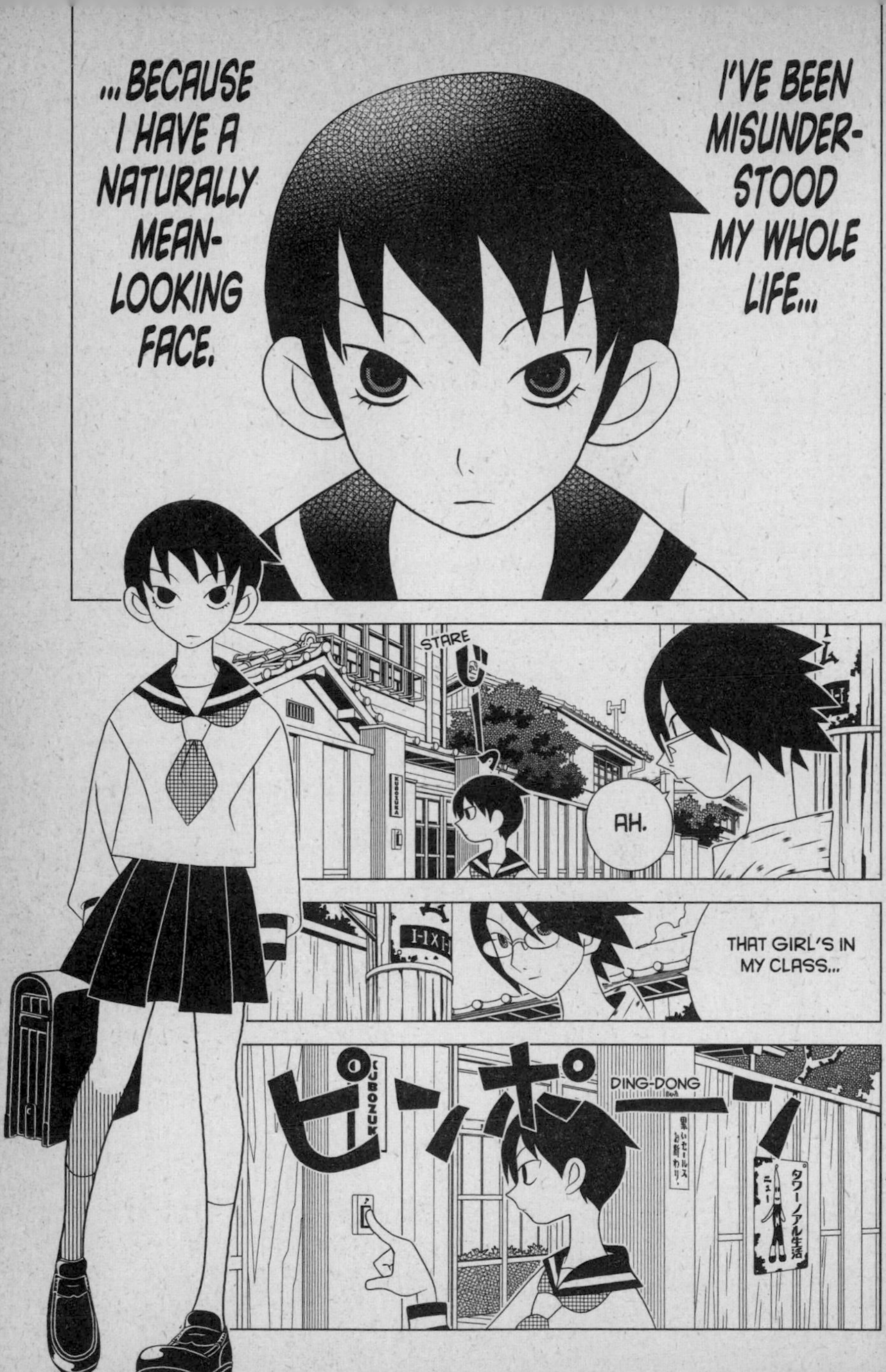
I'VE BEEN MISUNDERSTOOD MY WHOLE LIFE...
...BECAUSE I HAVE A NATURALLY MEAN-LOOKING FACE.
STARE
AH.
THAT GIRL'S IN MY CLASS...
DING-DONG

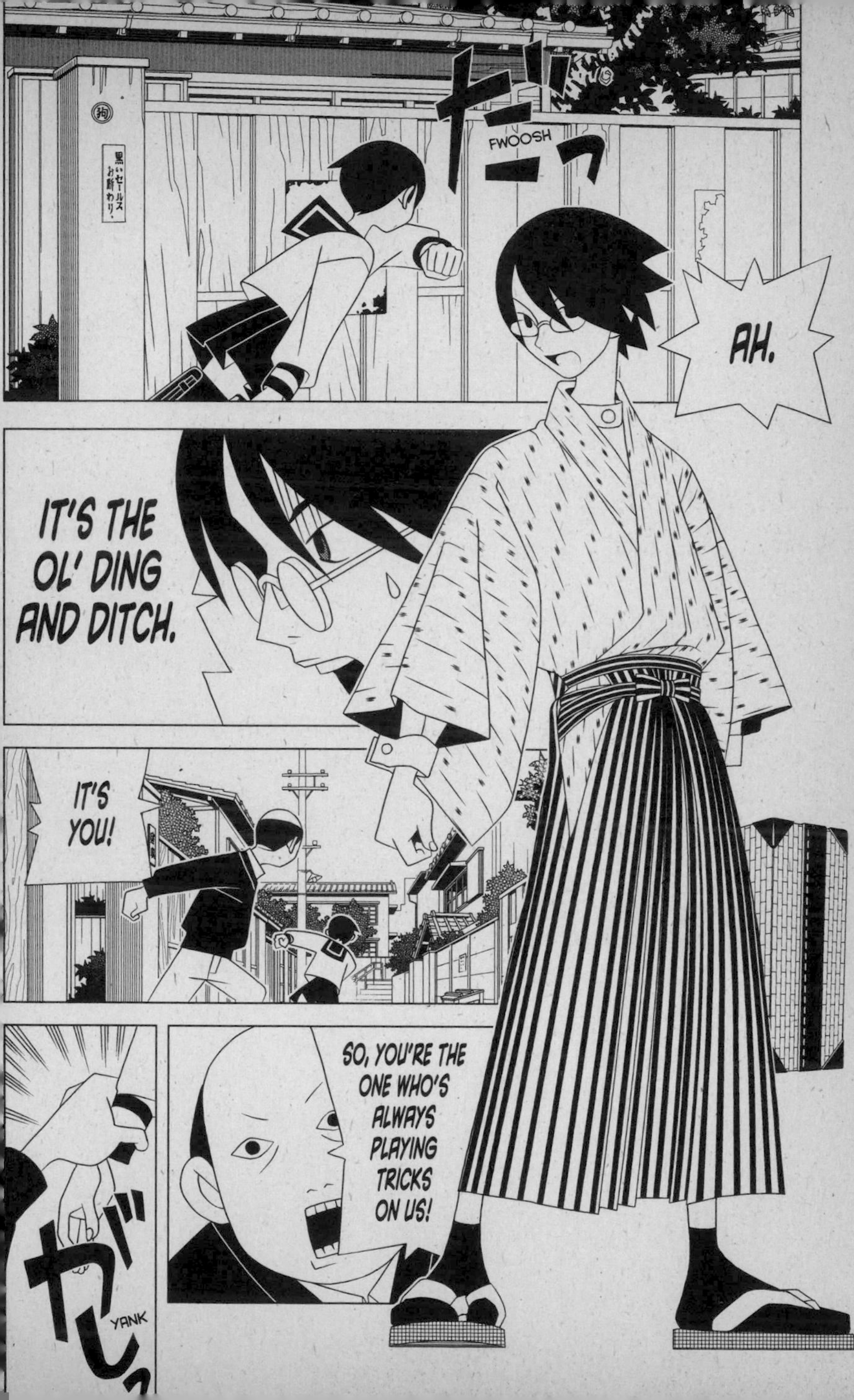
FWOOSH
AH.
黒いセールスお断わり。
IT'S THE OL' DING AND DITCH.
IT'S YOU!
SO, YOU'RE THE ONE WHO'S ALWAYS PLAYING TRICKS ON US!
YANK

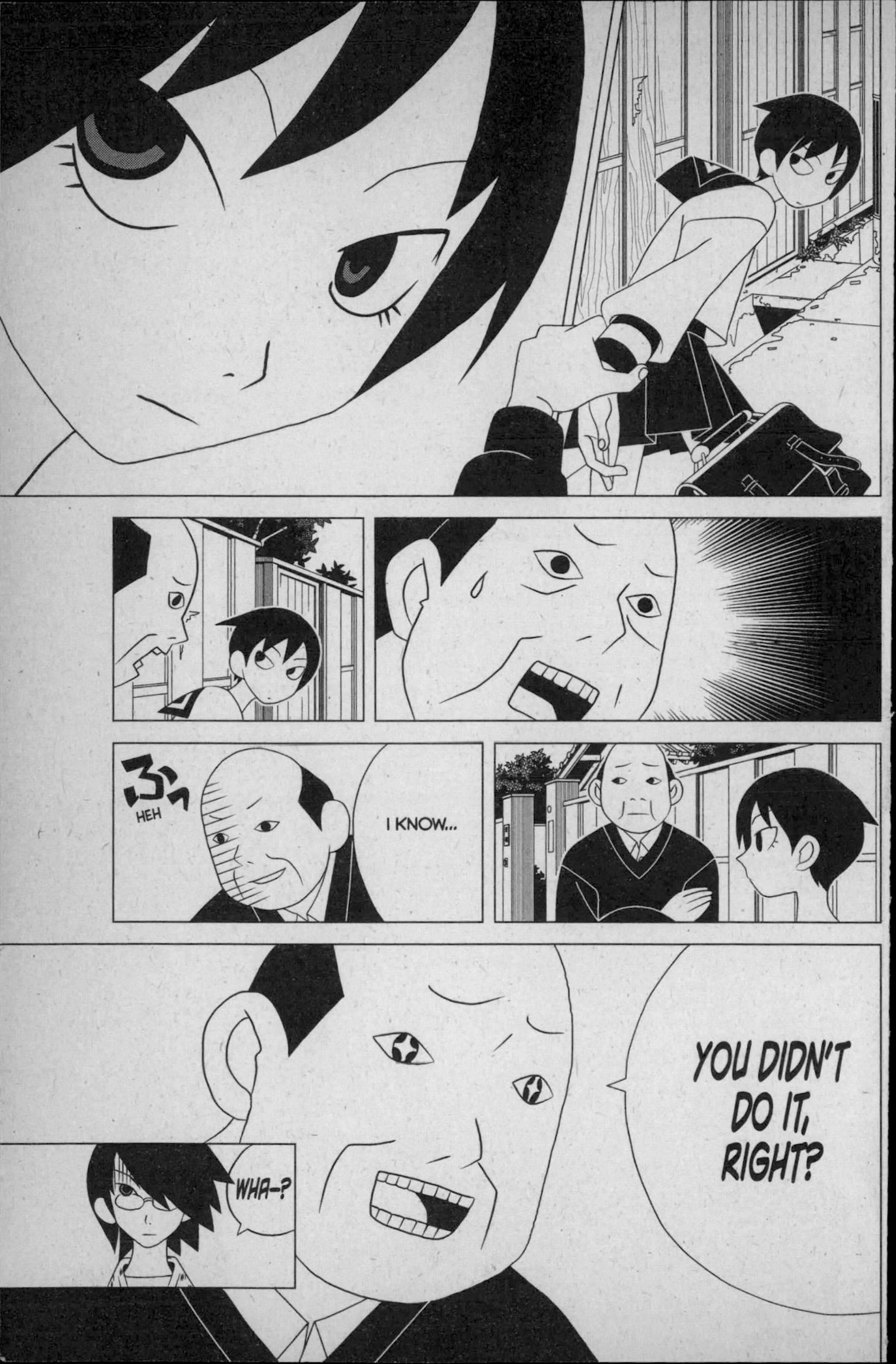
I KNOW...
ふっ
HEH
YOU DIDN'T DO IT, RIGHT?
WHA-?

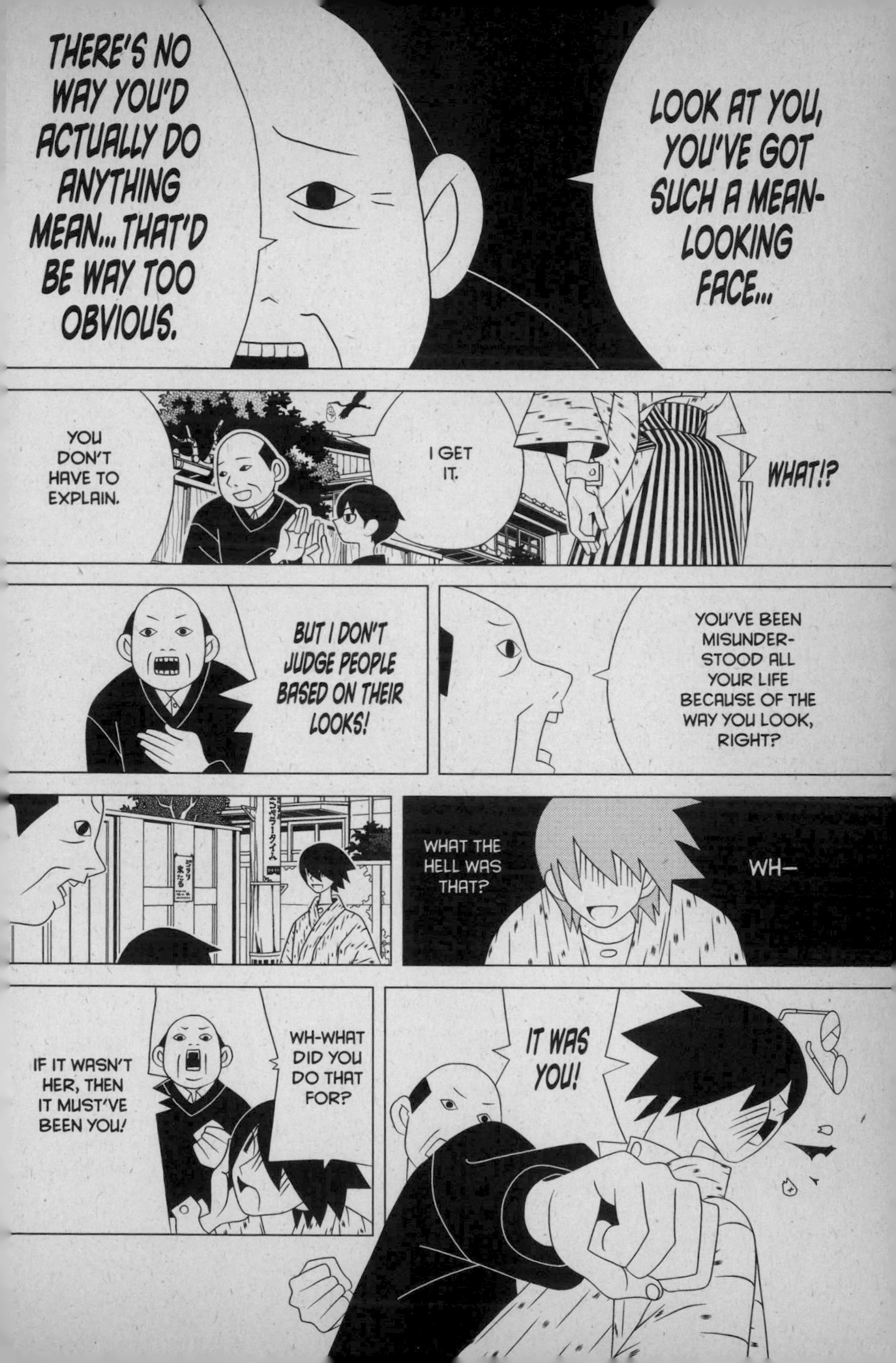
LOOK AT YOU, YOU'VE GOT SUCH A MEAN-LOOKING FACE...
THERE'S NO WAY YOU'D ACTUALLY DO ANYTHING MEAN...THAT'D BE WAY TOO OBVIOUS.
WHAT!?
I GET IT.
YOU DON'T HAVE TO EXPLAIN.
YOU'VE BEEN MISUNDER-STOOD ALL YOUR LIFE BECAUSE OF THE WAY YOU LOOK, RIGHT?
BUT I DON'T JUDGE PEOPLE BASED ON THEIR LOOKS!
WH-
WHAT THE HELL WAS THAT?
IT WAS YOU!
WH-WHAT DID YOU DO THAT FOR?
IF IT WASN'T HER, THEN IT MUST'VE BEEN YOU!

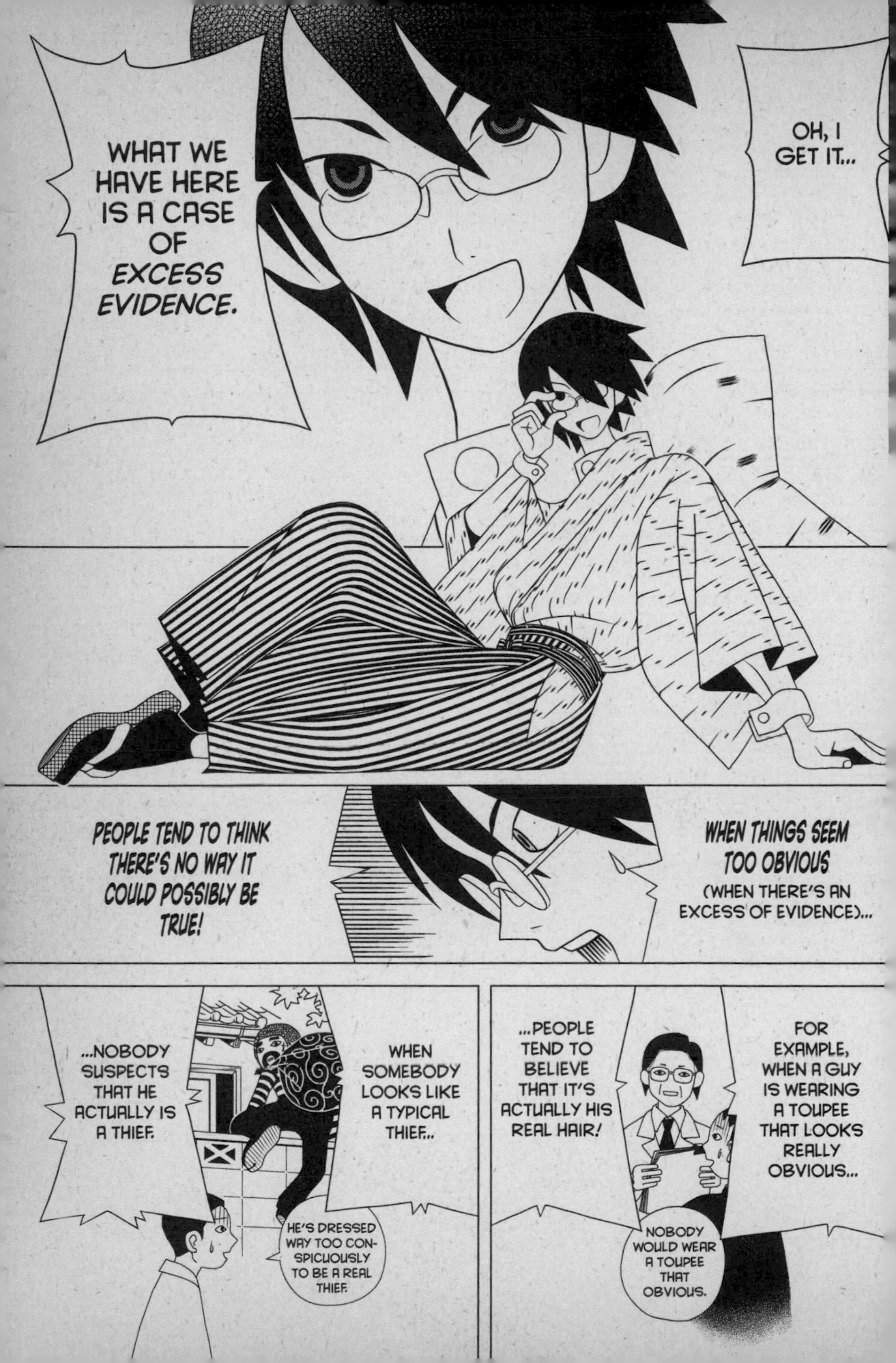
OH, I GET IT...
WHAT WE HAVE HERE IS A CASE OF *EXCESS EVIDENCE.*
WHEN THINGS SEEM TOO OBVIOUS (WHEN THERE'S AN EXCESS OF EVIDENCE)...
PEOPLE TEND TO THINK THERE'S NO WAY IT COULD POSSIBLY BE TRUE!
FOR EXAMPLE, WHEN A GUY IS WEARING A TOUPEE THAT LOOKS REALLY OBVIOUS...
...PEOPLE TEND TO BELIEVE THAT IT'S ACTUALLY HIS REAL HAIR!
NOBODY WOULD WEAR A TOUPEE THAT OBVIOUS.
WHEN SOMEBODY LOOKS LIKE A TYPICAL THIEF...
...NOBODY SUSPECTS THAT HE ACTUALLY IS A THIEF.
HE'S DRESSED WAY TOO CON-SPICUOUSLY TO BE A REAL THIEF.

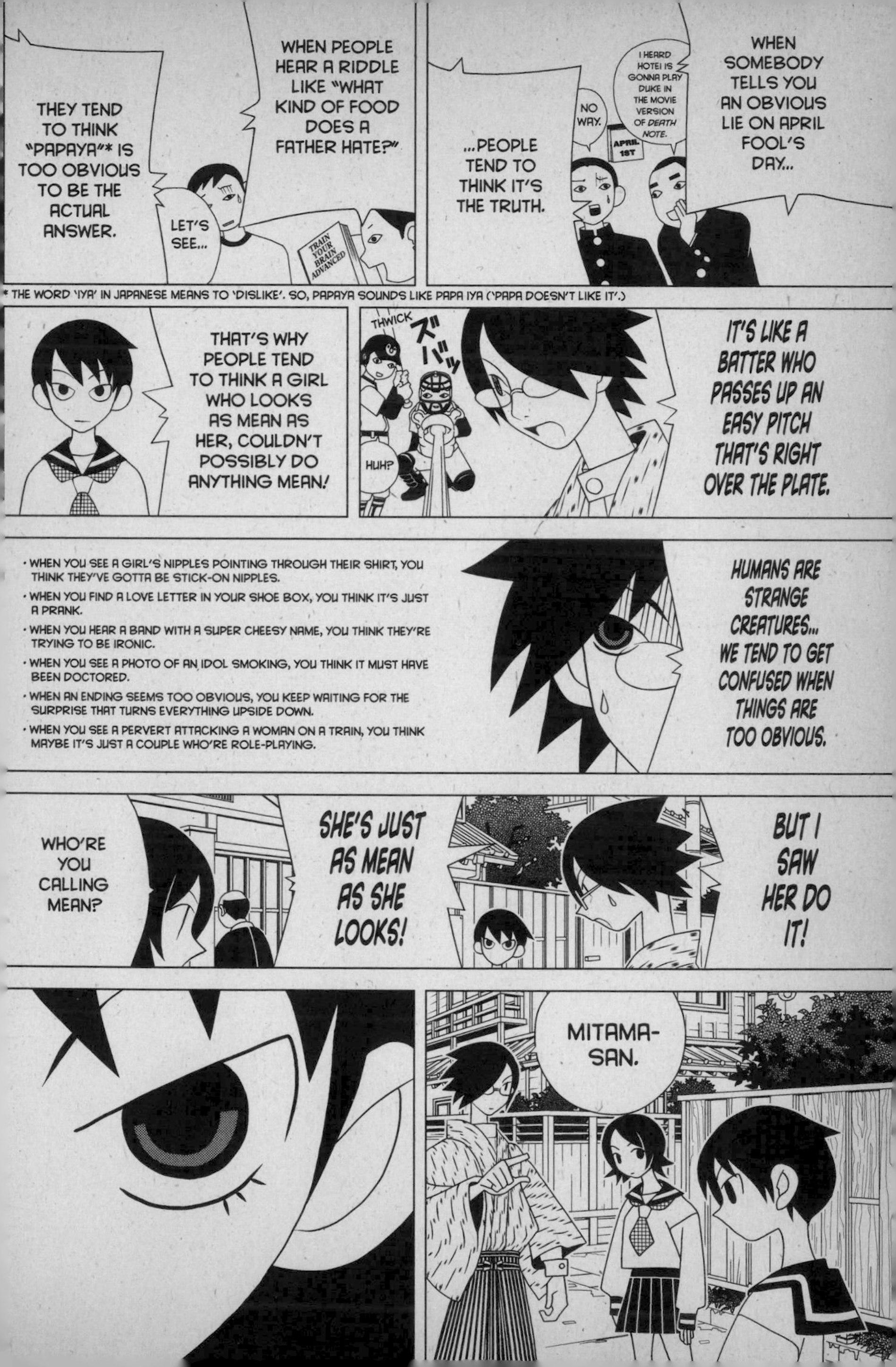
WHEN SOMEBODY TELLS YOU AN OBVIOUS LIE ON APRIL FOOL'S DAY...
I HEARD HOTEI IS GONNA PLAY DUKE IN THE MOVIE VERSION OF *DEATH NOTE.*
APRIL 1ST
NO WAY.
...PEOPLE TEND TO THINK IT'S THE TRUTH.
WHEN PEOPLE HEAR A RIDDLE LIKE "WHAT KIND OF FOOD DOES A FATHER HATE?"
TRAIN YOUR BRAIN ADVANCED
LET'S SEE...
THEY TEND TO THINK "PAPAYA"* IS TOO OBVIOUS TO BE THE ACTUAL ANSWER.
* THE WORD 'IYA' IN JAPANESE MEANS TO 'DISLIKE'. SO, PAPAYA SOUNDS LIKE PAPA IYA ('PAPA DOESN'T LIKE IT'.)
IT'S LIKE A BATTER WHO PASSES UP AN EASY PITCH THAT'S RIGHT OVER THE PLATE.
THWICK
ズバッ
HUH?
THAT'S WHY PEOPLE TEND TO THINK A GIRL WHO LOOKS AS MEAN AS HER, COULDN'T POSSIBLY DO ANYTHING MEAN!
HUMANS ARE STRANGE CREATURES... WE TEND TO GET CONFUSED WHEN THINGS ARE TOO OBVIOUS.
• WHEN YOU SEE A GIRL'S NIPPLES POINTING THROUGH THEIR SHIRT, YOU THINK THEY'VE GOTTA BE STICK-ON NIPPLES.
• WHEN YOU FIND A LOVE LETTER IN YOUR SHOE BOX, YOU THINK IT'S JUST A PRANK.
• WHEN YOU HEAR A BAND WITH A SUPER CHEESY NAME, YOU THINK THEY'RE TRYING TO BE IRONIC.
• WHEN YOU SEE A PHOTO OF AN IDOL SMOKING, YOU THINK IT MUST HAVE BEEN DOCTORED.
• WHEN AN ENDING SEEMS TOO OBVIOUS, YOU KEEP WAITING FOR THE SURPRISE THAT TURNS EVERYTHING UPSIDE DOWN.
• WHEN YOU SEE A PERVERT ATTACKING A WOMAN ON A TRAIN, YOU THINK MAYBE IT'S JUST A COUPLE WHO'RE ROLE-PLAYING.
BUT I SAW HER DO IT!
SHE'S JUST AS MEAN AS SHE LOOKS!
WHO'RE YOU CALLING MEAN?
MITAMA-SAN.

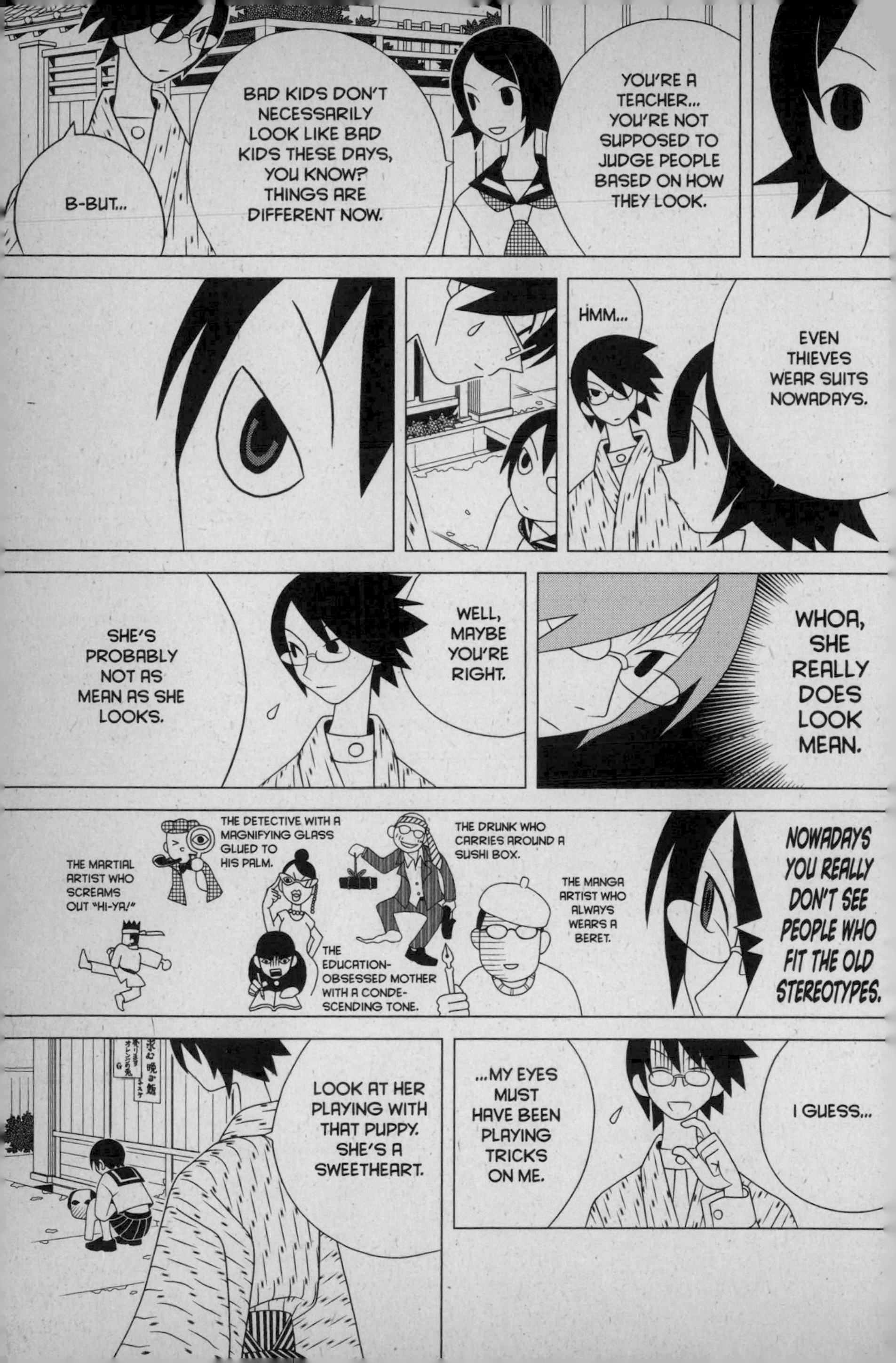
YOU'RE A TEACHER... YOU'RE NOT SUPPOSED TO JUDGE PEOPLE BASED ON HOW THEY LOOK.
BAD KIDS DON'T NECESSARILY LOOK LIKE BAD KIDS THESE DAYS, YOU KNOW? THINGS ARE DIFFERENT NOW.
B-BUT...
EVEN THIEVES WEAR SUITS NOWADAYS.
HMM...
WHOA, SHE REALLY DOES LOOK MEAN.
WELL, MAYBE YOU'RE RIGHT.
SHE'S PROBABLY NOT AS MEAN AS SHE LOOKS.
NOWADAYS YOU REALLY DON'T SEE PEOPLE WHO FIT THE OLD STEREOTYPES.
THE MANGA ARTIST WHO ALWAYS WEARS A BERET.
THE DRUNK WHO CARRIES AROUND A SUSHI BOX.
THE DETECTIVE WITH A MAGNIFYING GLASS GLUED TO HIS PALM.
THE EDUCATION-OBSESSED MOTHER WITH A CONDE-SCENDING TONE.
THE MARTIAL ARTIST WHO SCREAMS OUT "HI-YA!"
I GUESS...
...MY EYES MUST HAVE BEEN PLAYING TRICKS ON ME.
LOOK AT HER PLAYING WITH THAT PUPPY. SHE'S A SWEETHEART.

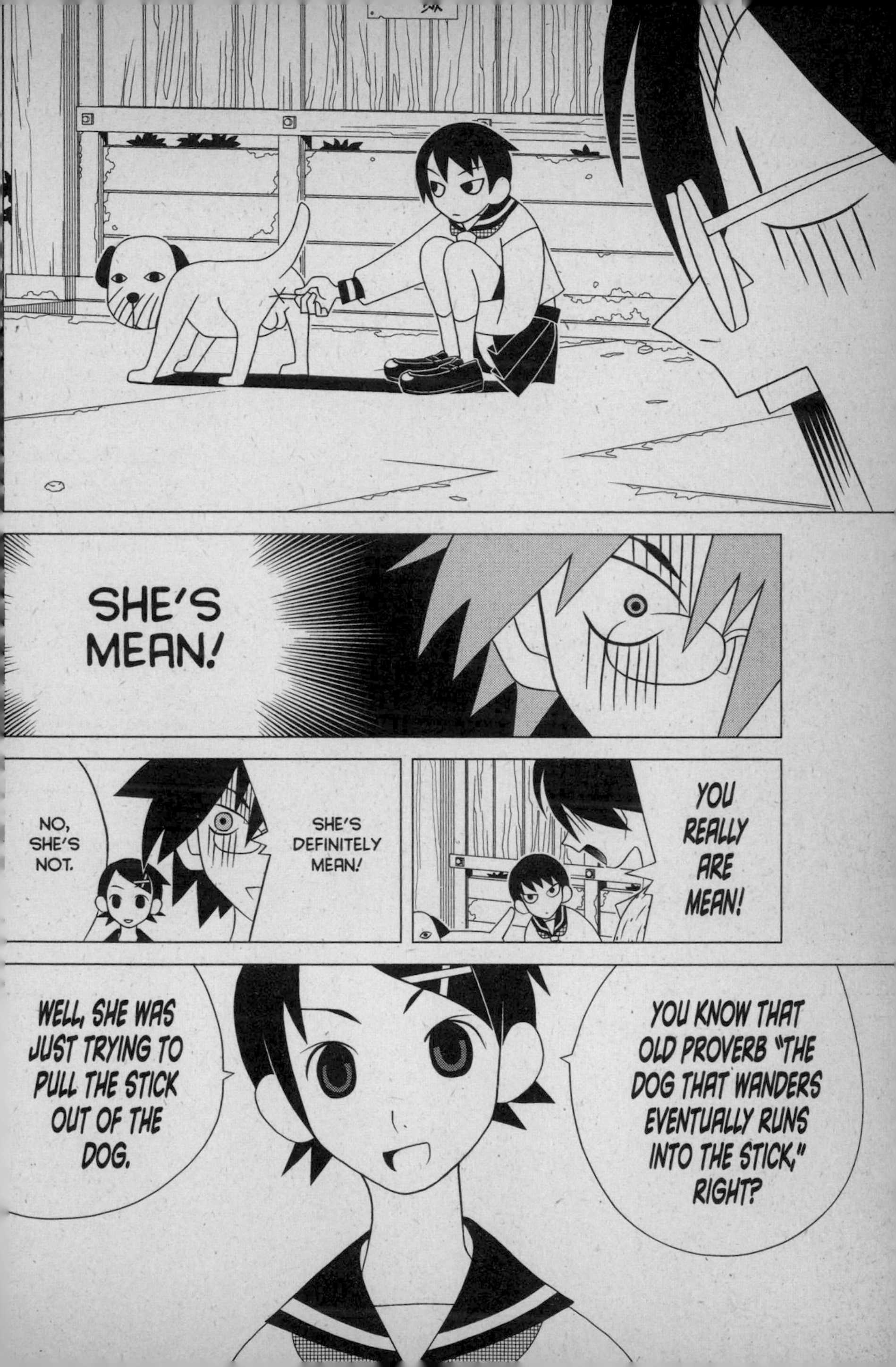
SHE'S MEAN!
YOU REALLY ARE MEAN!
SHE'S DEFINITELY MEAN!
NO, SHE'S NOT.
YOU KNOW THAT OLD PROVERB "THE DOG THAT WANDERS EVENTUALLY RUNS INTO THE STICK," RIGHT?
WELL, SHE WAS JUST TRYING TO PULL THE STICK OUT OF THE DOG.

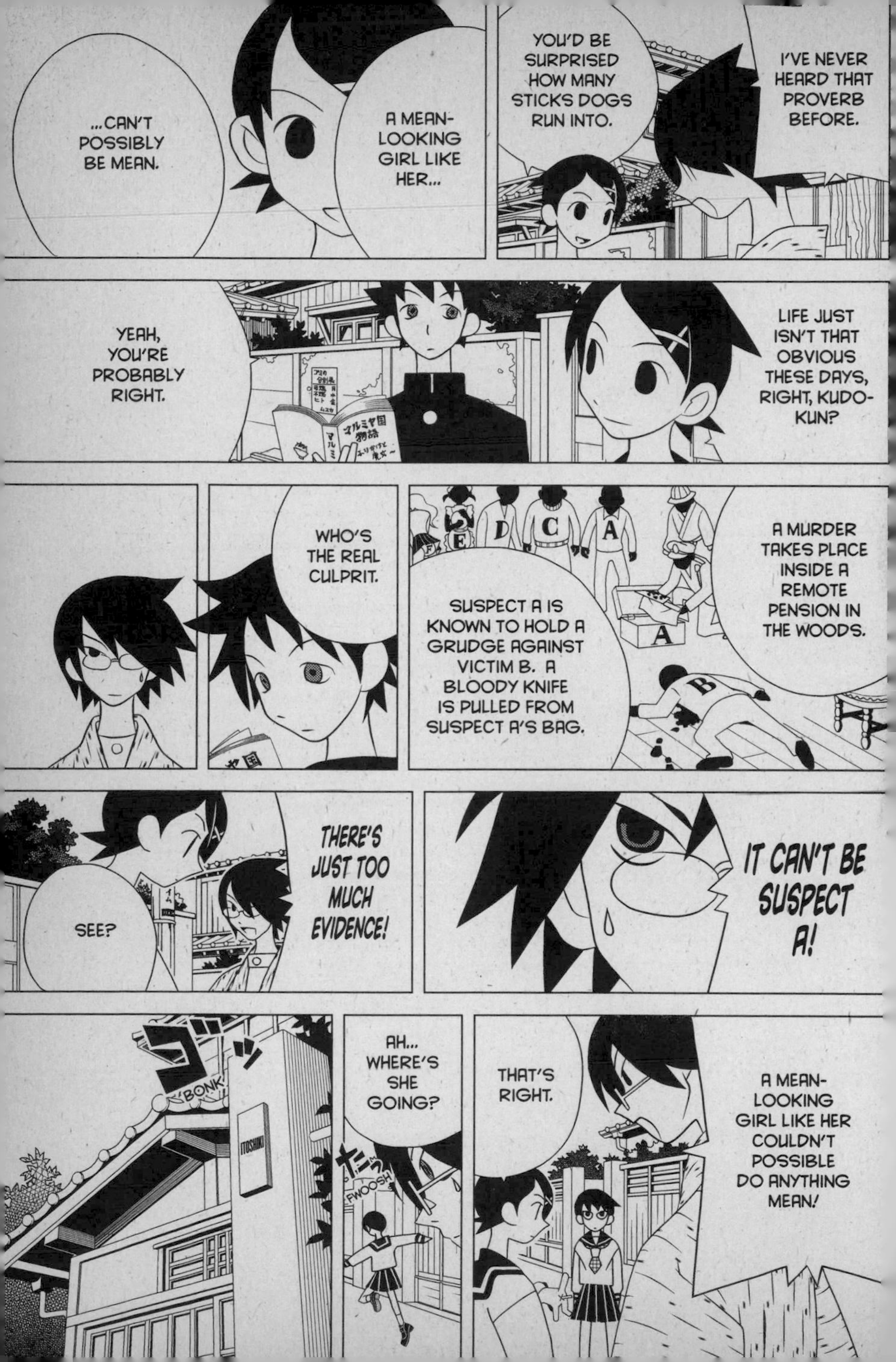
I'VE NEVER HEARD THAT PROVERB BEFORE.
YOU'D BE SURPRISED HOW MANY STICKS DOGS RUN INTO.
A MEAN-LOOKING GIRL LIKE HER...
...CAN'T POSSIBLY BE MEAN.
LIFE JUST ISN'T THAT OBVIOUS THESE DAYS, RIGHT, KUDO-KUN?
YEAH, YOU'RE PROBABLY RIGHT.
A MURDER TAKES PLACE INSIDE A REMOTE PENSION IN THE WOODS.
SUSPECT A IS KNOWN TO HOLD A GRUDGE AGAINST VICTIM B. A BLOODY KNIFE IS PULLED FROM SUSPECT A'S BAG.
WHO'S THE REAL CULPRIT.
IT CAN'T BE SUSPECT A!
THERE'S JUST TOO MUCH EVIDENCE!
SEE?
A MEAN-LOOKING GIRL LIKE HER COULDN'T POSSIBLE DO ANYTHING MEAN!
THAT'S RIGHT.
AH... WHERE'S SHE GOING?
FWOOSH
BONK
ITOSHIKI

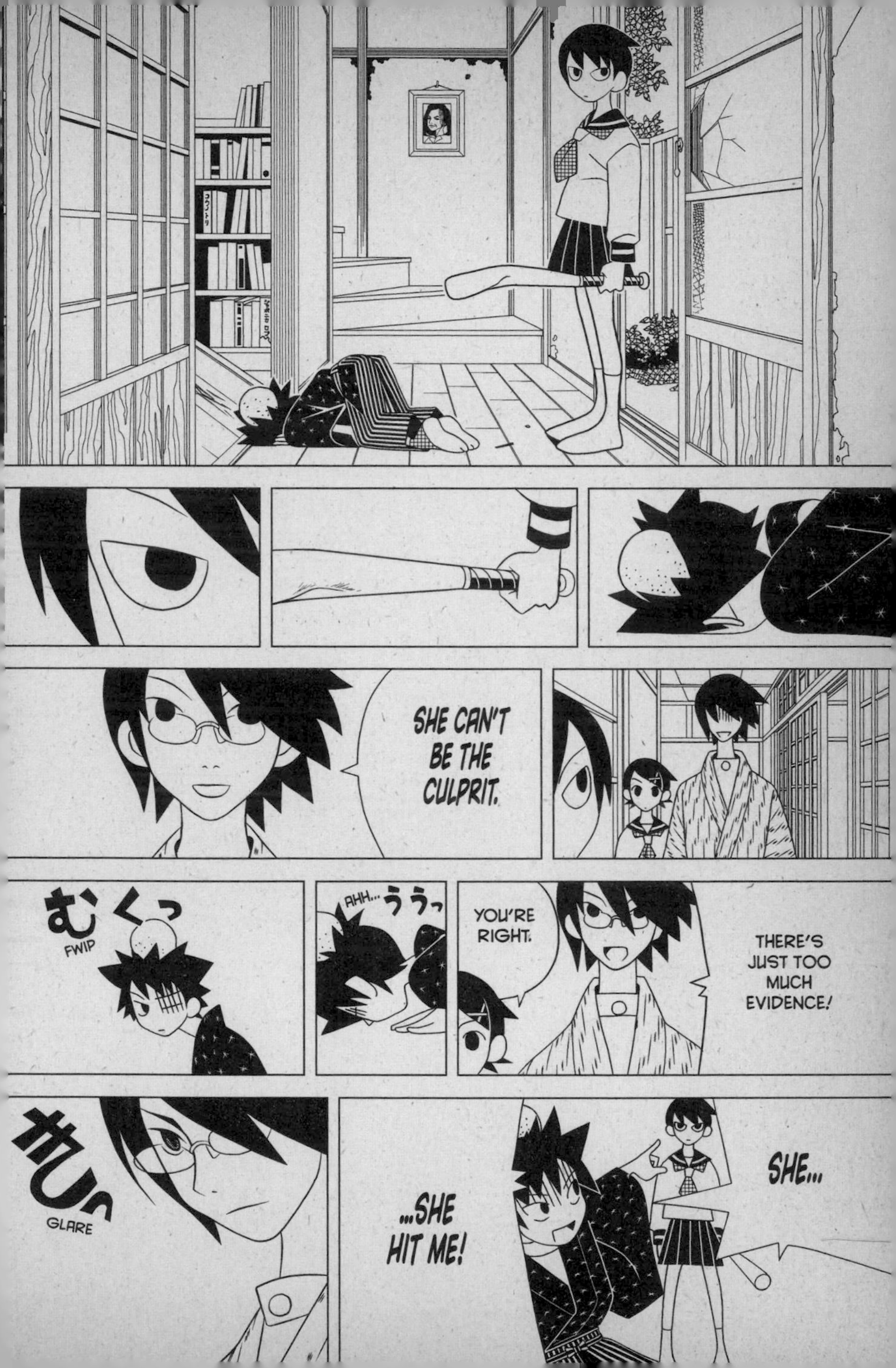
SHE CAN'T BE THE CULPRIT.
YOU'RE RIGHT.
THERE'S JUST TOO MUCH EVIDENCE!
AHH... うぅっ
むくっ
FWIP
SHE...
...SHE HIT ME!
GLARE

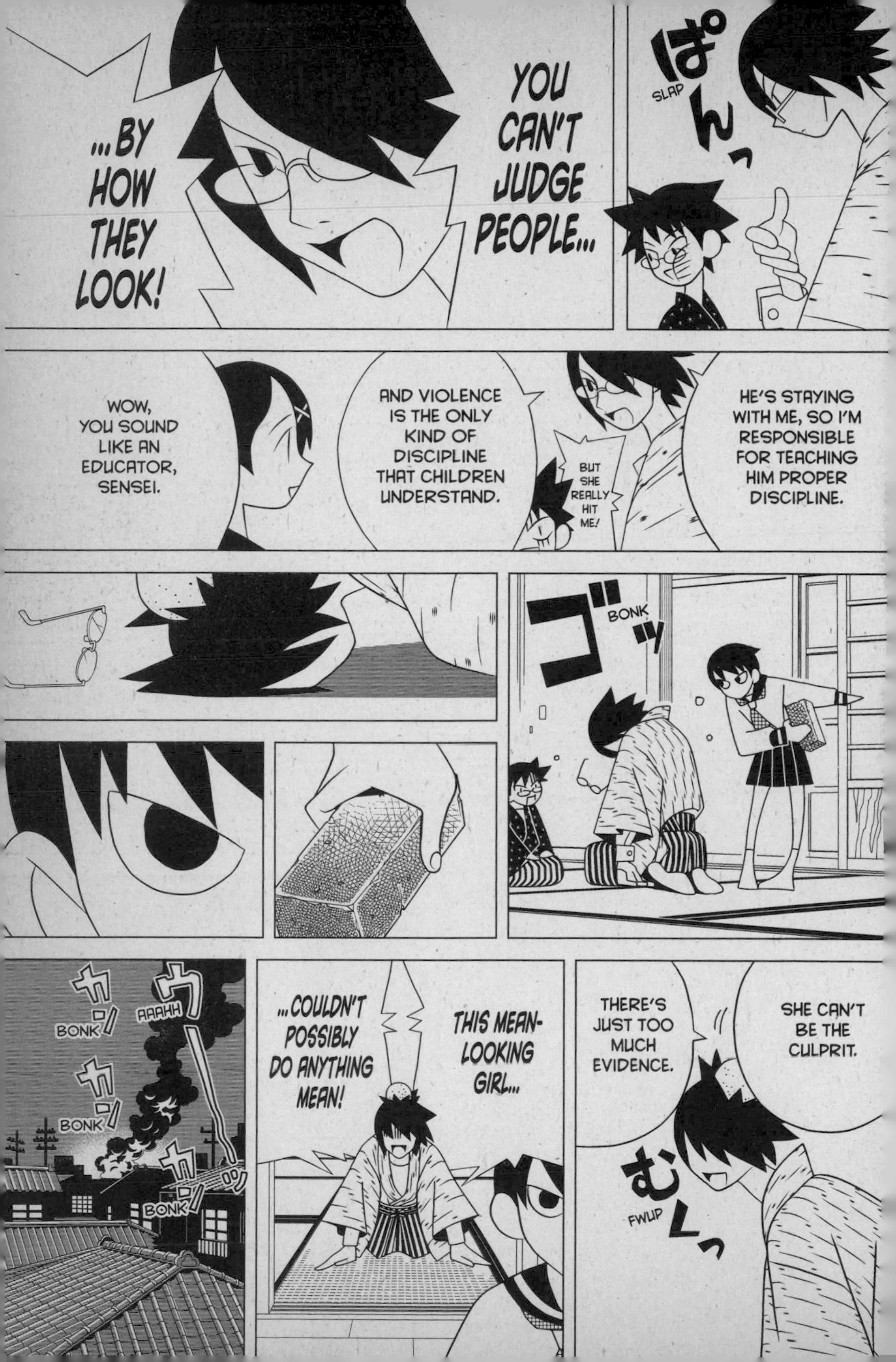
SLAP
YOU CAN'T JUDGE PEOPLE...
...BY HOW THEY LOOK!
HE'S STAYING WITH ME, SO I'M RESPONSIBLE FOR TEACHING HIM PROPER DISCIPLINE.
BUT SHE REALLY HIT ME!
AND VIOLENCE IS THE ONLY KIND OF DISCIPLINE THAT CHILDREN UNDERSTAND.
WOW, YOU SOUND LIKE AN EDUCATOR, SENSEI.
BONK
SHE CAN'T BE THE CULPRIT.
THERE'S JUST TOO MUCH EVIDENCE.
FWUP
THIS MEAN-LOOKING GIRL...
...COULDN'T POSSIBLY DO ANYTHING MEAN!
AAAHH
BONK
BONK
BONK

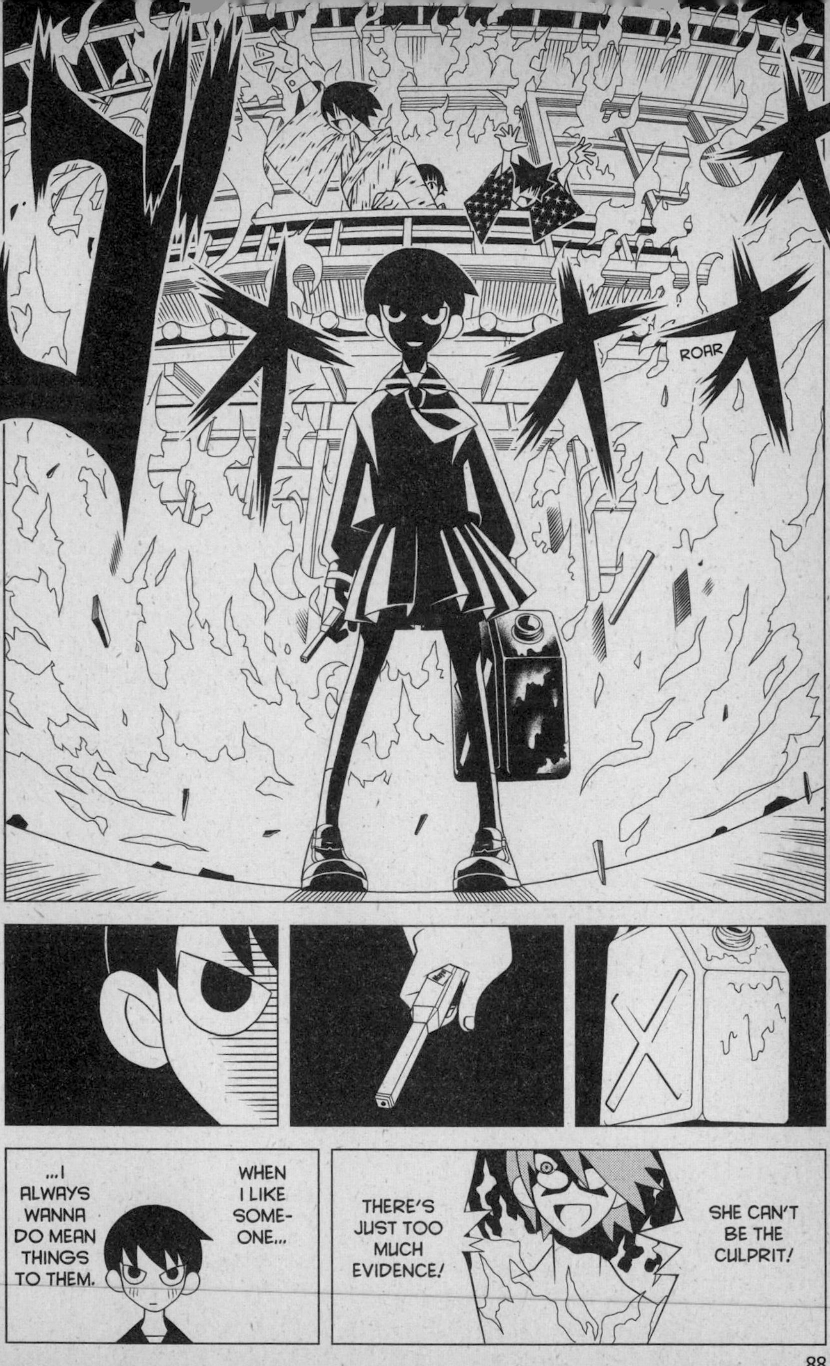
ROAR
SHE CAN'T BE THE CULPRIT!
THERE'S JUST TOO MUCH EVIDENCE!
WHEN I LIKE SOME-ONE...
...I ALWAYS WANNA DO MEAN THINGS TO THEM.

ATTENDANCE LIST
CLASS 2-HE

2006.04.12

ATTENDANCE NO. 30
MAYO MITAMA
MEAN-LOOKING GIRL

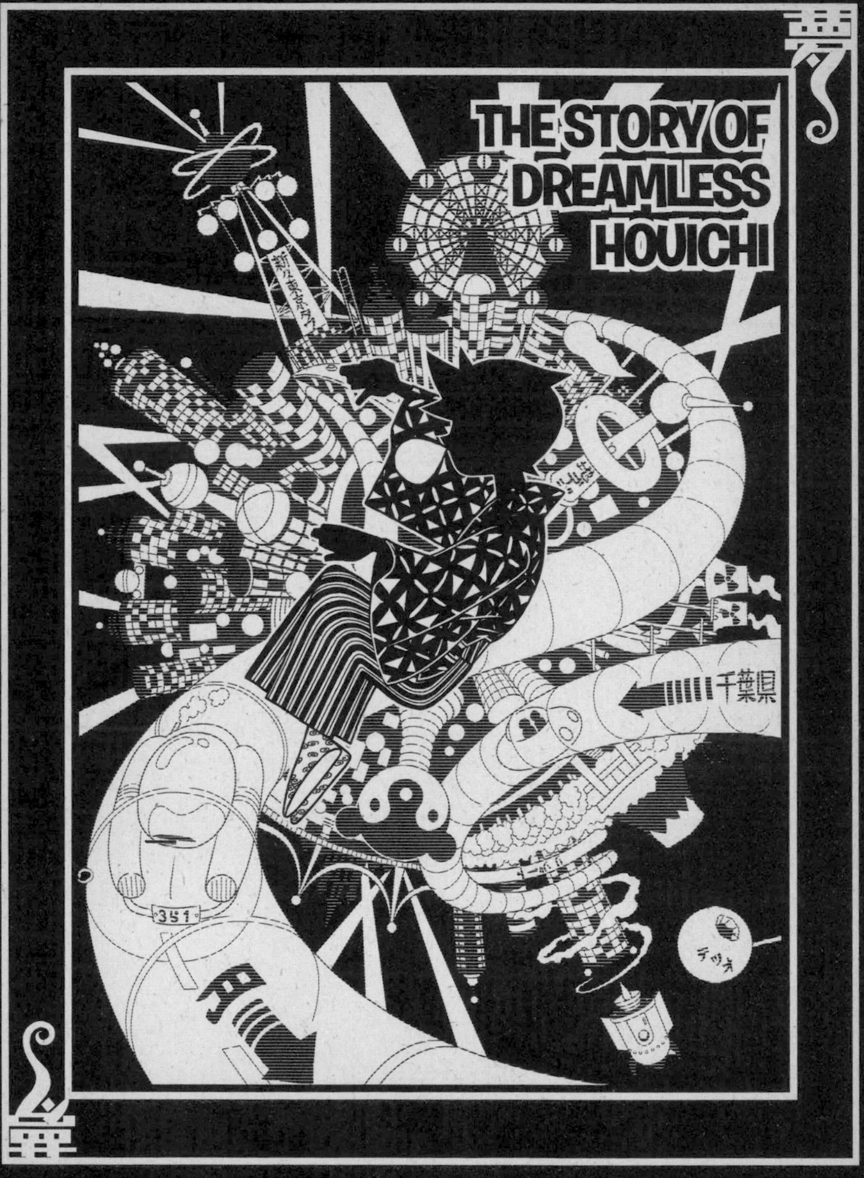
THE STORY OF DREAMLESS HOUICHI
千葉県
351

CHAPTER 47

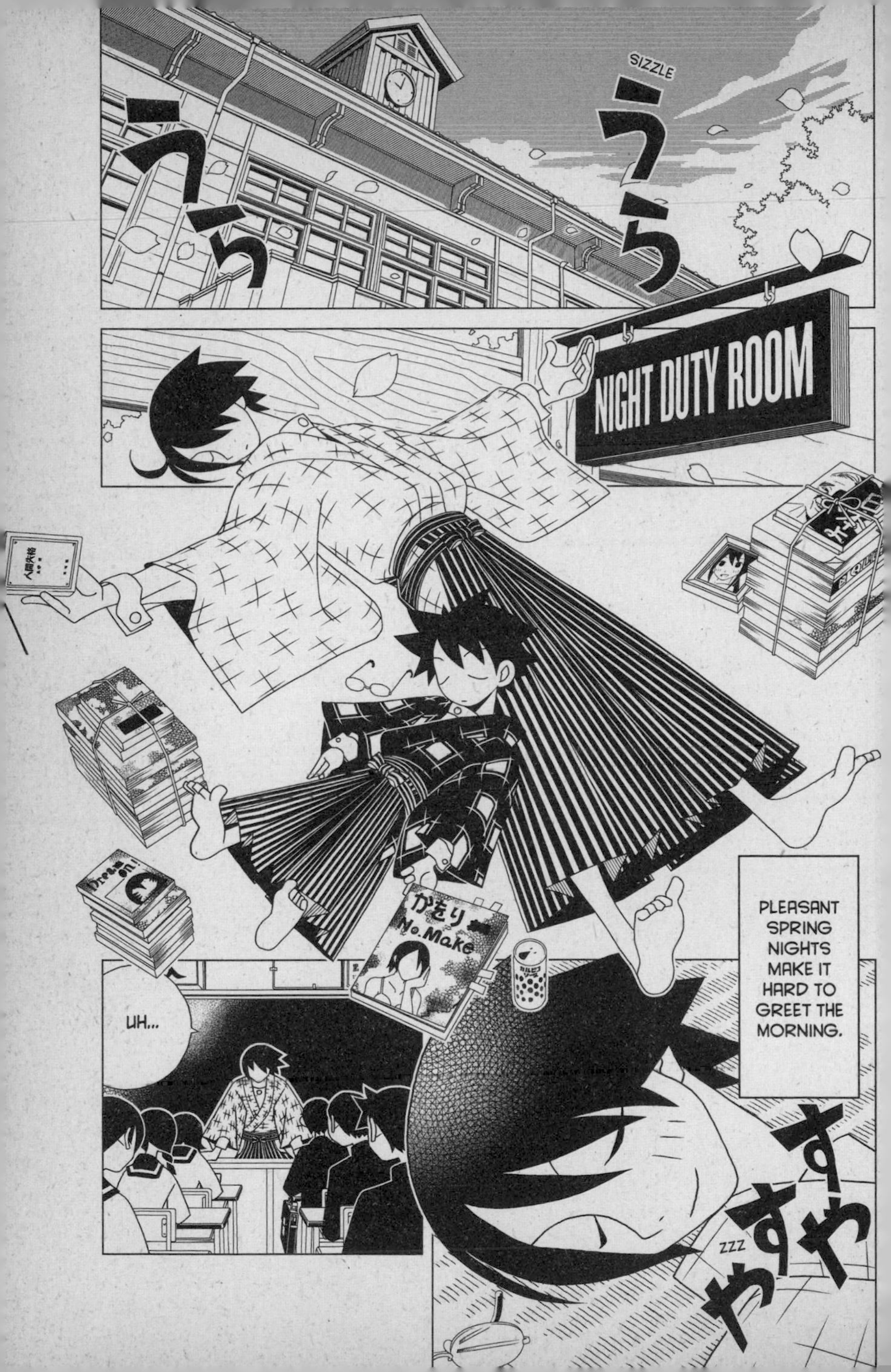

SIZZLE
うら
うら
NIGHT DUTY ROOM
PLEASANT SPRING NIGHTS MAKE IT HARD TO GREET THE MORNING.
すやすや
ZZZ
UH...

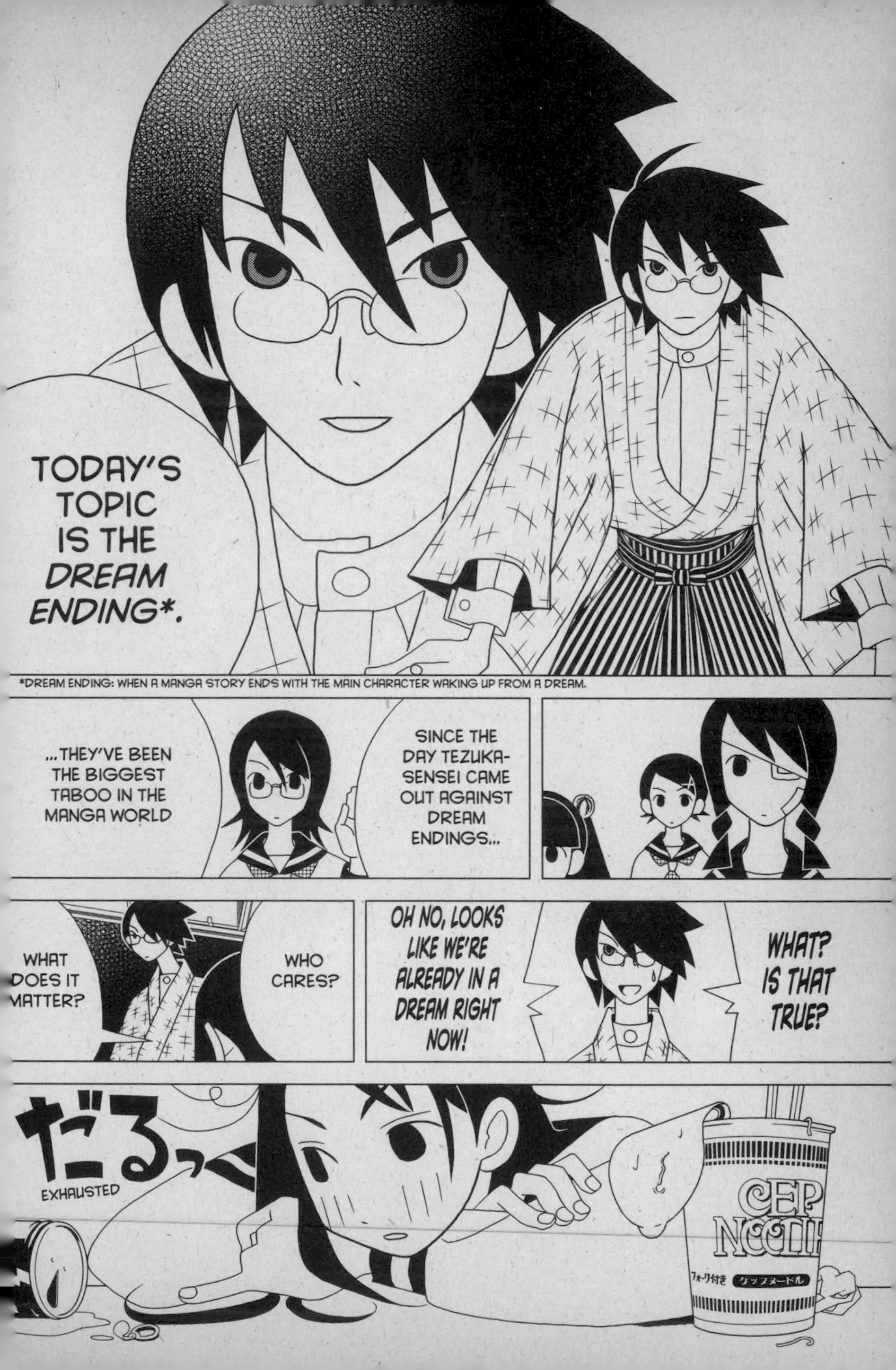
TODAY'S TOPIC IS THE *DREAM ENDING**.
*DREAM ENDING: WHEN A MANGA STORY ENDS WITH THE MAIN CHARACTER WAKING UP FROM A DREAM.
SINCE THE DAY TEZUKA-SENSEI CAME OUT AGAINST DREAM ENDINGS...
...THEY'VE BEEN THE BIGGEST TABOO IN THE MANGA WORLD
WHAT? IS THAT TRUE?
OH NO, LOOKS LIKE WE'RE ALREADY IN A DREAM RIGHT NOW!
WHO CARES?
WHAT DOES IT MATTER?
だるっ～
EXHAUSTED
フォーク付き
カップヌードル

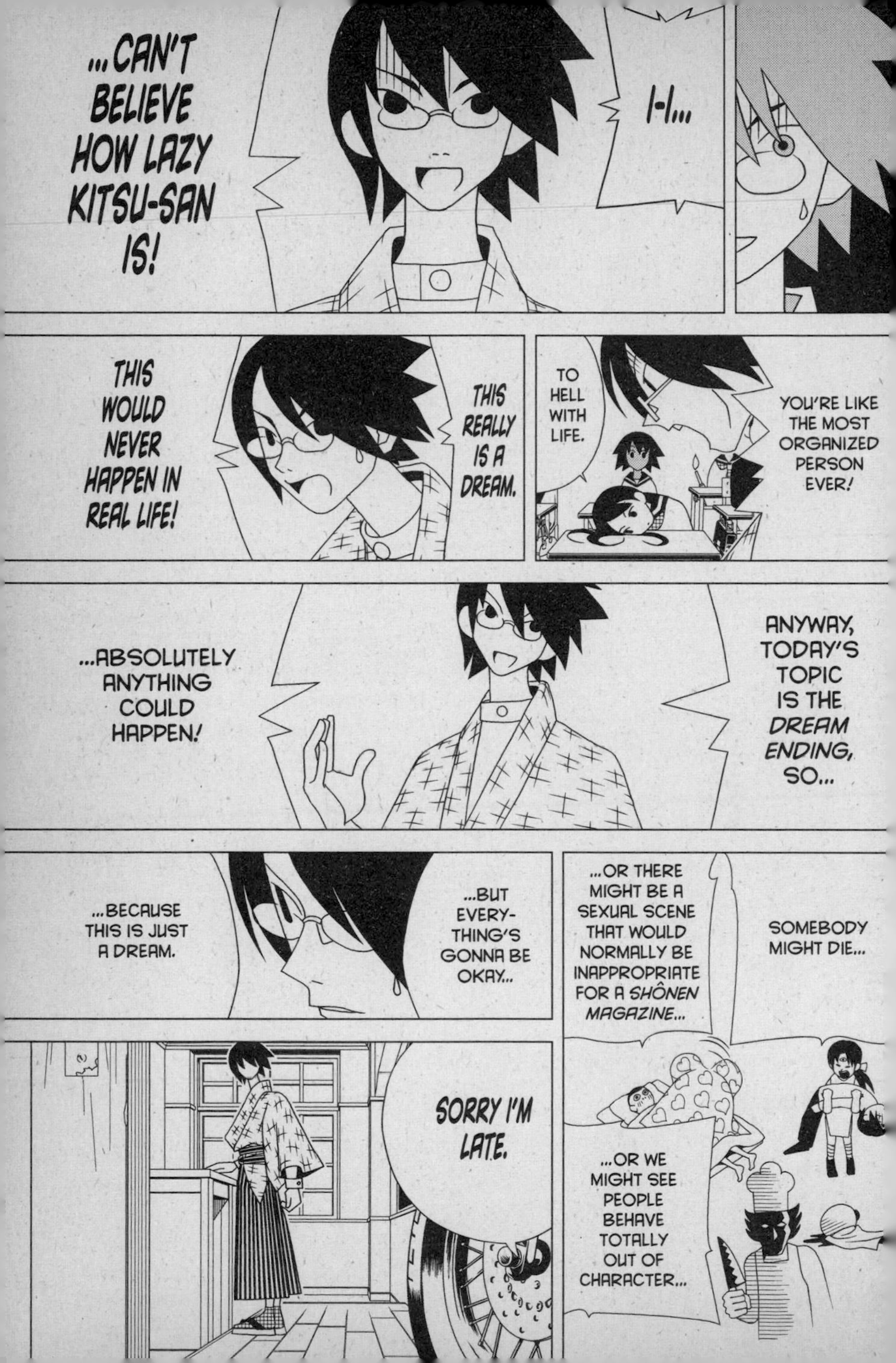
I-I...
...CAN'T BELIEVE HOW LAZY KITSU-SAN IS!
YOU'RE LIKE THE MOST ORGANIZED PERSON EVER!
TO HELL WITH LIFE.
THIS REALLY IS A DREAM.
THIS WOULD NEVER HAPPEN IN REAL LIFE!
ANYWAY, TODAY'S TOPIC IS THE *DREAM ENDING*, SO...
...ABSOLUTELY ANYTHING COULD HAPPEN!
SOMEBODY MIGHT DIE...
...OR THERE MIGHT BE A SEXUAL SCENE THAT WOULD NORMALLY BE INAPPROPRIATE FOR A *SHÔNEN MAGAZINE*...
...OR WE MIGHT SEE PEOPLE BEHAVE TOTALLY OUT OF CHARACTER...
...BUT EVERY-THING'S GONNA BE OKAY...
...BECAUSE THIS IS JUST A DREAM.
SORRY I'M LATE.

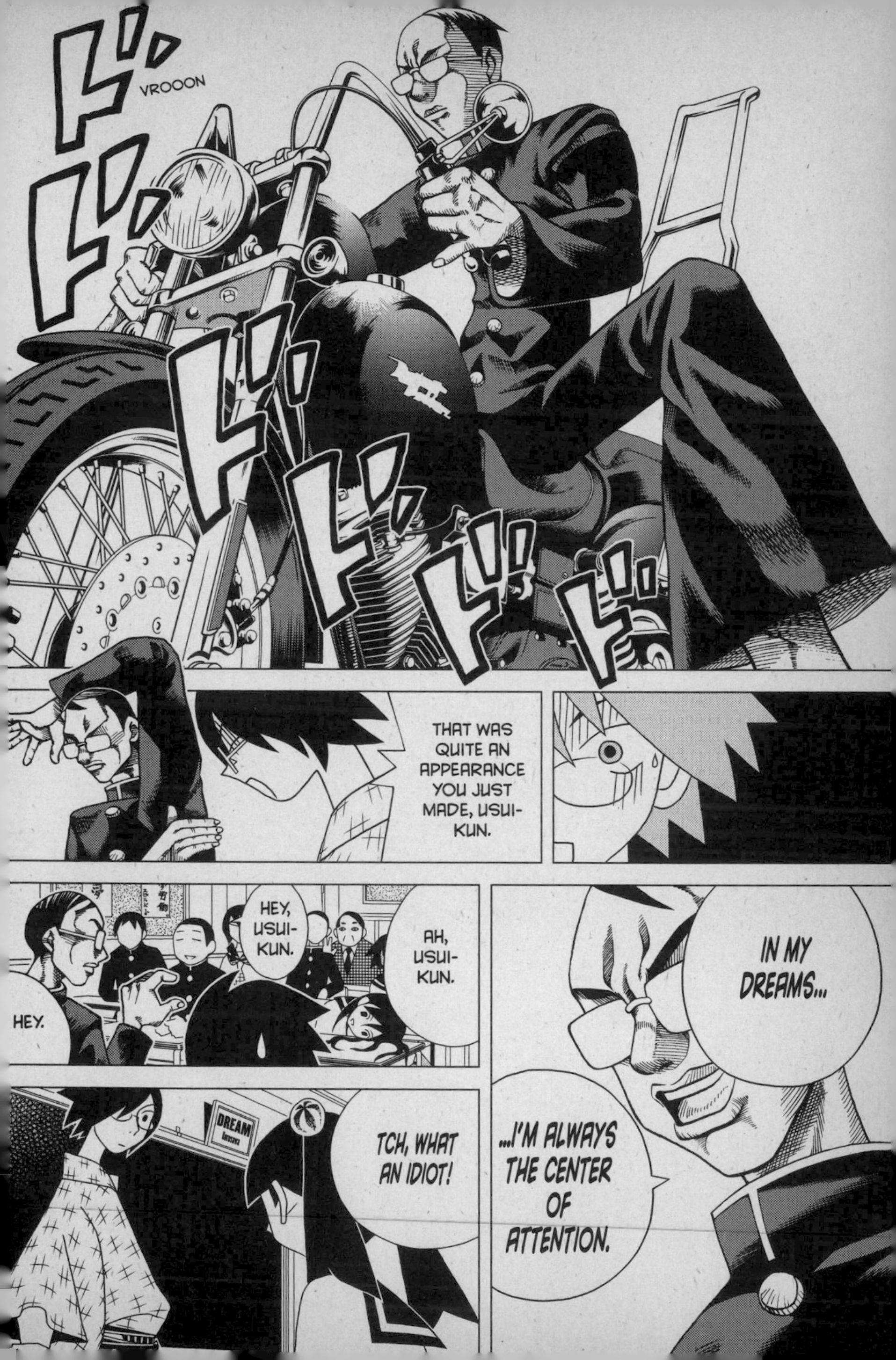
VROOON
THAT WAS QUITE AN APPEARANCE YOU JUST MADE, USUI-KUN.
IN MY DREAMS...
...I'M ALWAYS THE CENTER OF ATTENTION.
AH, USUI-KUN.
HEY, USUI-KUN.
HEY.
DREAM
TCH, WHAT AN IDIOT!

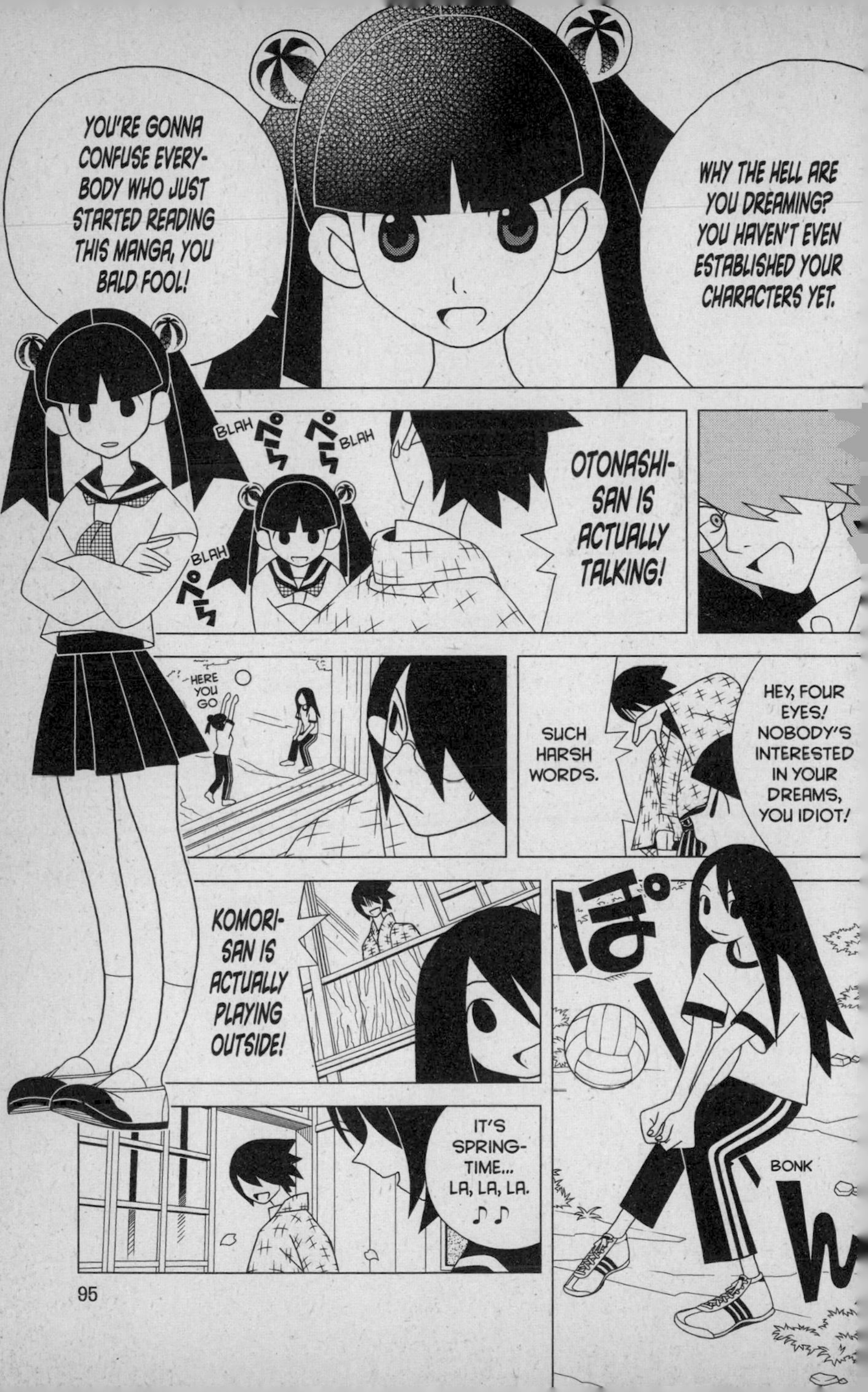
WHY THE HELL ARE YOU DREAMING? YOU HAVEN'T EVEN ESTABLISHED YOUR CHARACTERS YET.
YOU'RE GONNA CONFUSE EVERYBODY WHO JUST STARTED READING THIS MANGA, YOU BALD FOOL!
OTONASHI-SAN IS ACTUALLY TALKING!
BLAH
BLAH
BLAH
HEY, FOUR EYES! NOBODY'S INTERESTED IN YOUR DREAMS, YOU IDIOT!
SUCH HARSH WORDS.
HERE YOU GO
BONK
KOMORI-SAN IS ACTUALLY PLAYING OUTSIDE!
IT'S SPRING-TIME... LA, LA, LA. ♪♪

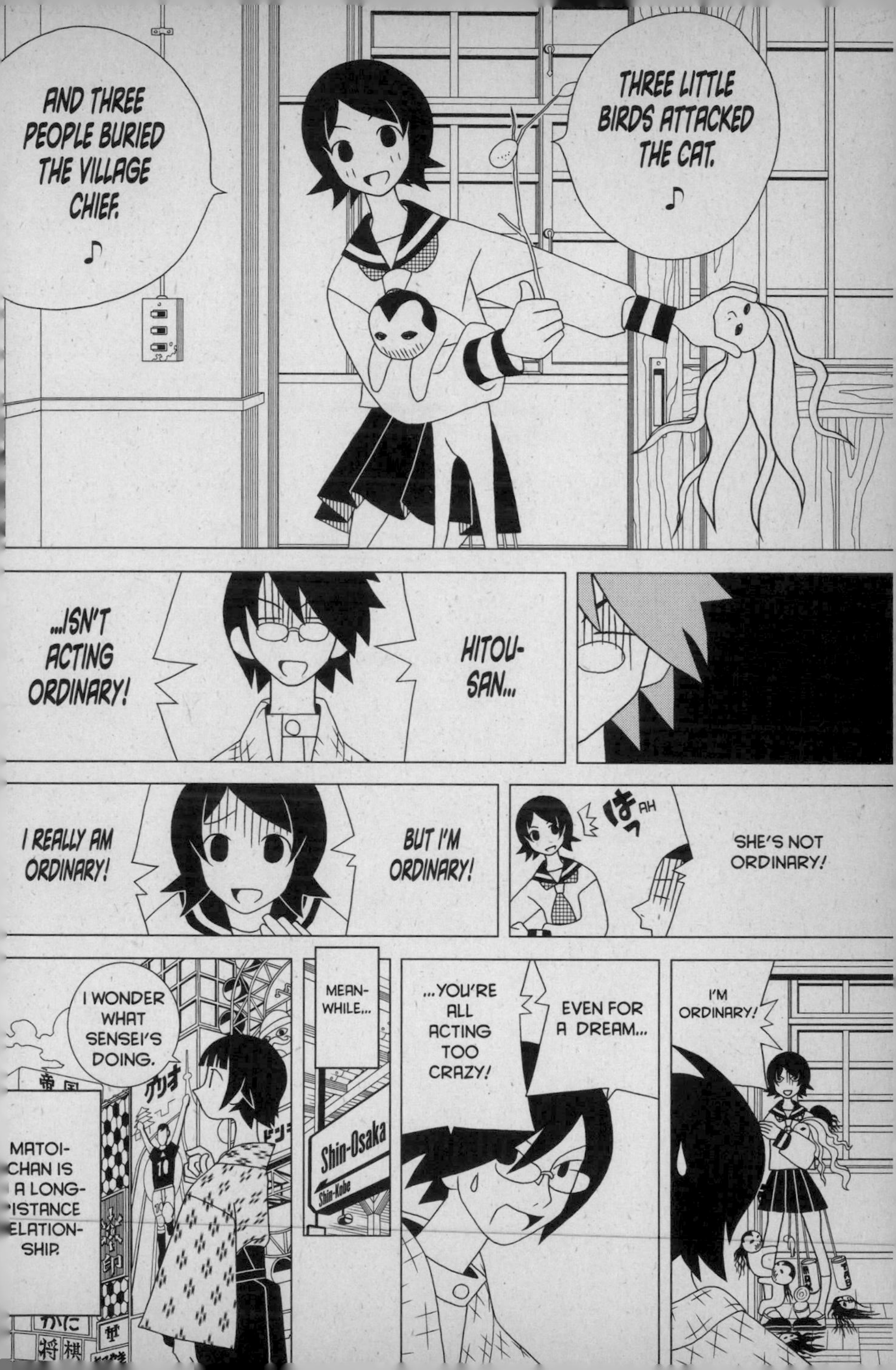

THREE LITTLE BIRDS ATTACKED THE CAT. ♪
AND THREE PEOPLE BURIED THE VILLAGE CHIEF. ♪
HITOU-SAN...
...ISN'T ACTING ORDINARY!
は AH
SHE'S NOT ORDINARY!
BUT I'M ORDINARY!
I REALLY AM ORDINARY!
I'M ORDINARY!
EVEN FOR A DREAM...
...YOU'RE ALL ACTING TOO CRAZY!
MEAN-WHILE...
Shin-Osaka
Shin-Kobe
I WONDER WHAT SENSEI'S DOING.
MATOI-CHAN IS A LONG-ISTANCE ELATION-SHIP.
かに
将棋

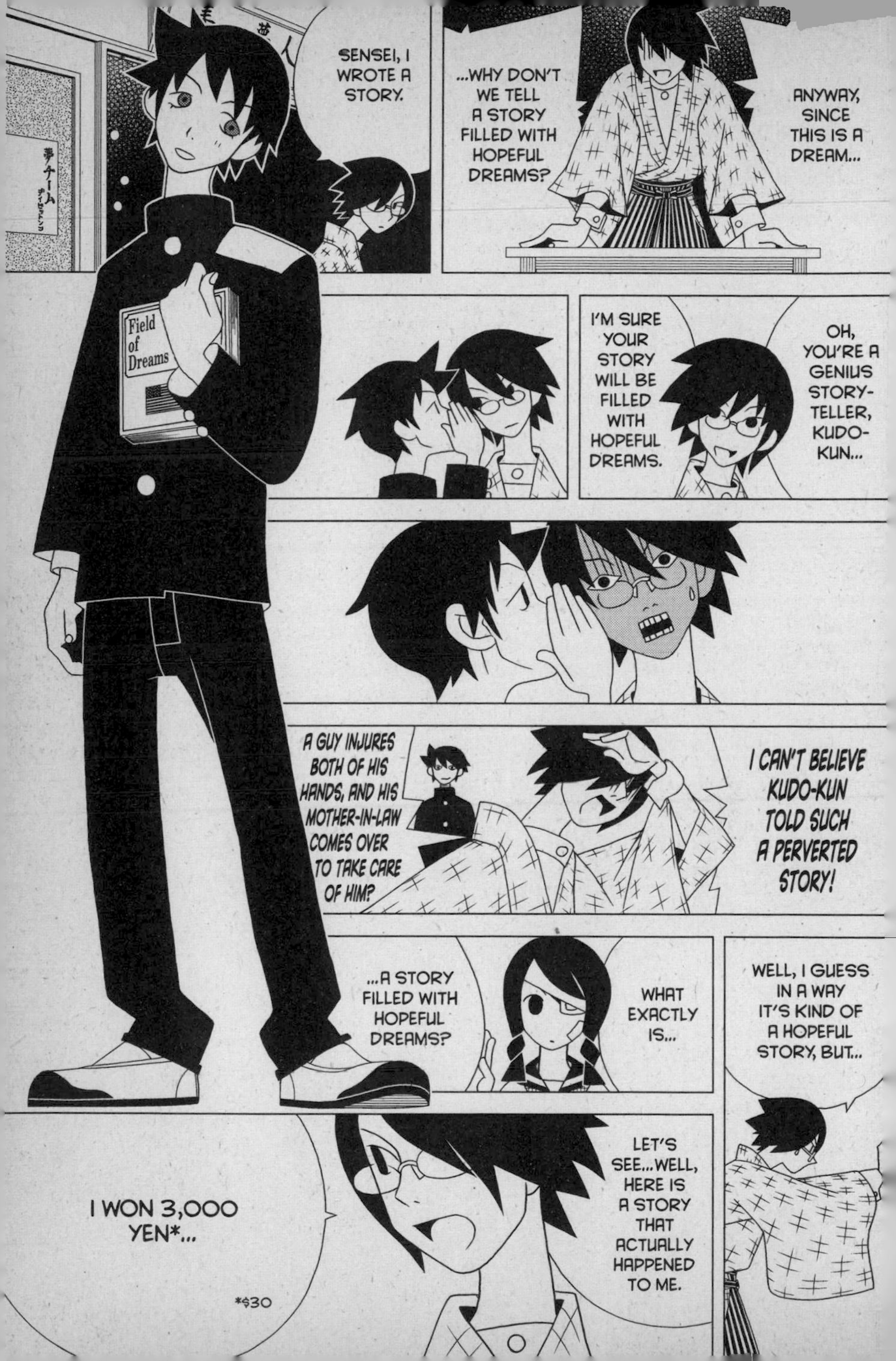
ANYWAY, SINCE THIS IS A DREAM...
...WHY DON'T WE TELL A STORY FILLED WITH HOPEFUL DREAMS?
SENSEI, I WROTE A STORY.
Field of Dreams
OH, YOU'RE A GENIUS STORY-TELLER, KUDO-KUN...
I'M SURE YOUR STORY WILL BE FILLED WITH HOPEFUL DREAMS.
I CAN'T BELIEVE KUDO-KUN TOLD SUCH A PERVERTED STORY!
A GUY INJURES BOTH OF HIS HANDS, AND HIS MOTHER-IN-LAW COMES OVER TO TAKE CARE OF HIM?
WELL, I GUESS IN A WAY IT'S KIND OF A HOPEFUL STORY, BUT...
WHAT EXACTLY IS...
...A STORY FILLED WITH HOPEFUL DREAMS?
LET'S SEE...WELL, HERE IS A STORY THAT ACTUALLY HAPPENED TO ME.
I WON 3,000 YEN*...
*$30

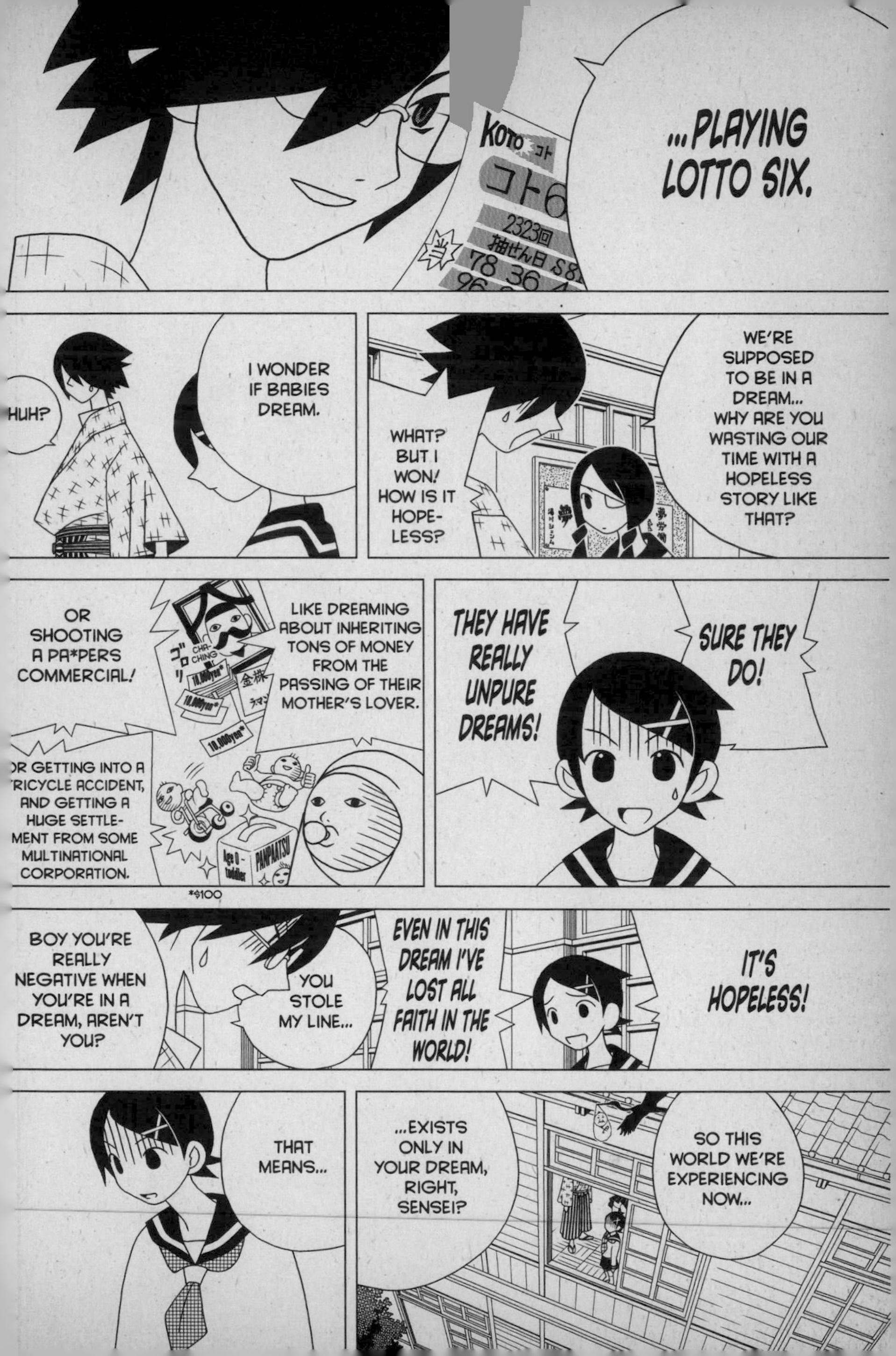
KOTO コト
コト6
2323回
抽せん日
...PLAYING LOTTO SIX.
WE'RE SUPPOSED TO BE IN A DREAM... WHY ARE YOU WASTING OUR TIME WITH A HOPELESS STORY LIKE THAT?
WHAT? BUT I WON! HOW IS IT HOPE- LESS?
I WONDER IF BABIES DREAM.
HUH?
SURE THEY DO!
THEY HAVE REALLY UNPURE DREAMS!
LIKE DREAMING ABOUT INHERITING TONS OF MONEY FROM THE PASSING OF THEIR MOTHER'S LOVER.
CHA- CHING
10,000yen*
10,000yen*
10,000yen*
OR SHOOTING A PA*PERS COMMERCIAL!
OR GETTING INTO A TRICYCLE ACCIDENT, AND GETTING A HUGE SETTLE- MENT FROM SOME MULTINATIONAL CORPORATION.
Age 0 - toddler
PANPAATSU
*$100
IT'S HOPELESS!
EVEN IN THIS DREAM I'VE LOST ALL FAITH IN THE WORLD!
YOU STOLE MY LINE...
BOY YOU'RE REALLY NEGATIVE WHEN YOU'RE IN A DREAM, AREN'T YOU?
SO THIS WORLD WE'RE EXPERIENCING NOW...
...EXISTS ONLY IN YOUR DREAM, RIGHT, SENSEI?
THAT MEANS...

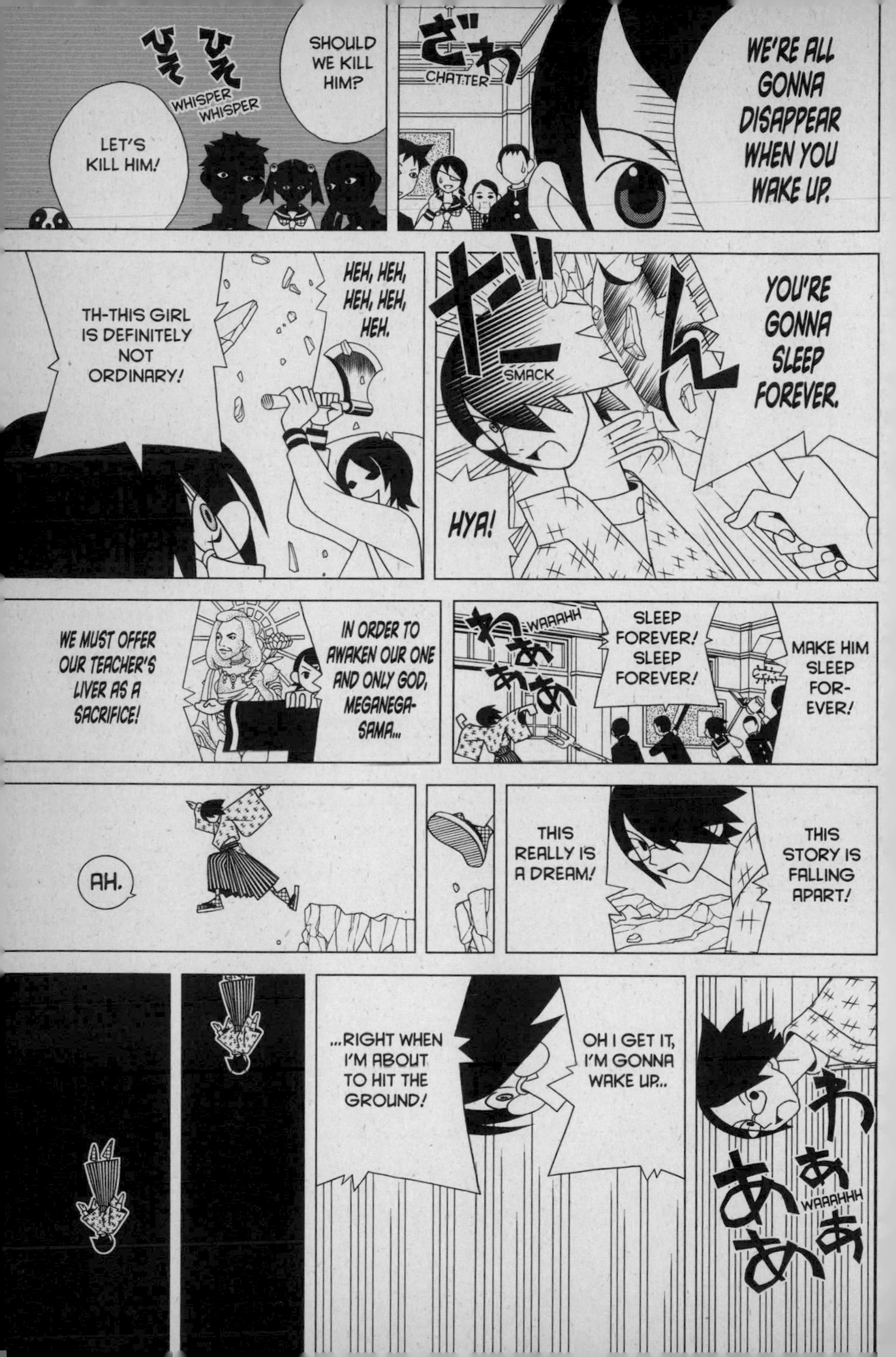
WE'RE ALL GONNA DISAPPEAR WHEN YOU WAKE UP.
ざわ
CHATTER
SHOULD WE KILL HIM?
ひそ ひそ
WHISPER WHISPER
LET'S KILL HIM!
YOU'RE GONNA SLEEP FOREVER.
だーん
SMACK
HYA!
HEH, HEH, HEH, HEH, HEH.
TH-THIS GIRL IS DEFINITELY NOT ORDINARY!
MAKE HIM SLEEP FOR-EVER!
SLEEP FOREVER! SLEEP FOREVER!
わあああ
WAAAHH
IN ORDER TO AWAKEN OUR ONE AND ONLY GOD, MEGANEGA-SAMA...
WE MUST OFFER OUR TEACHER'S LIVER AS A SACRIFICE!
THIS STORY IS FALLING APART!
THIS REALLY IS A DREAM!
AH.
わあああああ
WAAAHHH
OH I GET IT, I'M GONNA WAKE UP...
...RIGHT WHEN I'M ABOUT TO HIT THE GROUND!

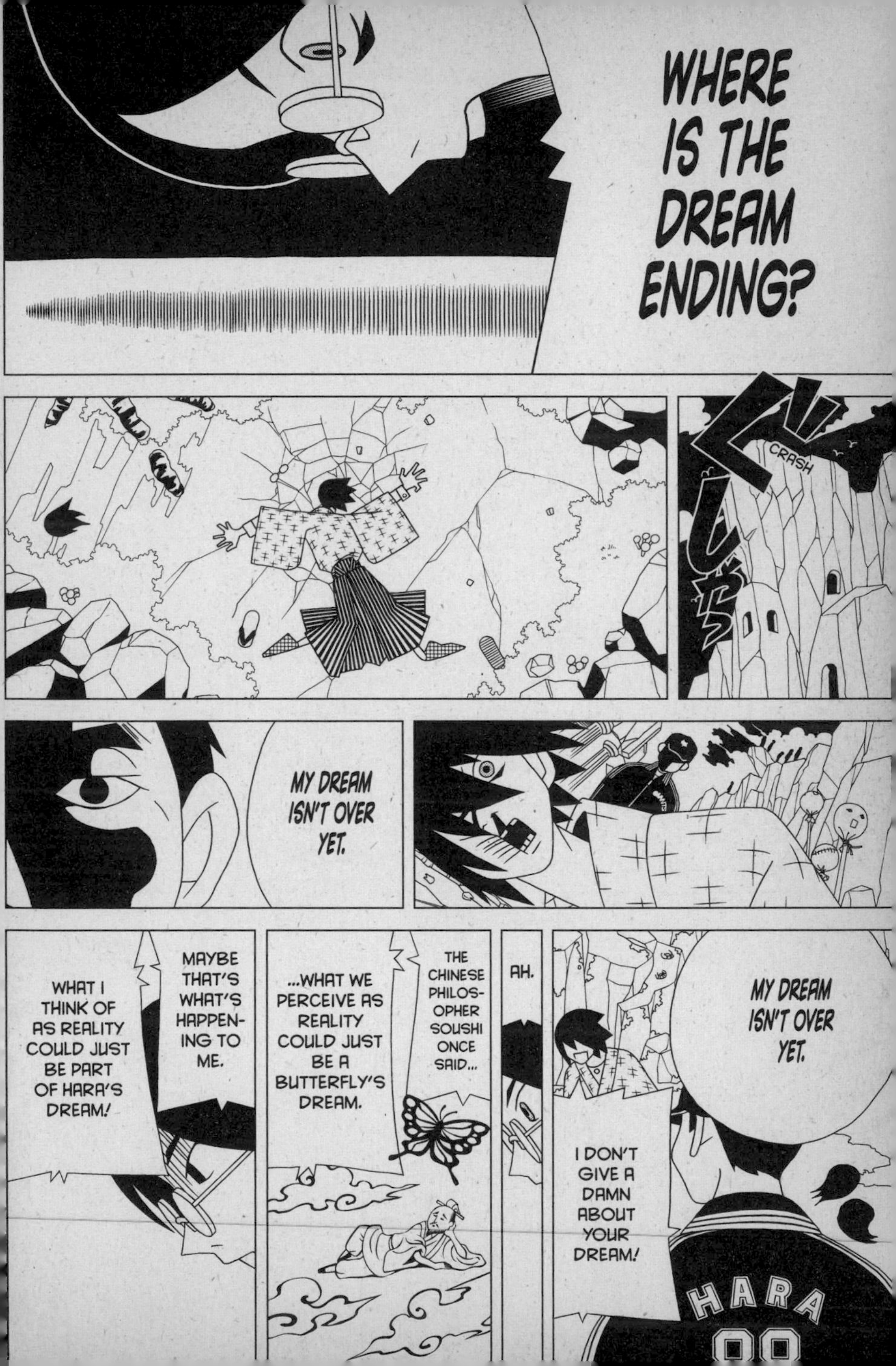
WHERE IS THE DREAM ENDING?
CRASH
MY DREAM ISN'T OVER YET.
MY DREAM ISN'T OVER YET.
I DON'T GIVE A DAMN ABOUT YOUR DREAM!
HARA
AH.
THE CHINESE PHILOSOPHER SOUSHI ONCE SAID...
...WHAT WE PERCEIVE AS REALITY COULD JUST BE A BUTTERFLY'S DREAM.
MAYBE THAT'S WHAT'S HAPPENING TO ME.
WHAT I THINK OF AS REALITY COULD JUST BE PART OF HARA'S DREAM!

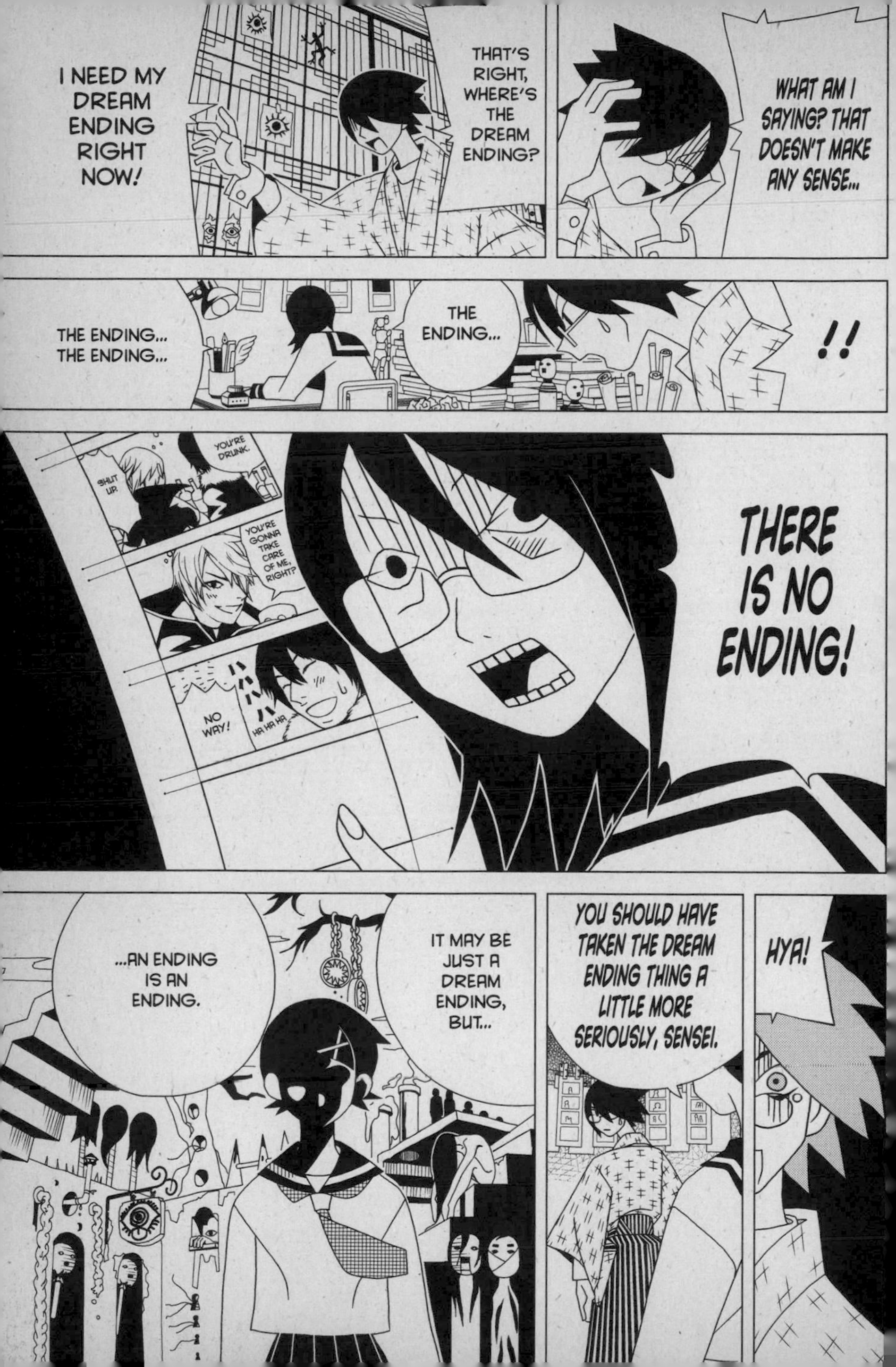
WHAT AM I SAYING? THAT DOESN'T MAKE ANY SENSE...
THAT'S RIGHT, WHERE'S THE DREAM ENDING?
I NEED MY DREAM ENDING RIGHT NOW!
!!
THE ENDING...
THE ENDING... THE ENDING...
THERE IS NO ENDING!
YOU'RE DRUNK.
SHUT UP.
YOU'RE GONNA TAKE CARE OF ME, RIGHT?
HA HA HA
NO WAY!
HYA!
YOU SHOULD HAVE TAKEN THE DREAM ENDING THING A LITTLE MORE SERIOUSLY, SENSEI.
IT MAY BE JUST A DREAM ENDING, BUT...
...AN ENDING IS AN ENDING.

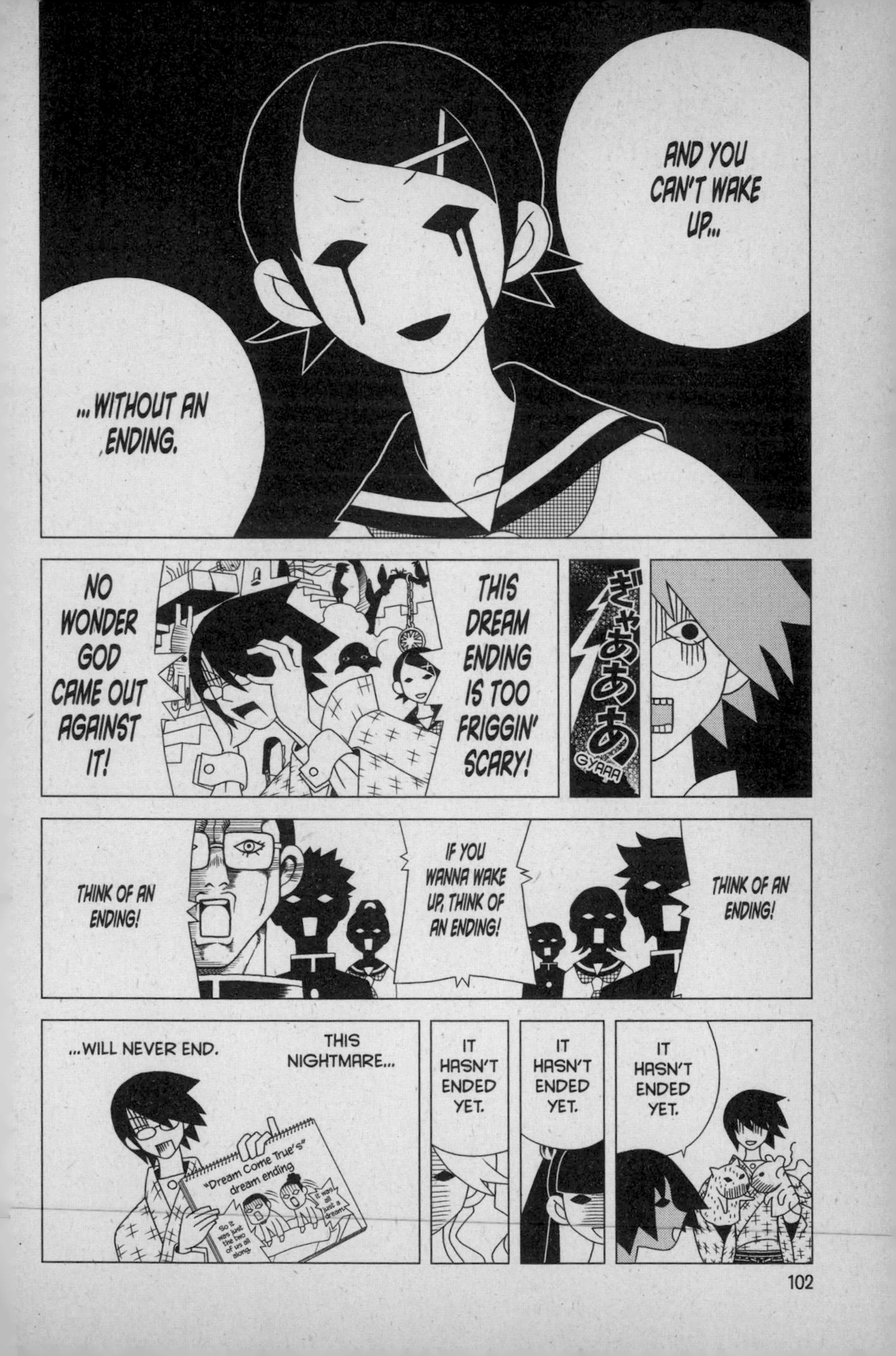
AND YOU CAN'T WAKE UP...
...WITHOUT AN ENDING.
ぎゃあああ
GYAAA
THIS DREAM ENDING IS TOO FRIGGIN' SCARY!
NO WONDER GOD CAME OUT AGAINST IT!
THINK OF AN ENDING!
IF YOU WANNA WAKE UP, THINK OF AN ENDING!
THINK OF AN ENDING!
IT HASN'T ENDED YET.
IT HASN'T ENDED YET.
IT HASN'T ENDED YET.
THIS NIGHTMARE...
...WILL NEVER END.
"Dream Come True's" dream ending
It was all just a dream.
So it was just the two of us all along.

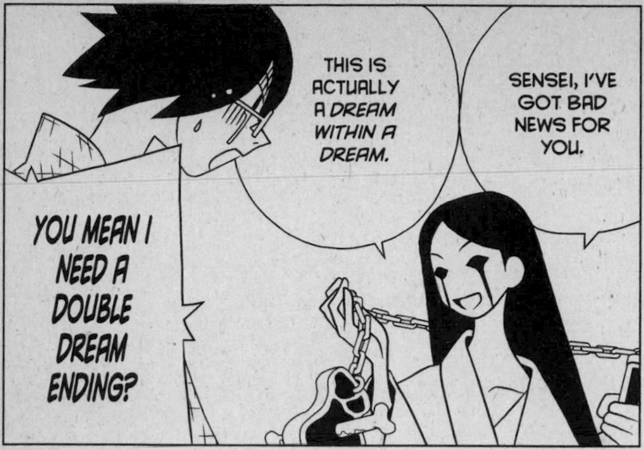
SENSEI, I'VE GOT BAD NEWS FOR YOU.
THIS IS ACTUALLY A *DREAM WITHIN A DREAM.*
YOU MEAN I NEED A DOUBLE DREAM ENDING?

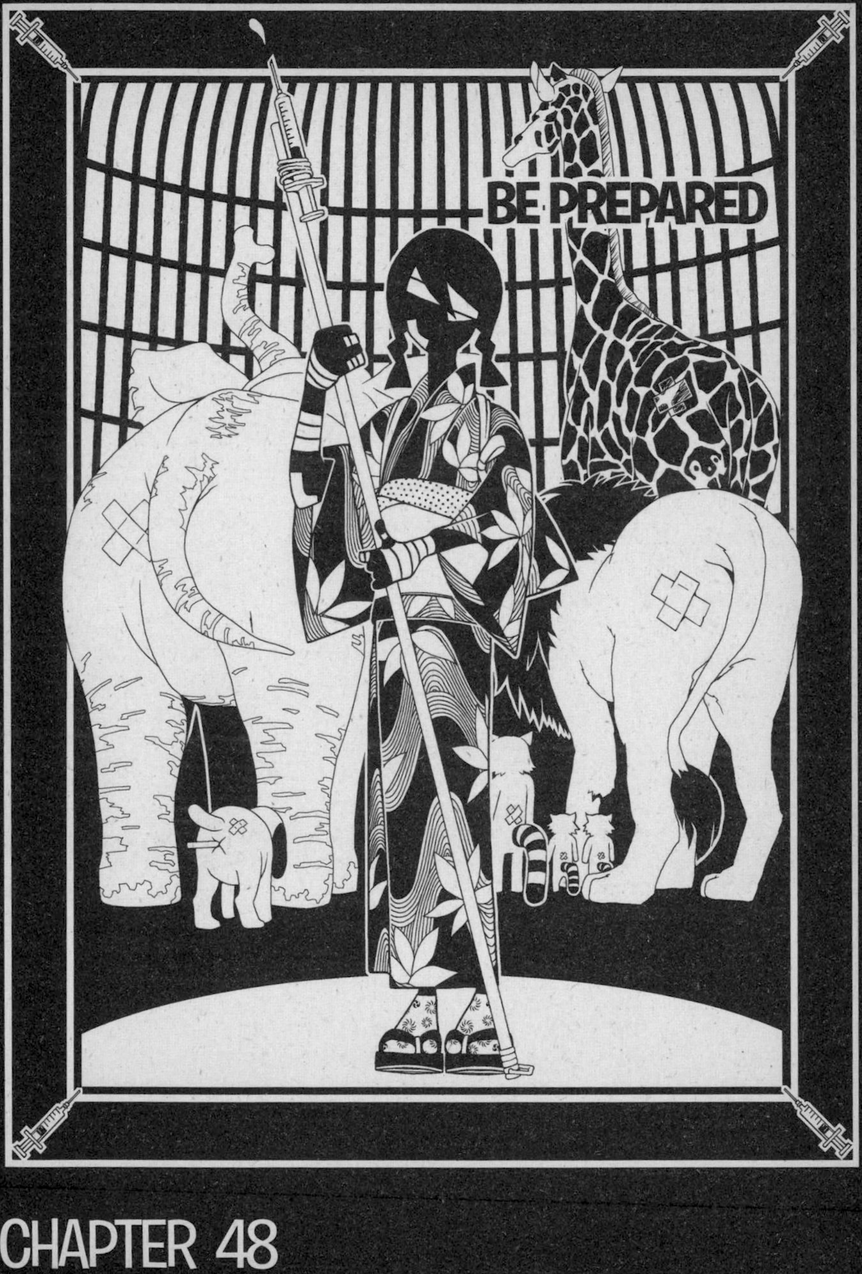
BE PREPARED

CHAPTER 48

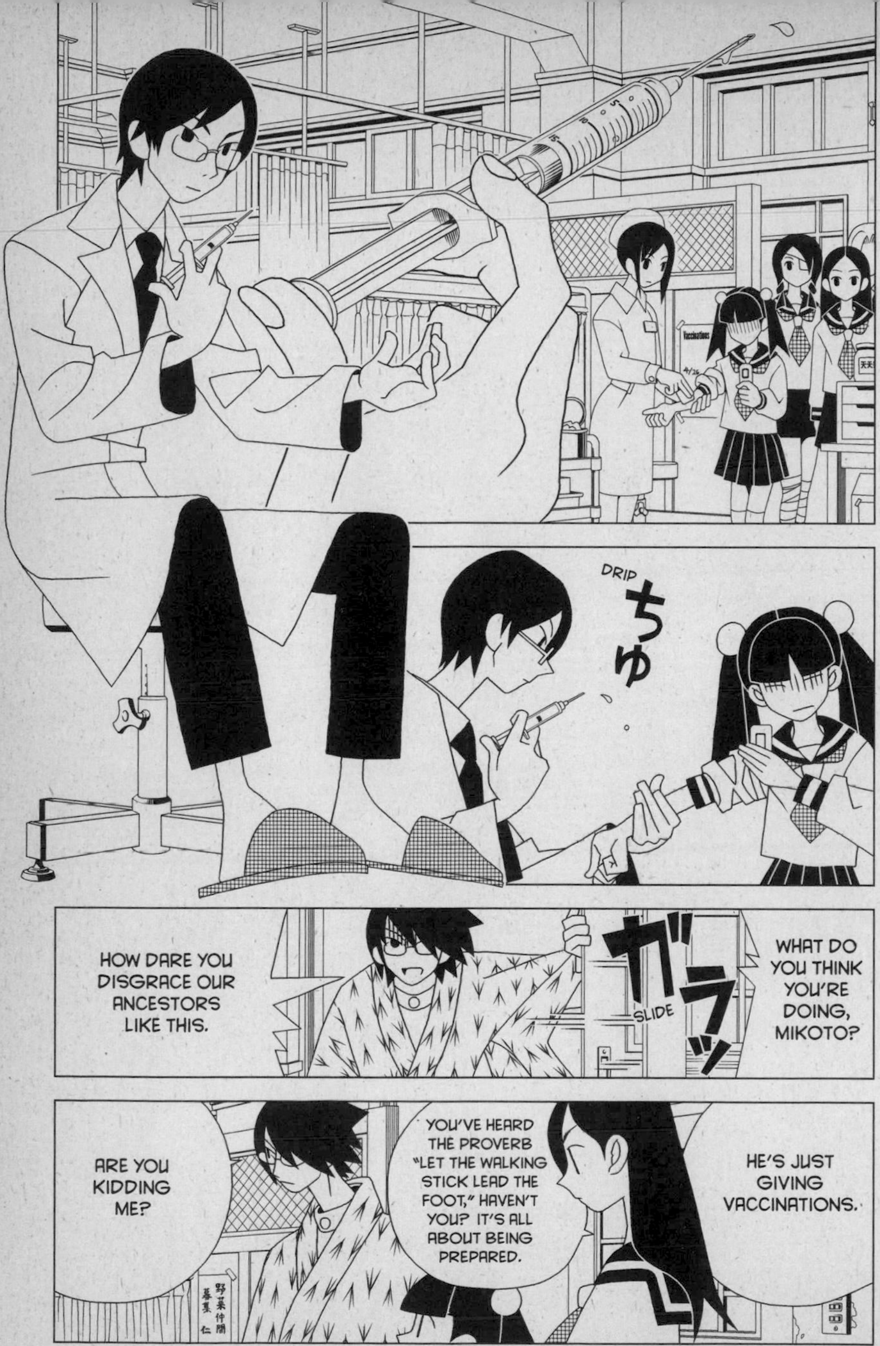
Vaccinations
4/26
DRIP
ちゅ
WHAT DO YOU THINK YOU'RE DOING, MIKOTO?
ガラッ
SLIDE
HOW DARE YOU DISGRACE OUR ANCESTORS LIKE THIS.
HE'S JUST GIVING VACCINATIONS.
YOU'VE HEARD THE PROVERB "LET THE WALKING STICK LEAD THE FOOT," HAVEN'T YOU? IT'S ALL ABOUT BEING PREPARED.
ARE YOU KIDDING ME?
野菜仲間募集 仁

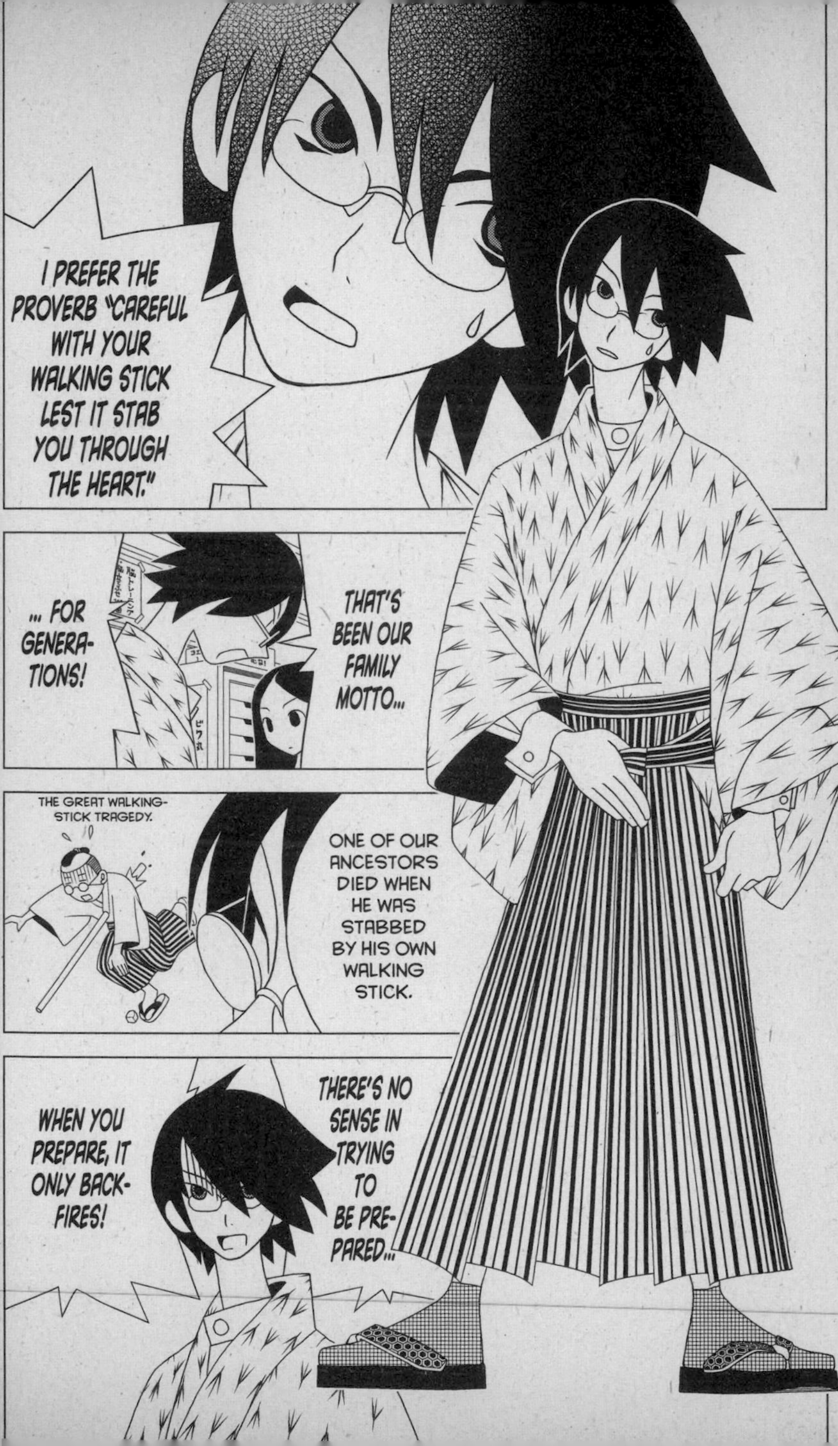
I PREFER THE PROVERB "CAREFUL WITH YOUR WALKING STICK LEST IT STAB YOU THROUGH THE HEART."
THAT'S BEEN OUR FAMILY MOTTO...
... FOR GENERA-TIONS!
ONE OF OUR ANCESTORS DIED WHEN HE WAS STABBED BY HIS OWN WALKING STICK.
THE GREAT WALKING-STICK TRAGEDY.
THERE'S NO SENSE IN TRYING TO BE PRE-PARED...
WHEN YOU PREPARE, IT ONLY BACK-FIRES!

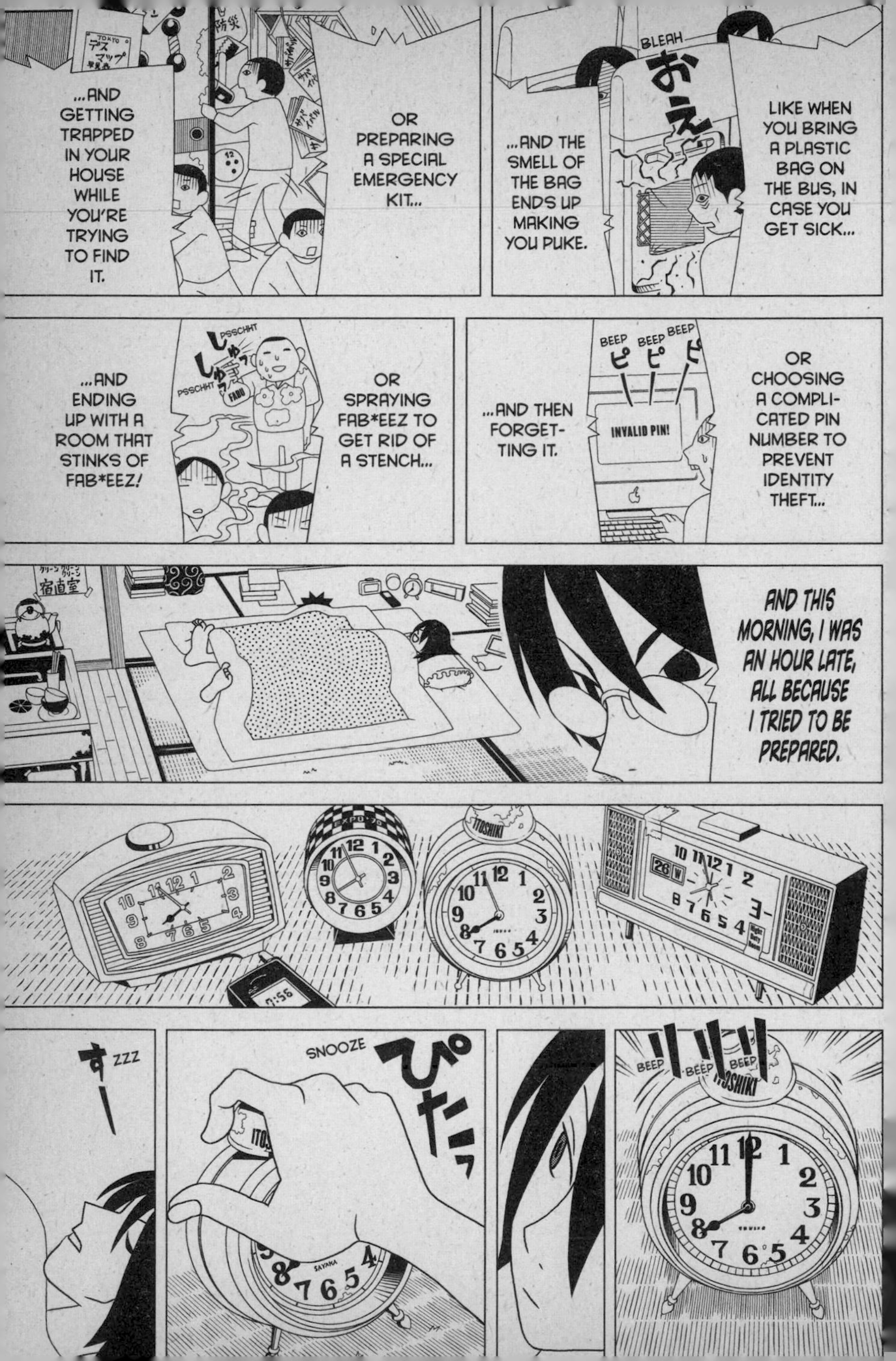

LIKE WHEN YOU BRING A PLASTIC BAG ON THE BUS, IN CASE YOU GET SICK...
BLEAH
おえ
...AND THE SMELL OF THE BAG ENDS UP MAKING YOU PUKE.
OR PREPARING A SPECIAL EMERGENCY KIT...
デスマップ
防災
...AND GETTING TRAPPED IN YOUR HOUSE WHILE YOU'RE TRYING TO FIND IT.
OR CHOOSING A COMPLICATED PIN NUMBER TO PREVENT IDENTITY THEFT...
BEEP BEEP BEEP
ピ ピ ピ
INVALID PIN!
...AND THEN FORGETTING IT.
OR SPRAYING FAB*EEZ TO GET RID OF A STENCH...
PSSCHHT
しゅっ
PSSCHHT
しゅっ
FABU
...AND ENDING UP WITH A ROOM THAT STINKS OF FAB*EEZ!
AND THIS MORNING, I WAS AN HOUR LATE, ALL BECAUSE I TRIED TO BE PREPARED.
宿直室
EXPO'70
ITOSHIKI
BEEP BEEP BEEP
リリリ
ITOSHIKI
SNOOZE
ぴたっ
SAYAKA
すー
ZZZ

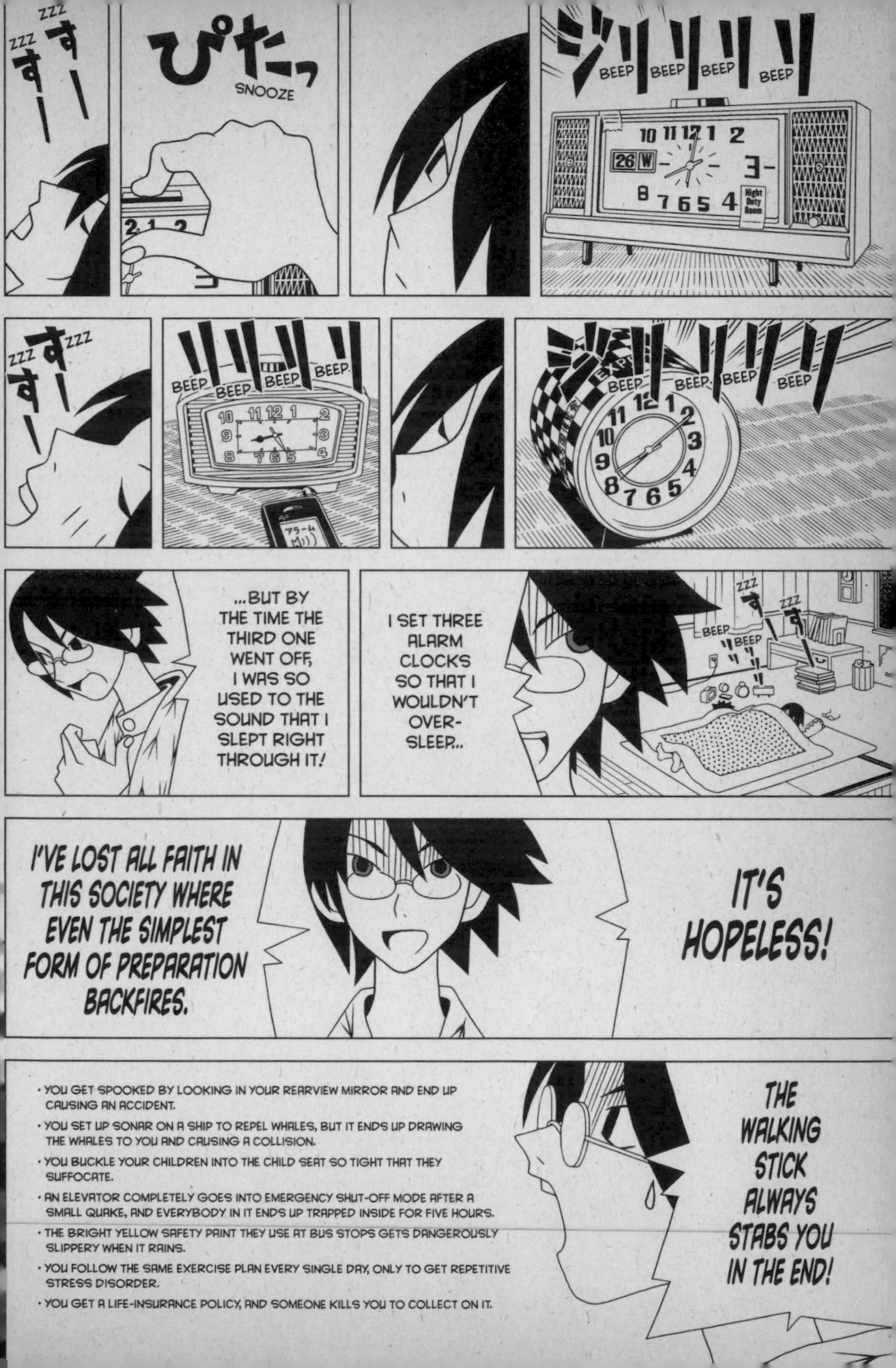

ジリリリリ
BEEP BEEP BEEP BEEP
Night Duty Room
ぴたっ
SNOOZE
すーすー
ZZZ ZZZ
ジリリリリリ
BEEP BEEP BEEP BEEP
リリリリリ
BEEP BEEP BEEP BEEP
アラーム
すーすー
ZZZ ZZZ
I SET THREE ALARM CLOCKS SO THAT I WOULDN'T OVER-SLEEP...
BEEP BEEP
ZZZ ZZZ
...BUT BY THE TIME THE THIRD ONE WENT OFF, I WAS SO USED TO THE SOUND THAT I SLEPT RIGHT THROUGH IT!
IT'S HOPELESS!
I'VE LOST ALL FAITH IN THIS SOCIETY WHERE EVEN THE SIMPLEST FORM OF PREPARATION BACKFIRES.
THE WALKING STICK ALWAYS STABS YOU IN THE END!
• YOU GET SPOOKED BY LOOKING IN YOUR REARVIEW MIRROR AND END UP CAUSING AN ACCIDENT.
• YOU SET UP SONAR ON A SHIP TO REPEL WHALES, BUT IT ENDS UP DRAWING THE WHALES TO YOU AND CAUSING A COLLISION.
• YOU BUCKLE YOUR CHILDREN INTO THE CHILD SEAT SO TIGHT THAT THEY SUFFOCATE.
• AN ELEVATOR COMPLETELY GOES INTO EMERGENCY SHUT-OFF MODE AFTER A SMALL QUAKE, AND EVERYBODY IN IT ENDS UP TRAPPED INSIDE FOR FIVE HOURS.
• THE BRIGHT YELLOW SAFETY PAINT THEY USE AT BUS STOPS GETS DANGEROUSLY SLIPPERY WHEN IT RAINS.
• YOU FOLLOW THE SAME EXERCISE PLAN EVERY SINGLE DAY, ONLY TO GET REPETITIVE STRESS DISORDER.
• YOU GET A LIFE-INSURANCE POLICY, AND SOMEONE KILLS YOU TO COLLECT ON IT.

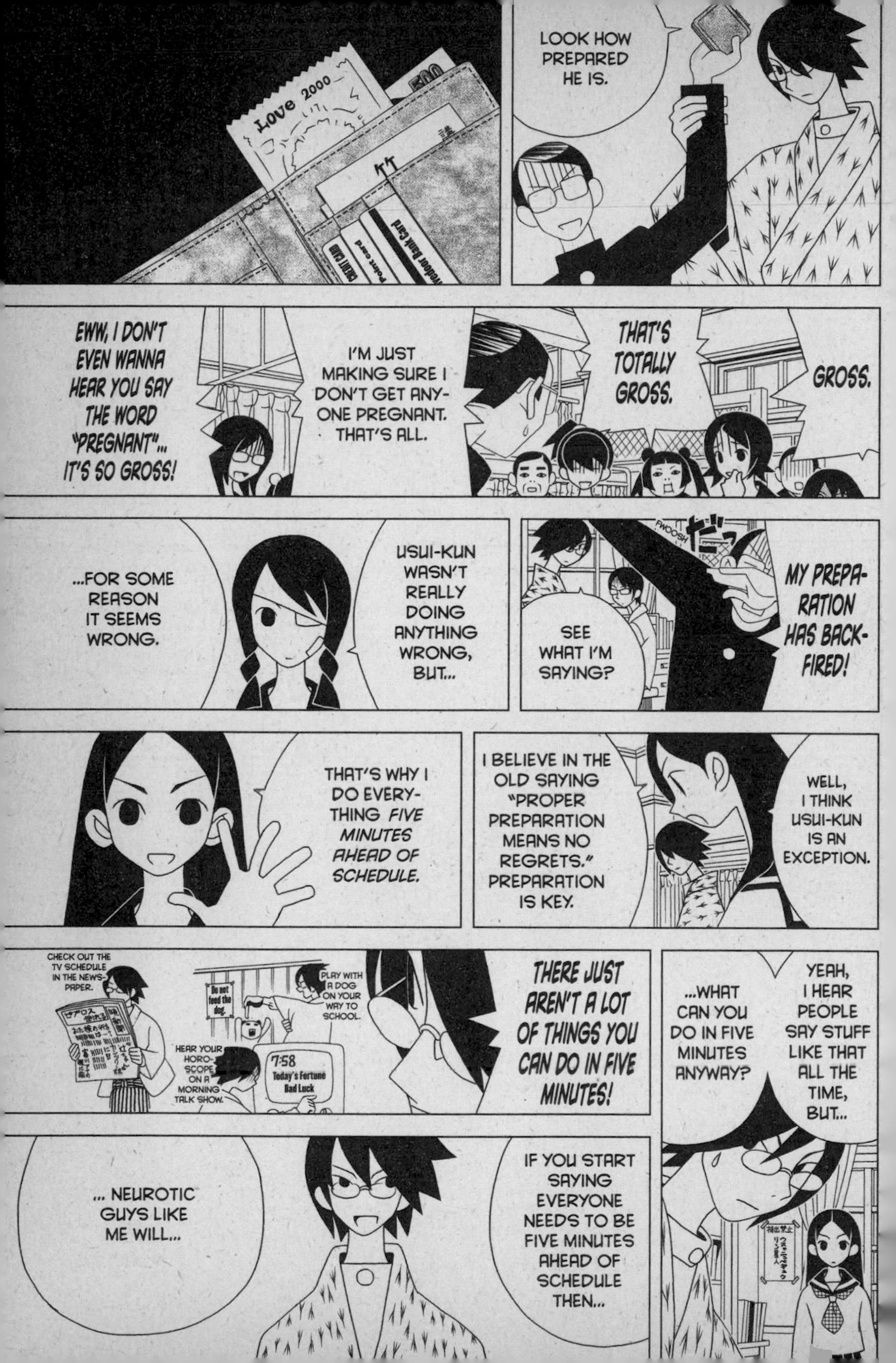
LOOK HOW PREPARED HE IS.
Love 2000
GROSS.
THAT'S TOTALLY GROSS.
I'M JUST MAKING SURE I DON'T GET ANYONE PREGNANT. THAT'S ALL.
EWW, I DON'T EVEN WANNA HEAR YOU SAY THE WORD "PREGNANT"... IT'S SO GROSS!
MY PREPARATION HAS BACKFIRED!
PWOOSH
SEE WHAT I'M SAYING?
USUI-KUN WASN'T REALLY DOING ANYTHING WRONG, BUT...
...FOR SOME REASON IT SEEMS WRONG.
WELL, I THINK USUI-KUN IS AN EXCEPTION.
I BELIEVE IN THE OLD SAYING "PROPER PREPARATION MEANS NO REGRETS." PREPARATION IS KEY.
THAT'S WHY I DO EVERYTHING *FIVE MINUTES AHEAD OF SCHEDULE.*
YEAH, I HEAR PEOPLE SAY STUFF LIKE THAT ALL THE TIME, BUT...
...WHAT CAN YOU DO IN FIVE MINUTES ANYWAY?
THERE JUST AREN'T A LOT OF THINGS YOU CAN DO IN FIVE MINUTES!
PLAY WITH A DOG ON YOUR WAY TO SCHOOL.
Do not feed the dog.
CHECK OUT THE TV SCHEDULE IN THE NEWSPAPER.
HEAR YOUR HOROSCOPE ON A MORNING TALK SHOW.
7:58
Today's Fortune
Bad Luck
IF YOU START SAYING EVERYONE NEEDS TO BE FIVE MINUTES AHEAD OF SCHEDULE THEN...
... NEUROTIC GUYS LIKE ME WILL...

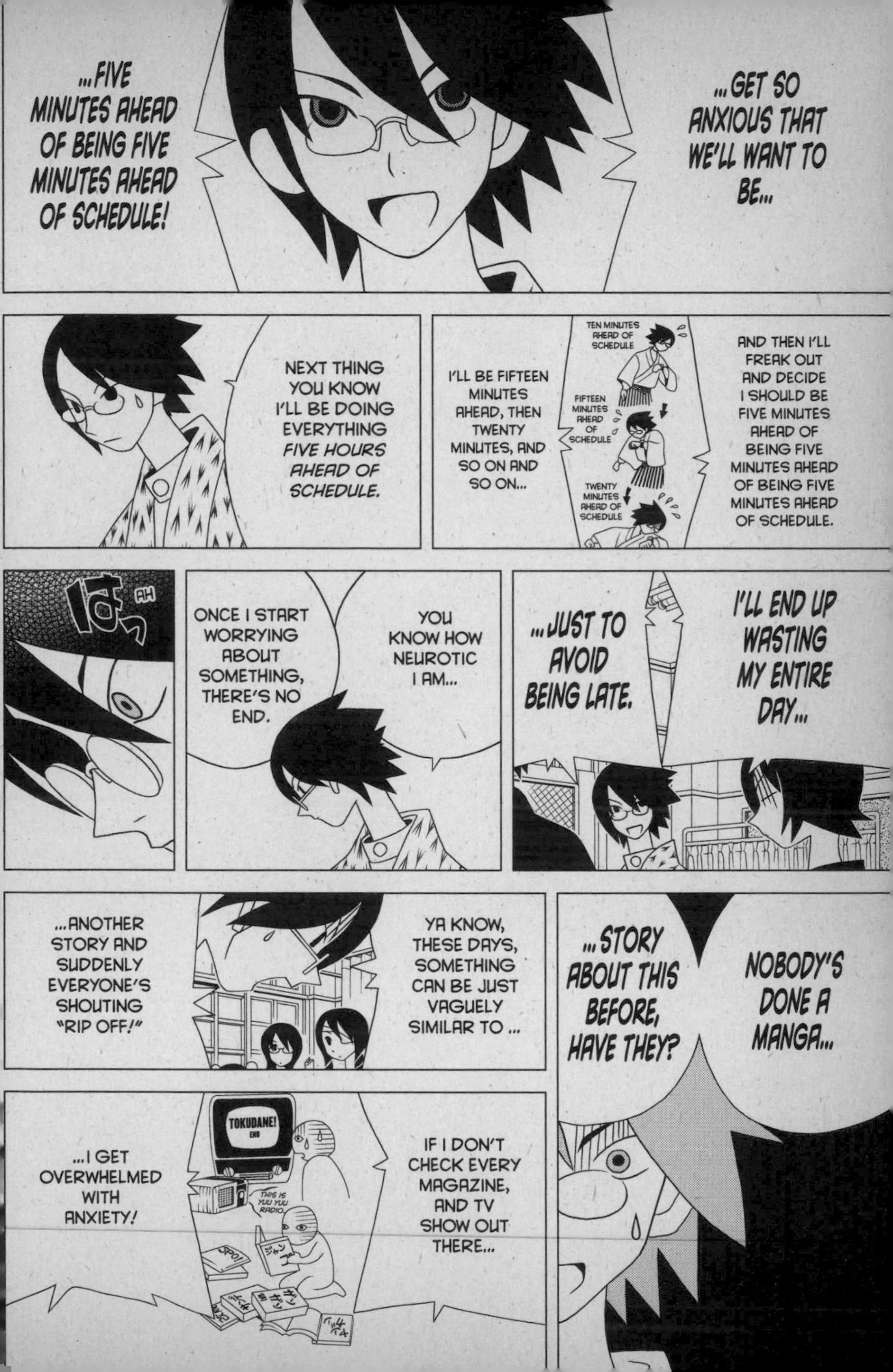
...GET SO ANXIOUS THAT WE'LL WANT TO BE...
...FIVE MINUTES AHEAD OF BEING FIVE MINUTES AHEAD OF SCHEDULE!
AND THEN I'LL FREAK OUT AND DECIDE I SHOULD BE FIVE MINUTES AHEAD OF BEING FIVE MINUTES AHEAD OF BEING FIVE MINUTES AHEAD OF SCHEDULE.
TEN MINUTES AHEAD OF SCHEDULE
FIFTEEN MINUTES AHEAD OF SCHEDULE
TWENTY MINUTES AHEAD OF SCHEDULE
I'LL BE FIFTEEN MINUTES AHEAD, THEN TWENTY MINUTES, AND SO ON AND SO ON...
NEXT THING YOU KNOW I'LL BE DOING EVERYTHING *FIVE HOURS AHEAD OF SCHEDULE.*
I'LL END UP WASTING MY ENTIRE DAY...
...JUST TO AVOID BEING LATE.
YOU KNOW HOW NEUROTIC I AM...
ONCE I START WORRYING ABOUT SOMETHING, THERE'S NO END.
はっ
AH
NOBODY'S DONE A MANGA...
...STORY ABOUT THIS BEFORE, HAVE THEY?
YA KNOW, THESE DAYS, SOMETHING CAN BE JUST VAGUELY SIMILAR TO ...
...ANOTHER STORY AND SUDDENLY EVERYONE'S SHOUTING "RIP OFF!"
IF I DON'T CHECK EVERY MAGAZINE, AND TV SHOW OUT THERE...
TOKUDANE!
END
THIS IS YUU YUU RADIO.
...I GET OVERWHELMED WITH ANXIETY!

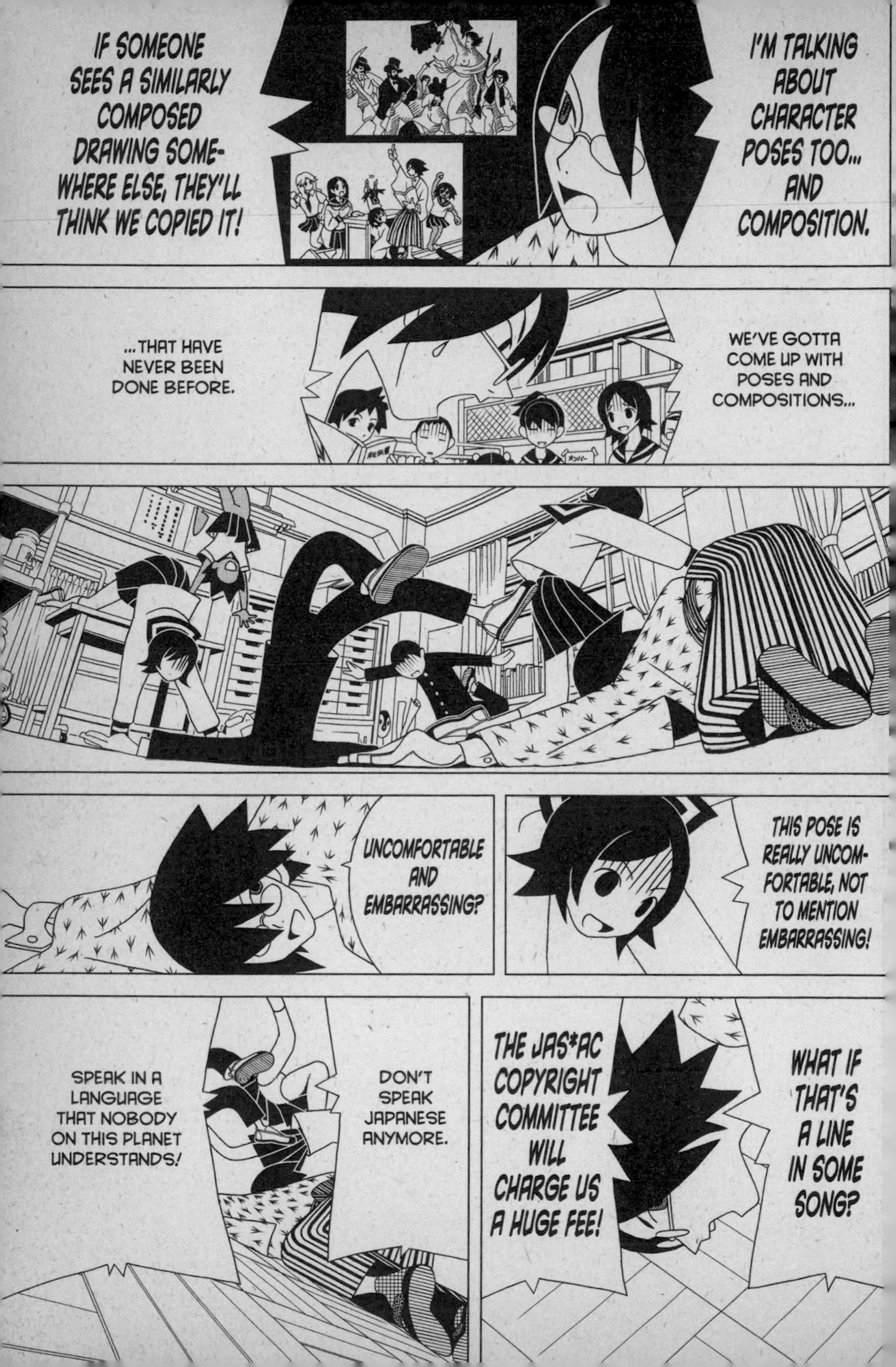
I'M TALKING ABOUT CHARACTER POSES TOO... AND COMPOSITION.
IF SOMEONE SEES A SIMILARLY COMPOSED DRAWING SOME-WHERE ELSE, THEY'LL THINK WE COPIED IT!
WE'VE GOTTA COME UP WITH POSES AND COMPOSITIONS...
...THAT HAVE NEVER BEEN DONE BEFORE.
THIS POSE IS REALLY UNCOM-FORTABLE, NOT TO MENTION EMBARRASSING!
UNCOMFORTABLE AND EMBARRASSING?
WHAT IF THAT'S A LINE IN SOME SONG?
THE JAS*AC COPYRIGHT COMMITTEE WILL CHARGE US A HUGE FEE!
DON'T SPEAK JAPANESE ANYMORE.
SPEAK IN A LANGUAGE THAT NOBODY ON THIS PLANET UNDERSTANDS!

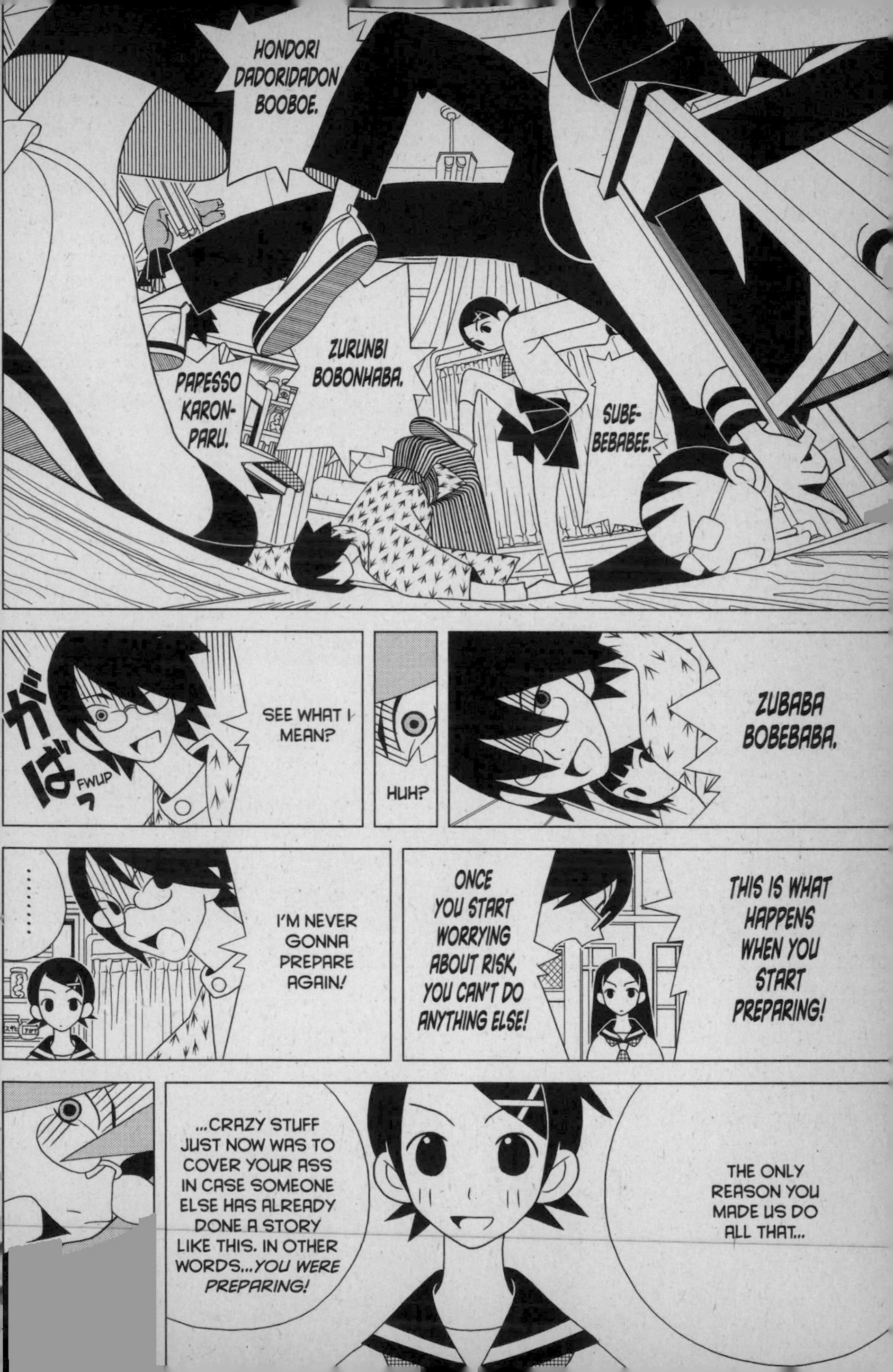
HONDORI DADORIDADON BOOBOE.
SUBE-BEBABEE.
ZURUNBI BOBONHABA.
PAPESSO KARON-PARU.
ZUBABA BOBEBABA.
HUH?
SEE WHAT I MEAN?
がばっ
FWUP
THIS IS WHAT HAPPENS WHEN YOU START PREPARING!
ONCE YOU START WORRYING ABOUT RISK, YOU CAN'T DO ANYTHING ELSE!
I'M NEVER GONNA PREPARE AGAIN!
......
THE ONLY REASON YOU MADE US DO ALL THAT...
...CRAZY STUFF JUST NOW WAS TO COVER YOUR ASS IN CASE SOMEONE ELSE HAS ALREADY DONE A STORY LIKE THIS. IN OTHER WORDS...*YOU WERE PREPARING!*

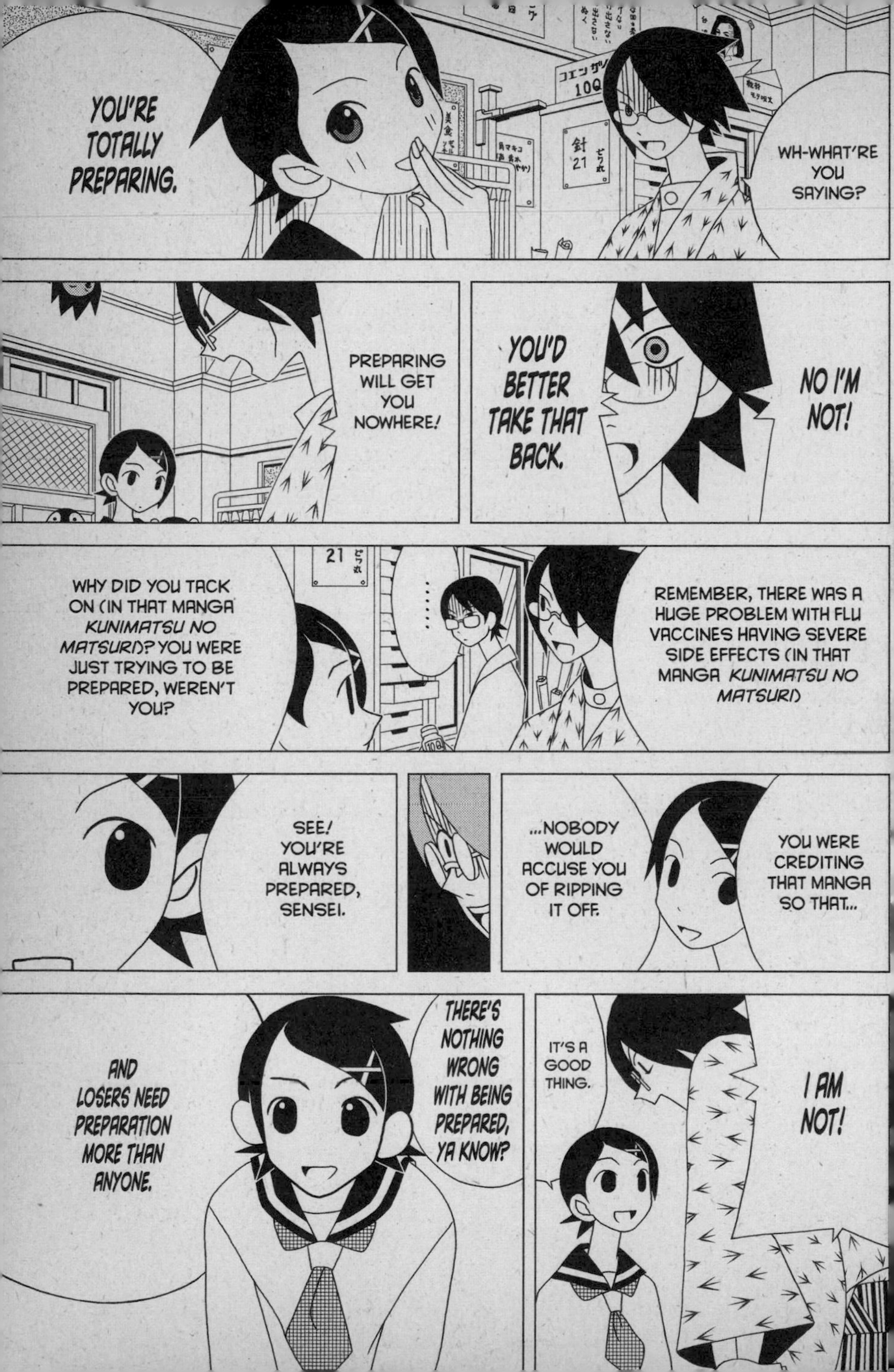

WH-WHAT'RE YOU SAYING?
YOU'RE TOTALLY PREPARING.
NO I'M NOT!
YOU'D BETTER TAKE THAT BACK.
PREPARING WILL GET YOU NOWHERE!
REMEMBER, THERE WAS A HUGE PROBLEM WITH FLU VACCINES HAVING SEVERE SIDE EFFECTS (IN THAT MANGA *KUNIMATSU NO MATSURI*)
......
WHY DID YOU TACK ON (IN THAT MANGA *KUNIMATSU NO MATSURI*)? YOU WERE JUST TRYING TO BE PREPARED, WEREN'T YOU?
YOU WERE CREDITING THAT MANGA SO THAT...
...NOBODY WOULD ACCUSE YOU OF RIPPING IT OFF.
SEE! YOU'RE ALWAYS PREPARED, SENSEI.
I AM NOT!
IT'S A GOOD THING.
THERE'S NOTHING WRONG WITH BEING PREPARED, YA KNOW?
AND LOSERS NEED PREPARATION MORE THAN ANYONE.

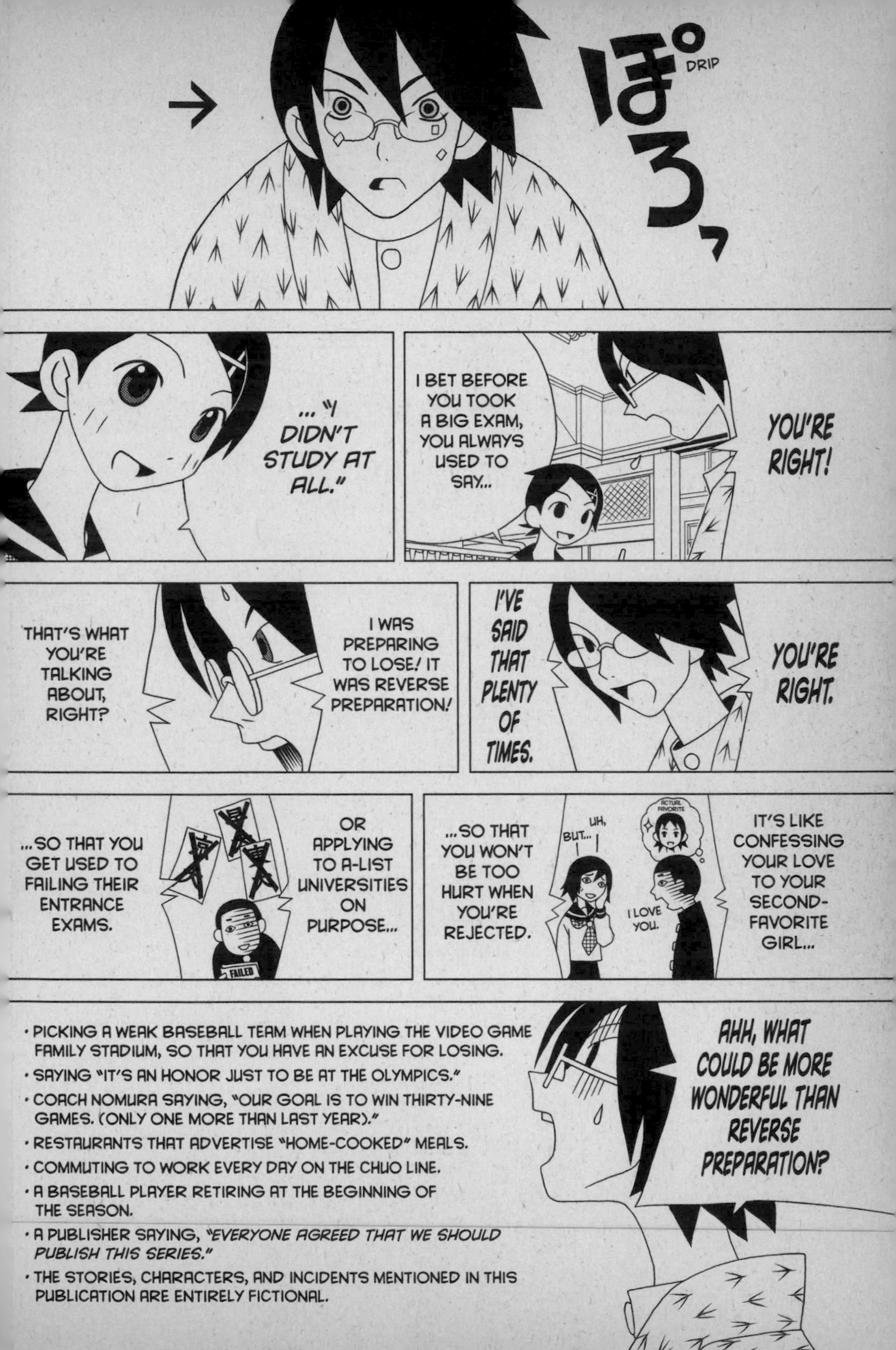
ぽろっ
DRIP
YOU'RE RIGHT!
I BET BEFORE YOU TOOK A BIG EXAM, YOU ALWAYS USED TO SAY...
..."I DIDN'T STUDY AT ALL."
YOU'RE RIGHT.
I'VE SAID THAT PLENTY OF TIMES.
I WAS PREPARING TO LOSE! IT WAS REVERSE PREPARATION!
THAT'S WHAT YOU'RE TALKING ABOUT, RIGHT?
IT'S LIKE CONFESSING YOUR LOVE TO YOUR SECOND-FAVORITE GIRL...
ACTUAL FAVORITE
I LOVE YOU.
UH, BUT...
...SO THAT YOU WON'T BE TOO HURT WHEN YOU'RE REJECTED.
OR APPLYING TO A-LIST UNIVERSITIES ON PURPOSE...
FAILED
...SO THAT YOU GET USED TO FAILING THEIR ENTRANCE EXAMS.
AHH, WHAT COULD BE MORE WONDERFUL THAN REVERSE PREPARATION?
• PICKING A WEAK BASEBALL TEAM WHEN PLAYING THE VIDEO GAME FAMILY STADIUM, SO THAT YOU HAVE AN EXCUSE FOR LOSING.
• SAYING "IT'S AN HONOR JUST TO BE AT THE OLYMPICS."
• COACH NOMURA SAYING, "OUR GOAL IS TO WIN THIRTY-NINE GAMES. (ONLY ONE MORE THAN LAST YEAR)."
• RESTAURANTS THAT ADVERTISE "HOME-COOKED" MEALS.
• COMMUTING TO WORK EVERY DAY ON THE CHUO LINE.
• A BASEBALL PLAYER RETIRING AT THE BEGINNING OF THE SEASON.
• A PUBLISHER SAYING, "EVERYONE AGREED THAT WE SHOULD PUBLISH THIS SERIES."
• THE STORIES, CHARACTERS, AND INCIDENTS MENTIONED IN THIS PUBLICATION ARE ENTIRELY FICTIONAL.

REVERSE PREPARATION IS AWESOME.

GROUP F
BRAZIL
ARGENTINA
ITALY
JAPAN

JAPAN'S WORLD CUP LOSS WOULD HAVE BEEN WAY LESS HUMILIATING IF THEY'D PLAYED AGAINST THESE TEAMS. AT LEAST THEY'D HAVE BEEN PREPARED FOR THEIR LOSS.

YOU NEED TO PREPARE WITH A POSITIVE ATTITUDE.

REVERSE PREPARATION IS DESPICABLE.

EVERY-BODY'S TALKING ABOUT ME BEHIND MY BACK.

...BEFORE THEY KILL ME.

I'D BETTER KILL THEM...

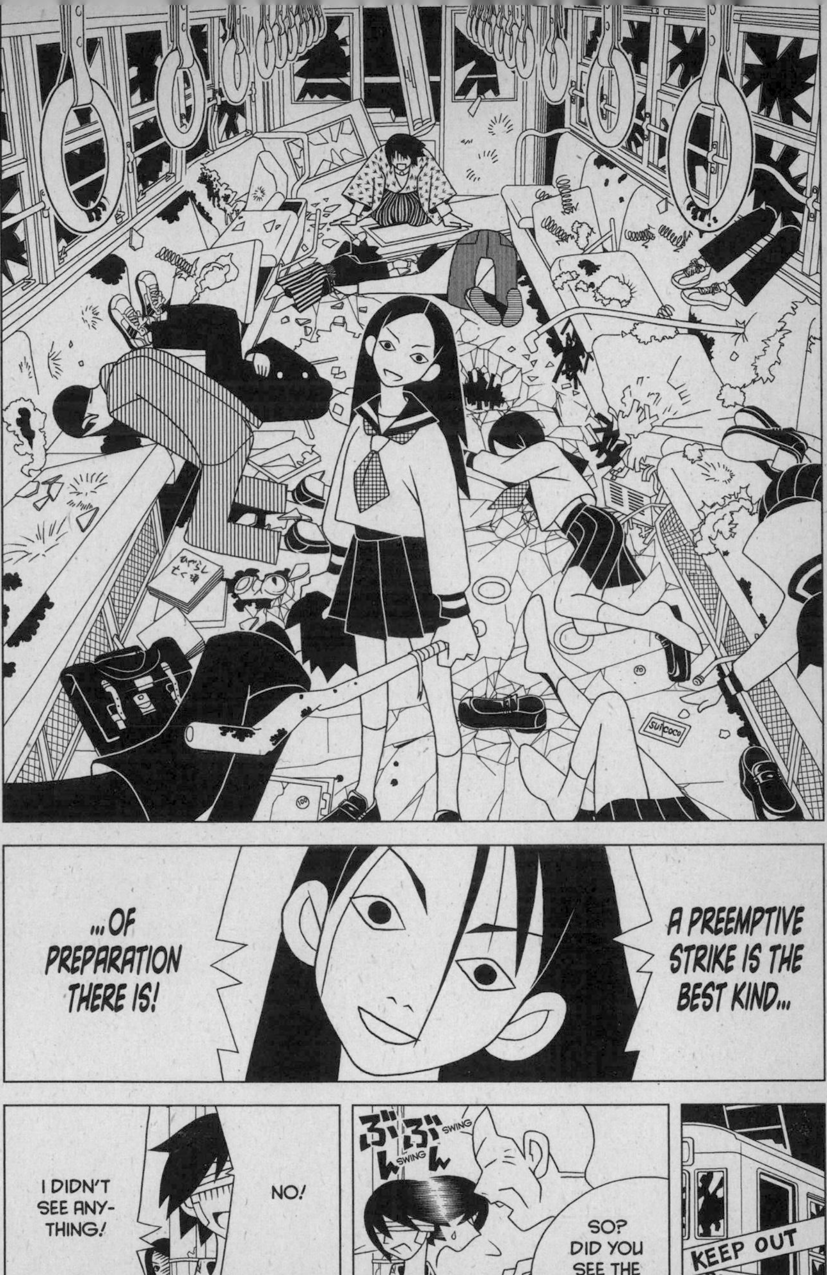
A PREEMPTIVE STRIKE IS THE BEST KIND...
...OF PREPARATION THERE IS!
KEEP OUT
OUT KEEP
ぶんぶん
SWING SWING
SO? DID YOU SEE THE ASSAILANT'S FACE?
NO!
I DIDN'T SEE ANY-THING!

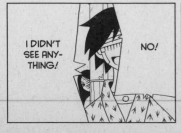

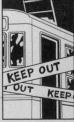

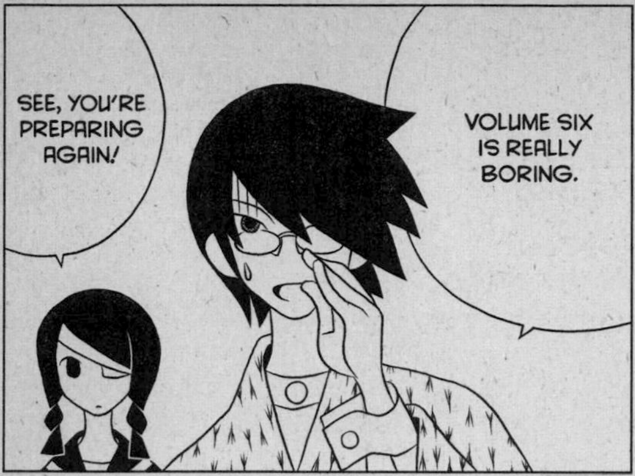
VOLUME SIX IS REALLY BORING.
SEE, YOU'RE PREPARING AGAIN!

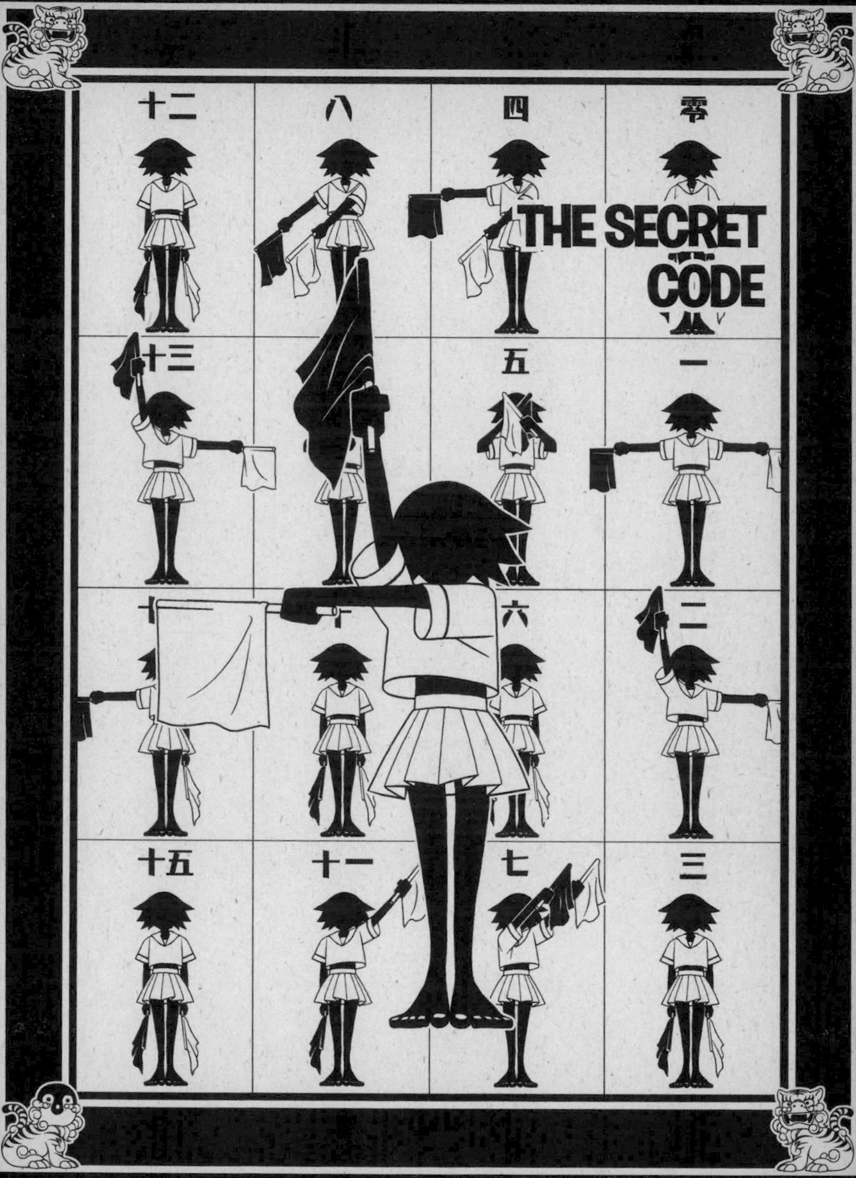
THE SECRET CODE
零
一
二
三
四
五
六
七
八
十一
十二
十三
十五

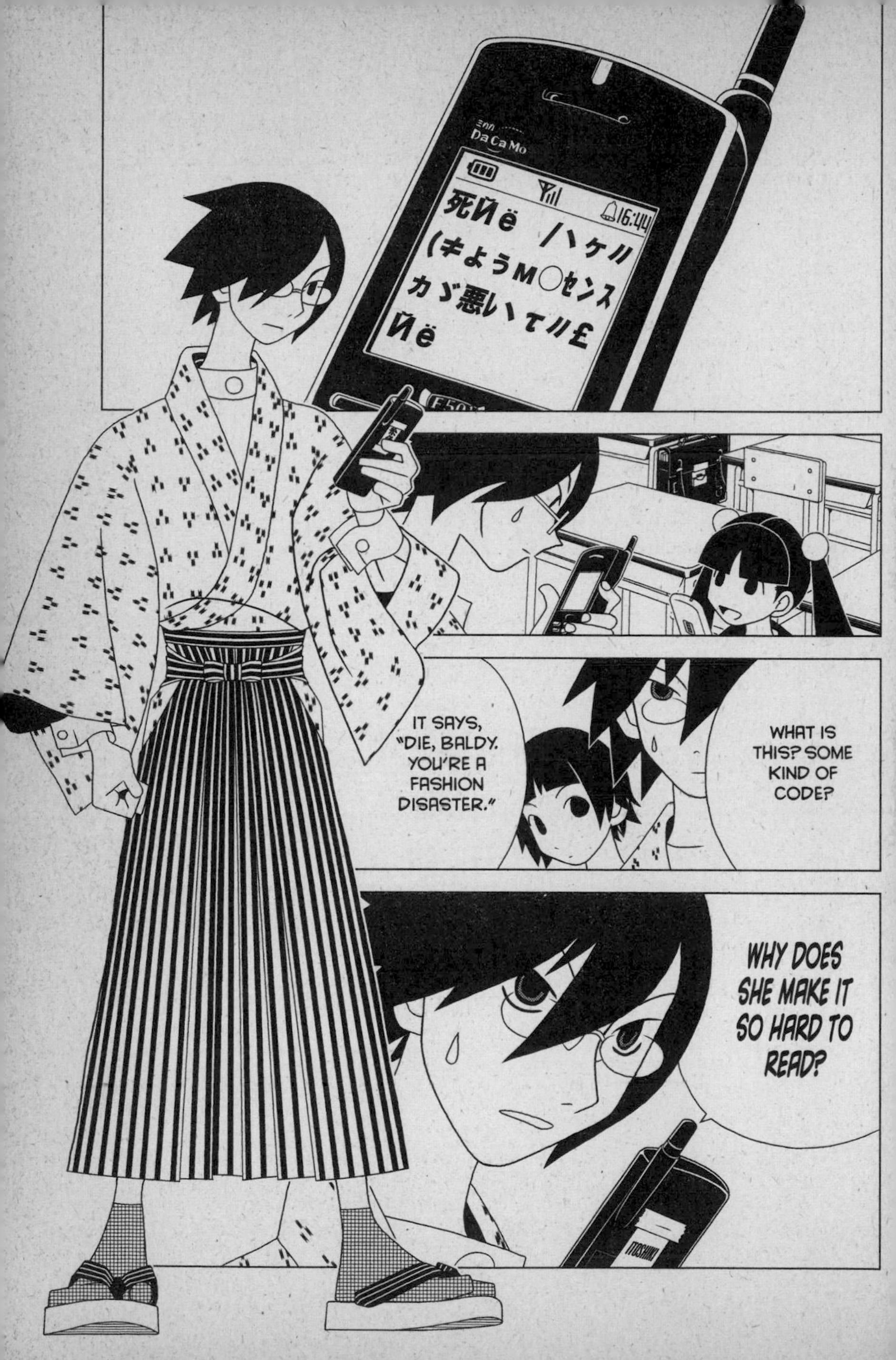
Da Ca Mo
16:44
死Йё ハヶ〃
(ｷょうM○センス
カゞ悪いて〃£
Йё
WHAT IS THIS? SOME KIND OF CODE?
IT SAYS, "DIE, BALDY. YOU'RE A FASHION DISASTER."
WHY DOES SHE MAKE IT SO HARD TO READ?

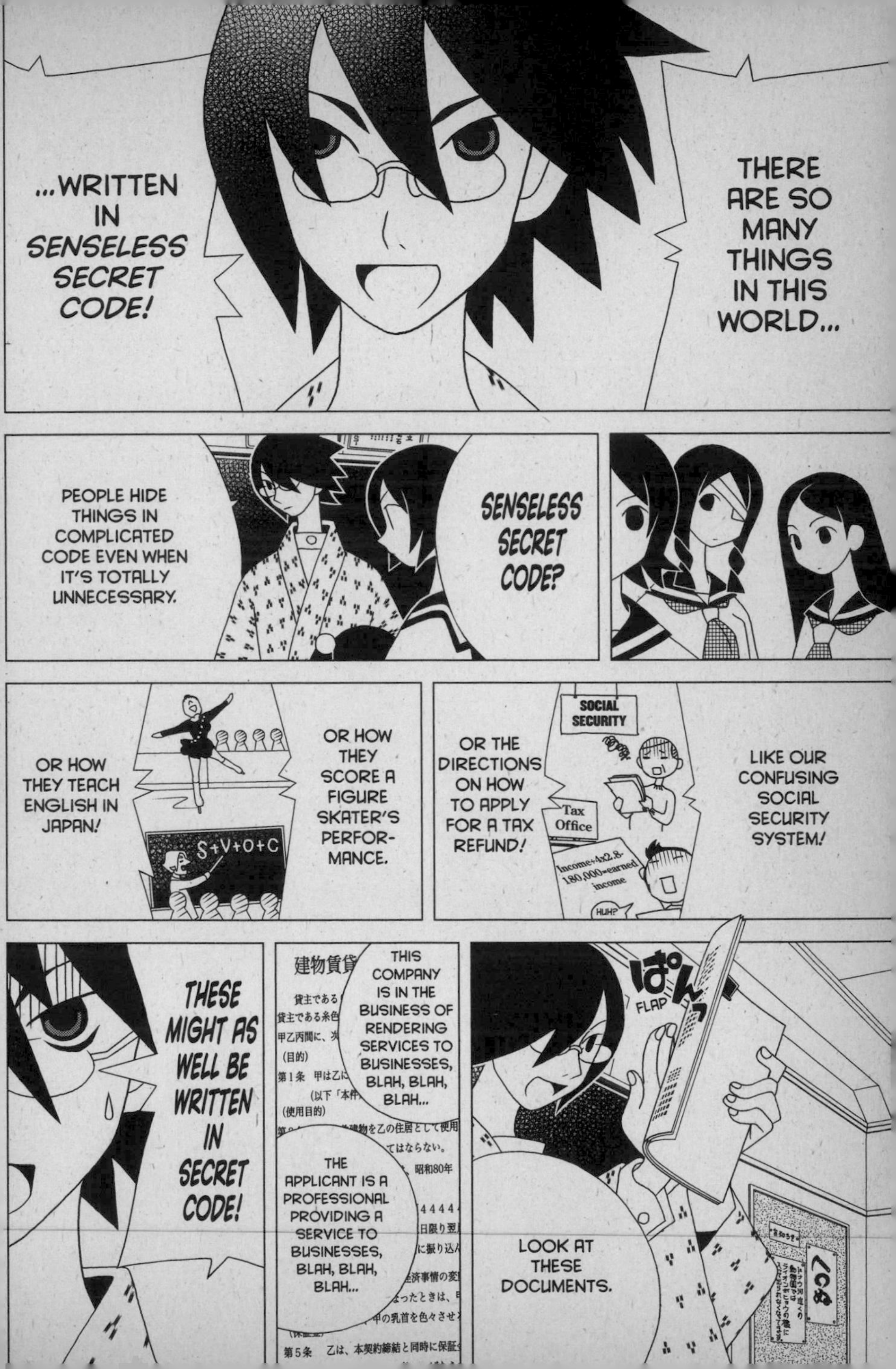
THERE ARE SO MANY THINGS IN THIS WORLD...
...WRITTEN IN SENSELESS SECRET CODE!
SENSELESS SECRET CODE?
PEOPLE HIDE THINGS IN COMPLICATED CODE EVEN WHEN IT'S TOTALLY UNNECESSARY.
LIKE OUR CONFUSING SOCIAL SECURITY SYSTEM!
SOCIAL SECURITY
Tax Office
Income÷4x2.8-180,000=earned income
HUH?
OR THE DIRECTIONS ON HOW TO APPLY FOR A TAX REFUND!
OR HOW THEY SCORE A FIGURE SKATER'S PERFORMANCE.
S+V+O+C
OR HOW THEY TEACH ENGLISH IN JAPAN!
ぱん
FLAP
LOOK AT THESE DOCUMENTS.
THIS COMPANY IS IN THE BUSINESS OF RENDERING SERVICES TO BUSINESSES, BLAH, BLAH, BLAH...
THE APPLICANT IS A PROFESSIONAL PROVIDING A SERVICE TO BUSINESSES, BLAH, BLAH, BLAH...
THESE MIGHT AS WELL BE WRITTEN IN SECRET CODE!

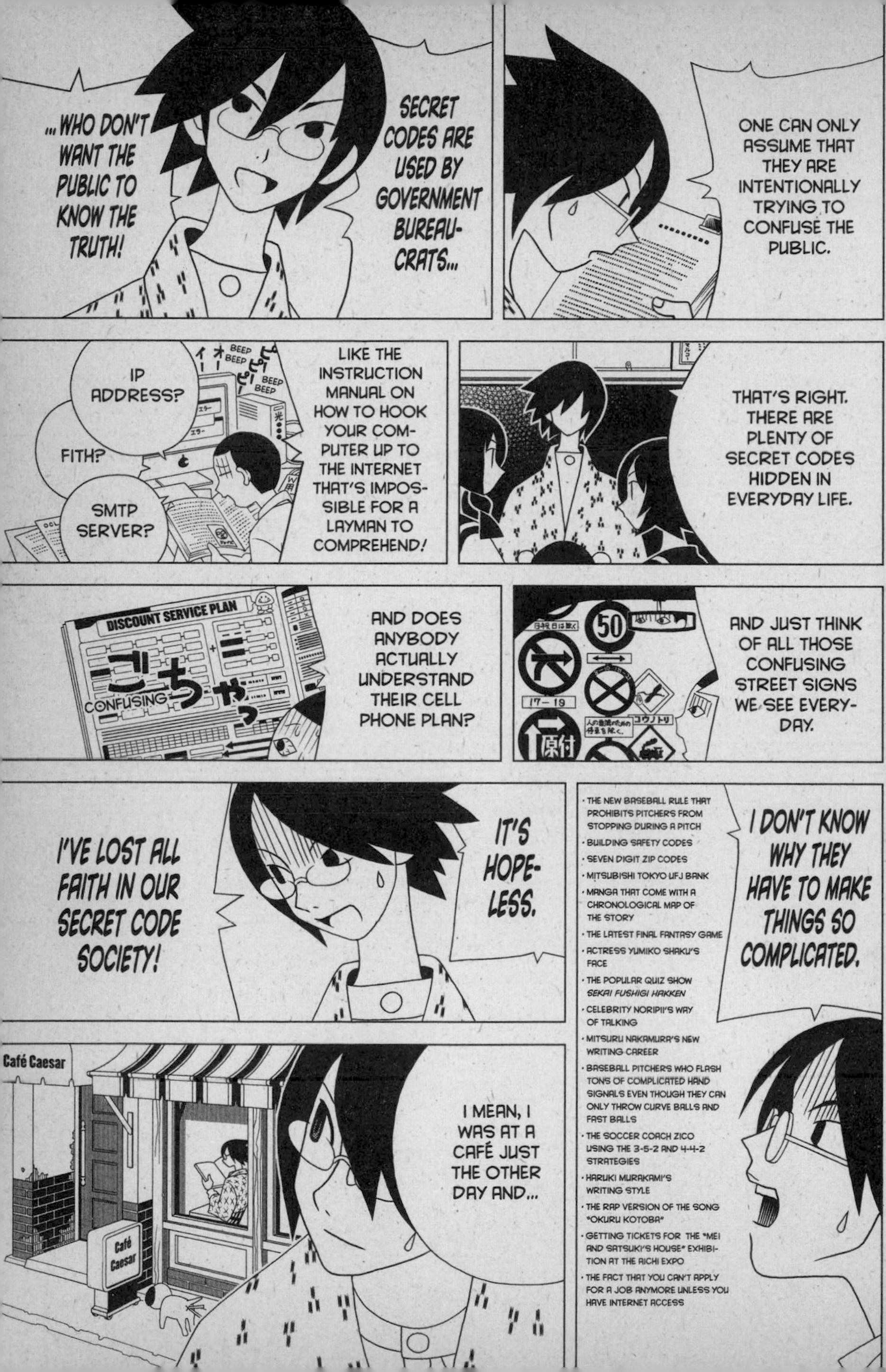
ONE CAN ONLY ASSUME THAT THEY ARE INTENTIONALLY TRYING TO CONFUSE THE PUBLIC.
SECRET CODES ARE USED BY GOVERNMENT BUREAU-CRATS...
...WHO DON'T WANT THE PUBLIC TO KNOW THE TRUTH!
THAT'S RIGHT. THERE ARE PLENTY OF SECRET CODES HIDDEN IN EVERYDAY LIFE.
LIKE THE INSTRUCTION MANUAL ON HOW TO HOOK YOUR COM-PUTER UP TO THE INTERNET THAT'S IMPOS-SIBLE FOR A LAYMAN TO COMPREHEND!
BEEP BEEP
BEEP BEEP
IP ADDRESS?
FITH?
SMTP SERVER?
AND JUST THINK OF ALL THOSE CONFUSING STREET SIGNS WE SEE EVERY-DAY.
50
17-19
原付
コウノトリ
AND DOES ANYBODY ACTUALLY UNDERSTAND THEIR CELL PHONE PLAN?
DISCOUNT SERVICE PLAN
ごちゃっ
CONFUSING
I DON'T KNOW WHY THEY HAVE TO MAKE THINGS SO COMPLICATED.
· THE NEW BASEBALL RULE THAT PROHIBITS PITCHERS FROM STOPPING DURING A PITCH
· BUILDING SAFETY CODES
· SEVEN DIGIT ZIP CODES
· MITSUBISHI TOKYO UFJ BANK
· MANGA THAT COME WITH A CHRONOLOGICAL MAP OF THE STORY
· THE LATEST FINAL FANTASY GAME
· ACTRESS YUMIKO SHAKU'S FACE
· THE POPULAR QUIZ SHOW *SEKAI FUSHIGI HAKKEN*
· CELEBRITY NORIPII'S WAY OF TALKING
· MITSURU NAKAMURA'S NEW WRITING CAREER
· BASEBALL PITCHERS WHO FLASH TONS OF COMPLICATED HAND SIGNALS EVEN THOUGH THEY CAN ONLY THROW CURVE BALLS AND FAST BALLS
· THE SOCCER COACH ZICO USING THE 3-5-2 AND 4-4-2 STRATEGIES
· HARUKI MURAKAMI'S WRITING STYLE
· THE RAP VERSION OF THE SONG "OKURU KOTOBA"
· GETTING TICKETS FOR THE "MEI AND SATSUKI'S HOUSE" EXHIBI-TION AT THE AICHI EXPO
· THE FACT THAT YOU CAN'T APPLY FOR A JOB ANYMORE UNLESS YOU HAVE INTERNET ACCESS
IT'S HOPE-LESS.
I'VE LOST ALL FAITH IN OUR SECRET CODE SOCIETY!
I MEAN, I WAS AT A CAFÉ JUST THE OTHER DAY AND...
Café Caesar
Café Caesar

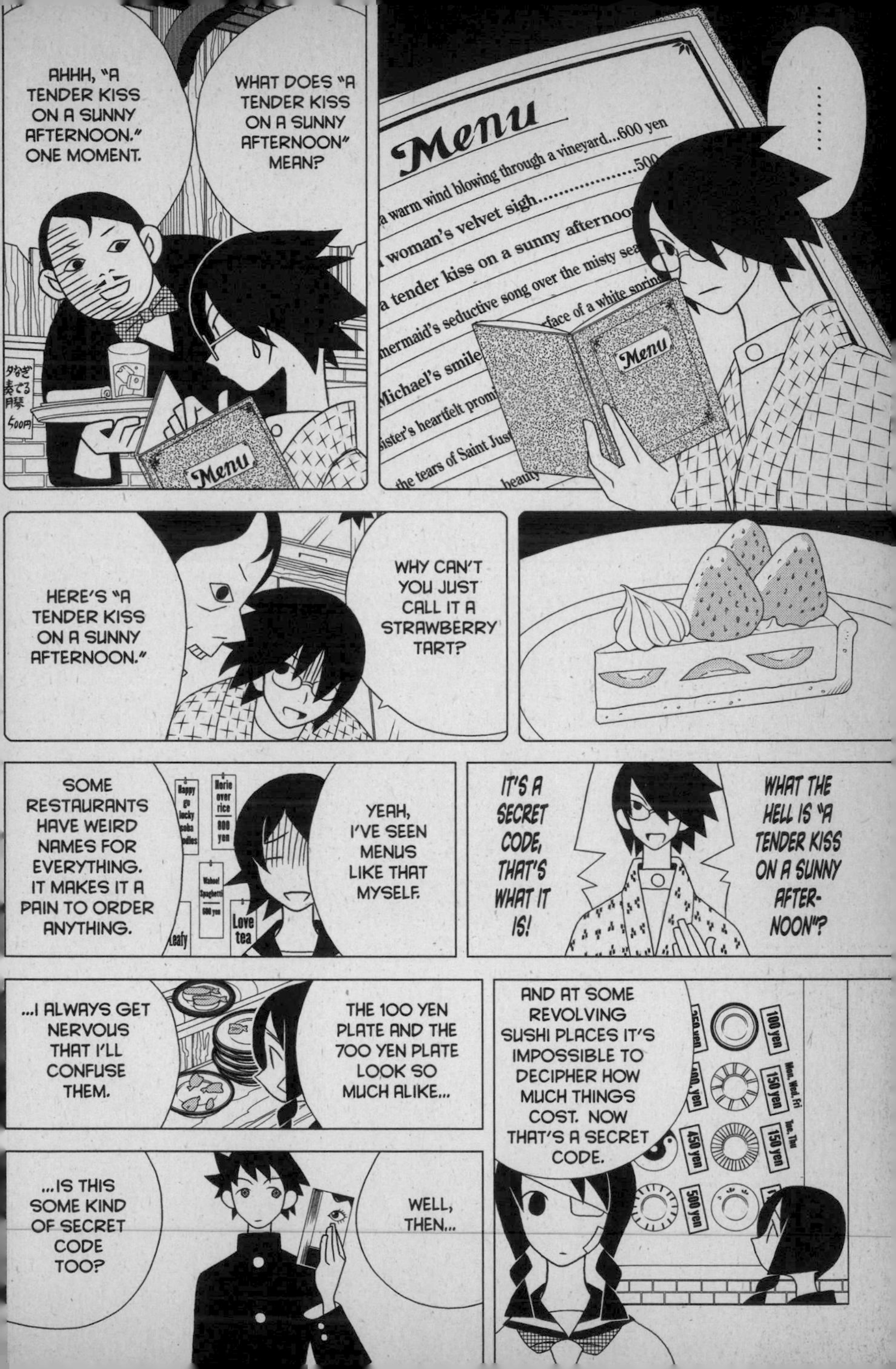
......
Menu
a warm wind blowing through a vineyard...600 yen
woman's velvet sigh
a tender kiss on a sunny afternoo
mermaid's seductive song over the misty sea
Michael's smile
sister's heartfelt promi
the tears of Saint Jus
Menu
WHAT DOES "A TENDER KISS ON A SUNNY AFTERNOON" MEAN?
AHHH, "A TENDER KISS ON A SUNNY AFTERNOON." ONE MOMENT.
夕なぎ奏でる月琴 500円
Menu
WHY CAN'T YOU JUST CALL IT A STRAWBERRY TART?
HERE'S "A TENDER KISS ON A SUNNY AFTERNOON."
WHAT THE HELL IS "A TENDER KISS ON A SUNNY AFTER-NOON"?
IT'S A SECRET CODE, THAT'S WHAT IT IS!
YEAH, I'VE SEEN MENUS LIKE THAT MYSELF.
SOME RESTAURANTS HAVE WEIRD NAMES FOR EVERYTHING. IT MAKES IT A PAIN TO ORDER ANYTHING.
Happy go lucky soba
Horie over rice 800 yen
Wahoo! Spaghetti 600 yen
Love tea
Leafy
AND AT SOME REVOLVING SUSHI PLACES IT'S IMPOSSIBLE TO DECIPHER HOW MUCH THINGS COST. NOW THAT'S A SECRET CODE.
100 yen
Mon. Wed. Fri
150 yen
Tue. Thu
150 yen
400 yen
450 yen
500 yen
THE 100 YEN PLATE AND THE 700 YEN PLATE LOOK SO MUCH ALIKE...
...I ALWAYS GET NERVOUS THAT I'LL CONFUSE THEM.
WELL, THEN...
...IS THIS SOME KIND OF SECRET CODE TOO?

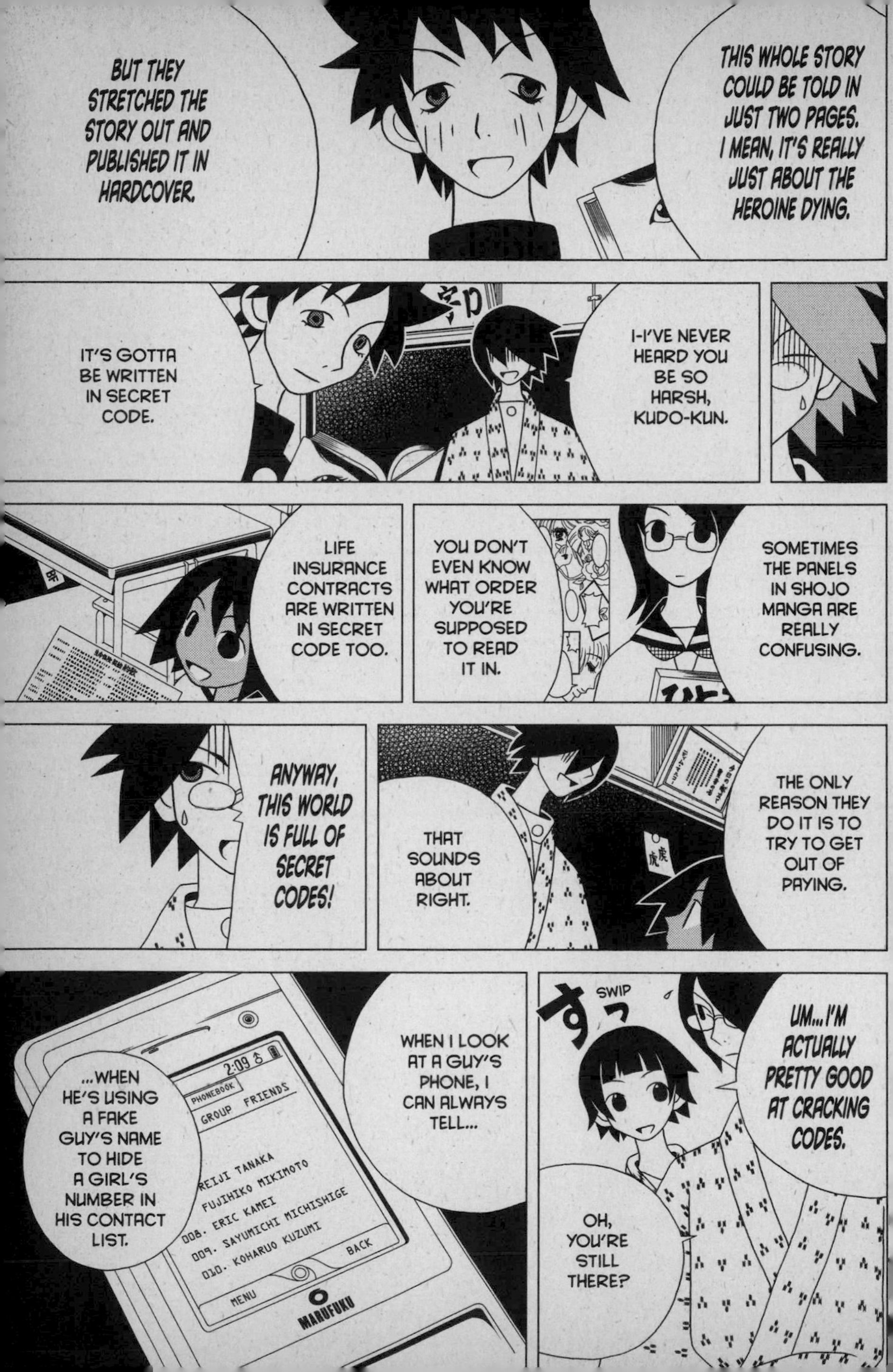
THIS WHOLE STORY COULD BE TOLD IN JUST TWO PAGES. I MEAN, IT'S REALLY JUST ABOUT THE HEROINE DYING.
BUT THEY STRETCHED THE STORY OUT AND PUBLISHED IT IN HARDCOVER.
I-I'VE NEVER HEARD YOU BE SO HARSH, KUDO-KUN.
IT'S GOTTA BE WRITTEN IN SECRET CODE.
SOMETIMES THE PANELS IN SHOJO MANGA ARE REALLY CONFUSING.
YOU DON'T EVEN KNOW WHAT ORDER YOU'RE SUPPOSED TO READ IT IN.
LIFE INSURANCE CONTRACTS ARE WRITTEN IN SECRET CODE TOO.
THE ONLY REASON THEY DO IT IS TO TRY TO GET OUT OF PAYING.
THAT SOUNDS ABOUT RIGHT.
ANYWAY, THIS WORLD IS FULL OF SECRET CODES!
すっ
SWIP
UM...I'M ACTUALLY PRETTY GOOD AT CRACKING CODES.
OH, YOU'RE STILL THERE?
WHEN I LOOK AT A GUY'S PHONE, I CAN ALWAYS TELL...
...WHEN HE'S USING A FAKE GUY'S NAME TO HIDE A GIRL'S NUMBER IN HIS CONTACT LIST.
2:09
PHONEBOOK
GROUP FRIENDS
REIJI TANAKA
FUJIHIKO MIKIMOTO
008. ERIC KAMEI
009. SAYUMICHI MICHISHIGE
010. KOHARUO KUZUMI
MENU
BACK
MARUFUKU

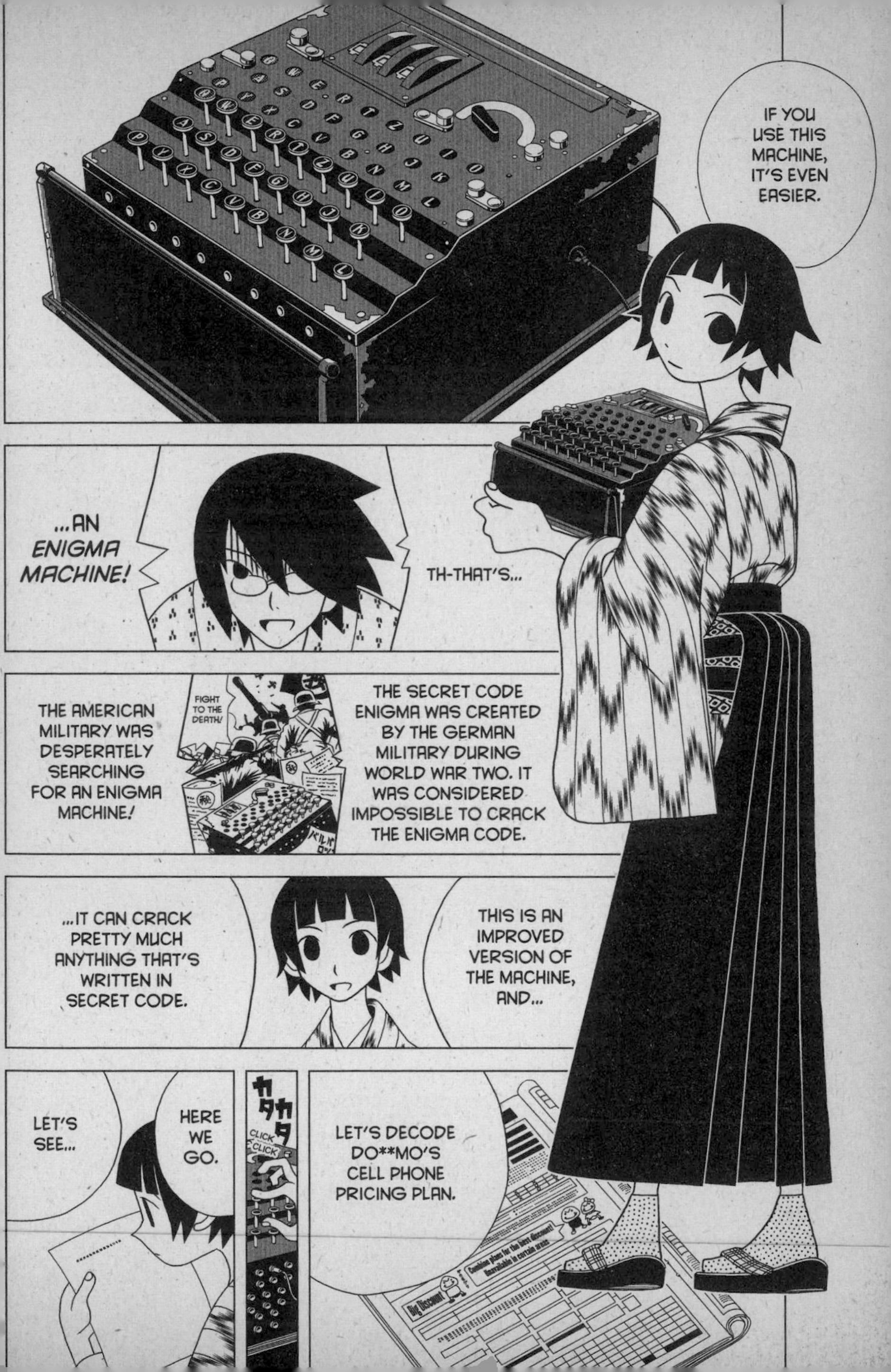
IF YOU USE THIS MACHINE, IT'S EVEN EASIER.
TH-THAT'S...
...AN *ENIGMA MACHINE!*
THE SECRET CODE ENIGMA WAS CREATED BY THE GERMAN MILITARY DURING WORLD WAR TWO. IT WAS CONSIDERED IMPOSSIBLE TO CRACK THE ENIGMA CODE.
FIGHT TO THE DEATH!
THE AMERICAN MILITARY WAS DESPERATELY SEARCHING FOR AN ENIGMA MACHINE!
THIS IS AN IMPROVED VERSION OF THE MACHINE, AND...
...IT CAN CRACK PRETTY MUCH ANYTHING THAT'S WRITTEN IN SECRET CODE.
LET'S DECODE DO**MO'S CELL PHONE PRICING PLAN.
カタカタ
CLICK CLICK
HERE WE GO.
LET'S SEE...

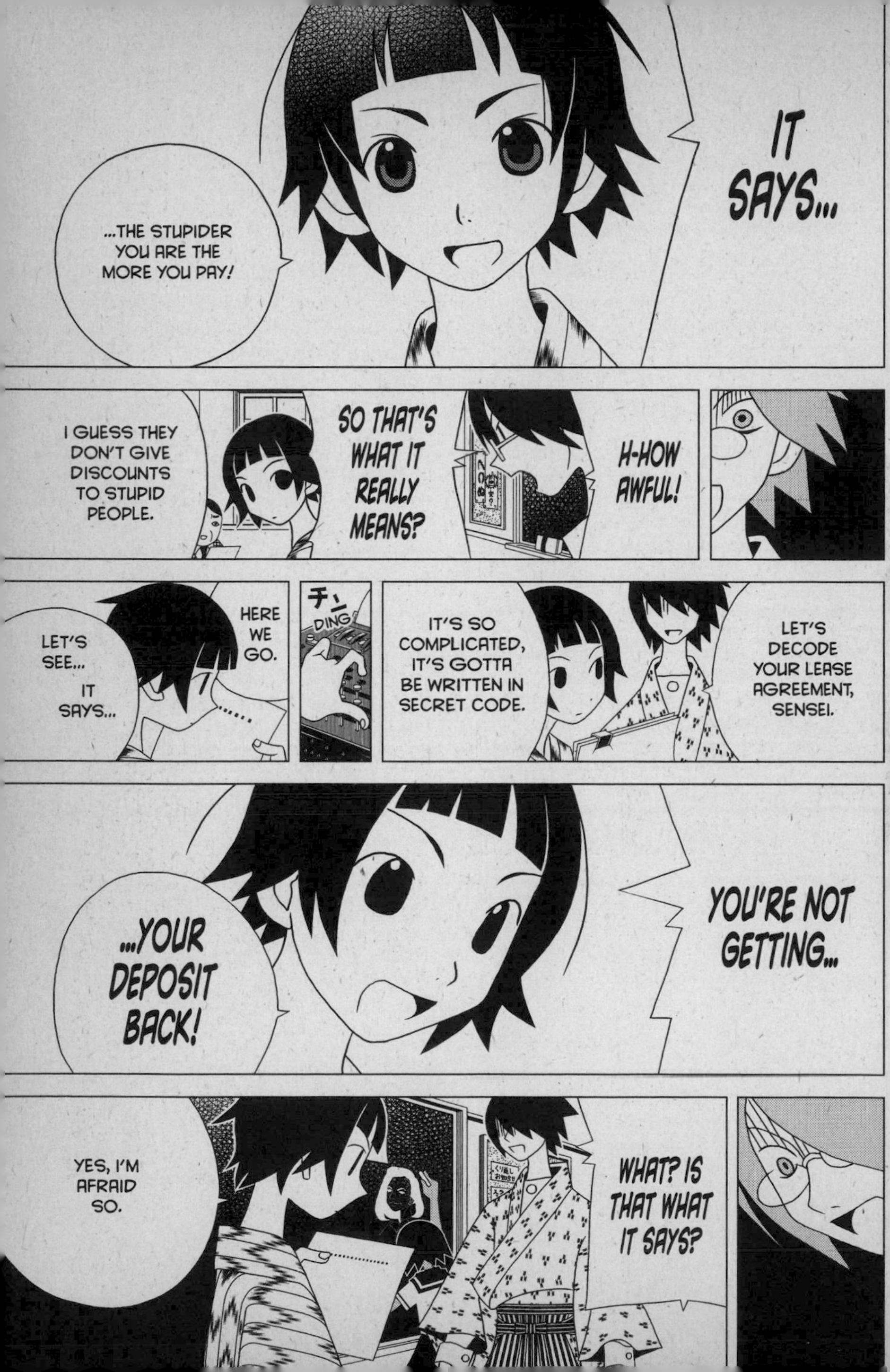
IT SAYS...
...THE STUPIDER YOU ARE THE MORE YOU PAY!
H-HOW AWFUL!
SO THAT'S WHAT IT REALLY MEANS?
I GUESS THEY DON'T GIVE DISCOUNTS TO STUPID PEOPLE.
LET'S DECODE YOUR LEASE AGREEMENT, SENSEI.
IT'S SO COMPLICATED, IT'S GOTTA BE WRITTEN IN SECRET CODE.
チン
DING
HERE WE GO.
LET'S SEE...
IT SAYS...
YOU'RE NOT GETTING...
...YOUR DEPOSIT BACK!
WHAT? IS THAT WHAT IT SAYS?
YES, I'M AFRAID SO.

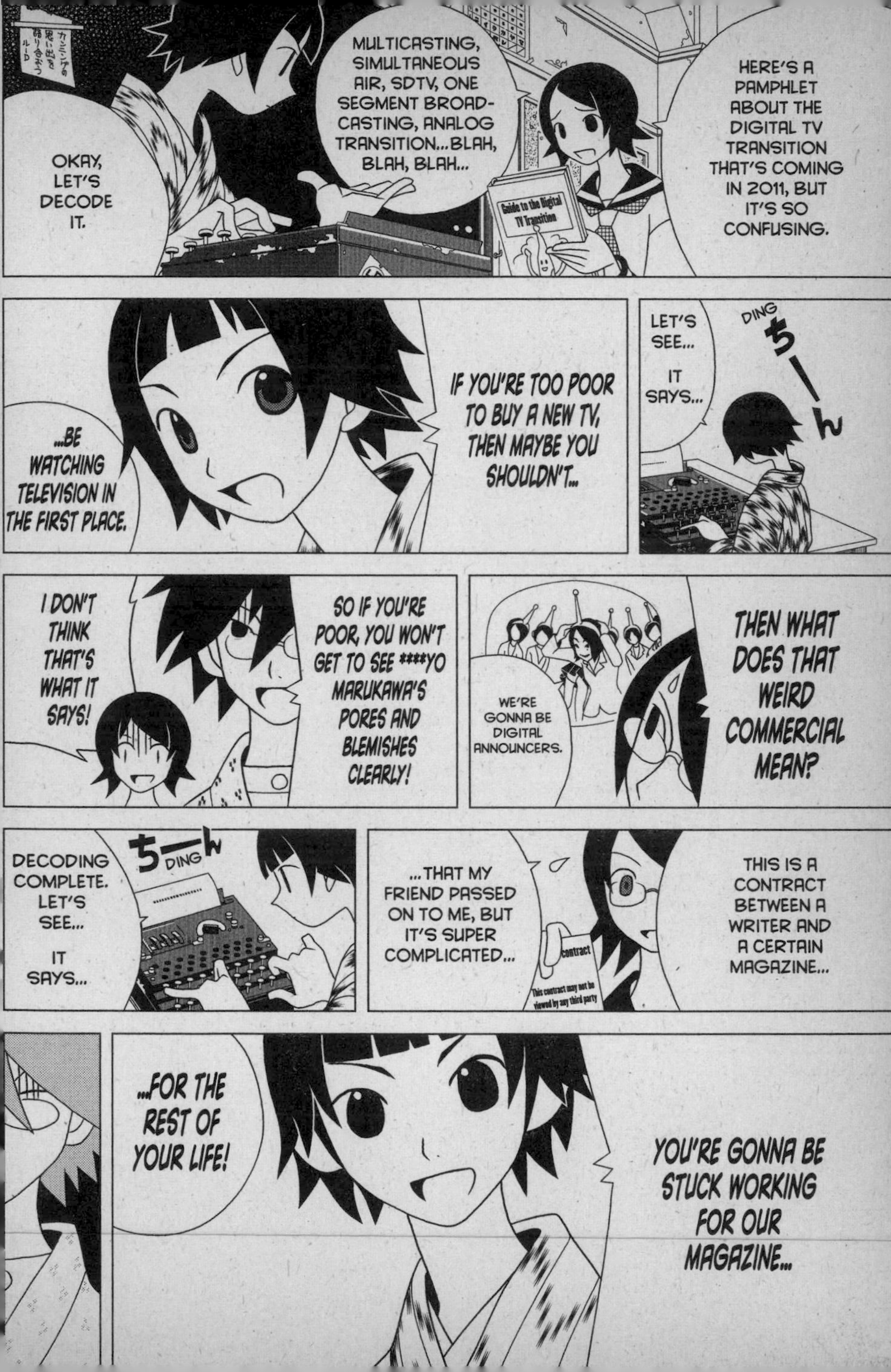
HERE'S A PAMPHLET ABOUT THE DIGITAL TV TRANSITION THAT'S COMING IN 2011, BUT IT'S SO CONFUSING.
Guide to the Digital TV Transition
MULTICASTING, SIMULTANEOUS AIR, SDTV, ONE SEGMENT BROADCASTING, ANALOG TRANSITION...BLAH, BLAH, BLAH...
OKAY, LET'S DECODE IT.
DING ちーん
LET'S SEE... IT SAYS...
IF YOU'RE TOO POOR TO BUY A NEW TV, THEN MAYBE YOU SHOULDN'T...
...BE WATCHING TELEVISION IN THE FIRST PLACE.
THEN WHAT DOES THAT WEIRD COMMERCIAL MEAN?
WE'RE GONNA BE DIGITAL ANNOUNCERS.
SO IF YOU'RE POOR, YOU WON'T GET TO SEE ****YO MARUKAWA'S PORES AND BLEMISHES CLEARLY!
I DON'T THINK THAT'S WHAT IT SAYS!
THIS IS A CONTRACT BETWEEN A WRITER AND A CERTAIN MAGAZINE...
...THAT MY FRIEND PASSED ON TO ME, BUT IT'S SUPER COMPLICATED...
contract
This contract may not be viewed by any third party
ちーん DING
DECODING COMPLETE. LET'S SEE... IT SAYS...
YOU'RE GONNA BE STUCK WORKING FOR OUR MAGAZINE...
...FOR THE REST OF YOUR LIFE!

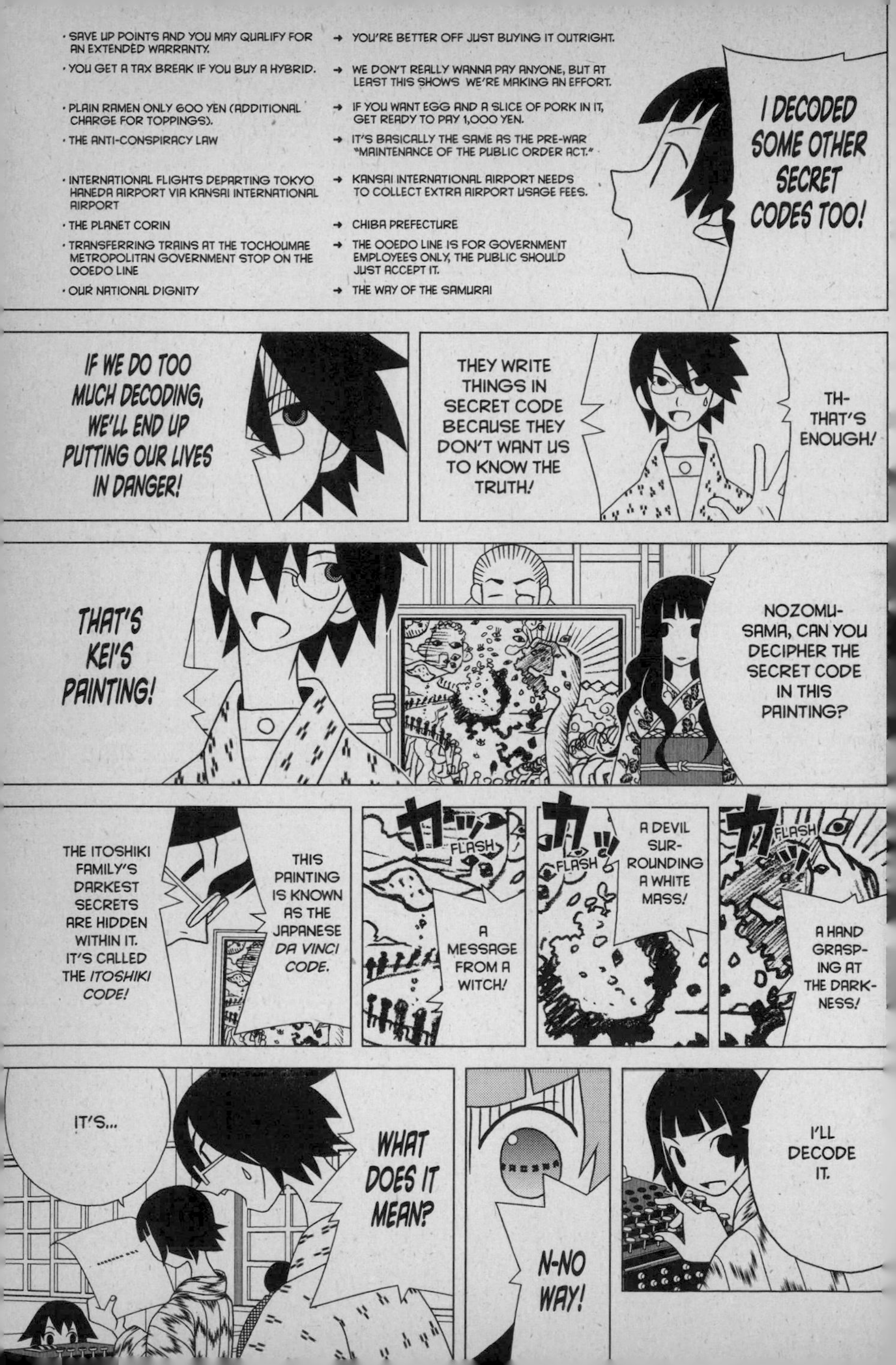
I DECODED SOME OTHER SECRET CODES TOO!
• SAVE UP POINTS AND YOU MAY QUALIFY FOR AN EXTENDED WARRANTY. → YOU'RE BETTER OFF JUST BUYING IT OUTRIGHT.
• YOU GET A TAX BREAK IF YOU BUY A HYBRID. → WE DON'T REALLY WANNA PAY ANYONE, BUT AT LEAST THIS SHOWS WE'RE MAKING AN EFFORT.
• PLAIN RAMEN ONLY 600 YEN (ADDITIONAL CHARGE FOR TOPPINGS). → IF YOU WANT EGG AND A SLICE OF PORK IN IT, GET READY TO PAY 1,000 YEN.
• THE ANTI-CONSPIRACY LAW → IT'S BASICALLY THE SAME AS THE PRE-WAR "MAINTENANCE OF THE PUBLIC ORDER ACT."
• INTERNATIONAL FLIGHTS DEPARTING TOKYO HANEDA AIRPORT VIA KANSAI INTERNATIONAL AIRPORT → KANSAI INTERNATIONAL AIRPORT NEEDS TO COLLECT EXTRA AIRPORT USAGE FEES.
• THE PLANET CORIN → CHIBA PREFECTURE
• TRANSFERRING TRAINS AT THE TOCHOUMAE METROPOLITAN GOVERNMENT STOP ON THE OOEDO LINE → THE OOEDO LINE IS FOR GOVERNMENT EMPLOYEES ONLY, THE PUBLIC SHOULD JUST ACCEPT IT.
• OUR NATIONAL DIGNITY → THE WAY OF THE SAMURAI
TH- THAT'S ENOUGH!
THEY WRITE THINGS IN SECRET CODE BECAUSE THEY DON'T WANT US TO KNOW THE TRUTH!
IF WE DO TOO MUCH DECODING, WE'LL END UP PUTTING OUR LIVES IN DANGER!
NOZOMU-SAMA, CAN YOU DECIPHER THE SECRET CODE IN THIS PAINTING?
THAT'S KEI'S PAINTING!
FLASH
A HAND GRASPING AT THE DARKNESS!
FLASH
A DEVIL SURROUNDING A WHITE MASS!
FLASH
A MESSAGE FROM A WITCH!
THIS PAINTING IS KNOWN AS THE JAPANESE *DA VINCI CODE*.
THE ITOSHIKI FAMILY'S DARKEST SECRETS ARE HIDDEN WITHIN IT. IT'S CALLED THE *ITOSHIKI CODE*!
I'LL DECODE IT.
N-NO WAY!
WHAT DOES IT MEAN?
IT'S...

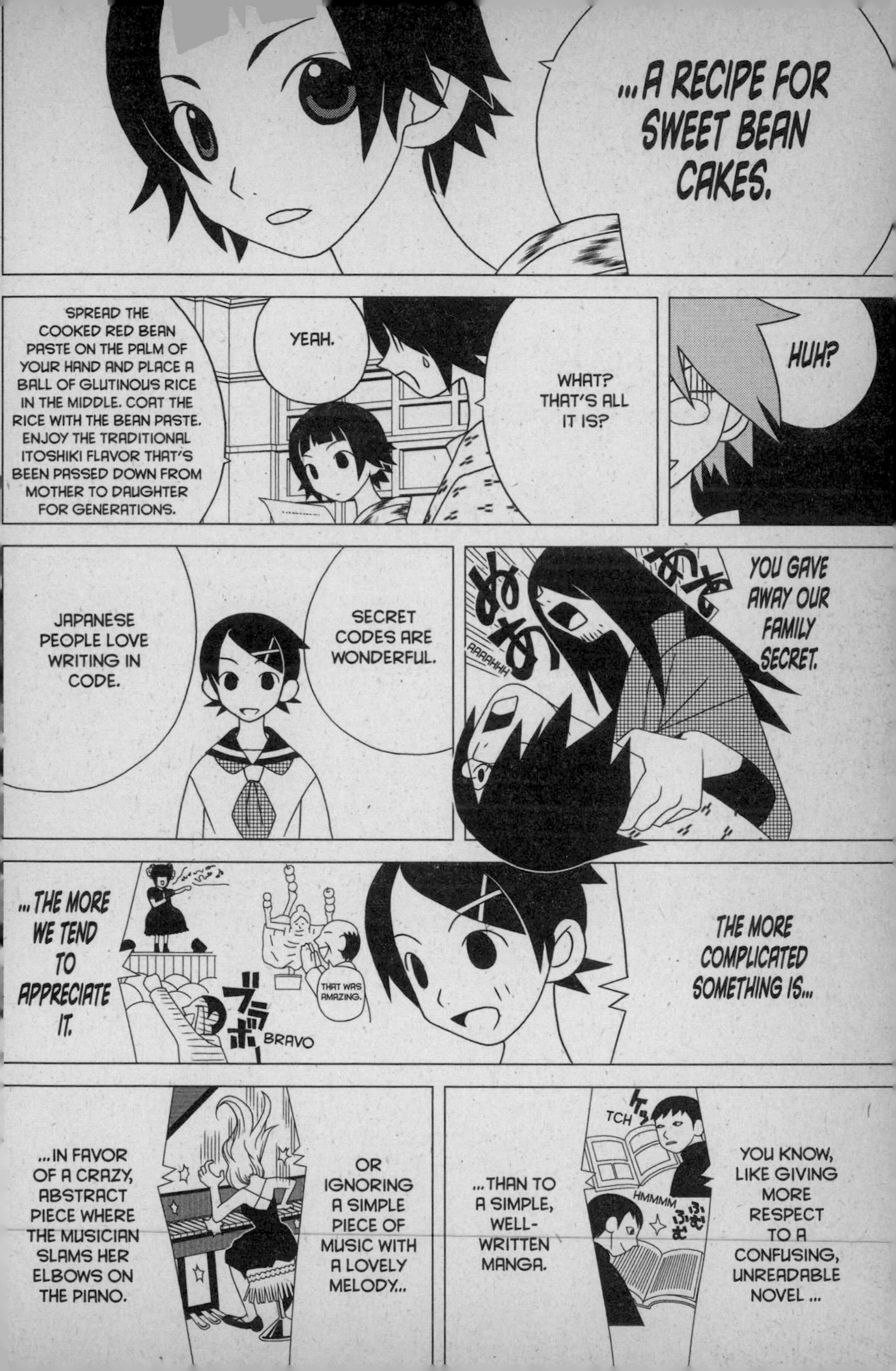
...A RECIPE FOR SWEET BEAN CAKES.
HUH?
WHAT? THAT'S ALL IT IS?
YEAH.
SPREAD THE COOKED RED BEAN PASTE ON THE PALM OF YOUR HAND AND PLACE A BALL OF GLUTINOUS RICE IN THE MIDDLE. COAT THE RICE WITH THE BEAN PASTE. ENJOY THE TRADITIONAL ITOSHIKI FLAVOR THAT'S BEEN PASSED DOWN FROM MOTHER TO DAUGHTER FOR GENERATIONS.
AAAAHHH
YOU GAVE AWAY OUR FAMILY SECRET.
SECRET CODES ARE WONDERFUL.
JAPANESE PEOPLE LOVE WRITING IN CODE.
THE MORE COMPLICATED SOMETHING IS...
THAT WAS AMAZING.
ブラボー
BRAVO
...THE MORE WE TEND TO APPRECIATE IT.
YOU KNOW, LIKE GIVING MORE RESPECT TO A CONFUSING, UNREADABLE NOVEL ...
ケッ
TCH
HMMMM
ふむふむ
...THAN TO A SIMPLE, WELL-WRITTEN MANGA.
OR IGNORING A SIMPLE PIECE OF MUSIC WITH A LOVELY MELODY...
...IN FAVOR OF A CRAZY, ABSTRACT PIECE WHERE THE MUSICIAN SLAMS HER ELBOWS ON THE PIANO.

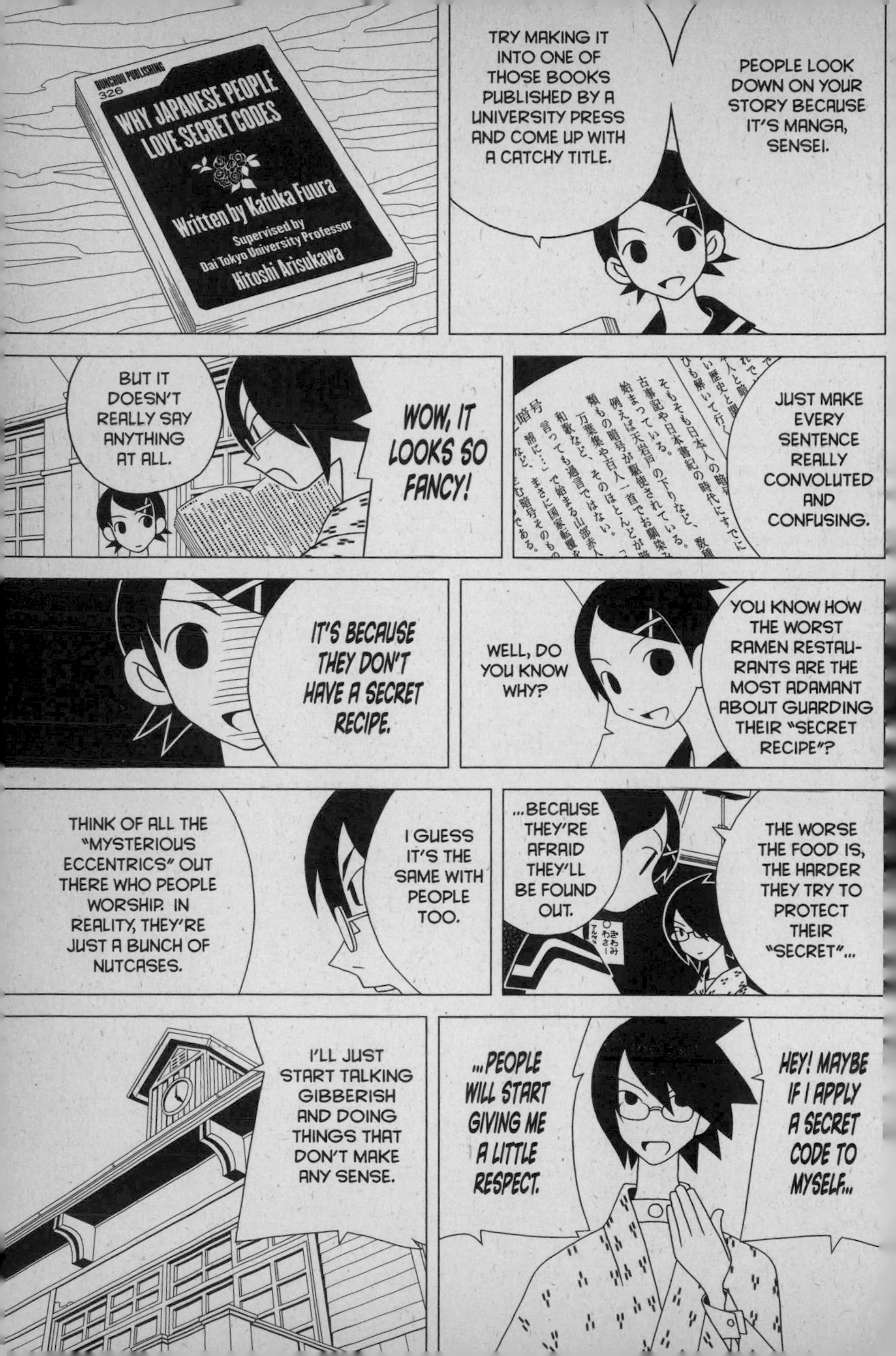
PEOPLE LOOK DOWN ON YOUR STORY BECAUSE IT'S MANGA, SENSEI.
TRY MAKING IT INTO ONE OF THOSE BOOKS PUBLISHED BY A UNIVERSITY PRESS AND COME UP WITH A CATCHY TITLE.
BUNCHOU PUBLISHING 326
WHY JAPANESE PEOPLE LOVE SECRET CODES
Written by Kafuka Fuura
Supervised by Dai Tokyo University Professor
Hitoshi Arisukawa
JUST MAKE EVERY SENTENCE REALLY CONVOLUTED AND CONFUSING.
WOW, IT LOOKS SO FANCY!
BUT IT DOESN'T REALLY SAY ANYTHING AT ALL.
YOU KNOW HOW THE WORST RAMEN RESTAURANTS ARE THE MOST ADAMANT ABOUT GUARDING THEIR "SECRET RECIPE"?
WELL, DO YOU KNOW WHY?
IT'S BECAUSE THEY DON'T HAVE A SECRET RECIPE.
THE WORSE THE FOOD IS, THE HARDER THEY TRY TO PROTECT THEIR "SECRET"...
...BECAUSE THEY'RE AFRAID THEY'LL BE FOUND OUT.
I GUESS IT'S THE SAME WITH PEOPLE TOO.
THINK OF ALL THE "MYSTERIOUS ECCENTRICS" OUT THERE WHO PEOPLE WORSHIP. IN REALITY, THEY'RE JUST A BUNCH OF NUTCASES.
HEY! MAYBE IF I APPLY A SECRET CODE TO MYSELF...
...PEOPLE WILL START GIVING ME A LITTLE RESPECT.
I'LL JUST START TALKING GIBBERISH AND DOING THINGS THAT DON'T MAKE ANY SENSE.

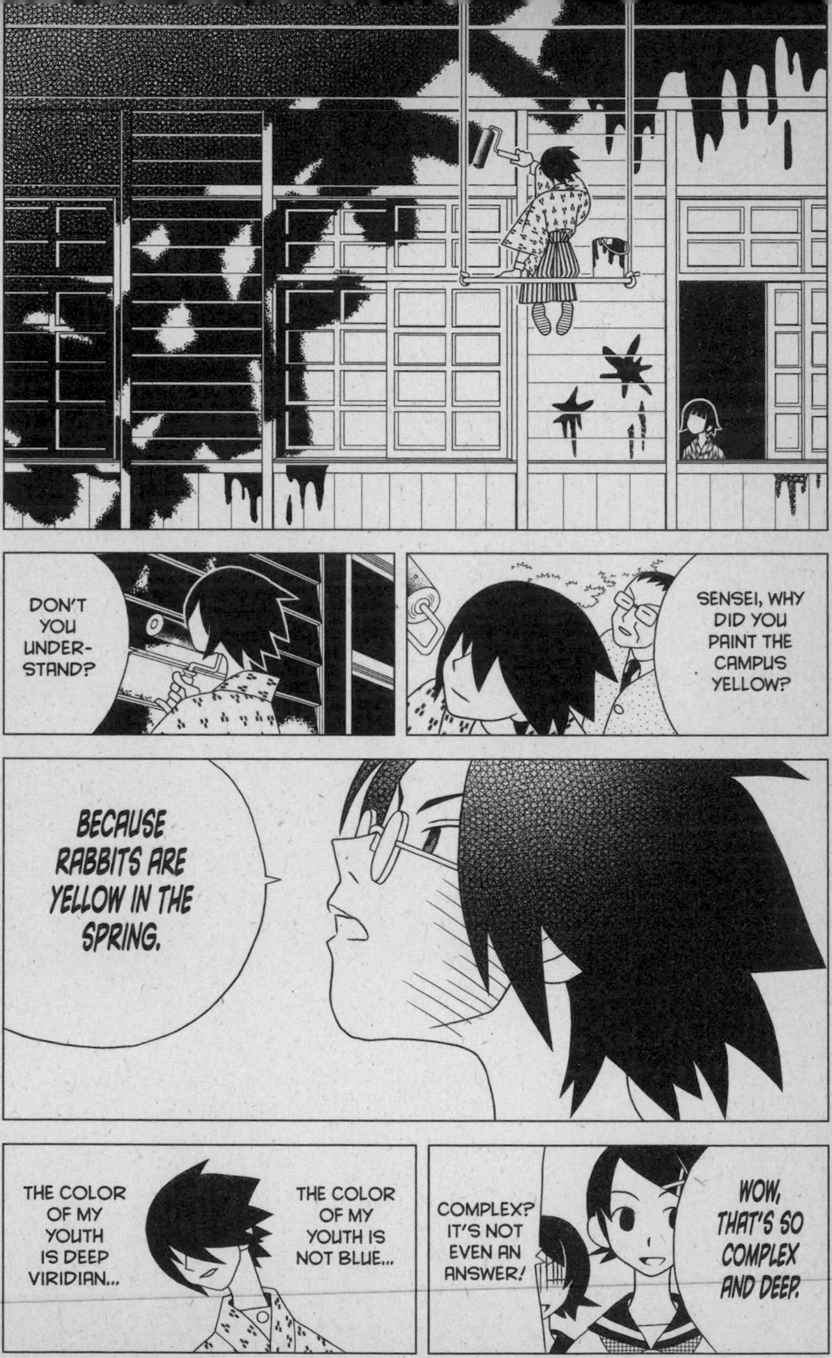
SENSEI, WHY DID YOU PAINT THE CAMPUS YELLOW?
DON'T YOU UNDERSTAND?
BECAUSE RABBITS ARE YELLOW IN THE SPRING.
WOW, THAT'S SO COMPLEX AND DEEP.
COMPLEX? IT'S NOT EVEN AN ANSWER!
THE COLOR OF MY YOUTH IS NOT BLUE...
THE COLOR OF MY YOUTH IS DEEP VIRIDIAN...

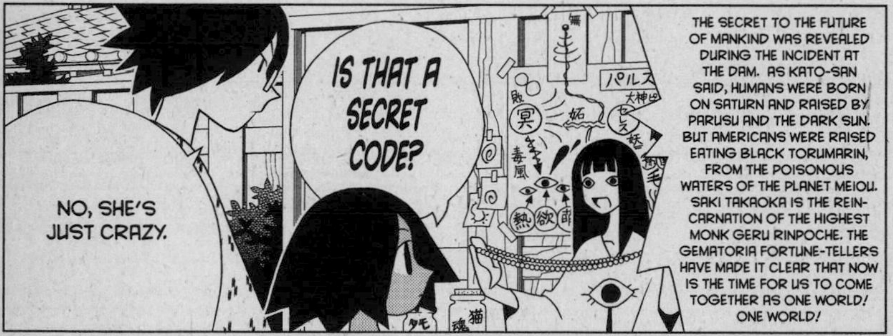
THE SECRET TO THE FUTURE OF MANKIND WAS REVEALED DURING THE INCIDENT AT THE DAM. AS KATO-SAN SAID, HUMANS WERE BORN ON SATURN AND RAISED BY PARUSU AND THE DARK SUN. BUT AMERICANS WERE RAISED EATING BLACK TORUMARIN, FROM THE POISONOUS WATERS OF THE PLANET MEIOU. SAKI TAKAOKA IS THE REINCARNATION OF THE HIGHEST MONK GERU RINPOCHE. THE GEMATORIA FORTUNE-TELLERS HAVE MADE IT CLEAR THAT NOW IS THE TIME FOR US TO COME TOGETHER AS ONE WORLD! ONE WORLD!
IS THAT A SECRET CODE?
NO, SHE'S JUST CRAZY.

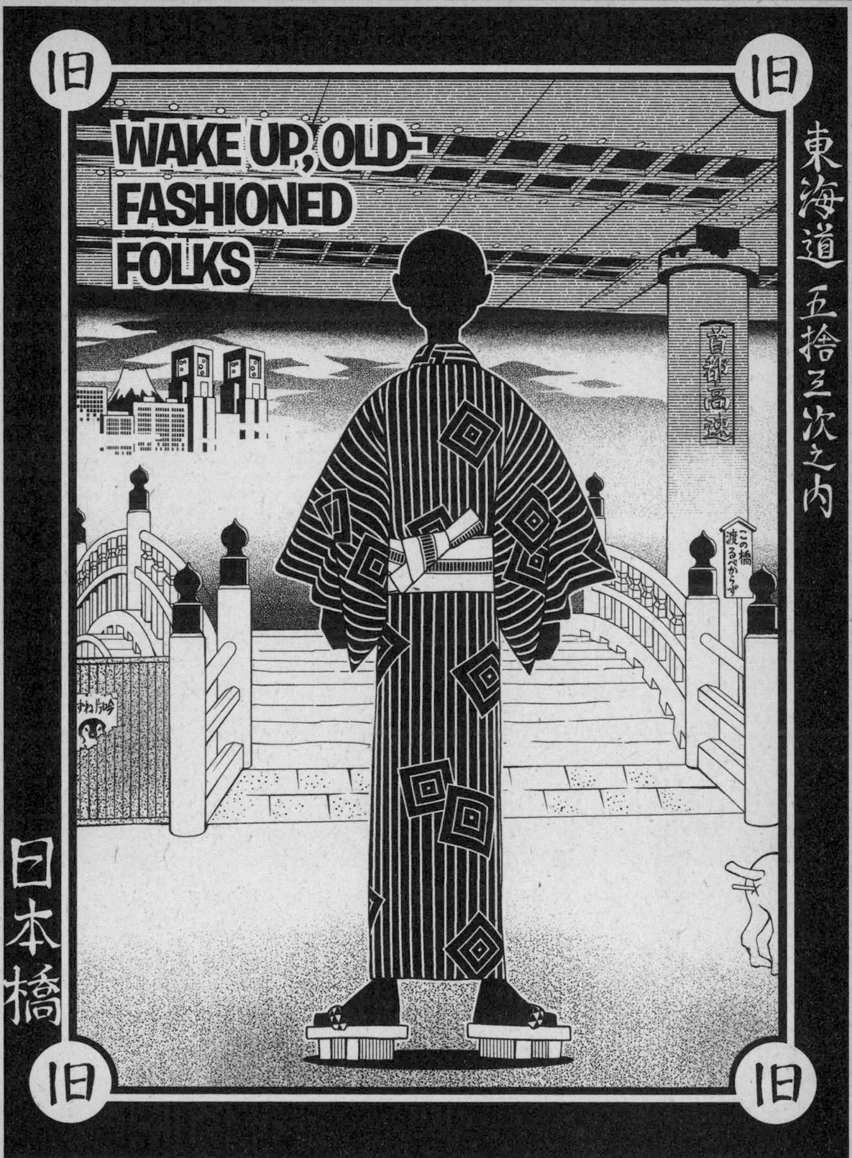
旧
旧
WAKE UP, OLD-FASHIONED FOLKS
東海道 五捨三次之内
首都高速
この橋渡るべからず
日本橋
旧
旧

CHAPTER 50

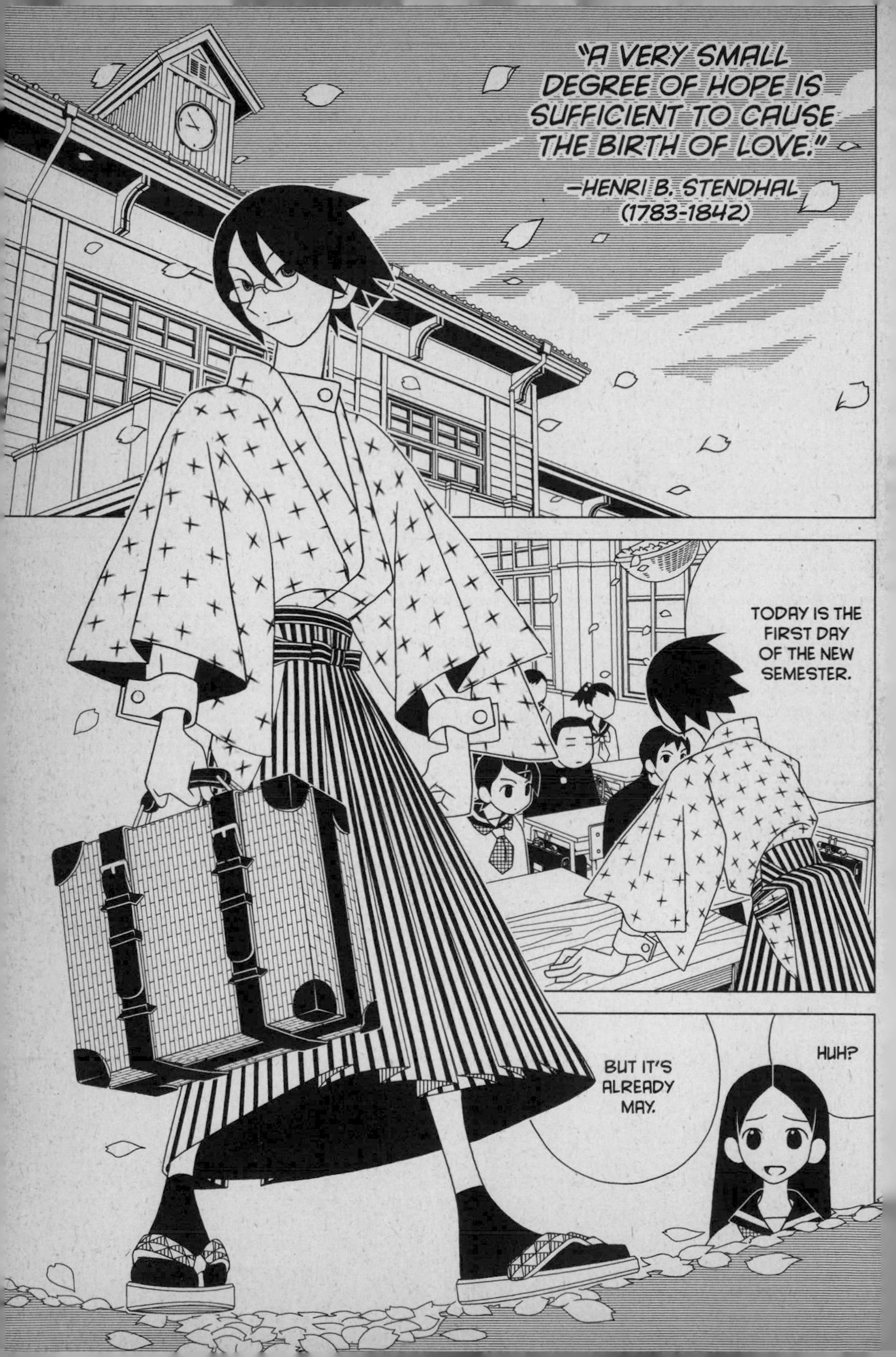
"A VERY SMALL DEGREE OF HOPE IS SUFFICIENT TO CAUSE THE BIRTH OF LOVE."
–HENRI B. STENDHAL (1783-1842)
TODAY IS THE FIRST DAY OF THE NEW SEMESTER.
HUH?
BUT IT'S ALREADY MAY.

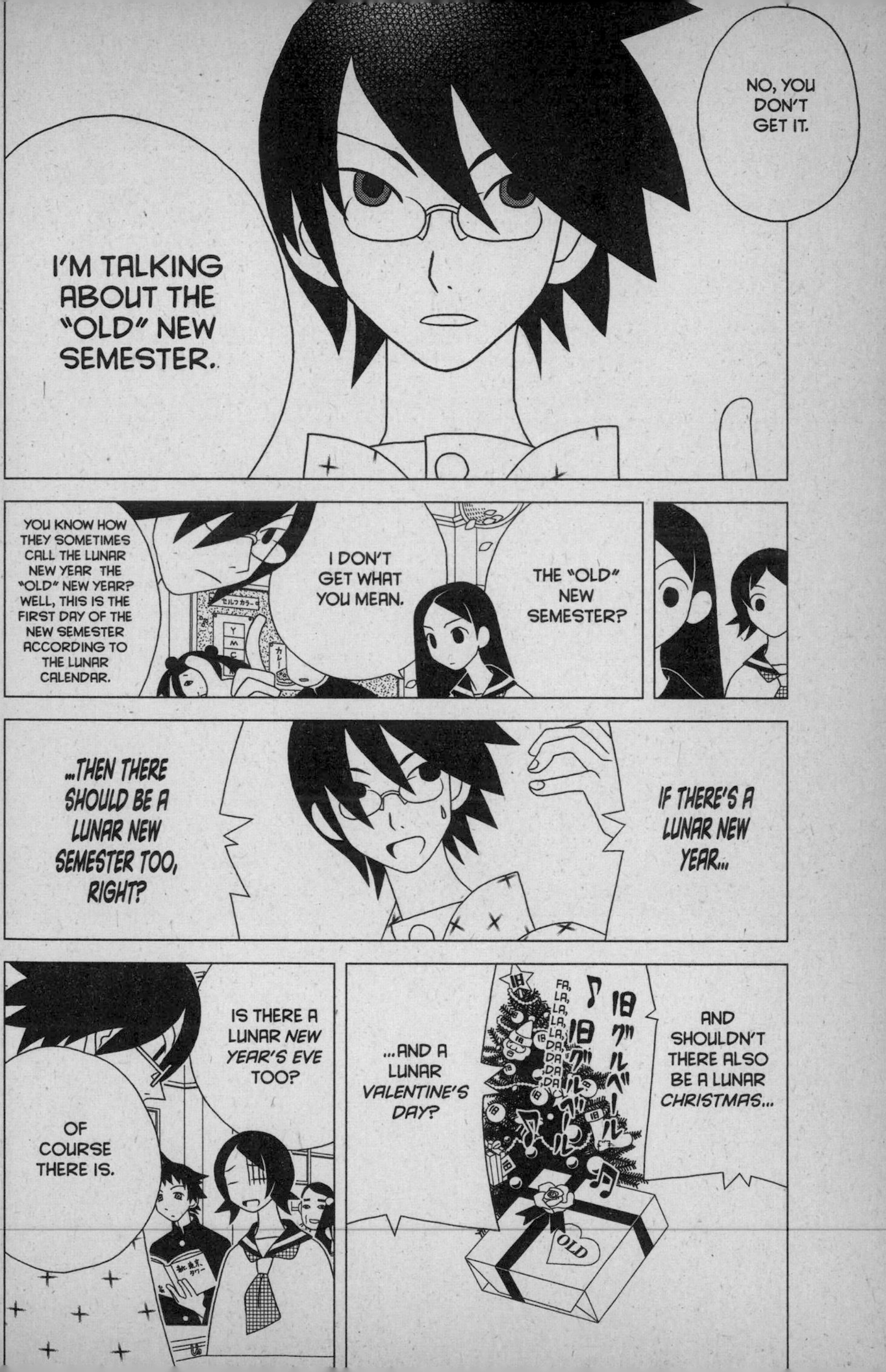
NO, YOU DON'T GET IT.
I'M TALKING ABOUT THE "OLD" NEW SEMESTER.
THE "OLD" NEW SEMESTER?
I DON'T GET WHAT YOU MEAN.
YOU KNOW HOW THEY SOMETIMES CALL THE LUNAR NEW YEAR THE "OLD" NEW YEAR? WELL, THIS IS THE FIRST DAY OF THE NEW SEMESTER ACCORDING TO THE LUNAR CALENDAR.
IF THERE'S A LUNAR NEW YEAR...
...THEN THERE SHOULD BE A LUNAR NEW SEMESTER TOO, RIGHT?
AND SHOULDN'T THERE ALSO BE A LUNAR *CHRISTMAS*...
FA, LA, LA, LA, LA, DA, DA, DA, DA
OLD
...AND A LUNAR *VALENTINE'S DAY*?
IS THERE A LUNAR *NEW YEAR'S EVE* TOO?
OF COURSE THERE IS.

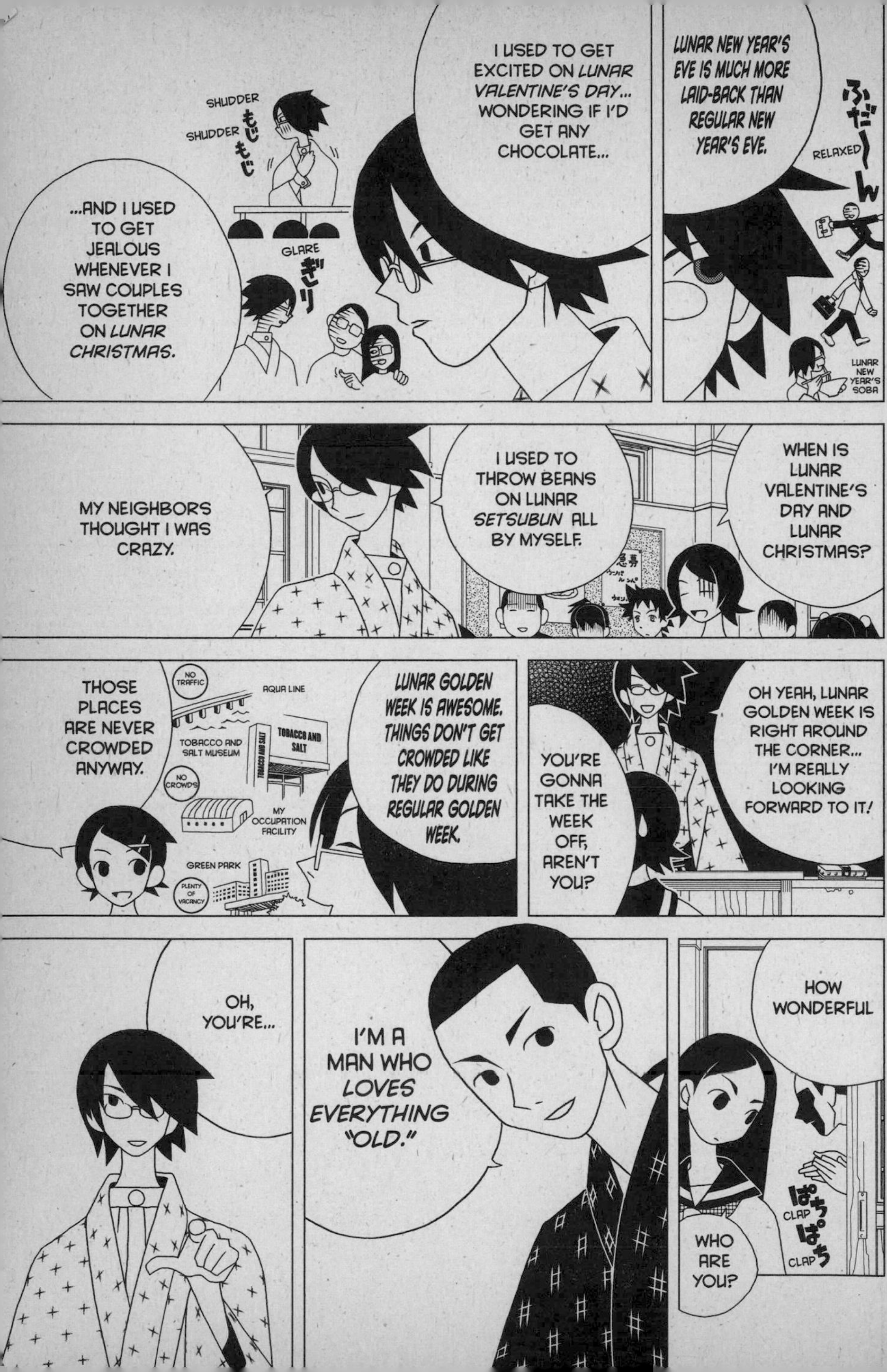
LUNAR NEW YEAR'S EVE IS MUCH MORE LAID-BACK THAN REGULAR NEW YEAR'S EVE.
ふだ～ん
RELAXED
LUNAR NEW YEAR'S SOBA
I USED TO GET EXCITED ON LUNAR VALENTINE'S DAY... WONDERING IF I'D GET ANY CHOCOLATE...
もじ
SHUDDER
もじ
SHUDDER
...AND I USED TO GET JEALOUS WHENEVER I SAW COUPLES TOGETHER ON LUNAR CHRISTMAS.
ぎろり
GLARE
WHEN IS LUNAR VALENTINE'S DAY AND LUNAR CHRISTMAS?
I USED TO THROW BEANS ON LUNAR SETSUBUN ALL BY MYSELF.
MY NEIGHBORS THOUGHT I WAS CRAZY.
OH YEAH, LUNAR GOLDEN WEEK IS RIGHT AROUND THE CORNER... I'M REALLY LOOKING FORWARD TO IT!
YOU'RE GONNA TAKE THE WEEK OFF, AREN'T YOU?
LUNAR GOLDEN WEEK IS AWESOME. THINGS DON'T GET CROWDED LIKE THEY DO DURING REGULAR GOLDEN WEEK.
THOSE PLACES ARE NEVER CROWDED ANYWAY.
NO TRAFFIC
AQUA LINE
TOBACCO AND SALT
TOBACCO AND SALT MUSEUM
NO CROWDS
MY OCCUPATION FACILITY
GREEN PARK
PLENTY OF VACANCY
HOW WONDERFUL
ぱちぱち
CLAP
CLAP
WHO ARE YOU?
I'M A MAN WHO LOVES EVERYTHING "OLD."
OH, YOU'RE...

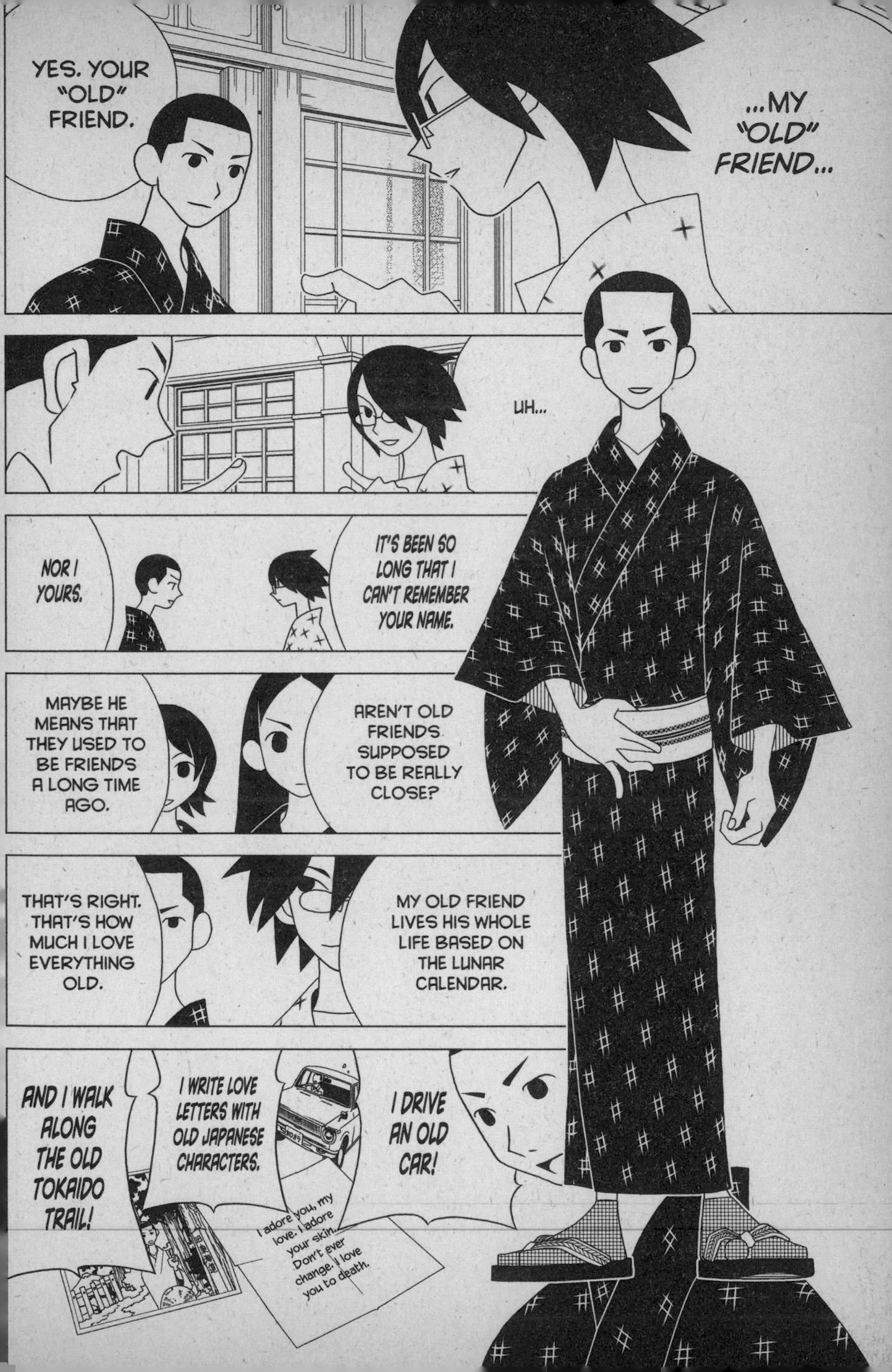

...MY "OLD" FRIEND...
YES. YOUR "OLD" FRIEND.
UH...
IT'S BEEN SO LONG THAT I CAN'T REMEMBER YOUR NAME.
NOR I YOURS.
AREN'T OLD FRIENDS SUPPOSED TO BE REALLY CLOSE?
MAYBE HE MEANS THAT THEY USED TO BE FRIENDS A LONG TIME AGO.
MY OLD FRIEND LIVES HIS WHOLE LIFE BASED ON THE LUNAR CALENDAR.
THAT'S RIGHT. THAT'S HOW MUCH I LOVE EVERYTHING OLD.
I DRIVE AN OLD CAR!
I WRITE LOVE LETTERS WITH OLD JAPANESE CHARACTERS.
I adore you, my love. I adore your skin. Don't ever change. I love you to death.
AND I WALK ALONG THE OLD TOKAIDO TRAIL!

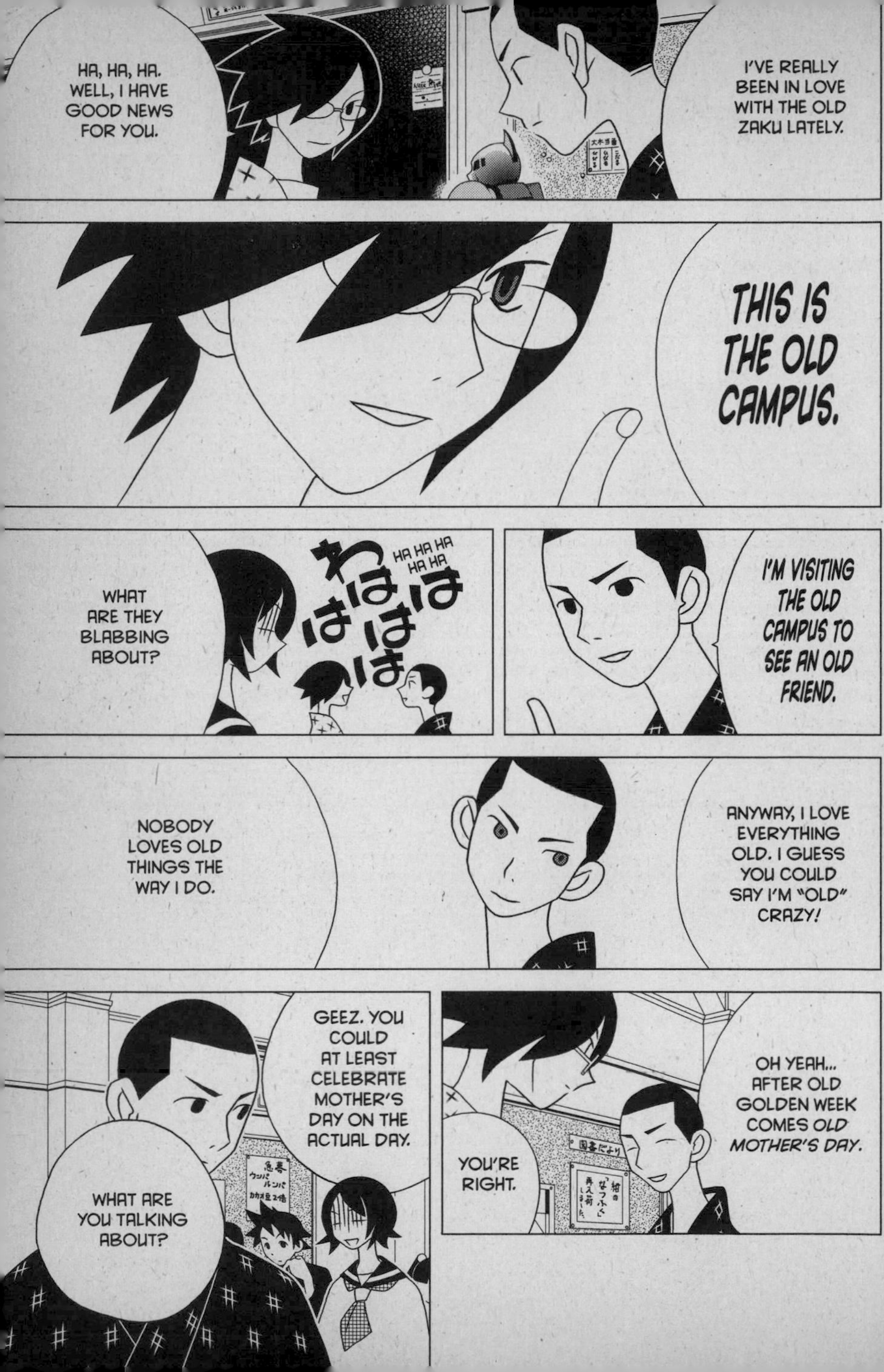
I'VE REALLY BEEN IN LOVE WITH THE OLD ZAKU LATELY.
HA, HA, HA. WELL, I HAVE GOOD NEWS FOR YOU.
THIS IS THE OLD CAMPUS.
I'M VISITING THE OLD CAMPUS TO SEE AN OLD FRIEND.
わははははは
HA HA HA HA HA
WHAT ARE THEY BLABBING ABOUT?
ANYWAY, I LOVE EVERYTHING OLD. I GUESS YOU COULD SAY I'M "OLD" CRAZY!
NOBODY LOVES OLD THINGS THE WAY I DO.
OH YEAH... AFTER OLD GOLDEN WEEK COMES *OLD MOTHER'S DAY*.
YOU'RE RIGHT.
GEEZ. YOU COULD AT LEAST CELEBRATE MOTHER'S DAY ON THE ACTUAL DAY.
WHAT ARE YOU TALKING ABOUT?

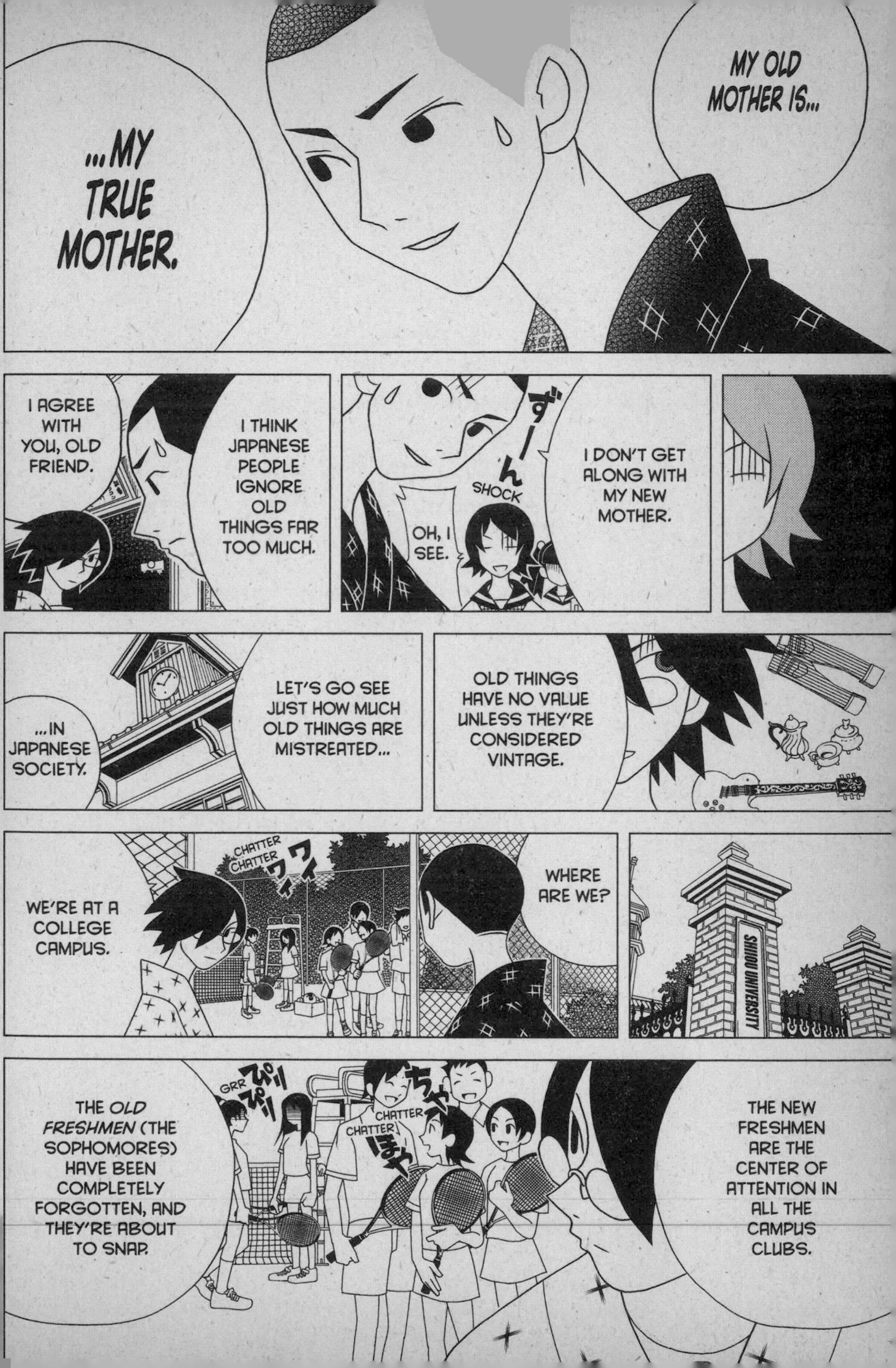
MY OLD MOTHER IS...
...MY TRUE MOTHER.
I DON'T GET ALONG WITH MY NEW MOTHER.
ずーん
SHOCK
OH, I SEE.
I THINK JAPANESE PEOPLE IGNORE OLD THINGS FAR TOO MUCH.
I AGREE WITH YOU, OLD FRIEND.
OLD THINGS HAVE NO VALUE UNLESS THEY'RE CONSIDERED VINTAGE.
LET'S GO SEE JUST HOW MUCH OLD THINGS ARE MISTREATED...
...IN JAPANESE SOCIETY.
SHIOU UNIVERSITY
WHERE ARE WE?
CHATTER CHATTER
ワイワイ
WE'RE AT A COLLEGE CAMPUS.
THE NEW FRESHMEN ARE THE CENTER OF ATTENTION IN ALL THE CAMPUS CLUBS.
CHATTER CHATTER
GRR
ぴりぴり
THE *OLD FRESHMEN* (THE SOPHOMORES) HAVE BEEN COMPLETELY FORGOTTEN, AND THEY'RE ABOUT TO SNAP.

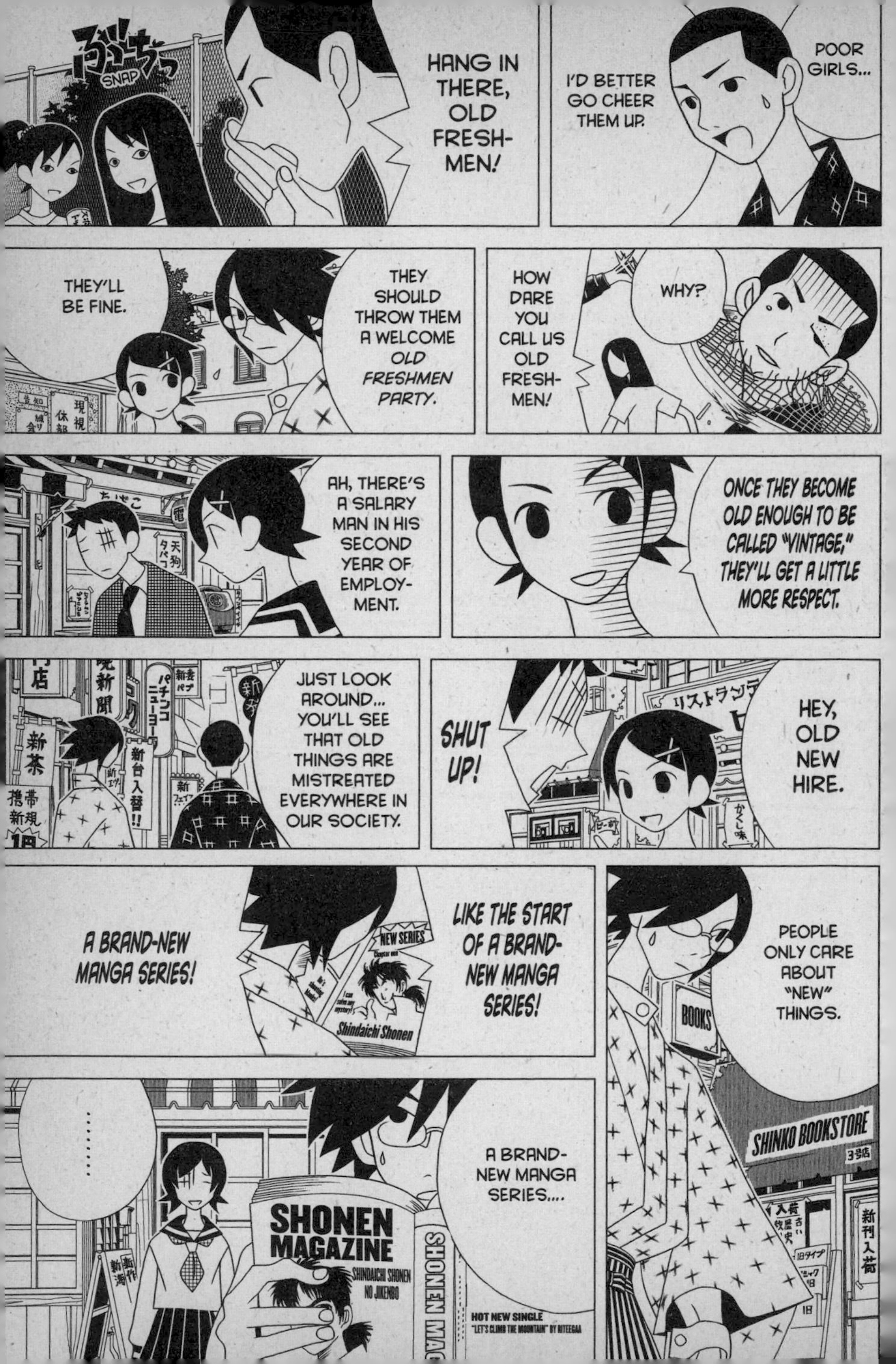

POOR GIRLS...
I'D BETTER GO CHEER THEM UP.
HANG IN THERE, OLD FRESHMEN!
SNAP
WHY?
HOW DARE YOU CALL US OLD FRESHMEN!
THEY SHOULD THROW THEM A WELCOME *OLD FRESHMEN PARTY.*
THEY'LL BE FINE.
ONCE THEY BECOME OLD ENOUGH TO BE CALLED "VINTAGE," THEY'LL GET A LITTLE MORE RESPECT.
AH, THERE'S A SALARY MAN IN HIS SECOND YEAR OF EMPLOYMENT.
HEY, OLD NEW HIRE.
SHUT UP!
JUST LOOK AROUND... YOU'LL SEE THAT OLD THINGS ARE MISTREATED EVERYWHERE IN OUR SOCIETY.
PEOPLE ONLY CARE ABOUT "NEW" THINGS.
BOOKS
SHINKO BOOKSTORE
LIKE THE START OF A BRAND-NEW MANGA SERIES!
NEW SERIES
Shindaichi Shonen
A BRAND-NEW MANGA SERIES!
A BRAND-NEW MANGA SERIES....
SHONEN MAGAZINE
SHINDAICHI SHONEN NO JIKENBO
SHONEN MAG
HOT NEW SINGLE
"LET'S CLIMB THE MOUNTAIN" BY NITEGAA
......

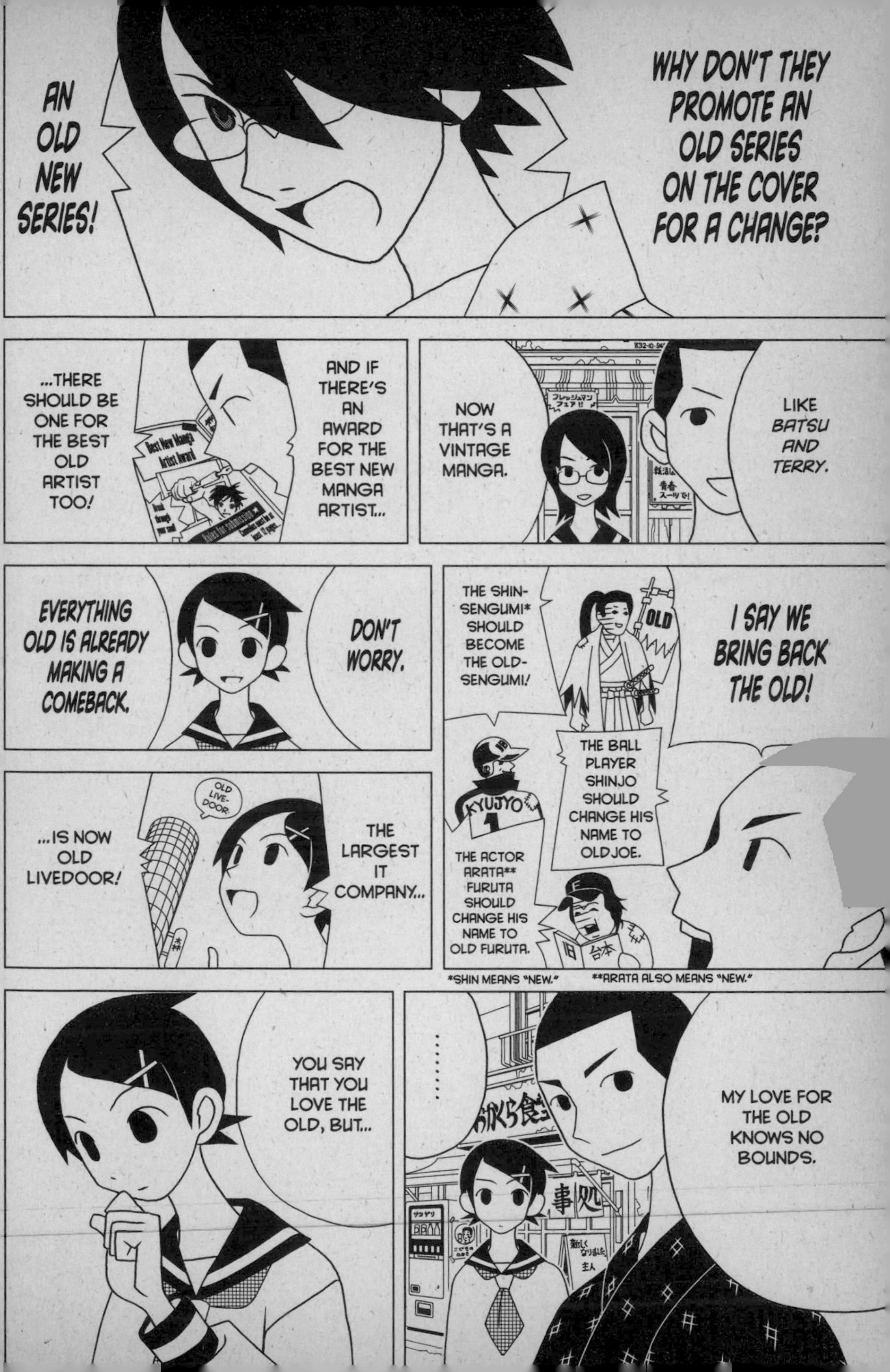
WHY DON'T THEY PROMOTE AN OLD SERIES ON THE COVER FOR A CHANGE?
AN OLD NEW SERIES!
LIKE BATSU AND TERRY.
NOW THAT'S A VINTAGE MANGA.
AND IF THERE'S AN AWARD FOR THE BEST NEW MANGA ARTIST...
...THERE SHOULD BE ONE FOR THE BEST OLD ARTIST TOO!
Best New Manga Artist Award
I SAY WE BRING BACK THE OLD!
THE SHIN-SENGUMI* SHOULD BECOME THE OLD-SENGUMI!
OLD
THE BALL PLAYER SHINJO SHOULD CHANGE HIS NAME TO OLDJOE.
KYUJYO
THE ACTOR ARATA** FURUTA SHOULD CHANGE HIS NAME TO OLD FURUTA.
旧 台本
DON'T WORRY.
EVERYTHING OLD IS ALREADY MAKING A COMEBACK.
THE LARGEST IT COMPANY...
OLD LIVE-DOOR.
...IS NOW OLD LIVEDOOR!
*SHIN MEANS "NEW."
**ARATA ALSO MEANS "NEW."
MY LOVE FOR THE OLD KNOWS NO BOUNDS.
......
YOU SAY THAT YOU LOVE THE OLD, BUT...

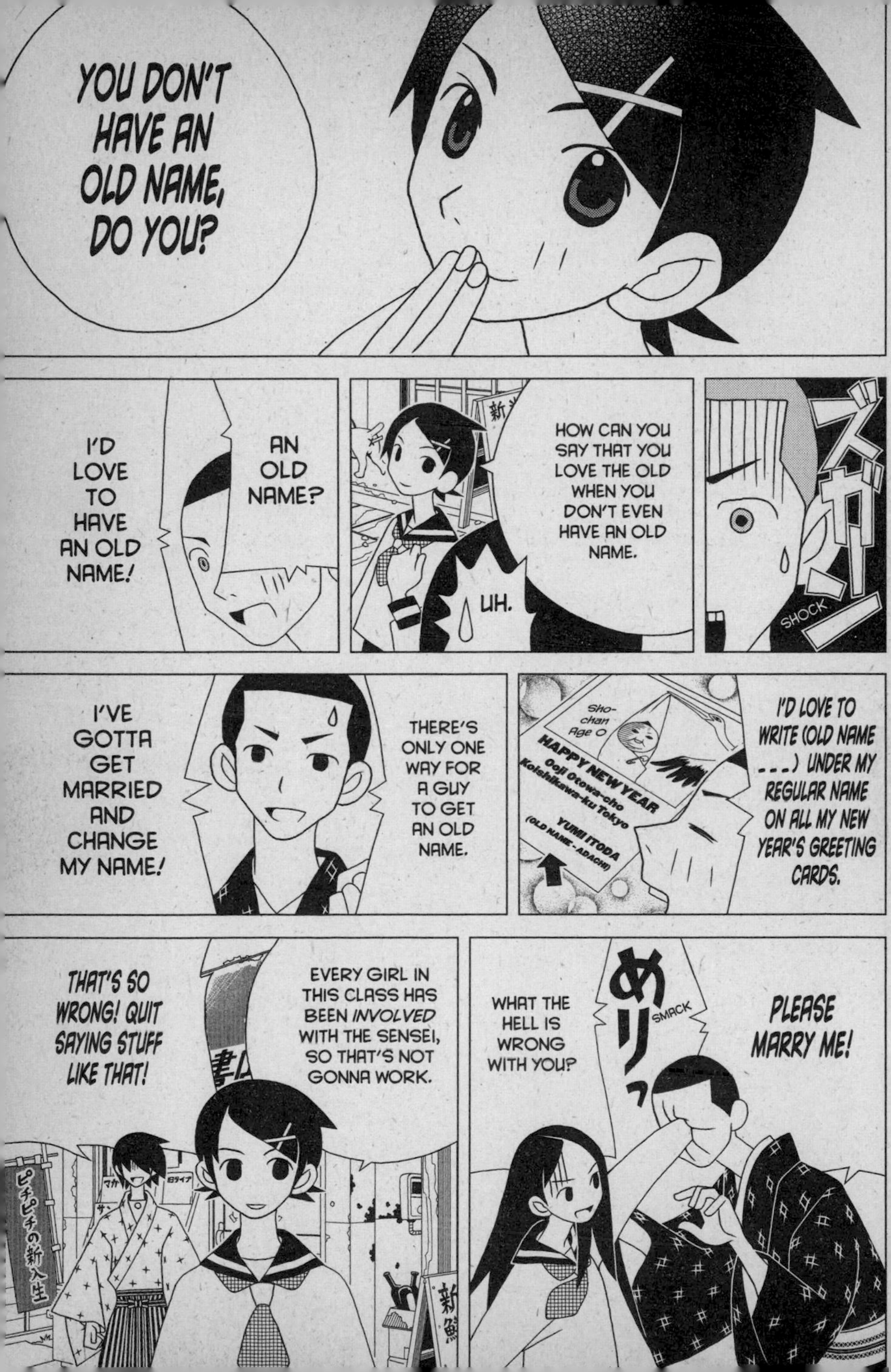
YOU DON'T HAVE AN OLD NAME, DO YOU?
ズガーン
SHOCK
HOW CAN YOU SAY THAT YOU LOVE THE OLD WHEN YOU DON'T EVEN HAVE AN OLD NAME.
UH.
AN OLD NAME?
I'D LOVE TO HAVE AN OLD NAME!
I'D LOVE TO WRITE (OLD NAME ---) UNDER MY REGULAR NAME ON ALL MY NEW YEAR'S GREETING CARDS.
Sho-chan Age 0
HAPPY NEW YEAR
Ooji Otowa-cho Koishikawa-ku Tokyo
YUMI ITODA
(OLD NAME - ADACHI)
THERE'S ONLY ONE WAY FOR A GUY TO GET AN OLD NAME.
I'VE GOTTA GET MARRIED AND CHANGE MY NAME!
PLEASE MARRY ME!
めりっ
SMACK
WHAT THE HELL IS WRONG WITH YOU?
EVERY GIRL IN THIS CLASS HAS BEEN *INVOLVED* WITH THE SENSEI, SO THAT'S NOT GONNA WORK.
THAT'S SO WRONG! QUIT SAYING STUFF LIKE THAT!
ピチピチの新入生

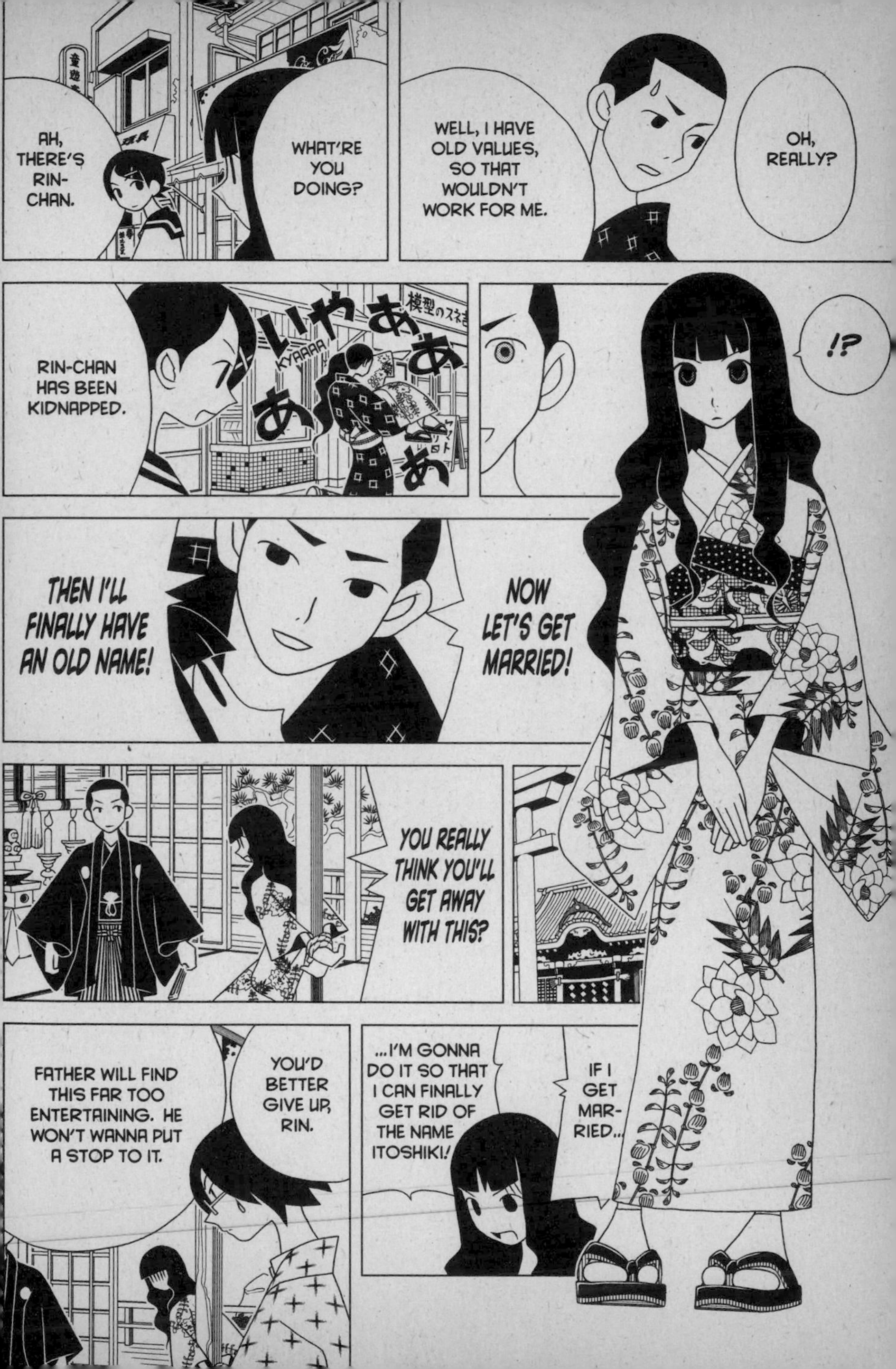
OH, REALLY?
WELL, I HAVE OLD VALUES, SO THAT WOULDN'T WORK FOR ME.
WHAT'RE YOU DOING?
AH, THERE'S RIN-CHAN.
!?
模型のスネ吉
いやあああ
KYAAAA
RIN-CHAN HAS BEEN KIDNAPPED.
NOW LET'S GET MARRIED!
THEN I'LL FINALLY HAVE AN OLD NAME!
YOU REALLY THINK YOU'LL GET AWAY WITH THIS?
IF I GET MARRIED...
...I'M GONNA DO IT SO THAT I CAN FINALLY GET RID OF THE NAME ITOSHIKI!
YOU'D BETTER GIVE UP, RIN.
FATHER WILL FIND THIS FAR TOO ENTERTAINING. HE WON'T WANNA PUT A STOP TO IT.

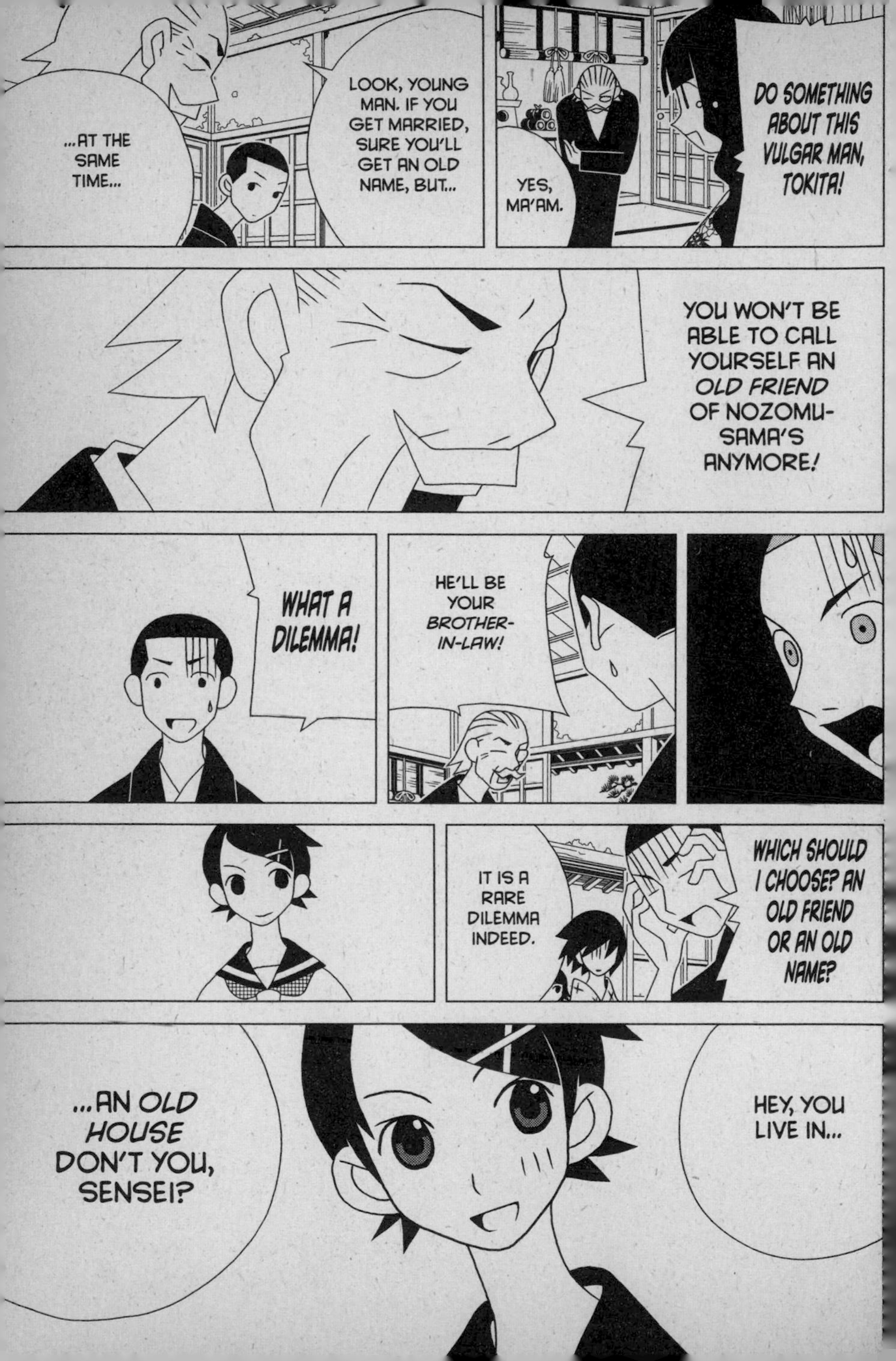
DO SOMETHING ABOUT THIS VULGAR MAN, TOKITA!
YES, MA'AM.
LOOK, YOUNG MAN. IF YOU GET MARRIED, SURE YOU'LL GET AN OLD NAME, BUT...
...AT THE SAME TIME...
YOU WON'T BE ABLE TO CALL YOURSELF AN *OLD FRIEND* OF NOZOMU-SAMA'S ANYMORE!
HE'LL BE YOUR *BROTHER-IN-LAW!*
WHAT A DILEMMA!
WHICH SHOULD I CHOOSE? AN OLD FRIEND OR AN OLD NAME?
IT IS A RARE DILEMMA INDEED.
HEY, YOU LIVE IN...
...AN *OLD HOUSE* DON'T YOU, SENSEI?

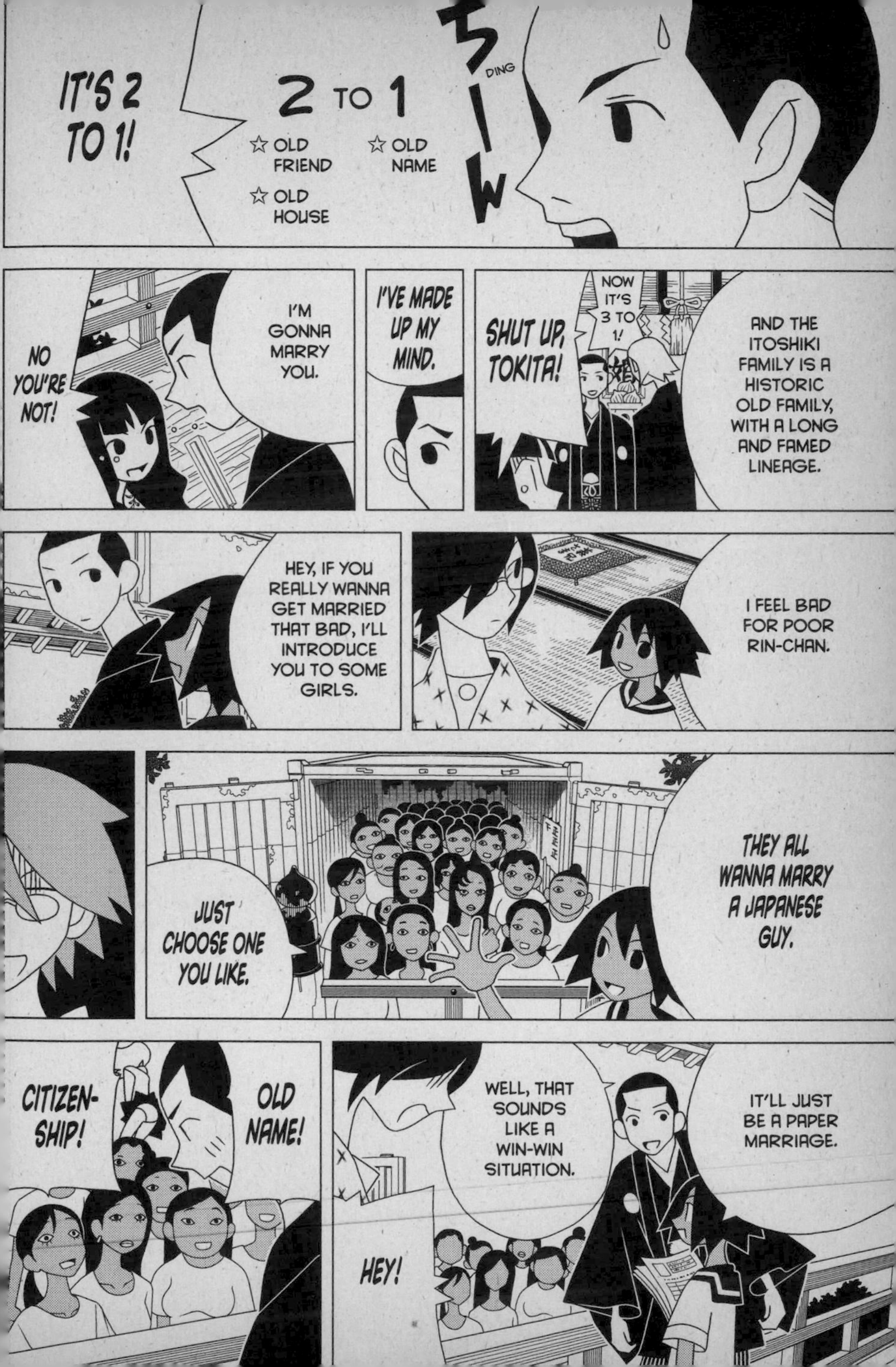
DING
2 TO 1
☆ OLD FRIEND
☆ OLD NAME
☆ OLD HOUSE
IT'S 2 TO 1!
AND THE ITOSHIKI FAMILY IS A HISTORIC OLD FAMILY, WITH A LONG AND FAMED LINEAGE.
NOW IT'S 3 TO 1!
SHUT UP, TOKITA!
I'VE MADE UP MY MIND.
I'M GONNA MARRY YOU.
NO YOU'RE NOT!
I FEEL BAD FOR POOR RIN-CHAN.
HEY, IF YOU REALLY WANNA GET MARRIED THAT BAD, I'LL INTRODUCE YOU TO SOME GIRLS.
THEY ALL WANNA MARRY A JAPANESE GUY.
JUST CHOOSE ONE YOU LIKE.
IT'LL JUST BE A PAPER MARRIAGE.
WELL, THAT SOUNDS LIKE A WIN-WIN SITUATION.
HEY!
OLD NAME!
CITIZEN-SHIP!

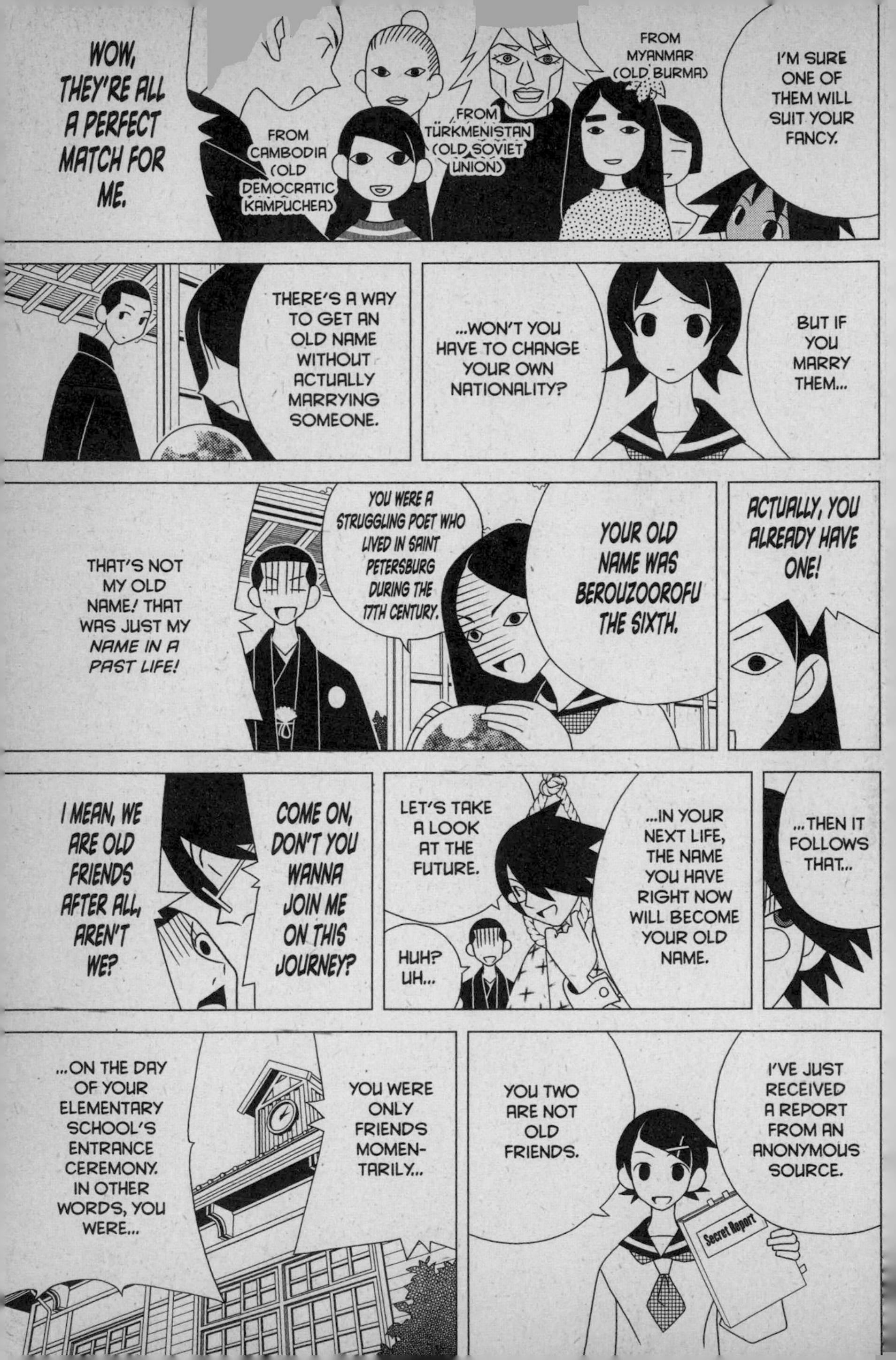
I'M SURE ONE OF THEM WILL SUIT YOUR FANCY.
FROM MYANMAR (OLD BURMA)
FROM TÜRKMENISTAN (OLD SOVIET UNION)
FROM CAMBODIA (OLD DEMOCRATIC KAMPUCHEA)
WOW, THEY'RE ALL A PERFECT MATCH FOR ME.
BUT IF YOU MARRY THEM...
...WON'T YOU HAVE TO CHANGE YOUR OWN NATIONALITY?
THERE'S A WAY TO GET AN OLD NAME WITHOUT ACTUALLY MARRYING SOMEONE.
ACTUALLY, YOU ALREADY HAVE ONE!
YOUR OLD NAME WAS BEROUZOOROFU THE SIXTH.
YOU WERE A STRUGGLING POET WHO LIVED IN SAINT PETERSBURG DURING THE 17TH CENTURY.
THAT'S NOT MY OLD NAME! THAT WAS JUST MY NAME IN A PAST LIFE!
...THEN IT FOLLOWS THAT...
...IN YOUR NEXT LIFE, THE NAME YOU HAVE RIGHT NOW WILL BECOME YOUR OLD NAME.
LET'S TAKE A LOOK AT THE FUTURE.
HUH? UH...
COME ON, DON'T YOU WANNA JOIN ME ON THIS JOURNEY?
I MEAN, WE ARE OLD FRIENDS AFTER ALL, AREN'T WE?
I'VE JUST RECEIVED A REPORT FROM AN ANONYMOUS SOURCE.
YOU TWO ARE NOT OLD FRIENDS.
Secret Report
YOU WERE ONLY FRIENDS MOMEN-TARILY...
...ON THE DAY OF YOUR ELEMENTARY SCHOOL'S ENTRANCE CEREMONY. IN OTHER WORDS, YOU WERE...

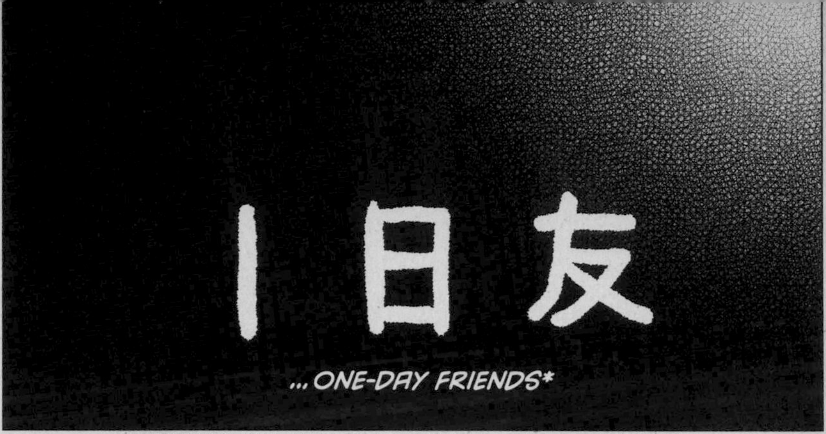
1日友
...ONE-DAY FRIENDS*

*WHEN COMBINED, THE CHARACTERS USED TO WRITE "ONE DAY" FORM THE CHARACTER FOR "OLD."

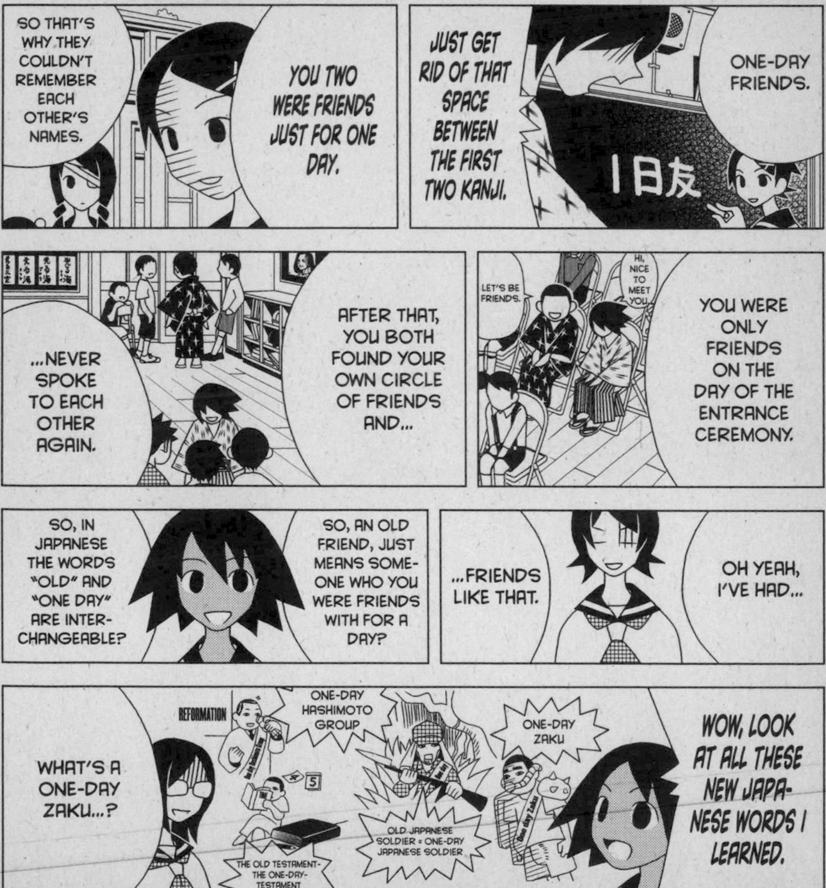
ONE-DAY FRIENDS.
1日友
JUST GET RID OF THAT SPACE BETWEEN THE FIRST TWO KANJI.
YOU TWO WERE FRIENDS JUST FOR ONE DAY.
SO THAT'S WHY THEY COULDN'T REMEMBER EACH OTHER'S NAMES.
YOU WERE ONLY FRIENDS ON THE DAY OF THE ENTRANCE CEREMONY.
HI, NICE TO MEET YOU.
LET'S BE FRIENDS.
AFTER THAT, YOU BOTH FOUND YOUR OWN CIRCLE OF FRIENDS AND...
...NEVER SPOKE TO EACH OTHER AGAIN.
OH YEAH, I'VE HAD...
...FRIENDS LIKE THAT.
SO, AN OLD FRIEND, JUST MEANS SOME-ONE WHO YOU WERE FRIENDS WITH FOR A DAY?
SO, IN JAPANESE THE WORDS "OLD" AND "ONE DAY" ARE INTER-CHANGEABLE?
WOW, LOOK AT ALL THESE NEW JAPA-NESE WORDS I LEARNED.
ONE-DAY ZAKU
OLD JAPANESE SOLDIER = ONE-DAY JAPANESE SOLDIER
ONE-DAY HASHIMOTO GROUP
REFORMATION
THE OLD TESTAMENT- THE ONE-DAY-TESTAMENT
WHAT'S A ONE-DAY ZAKU...?

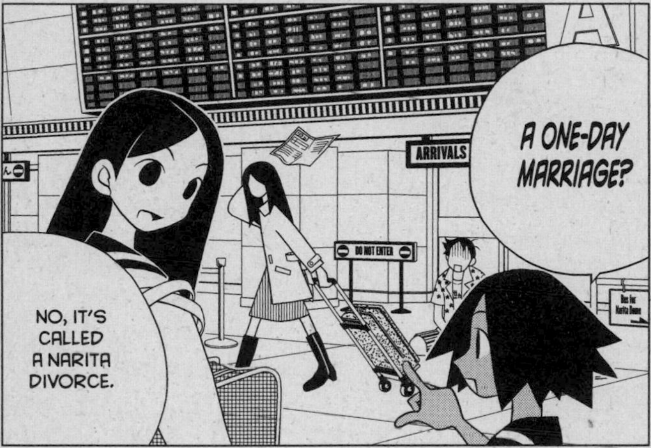
A ONE-DAY MARRIAGE?
ARRIVALS
DO NOT ENTER
NO, IT'S CALLED A NARITA DIVORCE.

CURRENT CHARGES FROM THIS ISSUE

LETTER OF ACCUSATION

PLAINTIFF:
OCCUPATION: STUDENT
NAME: KAERE KIMURA

DEFENDANT:
OCCUPATION: HOSTESS
NAME: N/A

DATE: MARCH 16
ATTN: CHIEF OF POLICE

- ACCUSATION

THE ACTS BY THE DEFENDANT AS STATED BELOW ARE CONSIDERED TO FALL UNDER CRIMINAL LAW, ARTICLE 203 (CRIME OF ATTEMPTED MURDER), AND THIS COMPLAINT IS MADE TO PURSUE SEVERE PUNISHMENT TO BE HANDED OUT TO THE DEFENDANT.

1. FACTS REGARDING THE ACCUSATION

 AT ABOUT 6:00 PM, WHEN MY FRIENDS AND I ARRIVED AT THE INN, THE DEFENDANT BECAME JEALOUS OF MY YOUTH AND BEAUTY, AND ATTEMPTED TO ASSASSINATE ME.

SHE TOOK ADVANTAGE OF HER ROLE AS HOSTESS AND SET A TRAP FOR ME IN THE INN'S BATHING AREA. SHE SET IT UP SO THAT I WOULD SLIP AND FALL TO MY DEATH AND IT WOULD APPEAR TO BE A MERE ACCIDENT.

WHEN HER PLAN FAILED, SHE FEIGNED IGNORANCE AND HANDED ME A BAND-AID. IT WAS OBVIOUS THAT SHE WAS TRYING TO CONCEAL ALL EVIDENCE.

THE AFOREMENTIONED ACTS ARE CONSIDERED TO FALL UNDER CRIMINAL LAW, ARTICLE 203 (CRIME OF ATTEMPTED MURDER), AND I HEREBY FILE THIS CHARGE IN ORDER TO INSURE THAT THE SUSPECT BE SENTENCED TO THE STRICTEST PUNISHMENT POSSIBLE.

2. EVIDENCE
    1. WITNESS: CLASSMATE A
    2. MEDICAL CERTIFICATE ISSUED BY A DOCTOR FROM THE UNIVERSITY HOSPITAL

        SUPPLEMENTARY DOCUMENTS
        THE ABOVE-MENTIONED MEDICAL CERTIFICATE - ONE CERTIFICATE

PAPER BLOGS

PREAMBLE | WHITE LIES | DETOX

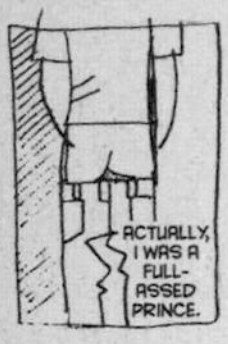
ACTUALLY, I WAS A FULL-ASSED PRINCE.

ALTHOUGH I HAD NO INTEREST WHATSOEVER, PEOPLE SEEMED PRETTY EXCITED OVER THIS SUMMER'S HIGH SCHOOL BASEBALL WORLD SERIES...HERE I AM, STARTING OFF WITH A GENERAL TOPIC. THE HANDKERCHIEF PRINCE IS QUITE POPULAR NOWADAYS. A LONG TIME AGO, PEOPLE USED TO CALL ME A HALF-ASSED PRINCE.

I'M NOT GONNA FORGIVE MYSELF FOR WHO I WAS WHEN I WAS YOUNGER. I'M PROBABLY NOT GONNA CHANGE MY MIND TILL THE DAY I DIE. I'M NOT GONNA FORGIVE MYSELF FOR WHO I WAS LAST YEAR. I'M NOT GONNA FORGIVE MYSELF FOR WHO I WAS YESTERDAY. I'M NOT GONNA FORGIVE MYSELF FOR WHO I WAS EARLIER. THE REASON I'M SUFFERING FROM A PULLED MUSCLE RIGHT NOW IS BECAUSE I WAS UNPREPARED IN THE PAST. WHEN I'M IN MY NEXT LIFE, I'M NOT GONNA FORGIVE MYSELF FOR WHO I WAS IN MY PAST LIFE.

PREAMBLE | **WHITE LIES** | DETOX

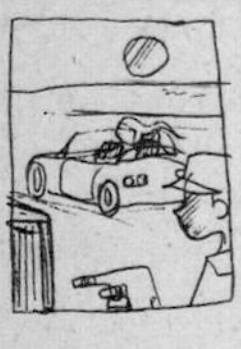

THERE ARE WHITE LIES TOLD WITH GOOD INTENTIONS AND BLACK LIES TOLD WITH EVIL INTENTIONS. I'VE ALSO HEARD PEOPLE TALK ABOUT RED LIES, SO I GUESS LIES COME IN ALL DIFFERENT COLORS. I WONDER WHAT OTHER COLORED LIES ARE LIKE. IF YOU LIED WHEN YOU WERE YOUNG, THAT WOULD BE A BLUE LIE. FOR EXAMPLE, IF YOU LIED ABOUT HAVING A SEXUAL EXPERIENCE DURING THE SUMMER...THAT'D BE A BLUE LIE. LET ME GIVE YOU AN EXAMPLE. SUMMER BREAK WAS ALMOST OVER. SOMEHOW, THE OCEAN LOOKED TOTALLY DIFFERENT IN THE SUMMER. I WAS WORKING AT A GAS STATION NEAR THE BEACH. ONE DAY, A RED ROADSTER CAME IN, AND THE DRIVER ASKED, "CAN YOU WASH THE WINDOWS FOR ME?" "SURE," I REPLIED. THAT WAS MY FIRST CONVERSATION WITH NAGISA. NAGISA WAS A COLLEGE STUDENT IN TOKYO. SHE WAS FOUR YEARS OLDER THAN ME. SHE WAS MATURE AND SEXY, YET AS INNOCENT AS A LITTLE GIRL. (TEXT PARTIALLY OMITTED) NAGISA SMILED AT ME, AND SUDDENLY PULLED INTO A MOTEL. "WHAT DO YOU WANNA DO, LITTLE BOY?" SHE SMILED AGAIN AND LOOKED ME UP AND DOWN WITH HER SEDUCTIVE EYES. (TEXT PARTIALLY OMITTED) THE SKIN BENEATH HER SHIRT WAS THE IVORY COLOR OF FINE WHITE LINEN. (TEXT PARTIALLY OMITTED) WHEN I PUT MY ARMS AROUND HER, I FELT HER BODY SHIVER. ALTHOUGH SHE SEEMED LIKE A PLAYGIRL ON THE OUTSIDE, SHE WAS AS PURE AND INNOCENT AS WHITE LINEN. (TEXT PARTIALLY OMITTED) I WAS INEXPERIENCED, AND THAT WAS AS FAR AS I COULD TAKE THINGS. WE ENDED UP STAYING UP ALL NIGHT TALKING ABOUT THE STARS....I GUESS YOU CAN CALL THIS A BLUE LIE. A LIE THAT'S "ALMOST TRANSPARENT BLUE" IS BLUE, BUT IT'S A VERY LIGHT KIND OF BLUE. A GOOD EXAMPLE OF A TRANSPARENT BLUE WOULD BE...LYING ABOUT MEETING A GIRL IN A *SWIMMING POOL*. HERE ARE SOME OTHER COLORS OF LIES: A GREEN LIE → LYING ABOUT RECYCLING, OR OTHER ENVIRONMENTALLY FRIENDLY ACTIVITIES....LIKE AN OIL COMPANY ADVERTISEMENT. A YELLOW LIE → WHEN AN INDIAN FRIEND TELLS YOU THAT A CURRY ISN'T THAT SPICY, WHEN IT'S ACTUALLY CRAZY HOT. THERE ARE LIES THAT GO WITH EVERY COLOR OF THE RAINBOW. WHAT COLOR ARE MY LIES, YOU ASK? HMMM....

PREAMBLE | WHITE LIES | **DETOX**

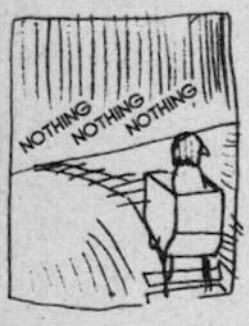
NOTHING NOTHING NOTHING

SOME PEOPLE COMPLAIN THAT I CAN BE TOO HARSH AND OTHERS THAT I AM NOT HARSH ENOUGH. I'VE CHOSEN SUCH AN UNFORTUNATE PATH. I CAN'T MAKE ANY MONEY ON THIS PATH. PEOPLE GET MAD WHEN I TALK SHIT ABOUT OTHER PEOPLE. BUT PEOPLE GET MAD WHEN I SAY NICE THINGS TOO. I'VE CHOSEN SUCH AN UNFORTUNATE PATH. I WANTED TO BE LOVED BY EVERYONE AND CREATE A MANGA THAT WOULD BE MADE INTO AN ANIME. I WANTED TO BE LOVED, AND MAKE LOTS OF MONEY AND LIVE IN A GORGEOUS CONDO WHERE I COULD GROW HERBS AND GO TO FINISHING SCHOOL. IS THAT EVER GONNA HAPPEN? WAIT, DOES SUCH A PATH EVEN EXIST?

SNOW MELTING | SELF-COMPLETING | MINOTAKE MEASUREMENT | TOO MUCH EVIDENCE

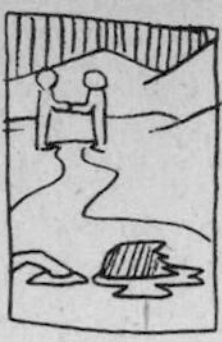

WHENEVER SOMEBODY EXPERIENCES "SNOW MELTING," I'M THE ONE WHO GETS SOAKED BY THE DIRTY, GRAY WATER. WHEN THE SNOW MELTS, IT TURNS INTO A RIVER, AND I GET SOAKED. WHEN I WAS IN JUNIOR HIGH, THE CAPTAIN AND THE COACH HAD A SNOW MELTING EXPERIENCE, AND I ENDED UP BEING BENCHED THE WHOLE SEASON. YEP, I GOT SOAKED BY GRAY WATER. ONE TIME, MY CHIEF EDITOR AND A CERTAIN MANGA ARTIST HAD A SNOW MELTING EXPERIENCE, AND I WAS ASKED TO QUIT WRITING FOR A MAGAZINE. YEP, I GOT SOAKED BY GRAY WATER. SNOW MELTING IS FINE ONCE IN A WHILE, BUT PEOPLE SHOULD KNOW THAT THERE'S ALWAYS SOMEBODY WHO GETS SOAKED BY THE RESULTING GRAY WATER. SO PLEASE STOP FIGHTING AND RECONCILING FOR GOD'S SAKE. THE DIRTY WATER ALWAYS FLOWS TO THE BOTTOM.

SNOW MELTING | **SELF-COMPLETING** | MINOTAKE MEASUREMENT | TOO MUCH EVIDENCE

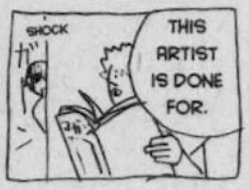
THIS ARTIST IS DONE FOR.
SHOCK

I HEARD SOMEBODY SAY, "THIS MANGA IS OVER" AFTER READING THE FIRST CHAPTER OF *ZETSUBOU SENSEI*. TO HIM, MY MANGA WAS ALREADY COMPLETE. WELL, SORRY THAT MY ALREADY "COMPLETED" SERIES HAS GONE ALL THE WAY TO VOLUME FIVE. THE END WAS ACTUALLY THE BEGINNING. NAH, THAT SOUNDS TOO COOL. IT WAS THE BEGINNING OF THE END. PEOPLE START TO GET OLD THE MOMENT THEY ARE BORN. I'D SAY THE SAME THING ABOUT THIS MANGA. THE MOMENT IT WAS BORN, IT WAS ALREADY OLD. IT'S AS IF A MAN WERE BORN AT THE AGE OF EIGHTY-EIGHT...AND COULD DIE AT ANY MOMENT. THAT'S WHAT THIS MANGA IS LIKE. PEOPLE OFTEN SAY, "I DON'T GET YOUR JOKES." WHAT CAN I SAY? I'M A SELF-COMPLETING MANGA ARTIST. I WRITE STORIES THAT MAKE ME LAUGH, BUT NOBODY LAUGHS AT MY JOKES. I'M LIKE A LONELY CLOWN SITTING ALL ALONE IN THE DARK. WELL, TO TELL YOU THE TRUTH, I DON'T FIND MY STORIES THAT FUNNY EITHER.

SNOW MELTING | SELF-COMPLETING | **MINOTAKE MEASUREMENT** | TOO MUCH EVIDENCE

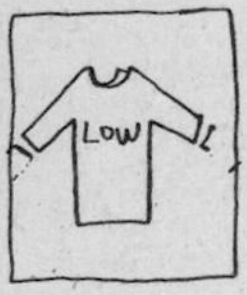
LOW

EVEN WHEN I TRY TO LIVE BEYOND MY MINOTAKE MEASUREMENT, FOR SOME STRANGE REASON, I'M ALWAYS FORCED TO LIVE ACCORDING TO MY MINOTAKE. WHEN I ORDER A SET MENU AT A RESTAURANT, THERE'S USUALLY ONE ITEM MISSING. THE RESTAURANT MUST'VE PREPARED MY MEAL ACCORDING TO MY MINOTAKE. WHEN I ORDER CURRY OVER RICE, THE ONLY TOPPING I GET IS THINLY SLICED ALMONDS...IT'S LIKE SAYING "THAT'S ALL YOU DESERVE, YOU PIECE OF TRASH." WHEN I ORDER PANCAKES, I DON'T GET ANY SYRUP. WHEN I ORDER A COFFEE FLOAT, I DON'T GET ANY ICE CREAM. ONE TIME A READER SENT ME CHOCOLATE, AND THERE WAS A TOOTH MARK IN IT. IT'S LIKE NOT GETTING FLORA WHEN YOU'RE PLAYING DRAGON QUEST. IT SEEMS LIKE MY LIFE IS MADE UP OF ONE LOSS AFTER ANOTHER, BUT I'M NOT GONNA COMPLAIN BECAUSE I'M JUST A SIMPLE, "PIECE OF TRASH." I BOUGHT A LONG-SLEEVED SHIRT THE OTHER DAY, BUT IT TURNED OUT TO HAVE THREE-QUARTER SLEEVES. I ALWAYS WALK ON THE EDGE OF THE STREET SO I WON'T GET IN ANYONE ELSE'S WAY.

SNOW MELTING | SELF-COMPLETING | MINOTAKE MEASUREMENT | **TOO MUCH EVIDENCE**

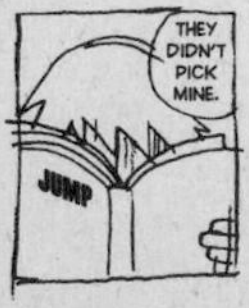
THEY DIDN'T PICK MINE.
JUMP

THERE'S JUST TOO MUCH EVIDENCE. THERE'S JUST TOO MUCH EVIDENCE THAT I'M A BAD MANGA ARTIST. I'VE BEEN WORKING FOR FIFTEEN YEARS, AND NOBODY EVEN NOTICES ME. I SENT AN ILLUSTRATION TO *JUMP BROADCASTING STATION* USING MY REAL NAME, AND IT WAS COMPLETELY IGNORED. I'VE NEVER EVEN MADE IT INTO THE TOOHAN MANGA RANKING. PRIME MINISTER ASO HAS NEVER SAID A WORD TO ME, AND MY NEIGHBORHOOD BOOKSTORE DOESN'T EVEN CARRY MY MANGA. THERE'S JUST TOO MUCH EVIDENCE THAT I'M NOT TALENTED...WAY TOO MUCH EVIDENCE. THERE'S SO MUCH EVIDENCE THAT IT MAKES IT HARD TO BELIEVE. IT MAKES ME THINK, THERE'S NO WAY I COULD REALLY BE THAT BAD. WAIT A MINUTE, MAYBE I'M NOT THAT BAD. THIS IS A NEW KIND OF POSITIVE THINKING. THERE'S NO WAY I'M BAD.

DREAM ENDING | BE PREPARED | SECRET CODE | OLD FRIEND

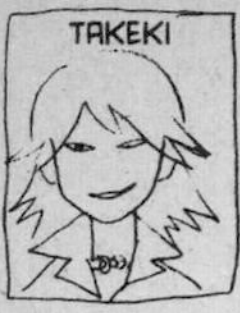
TAKEKI

I CAME UP WITH A COOL IDEA IN MY DREAM. I FORGOT IT THE MOMENT I WOKE UP, SO I WENT BACK TO SLEEP HOPING THAT IT WOULD COME BACK TO ME. I ENDED UP HAVING A DREAM ABOUT TAKAKO MATSU. IT WAS VERY REAL...MAYBE SHE WAS ACTUALLY HERE. I'M AN INSOMNIAC SO I HAVE A HARD TIME TELLING THE REAL WORLD FROM THE DREAM WORLD. THERE'S THIS EDITOR WHO ALWAYS APPEARS IN MY DREAMS WHEN I'M HALF ASLEEP. I'M NOT REALLY SURE IF HE'S REAL OR NOT. HIS NAME IS TETSUSUKE TAKEKI, AND IT'S HIS SECOND YEAR WORKING AS AN EDITOR. HE'S A RICH KID WHO LIVES IN A PENTHOUSE ALL BY HIMSELF. HE DRIVES AN ALFA ROMEO AND DATES MODELS EVERY WEEKEND. HE ALWAYS SAYS, "I'VE GOT AT LEAST SEVEN GIRLFRIENDS." HE REALLY GETS ON MY NERVES. HE'S ACTUALLY A MASOCHIST, AND HE ONCE SHOWED UP TO A MEETING WHILE CHAINED AND GAGGED BY A DOMINATRIX. WHAT MAKES HIM THINK HE CAN CONDUCT A MEETING WHILE HE'S BOUND AND GAGGED? I FELT TOTALLY ABANDONED. IT WAS AS IF I WAS BEING FORCED INTO HIS KINKY WORLD. THERE'S ALSO AN ASSISTANT NAMED KIMURA WHO APPEARS IN MY DREAMS. HE ALWAYS LOOKS DOWN ON ME. HE TELLS ME THAT MY DRAWING STYLE IS TOO OLD-FASHIONED AND WON'T PLAY TO A YOUNG AUDIENCE. YOU BASTARDS. QUIT MESSING WITH ME! SOMEDAY I'LL KILL YOU. I SWEAR.

DREAM ENDING | **BE PREPARED** | SECRET CODE | OLD FRIEND

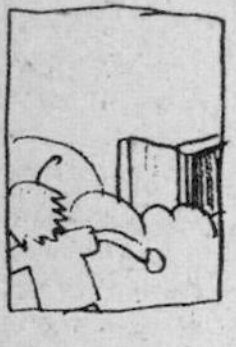

PREPARATION BACKFIRES 100% OF THE TIME. TRY USING A WALKING STICK, AND YOU END UP GETTING STABBED BY IT. I TRIP ON SLIP-PROOF FLOORS. I ALMOST SUFFOCATED MYSELF SLEEPING IN PADDED HEADGEAR. I GET A RASH WHENEVER I USE BUG SPRAY. IT MAKES TOTAL SENSE...SINCE I'M NOTHING BUT A LOWLY BUG. WHY WOULD A BUG USE BUG SPRAY? WHEN I PUT MOTHBALLS IN MY CLOSET, I END UP NOT BEING ABLE TO WEAR ANYTHING. IF MY APARTMENT WAS FUMIGATED, I'D MOVE OUT. WHAT ELSE COULD I DO? AFTER ALL, I'M JUST A LOWLY BUG. I'M THE LOWEST KIND OF BUG THERE IS. I'M A DUNG BEETLE. NO MATTER WHAT I DO TO PREPARE, IT ALWAYS BACKFIRES.

DREAM ENDING | BE PREPARED | **SECRET CODE** | OLD FRIEND

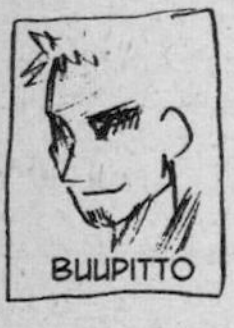
BUUPITTO

I DON'T KNOW IF YOU CAN CALL THIS A SECRET CODE, BUT LATELY I'VE BEEN USING WORDS THAT NOBODY ELSE SEEMS TO UNDERSTAND. I'M SPEAKING JAPANESE TO JAPANESE PEOPLE, BUT THEY STILL DON'T UNDERSTAND. ACTUALLY, I'VE ALWAYS HAD A TENDENCY TO USE WEIRD WORDS. I CALL 7-ELEVEN "SEREBU" FOR SHORT (MOST PEOPLE CALL IT "SEVEN"). AND I CALL AMPM "EMUPI" (MOST PEOPLE SAY "EEPII"). I ALSO CALL BRAD PITT "BUUPITTO" (MOST PEOPLE CALL HIM "BURAPI"). THE OTHER DAY I ASKED MAEDA-KUN, "HEY, IS YOUR MEBON ACTING UP?" AND MAEDA-KUN WAS LIKE "HUH???" "MEBON" IS SHORT FOR "METABOLIC SYNDROME." I USE IT ALL THE TIME. I'VE PROBABLY SAID IT SO MANY TIMES THAT I'VE CONVINCED MYSELF IT WAS NORMAL. HAVE YOU BOUGHT OHABI YET? IS MASENE ENTERTAINING? I WONDER HOW FUKAHIRE IS DOING.

DREAM ENDING | BE PREPARED | SECRET CODE | **OLD FRIEND**

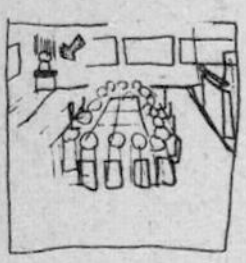

I DON'T HAVE ANY OLD FRIENDS. I DON'T HAVE ANY REGULAR FRIENDS EITHER. I HAVE NO FRIENDS. I'M SERIOUS. IT'S NOT LIKE I LOVE BEING ALONE. I JUST HAPPEN TO BE ALONE ALL THE TIME. THAT'S JUST MY FATE. I WENT TO A DINER THE OTHER DAY, AND I WAS SITTING ALONE IN THE NONSMOKING SECTION. THEN A GROUP OF THIRTY PEOPLE SHOWED UP. IT WAS A BUNCH OF LADIES WHO HAD JUST PICKED THEIR KIDS UP FROM NURSERY SCHOOL. THEY PUT SOME TABLES TOGETHER AND MADE ONE HUGE GROUP TABLE. I WAS ALL ALONE AGAIN. THERE WAS A HUGE GROUP IN THE MIDDLE AND THEN ME, ALL ALONE IN THE CORNER. I WAS COMPLETELY ISOLATED. IT REMINDED ME OF WHAT MY TEACHER USED TO DO TO ME BACK IN ELEMENTARY SCHOOL. TELL ME, GOD, WHAT AM I BEING PUNISHED FOR? THEN A CHILD STARED AT ME IN ASTONISHMENT WITH HIS PURE, INNOCENT LITTLE EYES. HE WAS PROBABLY THINKING, *WHY IS THERE A STRANGE OLD MAN SITTING IN THE SAME ROOM AS US?* THERE'S ONE THING THAT I LEARNED THAT DAY. IT GETS REALLY COLD IN A DINER WHEN THERE'RE NO OTHER TABLES AROUND YOU. THE AIR-CONDITIONER WAS BLOWING RIGHT AT ME, WITH NOTHING TO BLOCK THE ICY BREEZE.

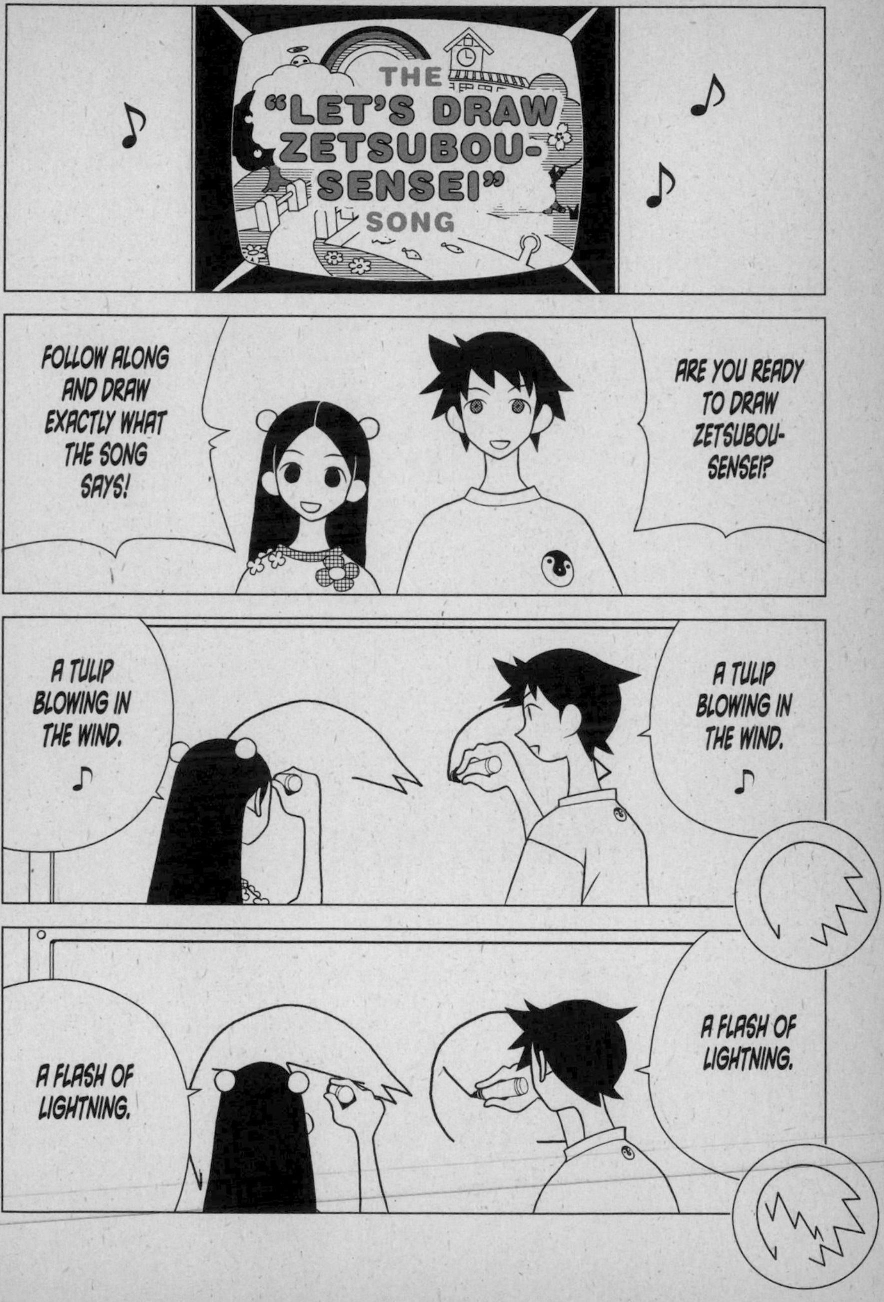
THE "LET'S DRAW ZETSUBOU-SENSEI" SONG
♪ ♪ ♪
ARE YOU READY TO DRAW ZETSUBOU-SENSEI!?
FOLLOW ALONG AND DRAW EXACTLY WHAT THE SONG SAYS!
A TULIP BLOWING IN THE WIND. ♪
A TULIP BLOWING IN THE WIND. ♪
A FLASH OF LIGHTNING.
A FLASH OF LIGHTNING.

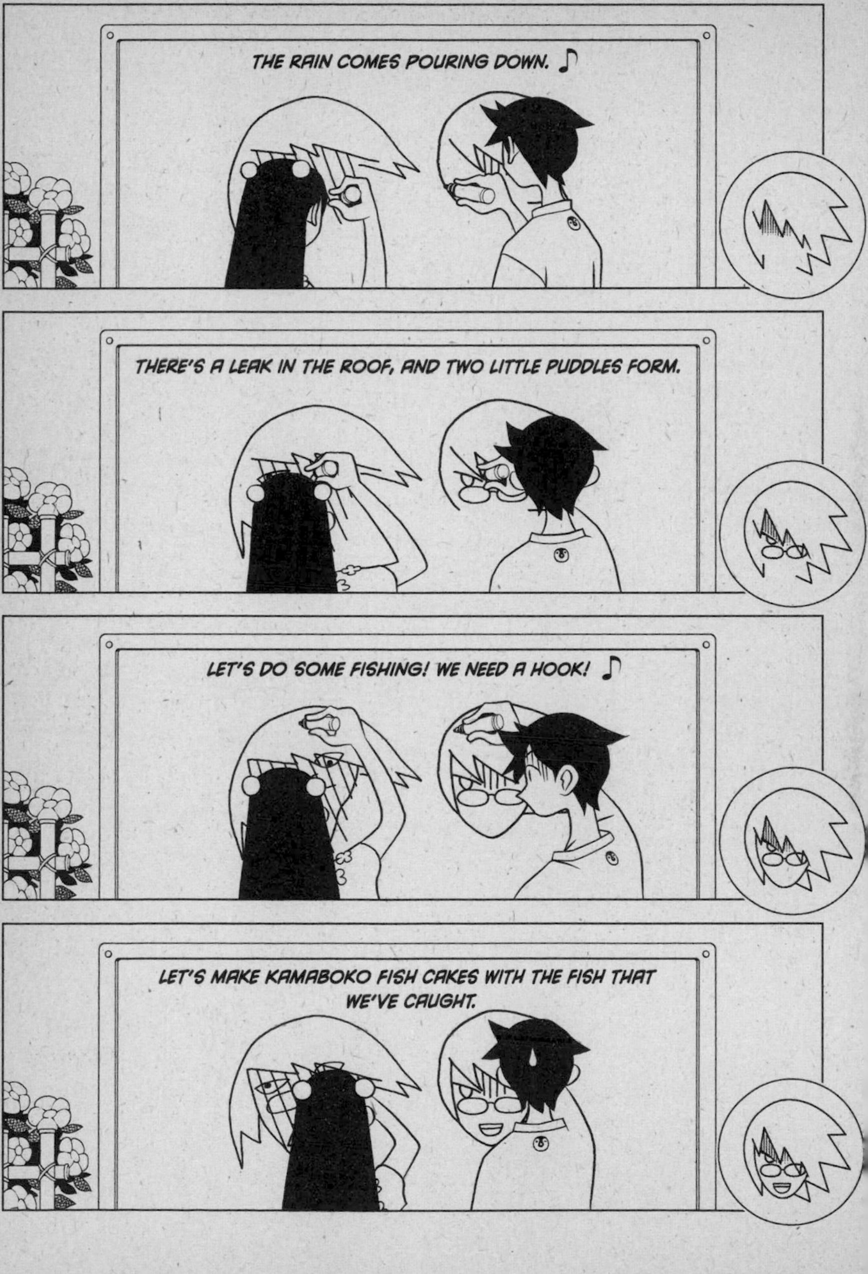
THE RAIN COMES POURING DOWN. ♪
THERE'S A LEAK IN THE ROOF, AND TWO LITTLE PUDDLES FORM.
LET'S DO SOME FISHING! WE NEED A HOOK! ♪
LET'S MAKE KAMABOKO FISH CAKES WITH THE FISH THAT WE'VE CAUGHT.

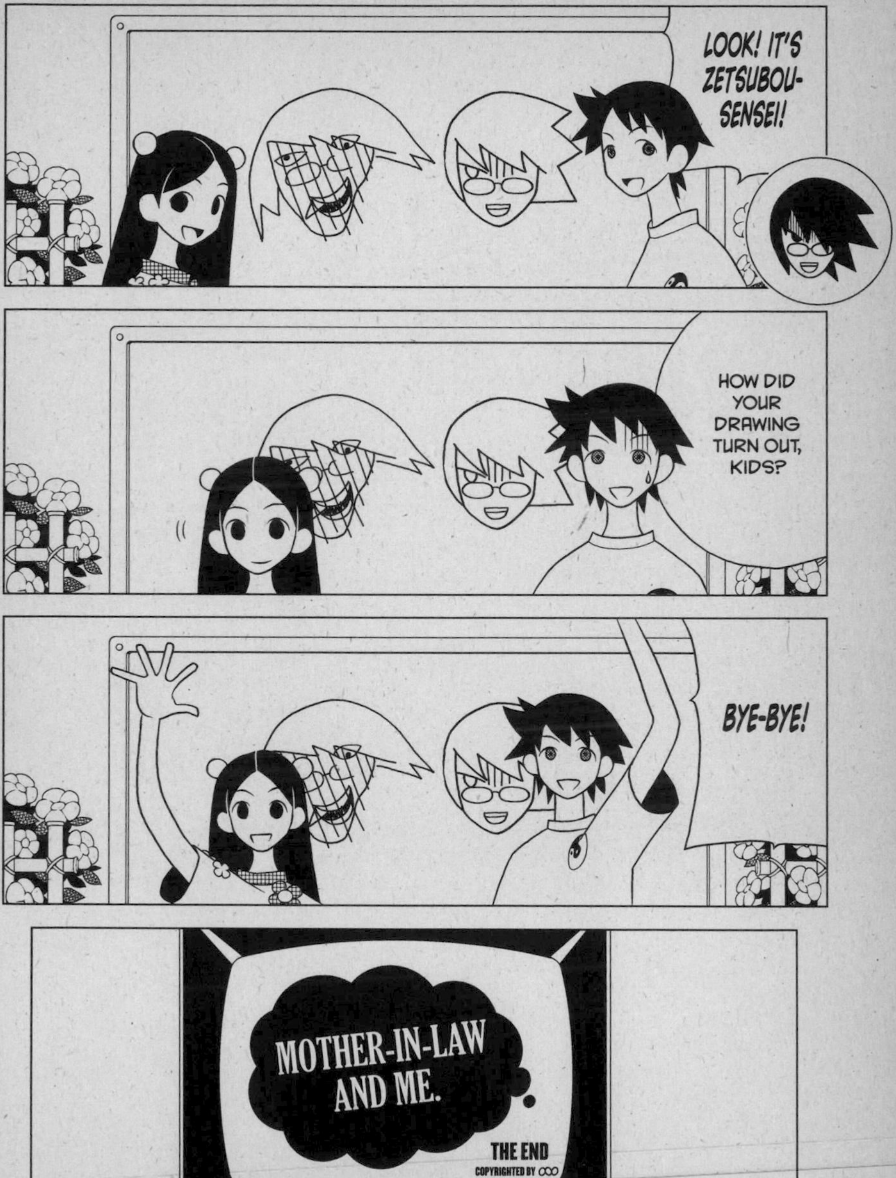
LOOK! IT'S ZETSUBOU-SENSEI!
HOW DID YOUR DRAWING TURN OUT, KIDS?
BYE-BYE!
MOTHER-IN-LAW AND ME.
THE END
COPYRIGHTED BY

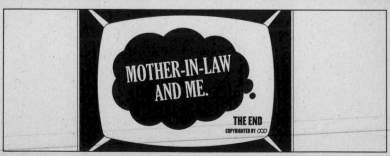

ZETSUBOU LITERARY COMPILATION

RODRIGO IN IZU

RODRIGO WAS FROM PUERTO RICO. HE LOOKED LIKE HE WAS ABOUT THIRTY-TWO. ONE TIME, I SAW RODRIGO COME RUNNING TOWARD ME FROM THE DARKNESS OF THE BATHROOM. HE WAS COMPLETELY NAKED AND HAD BOTH OF HIS ARMS STRETCHED OUT. HE GRABBED ME OUT OF THE BLUE. HE WASN'T EVEN HOLDING A TOWEL. THAT WAS RODRIGO.

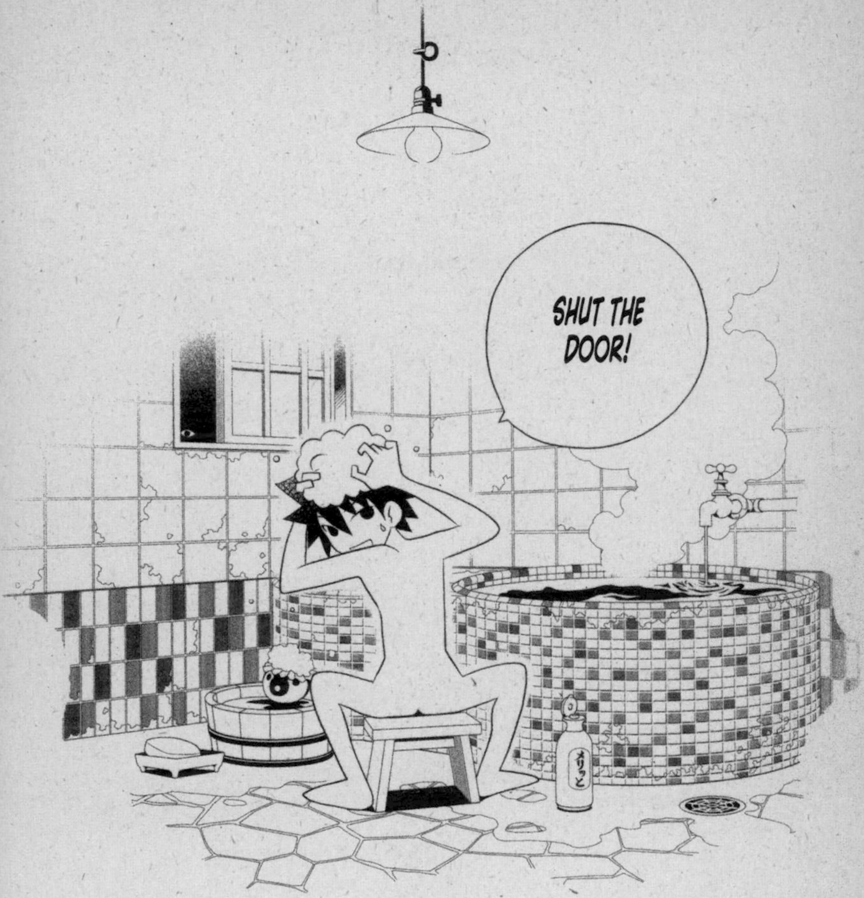
SHUT THE DOOR!

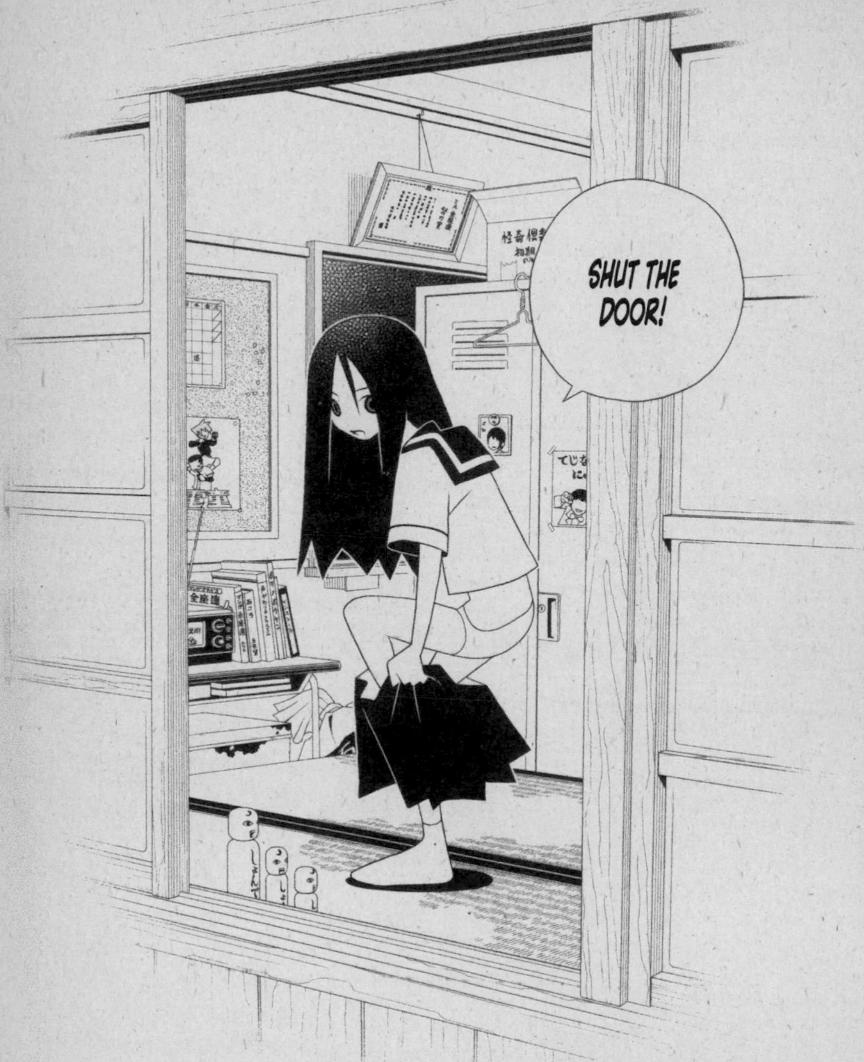
SHUT THE DOOR!

Translation Notes

Japanese is a tricky language for most Westerners, and translation is often more art than science. In the case of a text-dense manga like *Sayonara, Zetsubou-sensei*, it's a delicate art indeed. Although most of the jokes are universal, Koji Kumeta is famous for filling his manga with references to Japanese politics, entertainment, *otaku* culture, religion, and sports. Unless you're a true Japanophile, it's difficult to understand it all without some serious background knowledge of current events at the time the manga was running. Kumeta also uses references to foreign literature and politics, so even Japanese readers probably don't get all the humor. For your reading pleasure, here are notes on some of the more obscure references and difficult-to-translate jokes in *Sayonara, Zetsubou-sensei*.

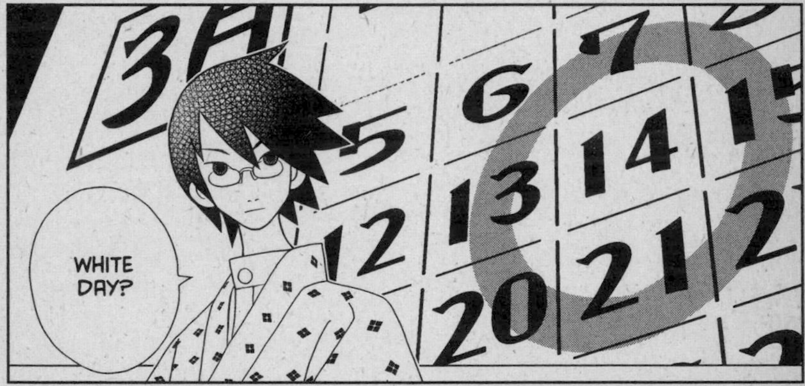
WHITE DAY?

"White Day", page 5

The Japanese version of Valentine's Day is a bit different than the American tradition. In Japan, Valentine's Day is a day when girls give presents to the boys they like (usually chocolate). This is followed by a holiday called White Day, when boys give presents to girls.

"It happens a lot in Africa," page 11

This is a reference to Nigerian-born TV personality Bobby Ologun. Ologun is a K-1 fighter and entertainer who was caught lying about his age.

"Welcome home, master," page 11

This is how maids greet their customers at Maid Cafés.

Conan-kun, Ran-chan, page 11

Conan-kun and Ran-chan are characters from the anime *Detective Conan*.

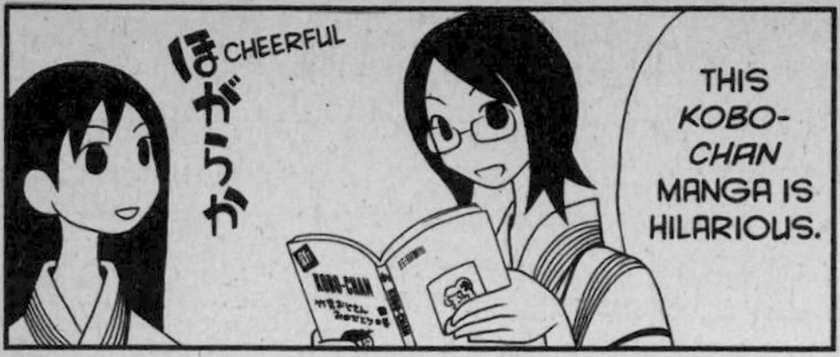
THIS KOBO-CHAN MANGA IS HILARIOUS.
ほがらか
CHEERFUL
KOBO-CHAN

Kobo-chan, page 26

Kobo-chan is a very clean manga about a five-year-old kid and his family.

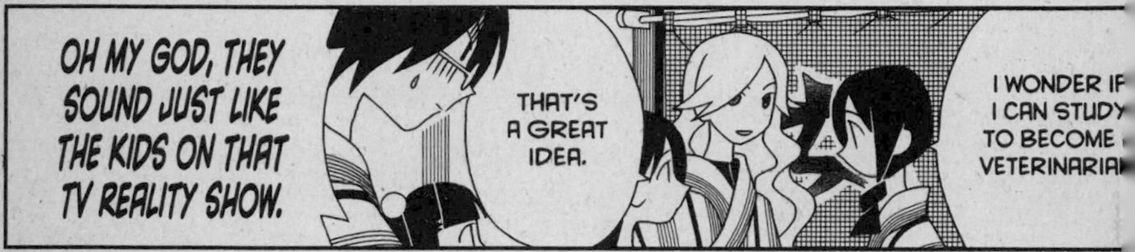
I WONDER IF I CAN STUDY TO BECOME VETERINARIA
THAT'S A GREAT IDEA.
OH MY GOD, THEY SOUND JUST LIKE THE KIDS ON THAT TV REALITY SHOW.

TV reality show, page 27

The teacher is actually saying, "They're talking like the kids in *Chuugakusei Nikki*. *Chuugakusei Nikki (Junior High School Diary)* is a reality series on NHK (PBC). The show follows real-life junior high kids and focuses on the challenges they face.

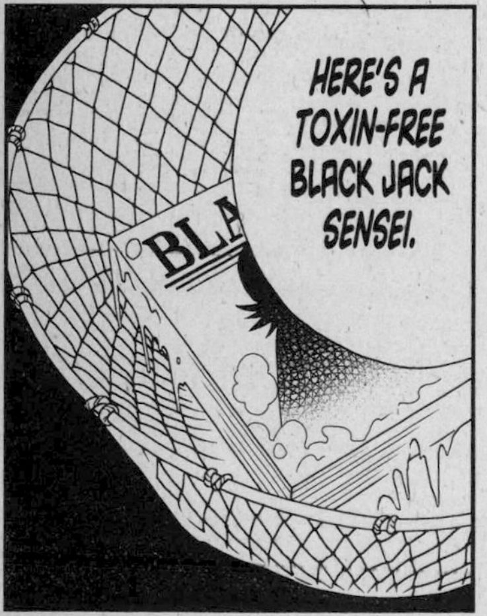
HERE'S A TOXIN-FREE BLACK JACK SENSEI.
BLA

Black Jack, page 27

Black Jack is a classic manga by Osamu Tezuka about a morally ambiguous doctor.

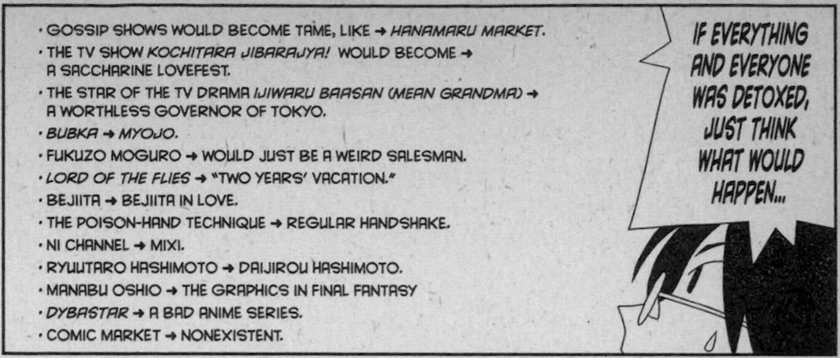

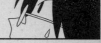

IF EVERYTHING AND EVERYONE WAS DETOXED, JUST THINK WHAT WOULD HAPPEN...
• GOSSIP SHOWS WOULD BECOME TAME, LIKE → HANAMARU MARKET.
• THE TV SHOW KOCHITARA JIBARAJYA! WOULD BECOME → A SACCHARINE LOVEFEST.
• THE STAR OF THE TV DRAMA IJIWARU BAASAN (MEAN GRANDMA) → A WORTHLESS GOVERNOR OF TOKYO.
• BUBKA → MYOJO.
• FUKUZO MOGURO → WOULD JUST BE A WEIRD SALESMAN.
• LORD OF THE FLIES → "TWO YEARS' VACATION."
• BEJIITA → BEJIITA IN LOVE.
• THE POISON-HAND TECHNIQUE → REGULAR HANDSHAKE.
• NI CHANNEL → MIXI.
• RYUUTARO HASHIMOTO → DAIJIROU HASHIMOTO.
• MANABU OSHIO → THE GRAPHICS IN FINAL FANTASY
• DYBASTAR → A BAD ANIME SERIES.
• COMIC MARKET → NONEXISTENT.

Kochitara Jibarajya!, page 29

This is a show within a TV show called *Toranomon*. In this show, director Kazuyuki Izutsu does movie reviews and critiques.

Ijiwaru Baasan, page 29

Ijiwaru Baasan is a TV dramedy series that starred Yukio Aoshima. Aoshima later became the governor of Tokyo.

Bubka, Myojo, page 29

Bubka is a gossip magazine that publishes celebrity scandals. *Myojo* is a more wholesome celebrity magazine.

Fukuzo Moguro, page 29

He is the main character of the dark manga *Laughing Salesman*.

Bejiita, page 29

Bejiita is a character in the manga *Dragon Ballz*.

Ni channel, page 29

Ni channel is a popular Internet site among *otaku* and is known for its harshness.

Mixi, page 29

Mixi is a social networking site. A Japanese version of MySpace.

Ryuutaro Hashimoto... Daijirou Hashimoto, page 29

These brothers are both politicians. Ryuutaro used to be the prime minister of Japan.

Manabu Oshio, page 29

Manabu Oshio is an actor/singer in his twenties. People were shocked when he married the actress, Akiko Yada.

Dybastar, page 29

Dybastar is the title of a late-night anime TV show.

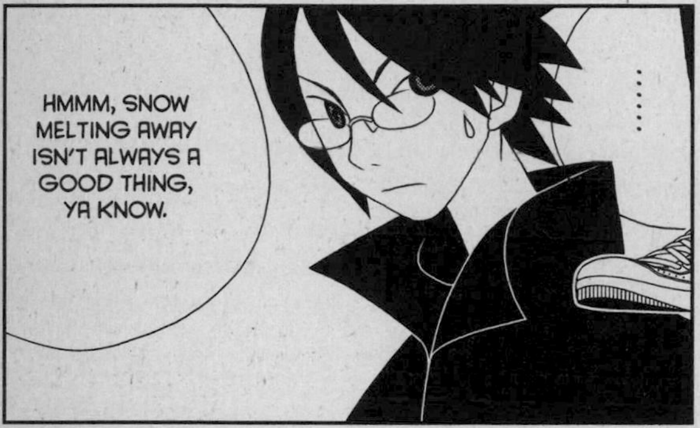

HMMM, SNOW MELTING AWAY ISN'T ALWAYS A GOOD THING, YA KNOW.

Yukidoke, page 34

In this chapter, the author uses the term "*yukidoke*" (melting snow) to refer metaphorically to the reconciliation, or "warming," of an icy relationship.

Doujinshi, page 40

A *doujinshi* is a homemade comic that is usually a parody of an existing manga or anime series.

A conflict between two nations is resolved thanks to a beautiful twelve-year-old girl, page 41

This is a reference to celebrity Saya Irie's effect on the relationship between China and Japan. Apparently, somebody posted a message with her photo on a Chinese website as a statement for world peace, which helped start some reconciliation between the two nations.

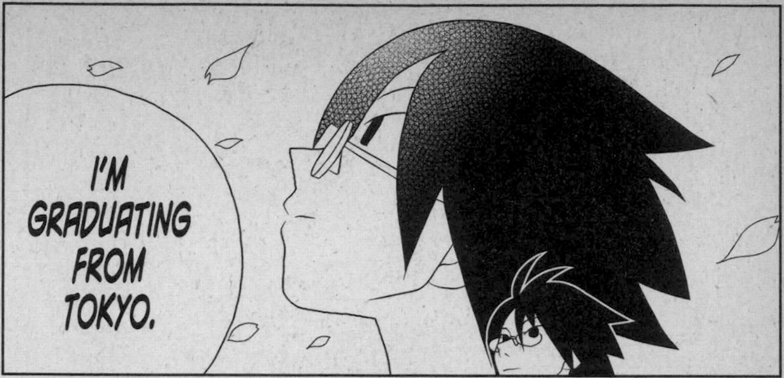
I'M GRADUATING FROM TOKYO.

"I'm graduating from Tokyo," page 48

This is a phrase spoken by the lead character Jun in the popular TV drama *Kita no Kuni kara*. He moves to Tokyo and decides to move back to Hokkaido after suffering through big city life.

Zekkei-sensei, page 56

Kafuka calls Kei Itoshiki "Zekkei-sensei" because when you combine the kanji "Ito" and "Shiki," it becomes "Zetsu." "Zetsu" and "Kei" together create the word "Zekkei," which means "fabulous view."

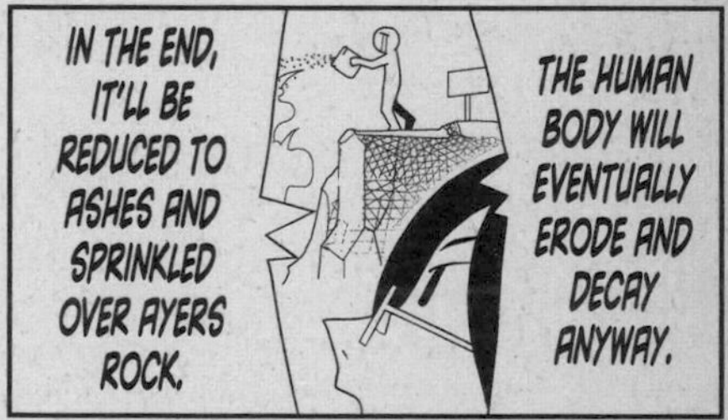
THE HUMAN BODY WILL EVENTUALLY ERODE AND DECAY ANYWAY.
IN THE END, IT'LL BE REDUCED TO ASHES AND SPRINKLED OVER AYERS ROCK.

Ayers Rock, page 62

This is a reference to the movie *Sekai no Chuushin de Ai wo Sakebu*. In the story, the lead character goes to Ayers Rock and sprinkles his lover's ashes there. Ayers Rock is known to some as the center of the planet. "Chuushin" means "center."

Fashion Center Shima**ra, page 64

Fashion Center Shimamura is a Japanese discount outlet.

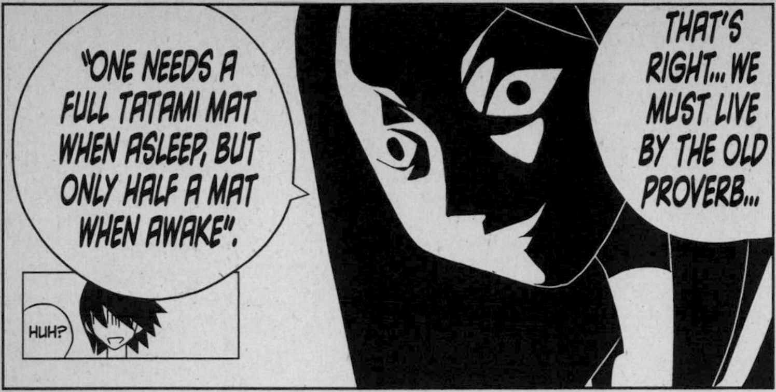
THAT'S RIGHT... WE MUST LIVE BY THE OLD PROVERB...
"ONE NEEDS A FULL TATAMI MAT WHEN ASLEEP, BUT ONLY HALF A MAT WHEN AWAKE".
HUH?

Tatami mat, page 69

This is an old Buddhist proverb about living modestly. The idea is that a monk only needs half a mat to pray on while awake, and while asleep he needs a full mat on which to lie.

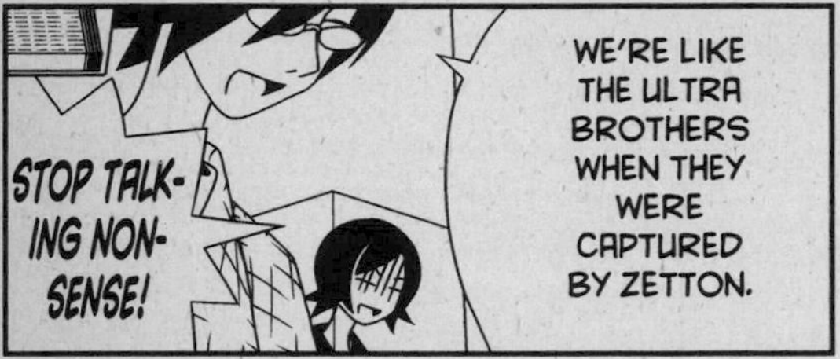
WE'RE LIKE THE ULTRA BROTHERS WHEN THEY WERE CAPTURED BY ZETTON.
STOP TALK-ING NON-SENSE!

Zetton, page 70

Zetton is the name of a monster that appeared in *Ultraman*.

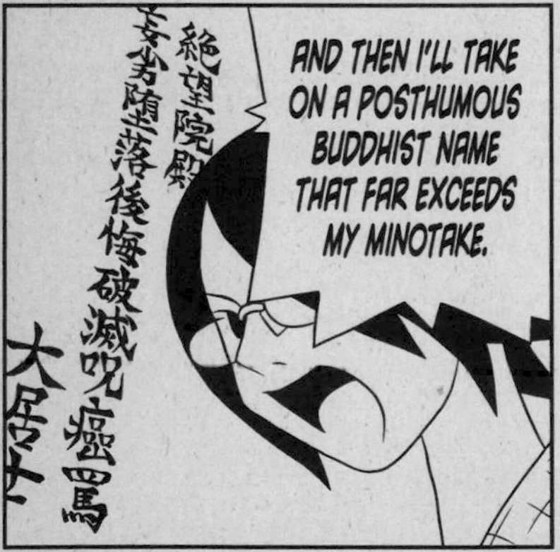
AND THEN I'LL TAKE ON A POSTHUMOUS BUDDHIST NAME THAT FAR EXCEEDS MY MINOTAKE.
絶望院殿
大居士

Posthumous Buddhist name, page 71

It is a Japanese tradition to give names after someone passes away.

Shougo Hamada, page 72

Shougo Hamada is a rock musician/songwriter in his fifties.

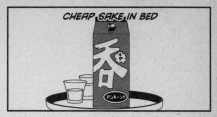

CHEAP SAKE IN BED

Don (Kizakura), page 75

Don is a name of cheap sake manufactured by Kizakura.

When you see a photo of an idol smoking..., page 82

This is referring to a scandal in which underaged female idol, Ai Kago, was caught smoking. She was fired from her agency and wasn't allowed to work for a year.

Dream ending, page 92

This refers to when a story ends with the main character waking up from a dream, thereby nullifying the entire story.

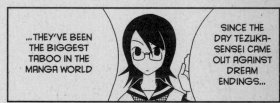

SINCE THE DAY TEZUKA-SENSEI CAME OUT AGAINST DREAM ENDINGS...
...THEY'VE BEEN THE BIGGEST TABOO IN THE MANGA WORLD

Tezuka-sensei, page 92

This is a reference to Osamu Tezuka, the grandfather of manga, who apparently didn't like dream endings.

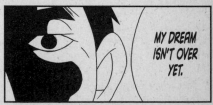

MY DREAM ISN'T OVER YET.

"My dream...," page 100

"My dream isn't over yet" were the words famously shouted by the Japanese pro-baseball team manager Hara.

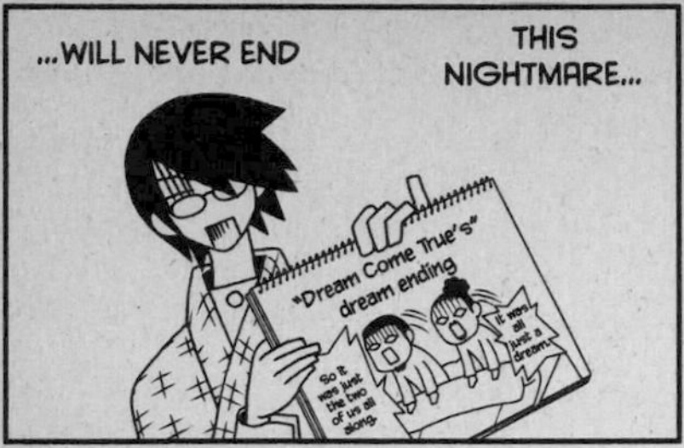
THIS NIGHTMARE...
...WILL NEVER END
"Dream Come True's" dream ending
It was all just a dream.
So it was just the two of us all along.

Dream Come True, page 102

Dream Come True is a band. They used to be a trio but one member quit the band years ago.

***Kunimatsu no Matsuri*,** page 113

Kunimatsu no Matsuri is the title of a manga series published in *Shônen Jump* from 2001–2005.

Horie over rice, page 122

Horie is the former CEO of the Japanese tech company Livedoor. He's currently in prison for fraud.

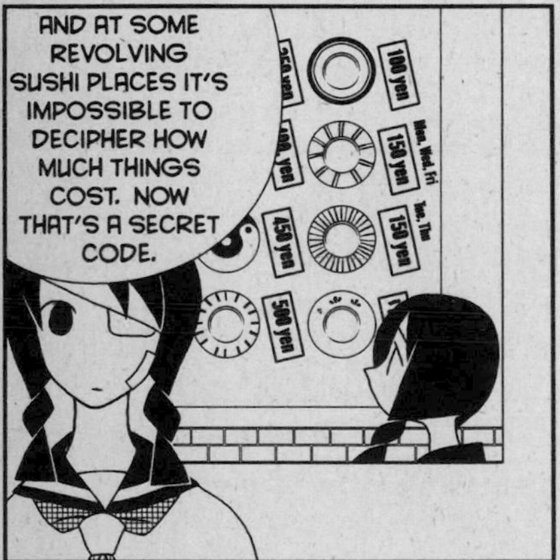
100 yen
Mon. Wed. Fri
150 yen
Tue. Thu
150 yen
450 yen
500 yen
AND AT SOME REVOLVING SUSHI PLACES IT'S IMPOSSIBLE TO DECIPHER HOW MUCH THINGS COST. NOW THAT'S A SECRET CODE.

Revolving sushi, page 122

Revolving sushi restaurants are a popular kind of low-cost, no frills alternative to high-end sushi bars. Plates of sushi rotate around on a conveyor belt and diners simply take the dishes they want. The price is generally determined by the color or pattern of the plates.

******yo Marukawa,** page 126

This is referring to Tamayo Marukawa, an announcer for TV Asahi.

"Maintenance of the Public Order Act," page 127

This was a draconian law aimed at stamping out anti-government sentiment in Japan.

The planet Corin, page 127

Celebrity Yuuko Ogura claims to be from the planet Corin, but she's actually from Chiba prefecture.

***Our National Dignity*,** page 127

This is the title of a bestselling book written by Masahiko Fujiwara. In one chapter he writes about the way of the samurai.

Lunar New Year's Soba, page 135

It is a Japanese tradition to eat soba noodles on New Year's Eve, this soba is called "toshikoshi soba." "Toshikoshi" literally means something like "Coming into the new year."

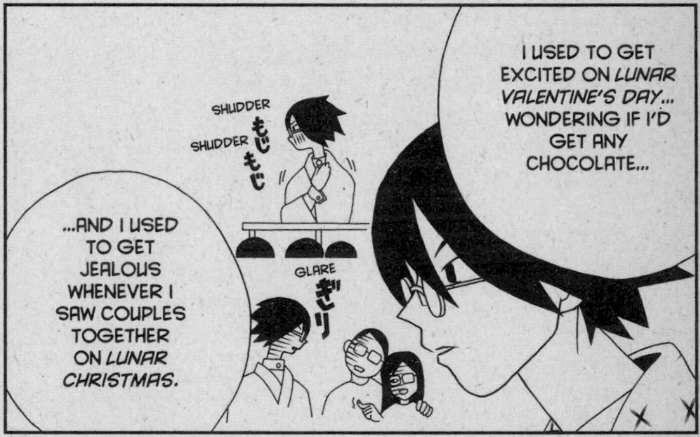
I USED TO GET EXCITED ON *LUNAR VALENTINE'S DAY*... WONDERING IF I'D GET ANY CHOCOLATE...
SHUDDER
SHUDDER
もじもじ
GLARE
ぎり
...AND I USED TO GET JEALOUS WHENEVER I SAW COUPLES TOGETHER ON *LUNAR CHRISTMAS*.

Lunar Christmas, page 135

In Japan, where less than 1 percent of the population identifies as Christian, Christmas is not celebrated as a religious holiday. Instead, Christmas Eve is somewhat similar to Valentine's Day in the United States. It's usually associated with couples and romance, hence Zetsubou-sensei's jealousy.

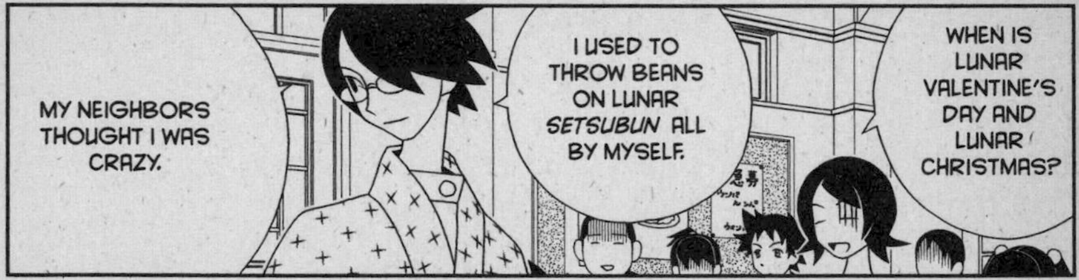
WHEN IS LUNAR VALENTINE'S DAY AND LUNAR CHRISTMAS?
I USED TO THROW BEANS ON LUNAR *SETSUBUN* ALL BY MYSELF.
MY NEIGHBORS THOUGHT I WAS CRAZY.

***Setsubun*,** page 135

Setsubun is the day before the first day of spring. It's a Japanese tradition to throw roasted soybeans inside and outside of the house, while saying out loud, "Oni wa soto [demons go outside], Fuku wa uchi [Good fortune come inside]."

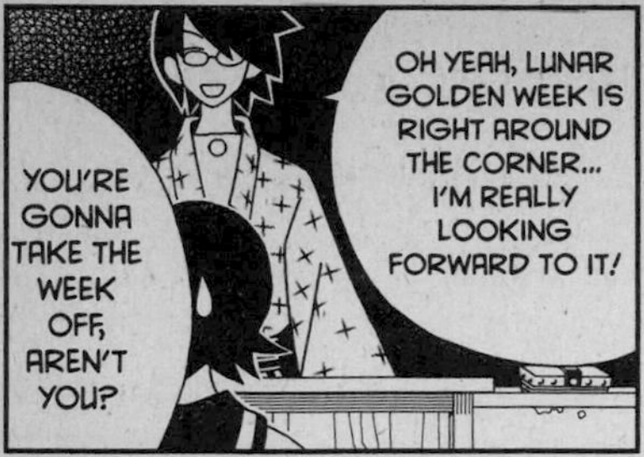
OH YEAH, LUNAR GOLDEN WEEK IS RIGHT AROUND THE CORNER... I'M REALLY LOOKING FORWARD TO IT!
YOU'RE GONNA TAKE THE WEEK OFF, AREN'T YOU?

Golden Week, page 135

Golden Week is a three-day holiday that usually falls in May. Golden Week is one of the busiest travel times in Japan.

My occupation facility, page 135

This is a facilty built and run by the Kyoto city government. It's supposed to provide students with information and training for various kinds of jobs. However, it's failed to draw crowds and is considered by many residents to be a colossal waste of taxpayer money.

Tokaido Trail, page 136

The old Tokaido Trail connects the cities of Osaka and Tokyo.

Zaku, page 137

Zaku is the name of a mobile suit that appears in the anime *Gundam*.

Welcome Old Freshmen, page 139

In Japan, school clubs often throw welcome parties for prospective freshmen members.

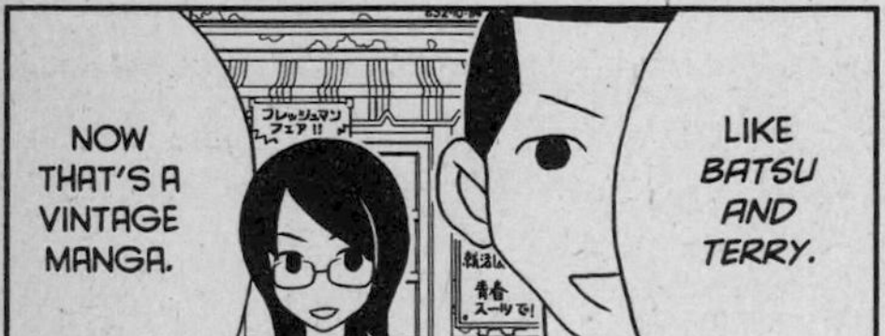
LIKE *BATSU AND TERRY.*
NOW THAT'S A VINTAGE MANGA.

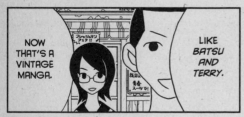

Batsu and Terry, page 140

This is the title of a manga that was published in *Shônen Magazine* 1982–1987.

Shinsengumi, page 140

Shinsengumi is the name of an army formed in Kyoto during the end of the Edo period. "Shin" means "new."

Shinjo, page 140

This is referring to Tsuyoshi Shinjo, a popular baseball player.

Arata Furuta, page 140

Arata Furuta is an actor. The word "arata" means "new" in Japanese.

Old Livedoor, page 140

This is a visual kanji pun. The Livedoor company symbol looks very similar to the Japanese kanji "kyuu," meaning "old."

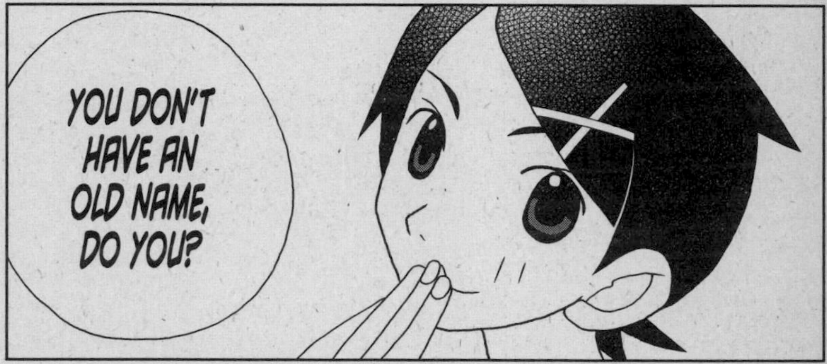
YOU DON'T HAVE AN OLD NAME, DO YOU?

Old name, page 141

In Japan, when a couple gets married, the bride generally takes on the groom's family name. When sending greeting cards, women sometimes write their maiden name in parentheses. Although it's rare, the groom can legally take on the family name of his bride. This usually happens when the wife is the only child of her family and her parents want the family name to live on.

One-day friends, page 146

This is a visual kanji pun. The character for "old" is actually made up of a combination of the character for "one" and the character for "day." The kanji characters in this panel read "one-day friend." However, if the first two characters were a bit closer together, it would read "old friend."

One-day Zaku, page 146

This is a reference to the manga *Gundam*. Zaku is the nickname of the mobile suit MS-05. The suit that appeared in the anime series was, in fact, the "new" version. The "old zaku" refers to the original version of the MS-05 mobile suit.

One-day Hashimoto group, page 146

This is a reference to a group of politicians that existed within the Liberal Democratic Party lead by Ryuutaro Hashimoto. When Hashimoto was defeated by Koizumi as the leader of the party in 2001, the group fell apart.

Old Japanese soldier, Page 146

The term “old soldier” here refers to World War Two–era Japanese troops who continued to fight even after the war had ended. Some troops were in such isolated areas of Asia, such as the jungles of the Philippines or Guam, that they continued to believe that they were still at war, years after the war had ended.

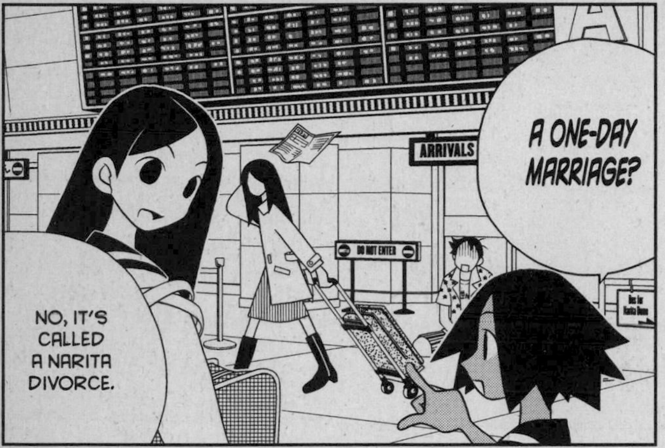
A ONE-DAY MARRIAGE?
ARRIVALS
DO NOT ENTER
NO, IT'S CALLED A NARITA DIVORCE.

Narita divorce, Page 147

A Narita divorce is when a couple gets divorced as soon as they return from their honeymoon. Narita is Tokyo’s international airport.

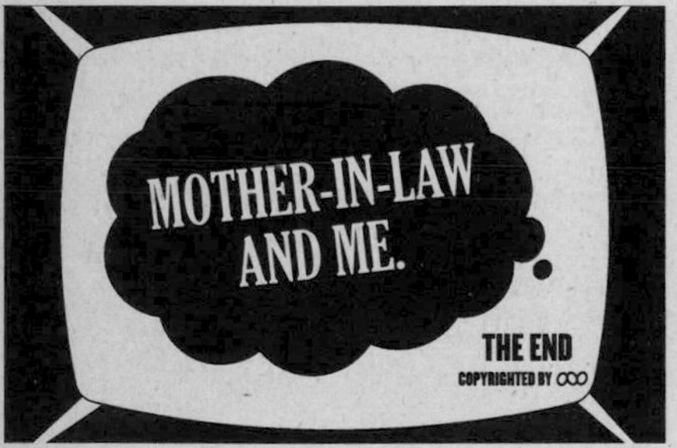
MOTHER-IN-LAW AND ME.
THE END
COPYRIGHTED BY

Mother-in-Law and Me, Page 154

This is a reference to the popular, long-running Japanese kids’ show *Mommy and Me*.

TOMARE! STOP

You're going the wrong way!

MANGA IS A COMPLETELY DIFFERENT TYPE OF READING EXPERIENCE.

TO START AT THE **BEGINNING**, GO TO THE **END**!

That's right!

Authentic manga is read the traditional Japanese way—from right to left, exactly the *opposite* of how American books are read. It's easy to follow: Just go to the other end of the book and read each page—and each panel—from right side to left side, starting at the top right. Now you're experiencing manga as it was meant to be!